Technology in Retrospect

Social Studies in
the Information Age 1984-2009

a volume in
International Social Studies Forum: The Series

Series Editors:
Richard Diem, *The University of Texas at San Antonio*
Jeff Passe, Towson University

International Social Studies Forum: The Series

Richard Diem and Jeff Passe, Series Editors

*Technology in Retrospect: Social Studies in
the Information Age 1984-2009* (2010)
edited by Richard Diem and Michael J. Berson

*Digital Geography: Geospatial Technologies in
the Social Studies Classroom* (2008)
edited by Andrew J. Milson and Marsha Alibrandi

Unsettling Beliefs: Teaching Theory to Teachers (2008)
edited by Josh Diem and Robert J. Helfenbein

*Democratic Education for Social Studies:
An Issues-Centered Decision Making Curriculum* (2006)
edited by Anna S. Ochoa-Becke

Social Justice in These Times (2006)
edited by James O'Donnell, Marc Pruyn, and Rudolfo Chávez Chávez

Social Studies and the Press: Keeping the Beast at Bay? (2006)
edited by Margaret Smith Crocco

Technology in Retrospect

Social Studies in
the Information Age 1984-2009

edited by

Richard Diem
The University of Texas at San Antonio

and

Michael J. Berson
University of South Florida

Information Age Publishing, Inc.
Charlotte, North Carolina • www.infoagepub.com

Library of Congress Cataloging-in-Publication Data

Technology in retrospect : social studies in the information age,
1984-2009 / edited by Richard Diem and Michael Berson.
p. cm. -- (International social studies forum: the series)
Includes bibliographical references.
ISBN 978-1-61735-038-2 (pbk.) -- ISBN 978-1-61735-039-9 (hardcover) --
ISBN 978-1-61735-040-5 (e-book)
1. Social sciences--United States--Computer-assisted instruction. 2.
Information technology--United States. 3. Educational technology--United
States. 4. Education--Effect of technological innovations on--United
States. I. Diem, Richard A. II. Berson, Michael J.
LB1584.7.T43 2010
300.78'5--dc22

                                                                    2010012639

Printed in the United States of America

CONTENTS

ACKNOWLEDGMENTS

We have a number of people to thank for their assistance in developing this book and promoting teaching, learning, and research with technology in the social studies. Special appreciation goes to George F. Johnson, President and Publisher of Information Age Publishing, who saw the promise of this book and provided steady support in guiding the manuscript through the publication process. We also wish to acknowledge many colleagues and students for their thoughtful reviews and valuable feedback, including Ilene R. Berson, University of South Florida; Ken Carano, University of South Florida; Natalie Keefer, University of South Florida; Peter Levine, The Center for Information and Research on Civic Learning and Engagement at Tufts University; George B. Lipscomb, Furman University; Jeffery A. Mangram, Syracuse University; Mark Pearcy, University of South Florida; Kerry D. Poole, University of South Florida; William B. Russell III, University of Central Florida; Caroline Sheffield, University of Louisville; Scott M. Waring, University of Central Florida; Stewart Waters, University of Central Florida; and Shannon White, University of Missouri.

We are extremely grateful to our families: Robbi, Josh, Erin, Sarah, Max , Rose, Ilene, Elisa, and Marc for sharing our long and winding journey through the ever changing technology landscape. They served as our inspiration and joy as we labored through the writing and editing process.

CHAPTER 1

AS IT WAS—1984

Richard A. Diem

BEGINNINGS

January 2009 marked the 25th anniversary of one of the most famous 3 minutes in television history. It was during half-time of the 1984 Supper Bowl that APPLE first show cased its new Macintosh computer in an avant-guard commercial. In the following 3 weeks sales of the new computer, in both public and private sectors, took off.

While the introduction of the "Mac," in and of itself, was a watershed event, it was only one of a series of like occurrences that unfolded during this time period. Announcements such as Microsoft's official release of the initial version of Microsoft Windows in November, 1983, Hewlett-Packard's introduction of the first laser jet printer in early 1984, and the public licensing of IBM compatible software in 1984 seemed to appear on almost a daily basis (Computer Hope.Com, n.d.). These seemingly endless new forms of publicly available information software and hardware led some to mark this era as the "true," or at least in public relations terms, onset of the "Information Age" or "micro-technic revolution."

Some 25 years before the flashy commercialization of computer technology was unleashed on the public, George Orwell (1949) presented a

Technology in Retrospect: Social Studies in the Information Age 1984-2009, pp. 1–12

1

somewhat differing vision of how information technology might be utilized in 1984:

> The telescreen received and transmitted simultaneously. Any sound that
> Winston made, above the level of a very low whisper, would be picked up by
> it; moreover, so long as he remained within the field of vision which the
> metal plaque commanded, he could be seen as well as heard. There was no
> way of knowing whether you were being watched at any given moment. How
> often, or on what system, the Thought Police plugged in on any individual
> wire was guesswork. It was even conceivable that they watched everybody all
> the time. But at any rate they could plug in your wire whenever they wanted
> to. You had to live—did live, from habit that became instinct-in the assump-
> tion that every sound you made was recorded. (pp. 6-7)

As we approach the second decade of the twenty-first century and contemplate both the Orwellian and the commercialized versions of an information age, it behooves us, given the continual changing nature of
information technology, as well as the variety of classroom applications
that have appeared over the past quarter century, to try to capture various
visions that have encompassed the use and application of information
technology as it relates to the social studies through a retrospective lens.
Noting the beginnings of the marriage of social studies and technology,
through its use and applications, can assist us in broadening our understanding of the effects that this type of technology has had and will have
on this important segment of the curriculum.

TECHNOLOGY AND INQUIRY—A LOOK BACK

For most of us our first ongoing interplay with information technology
was through television. Indeed, during the 1960s the number of TVs in
our homes surpassed the numbers of toilets and bathtubs we had available for use (United States Department of Commerce, 1970).

Commercial video networks, which set the norm for the types of
programs and video technology that was made available for most of the
general public, dominated the television market through which we gained
the majority of our information during most of the past half century.
These programs were enhanced by full color, dramatic scenery and vigor-
ous action, all of which generally overwhelmed verbal interactions.

This reliance on direct imagery was a quantum leap from the previous
50 years in which radio and telephone technology controlled the personal
entertainment market. In this context listening about information had
been the primary means by which one was "wired."

An analysis of most television shows of this period notes that many of its verbal messages were focused on commentary about the visual message. Viewers could probably have turned off the sound as they watched a typical commercial television program of this time and chances are they would have been able to follow the action. On the other hand, turning off the visual side and listening only to the verbal would have left something to be desired in the way of following most this age's television programming.

Another characteristic of these shows is that generally the message they carried was one of events and people and not one of ideas. Television comedies, soap operas, movie events, and even news are about what people do and rarely about a visual or verbal message with an abstract idea. Life is portrayed as concrete and not raised to an abstract level.

The intellectual quality of these shows was mirrored in a simple rhetoric. There was little ambiguity; the endings were established as well as the conditions. The viewers were left with little opportunity to make their own decisions, or to draw their own conclusions.

All of the characteristics of these programs bring out certain spectator traits. In this environment viewers are intellectually passive as they accept a whole series of conditions that lead to predefined answers. They are not asked to react or to change the observed material. They follow the leader accepting, and, maybe, absorbing. Intellectual passivity is rewarded in this context.

If the description of television and its programming sounds familiar to those who were part of the educational complex during this period—it should. Students throughout this time were consistently rewarded for listening and responding with "correct" answers to queries that emphasized base, or factual knowledge. To use a television analogy "Just gimme the facts!" (Jack Webb, *Dragnet*, circa 1955) was a familiar teaching tool in many social studies classrooms.

Into this context, in which the average amount of viewing television was over 6½ hours per day and where students in the American educational system left obligatory schooling having spent about 25% more hours watching television than attending class, appeared a new information focused tool, the classroom based computer (U.S. Department of Commerce, 1970). This new mechanism, with its attendant software, began to force students and teachers to move away from the passive knowledge settings they had become accustomed to rely on, and were comfortable with, towards interactive activities that not only rewarded those who knew the correct answers but also those who could ask the "best" questions.

As these new technologies began to appear in classrooms it was suggested that the best path for integrating these new tools within the school, and specifically the social studies, curriculum would begin be through the development of a series of computer, or technology, literacy skills.

COMPUTER LITERACY

Throughout the 1980s the prevailing view of how to develop general computer literacy in the schools, and the concurrent curriculum, can be encapsulated in the following:

> The entire information system handling curriculum should involve experiential learning at some level and to some minimal degree. The format envisioned is description of function, demonstration of how available tools can accomplish these functions, and practice by the students in using the available tools. However, now, administrators, teachers, and other adults may need to feel more "computer comfortable"—not necessarily becoming programmers. Curricula should be tailored to job role and relevance. An inverted pyramid approach would readily permit expansion of understanding and competence using technology based on interest and need, and built upon the familiar. (Hunter, 1985, pp. 220-221)

Those looking at the social studies were particularly focused on the "social uses of information and how people in society use information" (Seidel, Anderson, & Hunter, 1985). The suggested activities that sought to enforce this concept included problem solving and simulation activities that would "be used to teach the process of making decisions as well taking actions and taking responsibilities" (pp. 261-263).

Social studies educators of the time posited that the purpose of computer related social studies programs was to provide learning experiences that would lead to the acquisition, and development of the knowledge, attitudes, processes, and competencies essential for self development, positive human relationships, and participation in a democratic society. Within this context four distinctive areas were identified as primary to these programs: social responsibility and values, decision-making skills, the use of information in a democratic society, and the impact of technology, historically and in the future (Diem, 1985).

While there were articles in *Social Education* and *The Social Studies* as well as scholarship that described the impact of technology on specific issues, such as the energy crisis or regional development, there were no extant classroom materials, during this time that dealt specifically with computer literacy and social studies issues. There were, however, the beginnings of the first computer based social studies curricular materials.

SOFTWARE

In 1984 about 28% of all children aged 3 to 17 years of age had access to a computer at home while 15% of this same age group could use one at their school (Kominski, 1988). For most of these children there were four major categories of computer use: video games, school related activities, basic learning of the computer (computer literacy activities), and other activities (word-processing, and record keeping activities) (Kominski, 1988).

School-related computer usage was highly concentrated in mathematics, science, and computer literacy classes with applications in both the humanities and social sciences lagging behind these curricular offerings (Kominski, 1988). However, some very good software applications that directly related to the social studies were beginning to appear. The most noteworthy, and an excellent example of the direction that the technology oriented social curricula was taking, was the simulation game *The Oregon Trail*.

First developed by three student teachers, Don Rawitsch, Bill Heinemann, and Paul Dillenberger, at Carleton College in 1971, the game had became so popular by 1984 that it had been released, and re-released with several computer platform adaption's, three times (Educational Software Classics, n.d.). Each new version of the game kept its original simulation format where in students had to figure out how to survive their journey from Missouri to Oregon. Along the way they had to make choices about the amount food they would need as well as the types of game they needed to harvest to stay alive. Members of the student's wagon party were also subject to other forms of catastrophe such as snakebite and having their oxen fall ill.

This simulation game was one of the first that incorporated both social studies curriculum concepts as well as technological skill development while being "teacher-friendly" for those teachers who had minimal computer-based instructional experiences. It provided a vision of how information technology might be used as a means to deliver problem-solving concepts through an inquiry and critical thinking based platform.

HARDWARE

As new forms of educational and personal software were being developed and produced for mass markets the delivery systems, or personal computers, that were needed to actual use and manipulate information were also undergoing rapid structural and price changes in 1984. Noted below is a list of the hottest selling computer hardware circa 1983-84 as reported by *Time* magazine ("The Computer Moves In," 1983):

Under $1,000:

Timex Sinclair 1000 ($99)
Commodore VIC-20 ($299)
Atari 400 and 800 ($299 and $899)
Texas Instruments (TI) 99/4a ($450)
Epson HX-20 ($795)
TRS-80 Model III ($999)

Between $1,000 and$2,000:

Apple II Plus ($1,330)
IBM Personal Computer ($1,565)
Osborne 1 ($1,795)

Two of these, the Apple II Plus and the IBM Personal Computer, were far and away the "best sellers" during this period in terms of both public and private purchases. Indeed, the combined sales of these two machines were over 470,000 for the1981-82 period ("The Computer Moves In," 1983). By late 1984 Dell Computers, the Tandy 1000 and Apple Macintosh joined this list of top sellers. A large segment of these purchases were to schools, many of who were buying their initial small computer systems for classroom use, at both the pre-and postsecondary levels.

There were, however, lots of instances where schools and universities, often with limited funds and technological expertise, often bought cheap systems so that they could quickly provide their students with computer access. As these machines fell by the wayside due to competitive forces and, more often, lack of compatibility with changing industry standards and operating systems, students and teachers became limited in their ability to learn and apply technology to their classroom settings.

It should also be noted that during 1984 that the 3.5-inch floppy disk was also introduced. This device quickly became an information storage standard for and significantly expanded the possibilities of information sharing, retrieval, and creativity, in terms of individual authorship of technology applications, in a quantum leap from the old "floppy-disks" that had previously been in wide use as storage devices,

TEACHER TRAINING

As schools began to see the value, and necessity, of incorporating personal computer technology into classrooms it quickly became apparent that many pre- and in-service teachers did not have the knowledge or ability to use or effectively apply these new tools within their classrooms. To alleviate this situation teacher education programs began to include discussions of how to use computers as part of their instructional paradigms. For those already teaching professional development local education agencies, state service centers, professional education groups, and commercial vendors sponsored programs that focused on technology.

As training for technology applications and use evolved, its focus shifted from general education technology treatments to specific subject fields. Noted below is an example of the topics and readings that might have been included in social studies computer class for either pre or in-service educators in the 1980s (Naylor & Diem, 1987).

Topics

1. CAEMS: Computer Assisted Educational Management Systems: understanding data management and data retrieval from a broad administrative perspective

2. CAI: Computer Assisted Instruction: applications of computer technology for specific subject (social studies) areas

3. Tutorials: using computers for practice, reinforcement of concepts, remediation or enrichment

4. Drill and Practice: reinforcement of facts and knowledge in repetitive sequences through the use of computers

5. Simulations: simulating real or hypothetical events and allowing students to make choices and consequences of their decisions often using pre-packaged games

6. Data Bases: developing data based activities that incorporated, for example, historical facts, economic data, or demographic information, into excel spreadsheets

7. Programming Via the BASIC or LOGO Computer Languages: developing lessons and activities by authoring, or writing, a program in one of these computer-programming languages

8. Social Applications: discussion of the right to privacy and laws regarding stealing of information.

9. Evaluation of Software: learning how to select "appropriate and useful" software for social studies classes by using national subject based computer software standards

Class Readings

Abelson, R. B. (Ed.). (1983). *Using microcomputers in the social Studies.* Boulder, CO: Social Science Education Consortium. Practical guidelines for social studies teachers

Burnett, J. D. (1982). Logo: An introduction. Morris Plains, NY: Creative Computing Press. Discussion of Logo and its classroom applications.

Cannings T. R., & Brown S. W. (Eds.). (1986). *The information age classroom: Using the computer as a tool.* Irvine, CA: Franklin, Beedle & Associates. A general computer literacy textbook.

Diem, R. (Ed.) (1983). Technology and the social studies (Special Issue). *Social Education, 47,* 308-343. A special issue on the use of various new technologies in the social studies classroom.

Papert, S. (1980). *Mindstorms.* New York: Basic Books. The philosophy of the LOGO Computing language.

Robinson, S.B. (1982, December). Microcomputer software and the social studies. *ERIC Keeping Up.* List of computer software.

Ross, S. A. (1984). Social studies microcomputer evaluation guide-lines. *Social Education, 48,* 573-576.

Note that during this period there was an articulated emphasis on broad based subject matter applications and learning of computer languages with some discussion on self directed activities through the use of simulations and data base construction. Within these classes there were usually specific discussions that covered topics such as the right to privacy and the economic and social consequences of not becoming "computer literate." However, there was little consideration given to the emotional costs of embracing, whole-heartedly, this type of technology nor its effects on society as a whole. As Sherry Turkle (1984) noted in *The Second Self-Computers and the Human Spirit:*

> Most considerations of the computer concentrate on the "instrumental computer," on what the computer will do. But I am interested in the "subjective computer." This is the machine as it enters social life and psychological development, the computer as it affects the way we think, especially the way we think about ourselves. I believe that what fascinates me is the unstated question that lies behind much of our preoccupation with the computer's capabilities. The question is not what will the computer be like in the future, but what will *we* be like? What kind of people are we becoming? (pp. 18-19)

Interestingly, Turkle (1984) raised these issues near the birth of the first academic and social network systems and just before the world wide net, with its attendant unforeseen social, political, and economic impacts, had arrived.

SOCIAL NETWORKS

Beginning in 1979 the National Science Foundation (NSF) began to fund the development of a system that would link together various computer science departments in U.S. universities. Its goal was to allow scientists and other academicians to begin to share nonclassified research. In 1984 this work, through NSF funding, branched out to include the development of several regional supercomputing centers as well as the linking of these in a general purpose research sharing network (Merit Network, 1995). Within this new environment, called NSFNET, scientific information, experiments, and research discussions could proceed at unheard of speed. It was now possible to work on the same problem with colleagues across the country in "real" time.

Throughout its existence, which ended in 1995, NSFNET expanded to include social science applications as well as the development of various engineering break throughs including the development of computer "router" systems. Perhaps its most interesting, and widest, impact was the release of the *Hitchhiker's Guide to the Internet* (1989) and *The Whole Internet User's Guide & Catalog* (1992) that were both written, or cowritten, by one of the original NSF network managers Ed Krol.

At the same time that NSFNET began its "run" another telecommunication breakthrough was also being put into wide use. BITNET, "Because It's Time Network" became an early leader in network communications, especially in what came to be known as "e-mails." Based on IBM's internal e-mail system BITNET featured both e-mail and list serve software and supported interactive transmission of files and messages. At its height in the early 1990s this system connected over 3,500 educational organizations worldwide (Grier & Campbell, 2000). Through this system social studies researchers first began to look at the effects information technology and their applications had in classroom settings. However, it was not until a researcher, Tim Berners-Lee at the CERN laboratories in Switzerland proposed a new computer network that the effects of "the information revolution" would reach into and dramatically change, globally, educational systems.

Berners'-Lee technical paper titled "Information Management—A Proposal" brought the world its first computer browser and the concept of a world wide computer "web" (Bray, 2009). Latter, enhanced by others, this idea turned into the Mosaic, Netscape, Explorer, and Safari computer search engines. As each was released the numbers of Internet users rose, almost exponentially.

The social, cultural, and educational challenges brought forth by the web are still unfolding. As these have emerged the role of the social studies as the subject area that can develop the intersection of citizenship, and its responsibilities in a world in which instantaneous information and communication are now a given becomes even more important.

AS IT IS

Twenty-five years after Atari and Apple were commanding the attention of those who were computer literate, or sought to be, and Winston Smith stood before his telescreen, where are we, in terms of technology and the social studies?

Computer Literacy: Today's students from pre-K through college have always had a computer or other forms information technology, such as the cell phone or PDA, available to them throughout their entire lives. When they enter school there is no need to make them "computer literate" as they have surpassed all the expectations of the 1984 concepts of this term embraced. These same students still need to be taught the ever-changing social, political, and economic ramifications of technology and societal intersects as part of their instruction in citizenship education. In this light the role of the social studies is paramount.

Teacher Training: As with today's students, present day teachers no longer have to be taught basic information about computers. Instead they need to understand how to apply the new types of technology and web-based materials that are consistently arriving in the educational markets as well as understanding the history of present day information technology and the effects that these items have on the lives of their students.

Software: The type of social studies information based software that is now in use has its roots in early social studies decision-making and simulation games. Learning to manipulate various forms of historical and social science data and understanding the ramifications of how these data might be used in a real life situation is should be one of the basic outcomes in most social studies lessons. The challenge facing teachers in this context is not obtaining data for these purposes, but selecting the types of problems that will lead students to not only the "correct answer" but to understanding the process that they went through to get the answer.

Hardware: While every school throughout the United States has access to computers, the world wide, Internet, cable television, and in many cases a wireless network, there are still many classrooms that do not have a computer or, at best, have a single teacher based one. Access to computer technology is still an economic issue in many school communities. Interestingly, there is some evidence that more students have and use cell phones on a daily basis than computers (Bray, 2009).

Social Networks: The greatest difference, and challenge, from 1984 to now is the appearance of information technology based social networks.

Twenty-five years ago there were no social or technological visionaries who could even imagine the effect that websites such Facebook, MySpace, and Twitter would have on a global scale. No one predicted students "twittering" friends around the world during a class and no one can say what the long lasting effect of this phenomenon will be. The best that social studies educators can, and should, do is to note, for example, that postings to Facebook from the 2010 earthquake in Haiti appeared hours before any other information about this event was made available to the general public and then ask their students what this might mean for our established communication infrastructures like television and newspapers as well as its effects on their role in becoming an educated and informed citizen.

Control/Availability of Information: The issue of who owns and controls information is still evolving much as it was in 1984. With private companies and the government collecting data on almost everyone from the time of birth through, and after, death it is important for social studies instruction to still include discussions on the right to privacy, the accessing of public information, and the "fair" use this information in both public and private settings as part of their curriculum.

Commercial or Orwellian Influences: It is still an open question of how far the government can go in collecting information about individuals before it becomes unconstitutional. For example: Is it justified to pass laws such as the Patriot Act to protect us from terrorists while giving up certain privacy rights? Is it "ok" to track down those who would collect child pornography while, at the time, intruding on innocent users of the Internet? At the same time should those who write software programs be allowed to go into partnership with hardware vendors in an effort to dominate both markets? All these are topics for today and tomorrow's social studies classes.

The chapters that follow take these issues in the context of where computer and information technology within the venue of the social studies might be headed in the next 25 years. The authors present their views on these, and other, unthought of topics in 1984 terms while raising some that are yet to come.

REFERENCES

Bray, H. (2009, March). World-changing Web was born 20 years ago. *The Boston Globe*, 19-20.

Diem, R. (1985). Computer literacy in the social studies classroom. *Computer literacy: Issues and directions for 1985*. New York: Academic Press.

Educational Software Classics. (n.d.). Retrieved August 2009, from http://ldt.standford.edu/ldt199/Students/kemery/esc/otMain frame.htm

Computer Hope.Com (n.d.). Retrieved August 2009, from http://www.computerhope.com/history

Grier, D., & Campbell, M. (2000). *A social history of BITNET and Listserv, 1985, 1991*. Retrieved August 2009, from http://en.wikipedia.org/wiki/BITNET

Hunter, B. (1985). Computer literacy curriculum for Grades K-8. *Computer literacy: Issues and Directions for 1985*. New York: Academic Press.

Kominski, R. (1988). *Computer use in the United States: 1984*. Washington, DC: U.S. Department of Commerce.

Krol, E. (1989). *The hitchhiker's guide to the Internet*. Urbana, IL: University of Illinois Press.

O'Reilly, B., Krol, E., & Klopfenstein, B. (1992). *The whole Internet user's guide and catalog*. New York: Nutshell

Orwell, G. (1949). *1984*, London: Signet Classics

Merit Network. (1995). *The NSFNET Backbone Project, 1987-1995*. Washiington, DC: Merit Network.

Naylor, D., & Diem, R. (1987). *Elementary and middle school social studies*. New York: Random House.

Seidel, R., Anderson, R., & Hunter, B. (Eds.). (1982). *Computer literacy; Issues and directions for 1985*. New York: Academic Press.

The computer moves in. (1983, January 3). *Time*, 14-39.

Turkle, S. (1984). *The second self—Computers and the human spirit*. New York: Simon & Schuster.

United States Department of Commerce. (1970). Bureau of Census—1970 Report. Washington, DC: U.S. Government Printing Office.

CHAPTER 2

IN THE BEGINNING, APPLE

Ways in Which the Vision Progressed

Cheryl A. Franklin Torrez

When I began teaching the disks were floppy; now I have a SmartBoard in my class-room. I've always had a least one computer in my classroom. Years ago, I used it for record keeping ... eventually, when my students began using computers, my teaching changed. My current classroom has a lot of technology. This gives my students more access to knowledge, and gives me better teaching tools. I think one of the most important effects of the increased technologies is that education, or at least learning, is more equitable, more democratic. (T10)

The educational possibilities of computer-assisted instruction and other technologies such as hand-operated adding machines, microfilm, and eventually, calculators and LOGO had been suggested for decades (Machlowitz, 1976; Papert, 1978, 1980; Sells, 1959; Skinner, 1961; Wrigley, 1957) The seed was planted for a growing trend of educators seeking uses of technology for educational transformation. However, it was the introduction of the Apple computer into K-12 classrooms that set the vision for the technology use we commonly see and aspire to today.

In this chapter, the purposeful introduction of Apple computers in K-12 classrooms, the vision laid by this presence, and sustained evidence of

Technology in Retrospect: Social Studies in the Information Age 1984-2009, pp. 13–31

this vision will be presented. Alongside will be narratives from 15 K-12 classroom teachers who all began their teaching careers before or during the mid-1980s. Their professional careers parallel the 25 years of Macintosh/Apple.

> *When I began teaching, I had an overhead projector and a record player. The first time I had access to computers was in 1988—we had a lab with Apple II computers, and I got a brand new Apple IIc in my classroom. (T1)*
>
> *I had a tape recorder (earphones, too), a radio boom box, reel movies, and the first computer I received was a 1990 Apple. (T2)*
>
> *My first two years of teaching I only had access to an overhead projector. Then my third year of teaching my school purchased Josten computers which included word processing software for the most part. (T7)*
>
> *In my first years of teaching, we had no technology. The first computers available were Apple with 64 bits and then when the district decided to purchase computers for teachers, I was part of the Mac pilot in 1990. (T4)*

THE VISION: APPLE CLASSROOMS OF TOMORROW

Most notably, it was the Apple Classrooms of Tomorrow (ACOT) longitudinal study which began in 1985 and continued for a decade that marked a decisive effort towards improving and transforming teaching and learning through the use of technology. Until the ACOT project, little empirical evidence had been gathered or disseminated that examined the effects of computers on education. The technology focus was broadened to include student learning activities, teacher behaviors, competencies and characteristics, as well as teacher preparation and training. The framework and results of the ACOT studies are seminal to an understanding of technology in schools.

> *We had a lab with Apple II computers, and a colleague had a IIgs in his room. The disks were floppy—really, I mean they flopped. He taught me how to use a computer … those were darn good computers. (T12)*
>
> *My school had an Apple IIe lab which I didn't use (because of my teaching assignment), but I became quite proficient on the new IIe in the office—helped the secretary figure it out. (T3)*
>
> *Mostly, I used the Apple for word processing and then databases. I had to exchange floppies all the time. The printer paper for the dot-matrix printers had to be lined up so the holes would fit onto the roller sprockets. My students learned LOGO because I had learned it in my teacher training. (T15)*
>
> *Early on, my students did word processing and played simulation games and math skill games. We went to the lab once a week. Oregon Trail was huge. Students also practiced typing. We also did some basic Logo programming. (T1)*

ACOT Methods

ACOT cemented the notion of technology-infused classrooms and many subsequent documents have their foundation embedded in the findings of the ACOT project. ACOT was a research and development collaboration among public schools, universities, research agencies, and Apple, Inc. At the outset, the study consisted of seven classrooms representing a cross-section of America's elementary and secondary schools. The overall project goal was to study how the routine use of technology by teachers and students might change teaching and learning (Sandholtz, Ringstaff, & Dwyer, 1997).

Qualitative data were collected from 32 elementary and secondary teachers in 5 schools across 4 states throughout the 13 year study; over the course of the study more than 100 classrooms were involved. Project teachers were all volunteers selected by participating school districts. The gender and ethnic composition of the classes mirrored each school as a whole. Teachers ranged from novices to experienced veterans with over 20 years of classroom teaching and very few had worked with technology before joining the project.

In fall of 1986, each of the ACOT sites began with one classroom per school with additional classrooms, staff, and students joining in subsequent years. Although each site served students from various grade levels, none of the sites encompassed an entire school. In the first year of the study, each site was equipped with Apple IIe, IIgs, and Macintosh computers. In addition, Apple provided printers, scanners, laserdisc and videotape players, modems, CD-ROM drives, and a wide variety of software titles. This equipment was in addition to materials commonly found in classrooms. "The operating principle in ACOT classrooms was to use the media that best supported the learning goal." Initially, all participating students were provided two computers, one at school and one at home.

> Since hardware in 1986 was big and heavy, the two-computer formula was the only way to simulate a time when students and teachers would have constant access to technology by virtue of some future state of miniaturization, portability, and cost. (Sandholtz et al., 1997, p. 4)

The 32 ACOT teachers provided researchers with bi-monthly audiotapes on which they reflected about their experiences; weekly reports sent via electronic mail; and correspondence between sites. Independent researchers also provided reports based upon observations in project classrooms investigating the impact of technology on various aspects of learning and teaching. Throughout the duration of the project, students, teachers, classrooms and sites involved with the project changed as did the amount, type, and configuration of technology. "We learned that computer access was important but that access did not necessarily require a computer on every desk" (Sandholtz et al., 1997, p. 6). ACOT stopped providing a home computer for the students because "their teachers did not have time to develop appropriate assignments."

> Early on, my computer use with students was pretty much skill and drill until our district purchased HyperStudio and provided training for teachers during a summer institute. This was really the first user-friendly, multi-layer program students could use to create interactive presentations while exploring subject matter. (T1)
>
> At first, the movement was toward computer labs with 30 computers in one room. Then schools also tried to have 3-5 computers in each classroom in addition to the lab. So in a lab setting, students would type research papers and do graphing activities. (T6)
>
> In my 1st teaching assignment, there were no computers on the entire campus. Three years later, I was in a new assignment with one computer, a Mac, in my class and a Mac computer lab down the hall housing 6 computers. (T5)

ACOT and Knowledge Construction

The ACOT vision of technology in education was more far reaching than computers as teaching machines; "Technology was viewed as a tool to support learning across the curriculum" (Sandholtz et al., 1997, p. 6). This could be accomplished by supporting constructivist pedagogy. ACOT defined constructivism as a theory that

> defines knowledge as temporary, developmental, socially and culturally mediated, and thus, non-objective. Learning from this perspective is understood as a self-regulating process of resolving inner cognitive conflicts that often become apparent through concrete experience, collaborative discourse, and reflection. (Sandholtz et al., 1997, p. 12)

The purpose and vision was to transform traditional *knowledge instruction* classrooms into *knowledge construction* classrooms. ACOT viewed technology as a necessary and catalytic part of such a transformation. A knowledge construction classroom would emphasize problem solving, conceptual development, and critical thinking rather than rote memorization that one would traditionally find in a knowledge instruction classroom. During the 1980s, schools engaged in traditional forms of instruction raised test scores but students were unable to solve problems or think critically.

> When teachers and administrators became more accountable for student test scores, they increasingly limited instruction to drill and practice of the

kinds of skills and disjointed facts that nationally normed tests emphasized. As a result of state-mandated accountability systems that began as early as 1972, "public schools showed a decline in the use of such methods as student-centered discussion, the writing of essays or themes, and projects or laboratory work." (Darling-Hammond, 1990, p. 290)

In other words, while schools focused, albeit successfully, on raising test scores, the classroom demand for higher-order cognitive performance virtually disappeared. "Students became better test takers but at a terrible cost" (Sandholtz et al., 1997, p. 12). The educational climate was conducive to change, and computer integration in schools provided a vehicle for reform.

I was committed to cooperative learning for my students, and one of the first computer activities I used was having groups develop Hyperstacks about the Gold Rush using HyperCard. I used the state Social Studies Framework and decided that each unit would include some form of computer use by students. (T10)

ACOT set forth contrasting views of instruction and construction (see Table 2.1) and indicated that the cognitive premises of the theory of constructivism cannot dictate specific teaching methods, but rather offer guidelines for good teaching.

Table 2.1.   Contrasting Views of Instruction and Construction

	Instruction	*Construction*
Classroom activity	Teacher centered Didactic	Learner centered Interactive
Teacher role	Fact teller Always expert	Collaborator Sometimes learner
Student role	Listener Always learner	Collaborator Sometimes expert
Instructional emphasis	Facts Memorization	Relationships Inquiry and invention
Concept of knowledge	Accumulation of facts	Transformation of facts
Demonstration of success	Quantity	Quality of understanding
Assessment	Norm referenced Multiple-choice items	Criterion referenced Portfolios and performances
Technology use	Drill and practice	Communication, collaboration, information access, expression.

Source: Sandholtz et al. (1997, p. 14).

The body of work resulting from the ACOT study provided a foundation for educational technology in schools. The ACOT researchers clearly stated that the marriage of constructivism and technology could revolutionize K-12 education. They held a vision of reform and built their conceptual framework upon the work of educational reformists (Sandholtz et al., 1997).

> *Apple focused on schools, and it made all the difference, didn't it? In the late 80s, I was developing databases for my students to use—that was considered interactive at the time. One project I developed was a database of all the Donner Party members. This included gender, age, family, and survivorship. Then my students could develop their own questions about the Donner Party and inquire using the database. Eventually, the students made their own databases for the expansion and settlement of the West. (T13)*

Units of Practice

In order to integrate technology into curriculum, ACOT developed the unit of practice (UOP). The UOP was to exemplify both technology integration and constructivist theory via project-based learning. The UOP was a tool designed to encourage teachers to experiment with, learn, and implement new approaches to teaching and grew out of the ACOT staff's desire to develop an instrument that could be used across all ACOT sites as an indicator of classroom change. The UOP did not refer to "a teaching unit in the traditional sense, nor is the process synonymous with lesson planning." At the outset of the UOP process, a teacher selects a teaching episode that has been successful in the past and then thinks about how she might enhance or extend it using technology.

> If technology is effectively integrated into the lesson and not simply added on, teachers implementing the UOP process learn quickly that changing one component of a lesson—in this instance, adding a new technological tool—has ramifications for other components of the teaching episode. (Sandholtz et al., 1997, p. 123)

The components of a learning activity thusly become one integrated whole consisting of standards, tasks, interactions, tools, situations, and assessments. The authors likened it to the ancient Chinese game, the tangram. Tiles of different shapes and sizes can be arranged to make a square but also be arranged to make a variety of figures such as birds, trees, houses or boats. No piece can be defined or fully understood except in relation to the others.

I remember being trained in UOPs as part of our inservices [professional development] in the late 1980s; these pretty much established how I designed and still design lessons. I used to make myself think of ways to integrate technology; now it is just a routine part of what I do. (T9)

We used the UOP model during our workshops for our PT3 grants in late 90s and early 2000s. Nearly every teacher in our district used this framework; many of them still do. It remains an authentic way to effectively integrate technology and curriculum. (T12)

Stages of Instructional Evolution

The ACOT study also resulted in widespread use of stages of teachers' progress as they learned how to incorporate technology into classroom environments (see Table 2.2). This framework continues to be used as a tool to analyze and describe technology use in classrooms (for example, Cuban, 2001). Some of the major themes of the ACOT research were collaboration, communication, multiple representations of ideas, intelligent applications and modeling, information analysis, and assessment.

By the late 80's my colleagues and I were redesigning our thematic units, usually focused around a social studies concept, and integrating technology into them. We had arguments over which software to buy site licenses for, and long discussions about checking out laser discs. Fortunately, our school was a Title I site and we had funds for the technology we needed. Students used the Oregon Trail when we studied the

Table 2.2. ACOT Stages

Stage	Examples of What Teachers Do
Entry	Learn the basics of using the new technology
Adoption	Use new technology to support traditional instruction
Adaptation	Integrate new technology into traditional practice. Here, they often focus on increased student productivity and engagement by using word processors, spreadsheets, and graphics tools.
Appropriation	Focus on cooperative, project-based, and interdisciplinary work—incorporating the technology as needed and as one of many tools.
Invention	Discover new uses for technology tools, for example, developing spreadsheet macros for teaching algebra or designing projects that combine multiple technologies.

Source: Sandholtz et al. (1997).

West and Storybook Weaver in the computer lab (my site just cleaned the lab and threw these away). We were really trying to have students learn and construct knowledge, and we wanted to use as much technology as we could. (T8)

From 1994-2000 technology use in my classroom expanded. I worked at a site which was networked schoolwide (sic.). We created HyperStudio and PowerPoint projects that incorporated video, data, text, and links to Internet areas of student interest. My fifth graders developed training projects to instruct their parents, and we presented during evening sessions in our lab. We created the first electronic yearbook with a HP grant. Students began video editing during that time. Our site was dynamic with technology. Many teachers were struggling up the steep learning curve, so we developed a variety of on-site training opportunities to teach each other. We organized a total school computer upgrade with 30 volunteers to upgrade our 75, five-year old computers in 1999. (T1)

I first began using software programs like Decisions, Decisions in my Civics class and Inspiration for all of my classes. My district had support from Apple, and this may be one of the reasons I wanted my students to use technology to empower themselves. My school has a high percentage of English language learners, and computers gave my students a way to show what they learned in a variety of ways. (T9)

In its early stages, ACOT focused on computer-saturated environments in single classrooms rather than entire school sites and a primary intent was to reform educational settings. As the project progressed, additional classrooms at each project site were added but, still, none of the sites encompassed an entire school. By focusing on classrooms, attention was given to teachers' development through the ACOT stages. Changing teachers' beliefs was a necessary condition for instructional change. One of the lessons learned as a result of ACOT is that technology alone cannot improve teaching and learning and that technology must be "grounded firmly in curriculum goals, incorporated in sound instructional processes, and deeply integrated with subject-matter content" (Baker, Herman, & Gearhart, 1996, p. 201). In order for this to be accomplished within the technology-rich classroom, teachers' beliefs about teaching and learning became fundamental.

The findings from the ACOT study indicated that technology has the potential to transform education in positive ways. ACOT also helped us understand that the numerous factors contribute to successful integration of technology. These included the physical and contextual environment, teacher beliefs and training, and technology integration into sound and meaningful curriculum and instruction. The visionary foundation laid by Apple showed us that technology could help create knowledge construction classrooms as well as providing a framework for the stages of instructional evolution (see Table 2.2) that remain pervasive in the current educational world.

SUSTAINED EVIDENCE OF THE VISION

Vestiges of this early ACOT work appear in many of the educational technology standards in existence today. These include content standards, technology standards, and standards for teachers. Woven throughout all of these standards, as they relate to technology, is the thread of technology as a catalyst for change in schools, for improved teaching, and greater learning.

Content Standards

The National Council for the Social Studies (NCSS, 1997, 2002, 2008) included technology as a component in their standards documents, "Social Studies teaching and learning integrate effective uses of technology" (NCSS, 1994, p. 11). These documents emphasized content with technology being a tool to support content. The NCSS document stated:

Teachers of the early grades can help learners use their own experiences with science and technology to develop an understanding of the role that science and technology play in shaping human experience. They can have them consider how inventions have altered the course of history and how society has employed technologies to modify the physical environment. They can also provide opportunities for learners to consider instances in which changes in values, beliefs, and attitudes have resulted from the communication and acceptance of scientific and technological knowledge. Teachers of young learners can also challenge them to consider ways to monitor individual rights, and the common good. (NCSS, 1997, para. 11)

In social studies ... I used to use simulations like Oregon Trail and Caesar; then interactive CDs on specific topics. We also had access to text-related sites that led students through course content, mostly videos and online quiz type formats. Now, I use video and image content from the Internet. Our social studies text has videos that illustrate concepts and online access to standards based test prep materials. I can prepare quizzes and assessment rubrics online that correlate with the text. (T1)

Initially, I used technology during social studies by researching topics that are part of my curriculum and sharing the information with my students. We study the geography of Canada, and I was able to put together a PowerPoint of the region in which we were studying so the students could have a connection. As time progressed, not only did I use the computer and internet as a tool, but I also have taught my students to do the same. Students complete several research projects through the course of the year using technology as a way to collect information and organize it before sharing it with peers. For example, Canadian explorers PowerPoint, primary/secondary sources exploration and presentation. Now, I take my students on electronic fieldtrips to places we study, create PowerPoint presentations of curriculum content, current information about geography and history of the western hemisphere is easily shared on my SmartBoard. And I share and collect ideas from other teachers around the world. (T4)

The NCSS has also published its *Technology Position Statement and Guidelines* that sets forth a rationale and vision for technology integration into the social studies. These guidelines call for educators to seamlessly weave technology into the social studies curriculum (NCSS, 2006, para. 8). The premise of integrating technology into curriculum and assessment has its roots in ACOT. Additionally, in this position statement, we see a vision of knowledge construction social studies classrooms. Having students use technology to construct social studies knowledge is also grounded in the foundation laid by Apple. The *Position Statement and Guidelines* refer the social studies educator additional standards that are addressed next. The interweaving of these standards provides additional evidence of their roots in ACOT.

Technology Standards

In addition to content area standards, *National Educational Technology Standards* [NETS] reflect the ACOT vision. The *NETS for Students* serves as a guide for classroom teachers and describes what students should know about technology, be able to do with technology, and provides curriculum examples of effective use of technology (International Society for Technology in Education [ISTE], 2000, 2007). This document defined curriculum integration and stated

Curriculum integration with the use of technology involves the infusion of technology as a tool to enhance the learning in a content area or multidisciplinary setting. Technology enables students to learn in ways not previously possible. Effective integration of technology is achieved when students are able to select technology tools to help them obtain information in a timely manner, analyze and synthesize the information, and present it professionally. The technology should become an integral part of how the classroom functions—as accessible as all other classroom tools. (ISTE, 2000, p. 6)

The focus on curriculum outcomes instead of a myopic view on technology proliferation is another example of the continued philosophical emphasis of the ACOT project. NETS and ACOT both view technology as a tool to support learning across the curriculum. Positioning technology integration in curriculum, student learning and understanding, communication and collaboration, all of which are evident in NETS, has its roots in the ACOT project.

*As Web 2.0 technologies have become more widely available, students are now creat-
ing their own websites, blogging, and using discussion boards. Technology has moved
from teacher- developed activities to more student created-published activities. There
has also been a move away from teaching technology skills (typing, word processing,
file management) in isolation. These skills are more embedded. (T6)*

*In a nutshell, technology has democratized information. This has changed the way
my students communicate and learn, and the way I teach, communicate, and learn.
Learning is more connected, interactive and global. Access to information is free and
easy. I think the world is smaller for my students. (T12)*

Standards for Teachers

Additional evidence of the ACOT vision is found in *NETS for Teachers*
regarding teacher preparation:

> the technology use in elementary teacher professional preparation must
> focus on preparing the elementary teacher in all curriculum areas instead of
> just one or two. The program must emphasize student-centered approaches
> to working in a flexible environment, coping with a host of ways to access
> equipment and software in the context of addressing the needs of second
> language learners. (ISTE, 2002, p. 130)

Without teachers who are well prepared to integrate curriculum and
instruction, K-12 students will not tap into the potential of technology
and its educational possibilities. The emphasis of *NETS for Teachers* is on
teacher preparation. "A combination of essential conditions is required
for teachers to create learning environments conducive to powerful uses
of technology" (ISTE, 2002, p. 16). Teachers are expected to integrate
technology into subject matter, and to design, develop, and evaluate
authentic learning experiences and assessment incorporating contemporary tools and resources to maximize content learning in context, and to
engage in professional growth (ISTE, 2008). Evidence of the ACOT vision
is prominent in these standards: curriculum and content remain fundamental and technology provides a vehicle for outstanding learning
opportunities.

*A huge worry for me during my teacher preparation program was being able to learn
to use a movie projector and a slide projector. In order to complete the program, we
had to show proficiency operating these machines. My current student teacher has our
students making documentaries using little digital cameras and websites. This is a
culmination of a service learning project. Over the past thirty years, technology has
improved and it has made a difference in schools. I'd still like to see more reform
though. We've been stuck for a few years with computers being used for testing. (T11)*

Our district has loaded us with technology---audio systems, ceiling mounted projectors, ELMOs. We just had Smart Boards installed throughout the school. Unfortunately, we are throwing technology at schools without really looking at effective instruction and teacher training. Instead, the district is relying on the marketing and training of the companies we're buying from to justify purchases and guide usage. (T3)

Similar to the NETS Standards for Teachers, The National Council for Accreditation of Teacher Education (NCATE) also provides standards for "knowledge and use of technology." These standards state that preservice teachers should learn how to use computers to teach content area curriculum as well as learn how to use technology for assessment and professional productivity. These foci have their roots in the ACOT foundation; technology should be integrated into curriculum, assessment and professional work.

Teacher training was pivotal to the ACOT project and a key outcome of the project. The College and University Faculty Assembly (CUFA) of the NCSS, in its *Guidelines for Using Technology to Prepare Social Studies Teachers* has suggested ways for social studies teacher educators to infuse technology in teacher preparation programs. The principles offered include (a) extending learning beyond what could be done without technology, (b) introducing technology in context, (c) including opportunities for students to study relationships among science, technology, and society, and (d) fostering the development of the skills, knowledge, and participation as good citizens in a democratic society (Mason, Berson, Diem, Hicks, Lee, & Dralle, 2000). These principles have their roots in Apple as they call for using technology in innovative ways and insist on maintaining emphasis on subject matter content; they call for knowledge construction classrooms.

Combined technology standards, whether for inservice teachers, preservice teachers or teacher education faculty, have resulted in concerted efforts to infuse computer technology into all levels of public education. In many respects effective use of technology goes hand-in-hand with educational reform. Using computers as multipurpose tools to enhance learning, to empower students, and to situate educational innovation at the forefront of progressive educational change was the aim of ACOT.

Technology is now a part of my everyday instruction. I use a SmartBoard, document camera and projector attached to my computer for almost every lesson I teach. Students use the computer as a teacher in the PLATO software. (T4)

We have SmartBoards in every classroom. I LOVE its interactivity. My students are thinking and being creative. Technology in my teaching is no longer a tool to present information. I teach 2nd/3rd grade and have a huge focus on local history. A colleague and I rewrote our social studies units so we can better use the SmartBoard technology. The first unit is on the local salt marshes and how they have impacted our area. We wrote the coolest programs and uploaded them to the Interactive Tool Box for Educators. Teachers in the district and around the world can access these and use them immediately with their SmartBoards. (T2)

For many, technology has the potential to dramatically reform education. And, although no one innovation will address all of the challenges that confronting education, ACOT sought to transform education using technology as a vehicle of reform. According to Cuban (2001), reform was the response to the 1983 report, *A Nation at Risk*, by the National Commission on Excellence on Education. Technology in schools soon became viewed as a transformative panacea. However, it was this goal of reform that provided fertile ground for the fast-growing technology industry, including Apple Computer. Apple purposefully partnered with K-12 schools to infuse technology and reform education.

Throughout the late 1980s and 1990s, public officials, corporate executives, vendors, parents and policymakers included in their reform agendas the common goal of creating more access to technology in schools. These reform efforts have not always been successful because the nature of traditional school and classroom organizations do not easily allow for computers to be used for knowledge construction models of instruction (Cuban, 2001).

I began teaching in 1985 and the technology available to me consisted of a slide projector, film projector, and an overhead transparency machine. Shortly thereafter, we had 3 computer labs: Apple, PC, and Mac. Ten years later, we were communicating with parents via email, posting midterm scores and progress reports for parents to access, doing other administrative duties with computers and having students do much of their research for my history class online. This was one of the most progressive schools in the state as the Internet wasn't as robust in 1995 as it is now—schools are often slow to catch on. One of the most interactive things I did then was to have students make an alphabet book focusing on the 1920s and 1930s; they got firewalled when researching the Valentine's Day Massacre. It was frustrating for my high school students and me—we couldn't get to the sites we needed; we couldn't use the technology as it was designed. I know this is a persistent problem for a lot of teachers, but it's ridiculous. Our students are much more engaged with technology outside of school than while at school. Now they live in a Web 2.0 world—they create and upload their lives for the world to see. (T14)

Shortly after the ACOT project began in 1995, and in response to the numerous calls for educational reform and increased computer availability in classrooms, there is clear evidence that policy and legislation impacted technology in education.

PARALLEL POLICY

As the diffusion of technology became more widespread in the 1990s, public interest in technology, especially personal computing, increased the role of policy and legislation in technology integration. Technology literacy came to be viewed as a necessary basic skill by the public and policymakers alike. The federal government exerted influence and leadership in the area of educational technology by means of funding. Within this arena, the "image of technology as a catalyst for change is almost universally shared" (Culp, Honey, & Mandinach, 2005, p. 5). Here again we see evidence of the ACOT vision.

During the 1990s, federal programs addressing educational technology gained impetus and the United States spent billions of dollars to bring computer and Internet access to public schools. This trend carried well through the 1990s into the new millennium. At the same time, legislative interest in the 1990s marked the beginning of federal mandates related to not only access issues but also curricular issues. For instance, *The Goals 2000: Educate America Act* enacted in 1994 was legislation designed to enhance educational technology in the nation's schools. Included with these goals was a call for all teachers to have continuing opportunities to acquire additional knowledge and skills needed to teach challenging subject matter and to use emerging new methods, forms of assessment, and technologies.

In order to accomplish these goals, various federal initiatives were implemented. These included the opening of the Office of Educational Technology, the development of a national technology plan, the establishment of the *Regional Technology in Education Consortia* (2002). Numerous grant projects became available under the umbrella of the Technology Literacy Challenge. These provided funding to states for the purchase of hardware, educational software and online applications, Internet connectivity and teacher training. National industry and educational leaders were also encouraged to collaborate on supporting educational technology. Another key initiative was the creation of *Preparing Tomorrow's Teachers to Use Technology* (PT3), which supported planning, implementation and the development of state and national efforts to integrate technology into teacher preparation programs. This Department of Education (DOE) program awarded grants to colleges, school districts, and state education agencies in order to support better preparation of future teachers to integrate technology into their teaching. Over $335 million was spent on these grants. These grants, served as a catalyst for teacher educators to partner with K-12 schools around technology integration and provided a fertile research field for educational researchers.

I was involved with several PT3 grants. Apple partnered with us and we spent a significant amount of time at their campus. We loosely adopted a "train the trainers" model in which several teachers were trained extensively by Apple in technology integration and these teachers trained their colleagues. It was a great success and helped us prepare a generation of teachers to effectively integrate technology into their teaching … transformation was the purpose of these grants. (T12)

The decade of the 1990s proved to be a great boon to educational technology. This paralleled the growth of technology in the nation, not only in the business and technology sectors, but in private households as well (Solomon, 2002). Just as national policy provided support via funding for technological availability within K-12 schools in the last century, the national policy in the first decade of the twenty-first century provided a focus as well.

Let's be honest. For most of my career, I've viewed technology as transformational; I still think it has huge potential to radically improve our schools. Wasn't that part of the focus of Apple along with marketing? I still buy Apple and Mac. Then, after 2000, much of it went to hell in our district. (T11)

The No Child Left Behind (NCLB) Act of 2001 sought to "improve student academic achievement through the use of technology" in K-12 schools. The federal technology plan indicated that systemic change was needed in order to address "the national crisis that underscores the demand for accountability in education" (p. 12). The 2001 NCLB legislation superseded and eliminated many of the 1999 national educational technology goals. In an attempt to relegate authority to the states and minimize paperwork, the potential for losing the ground gained in the 1990s was great. Underlying this legislation was the notion that if educational technology is not being used to raise standardized test scores, there is no need for the technology or for its funding. Whether the consequences were intended or unintended, many veteran teachers felt diminishment of the technology vision in schools while technological advances were significant outside of schools.

All of this changed when high-stakes testing reared its ugly head. Suddenly, if the training didn't justify meeting a state standard tested in April, it wasn't a priority. Tech training essentially fizzled, emphasis on technology faltered, and our school site had to develop covert operations to spend time on technology- rich projects instead of the pacing guide activities we were required to do. No Child Left Behind left technology behind at our site. Currently more of our textbooks have a technology component, but it's pseudo interactive, sort of like worksheets online. I have found many websites that are interactive and educational for my students that I use often. Most work well now that we have better bandwidth, or whatever it's now called. Students at the 3rd grade level aren't proficient computer users by any means, and proficiency for school applications has degraded in the last ten years, even with the huge influx of technology in their lives. Unless a child is interested in computers and pursues this interest independently, they definitely don't have the technology opportunities they had 10 years ago, at least at our site. (T1)

Overall, great strides were made as a result of federal policy and funding for technology in schools. Policy and funding impacted not only the integration of technology into schools, but also research on technology. As technology continues to rapidly advance and change, continued federal funding remains crucial to both the diffusion of technology as well as research in the field.

PRESENTLY

Currently, each of the educators who shared their technology histories in this chapter has access to a variety of technologies. They work within the constraints of their districts and states, and despite some grumbling, all have indicated that they are able to integrate technology into their teaching of social studies. However, their current level of technology integration is inadequate and frustrating. This is due to many of the external constraints placed upon them.

In my classroom, I have an LCD, Interwrite, all wireless, streaming. This allows me to relate past history to today by showing clips from news, primary images, etc. (T2)

I use websites I find that are interactive to help teach my 3rd graders about history and social science—I also integrate science. Students create projects incorporating research done on the computer, video and photos. We create movies to promote civic engagement. We use the Office Suite for word processing and presentations. Students collect data with video cameras and download and edit video using Pinnacle Studio. (T1)

I am now developing most units right in my Smart Notebook where I can capture on-line resources to show students. I recently scanned and put all state test prep materials into this format also (I hope this might make it more meaningful to students). In social studies, the students take virtual field trips and I'm using digital primary source artifacts quite often. I used to only use Jackdaw materials that came in boxes, but now my students and I can locate more than I ever dreamed of. We still have too many required tests, but Web 2.0 and Open Source software are also allowing my students to engage in history authentically, to engage in inquiry. Not only are they inquiring and analyzing, but they are also producing content for others. (T5)

Perhaps most interesting to me is that I am easily able to download primary source material (e.g,. letters between John and Abigail Adams). I download lots of pictures of historical sites and video reenactments, as well as paintings and engravings of historical events. My students love virtual field trips ... most of my students have never left their neighborhood, so the world is wide open to them now. (T3)

Apple Classrooms of Tomorrow—Today (ACOT²)

Apple, Inc. continues to be involved in educational reform. In addition to various laptop initiatives, Apple is currently engaged in a new collaborative project focusing on high schools. ACOT² assumes as its starting point that time-honored yet outmoded approaches to education and education reform must be replaced with new and creative ways of thinking about designing learning environments for this generation of students" (Apple, 2008). This project has established a focus on high school redesign with six guiding principles which reflect the initial ACOT vision of transforming education with attention to curriculum, assessment, communication, collaboration as well as ubiquitous access to technology (for more information, see http://www.acot2.com).

I most likely do view technology in education in a way that reflects the influence of Apple. Apple has been ubiquitous in education since I began teaching. I'm not sure how I could separate the two ... I do miss the focus on technology that we used to have. (T5)

In the beginning, there was Apple. The diffusion of the ACOT vision has permeated much of the educational thinking concerning technology and the transformational possibilities technology provides. The ACOT vision remains evident in national standards, policy and legislation, and more importantly, in many K-12 social studies classrooms.

I am very hopeful about the future. I've been teaching long enough to know that policies and ideas are cyclical. We were screaming about too much testing in the 80s, and we're doing it again. I'm hopeful because I know that technology will continue to make a difference in the lives of my students. I'm hopeful because I know that using technology in my teaching really does help my students construct meaning and understanding. (T12)

REFERENCES

Apple Inc. (2008). *Apple classrooms of tomorrow—today*. Retrieved August 20, 2009, from http://ali.apple.com/acot2/program.shtml

Baker, E. L., Herman, J. L., & Gearhart, M. (1996). Does technology work in schools? Why evaluation cannot tell the full story. In C. Fisher, Dwyer, D. C., & Yocam, K (Ed.), *Education and technology: Reflections on computing in classrooms* (pp. 185-202). San Francisco, CA: Jossey-Bass.

Cuban, L. (2001). *Oversold and underused: Computers in the classroom*. Cambridge, MA: Harvard University Press.

Culp, K. M., Honey, M., & Mandinach, E. (2005). A retrospective on twenty years of education technology policy. *Journal of Educational Computing Research, 32*(3), 279-307.

Darling-Hammond, L. (1990). Achieving our goals: Superficial or structural reforms. *Phi Delta Kappan, 19*(19), 286-295.

Goals 2000: Educate America Act. (1994). *One hundred and third Congress* (2nd session). Washington, DC.

Gooden, A. R. (1996). *Computers in the classroom.* San Francisco, CA: Jossey-Bass.

International Society for Technology in Education. (2000). *National educational technology standards for students: Connecting curriculum and technology* (1st ed.). Eugene, OR: Author.

International Society for Technology in Education. (2002). *National educational technology standards for teachers: Preparing teachers to use technology* (1st ed.). Eugene, OR: Author.

International Society for Technology in Education. (2007). *National educational technology standards for students* (2nd ed.). Eugene, OR: Author.

International Society for Technology in Education. (2008). *National educational technology standards for teachers* (2nd ed.). Eugene, OR: Author.

Machlowitz, E. (1976). Electronic calculators. *Education Digest, 41*(8), 46-48.

Mason, C., Berson, M., Diem, R., Hicks, D., Lee, J., & Dralle, T. (2000). Guidelines for using technology to prepare social studies teachers. *Contemporary issues in technology and teacher education, 1*(1), 107-116.

National Commission on Excellence in Education. (1983). *A nation at risk: The imperative for educational reform.* Retrieved August 25, 2008, from http://www.ed.gov/pubs/NatAtRisk/index.html

National Council for Accreditation of Teacher Education. (2001). *Technology and teacher education.* Retrieved February 1, 2006, from http://www.ncate.org/states/technology21.asp?ch=113

National Council for the Social Studies. (1994). *Curriculum standards for social studies: Expectations of excellence.* Silver Spring, MD: Author.

National Council for the Social Studies. (1997). *National standards for social studies teachers.* Silver Springs, MD: Author. Retrieved August 30, 2006, from http://www.socialstudies.org/standards/teachers/vol1/thematic

National Council for the Social Studies. (2002). *National standards for social studies teachers.* Silver Springs, MD: Author. Retrieved August 30, 2006, from http://www.socialstudies.org/standards/teachers/vol1/thematic

National Council for the Social Studies. (2006). *Technology position statement and guidelines.* Silver Springs, MD: Author. Retrieved August 12, 2009, from http://www.socialstudies.org/positions/technology

National Council for the Social Studies. (2008). Curriculum standards for social studies (draft revision). Silver Springs, MD: Author. Retrieved August 1, 2009, fromhttp://www.socialstudies.org/system/files/StandardsDraft10_08.pdf

Papert, S. (1978). *Interim report of the LOGO project in the Brookline public schools: An assessment and documentation of a children's computer laboratory. Artificial Intelligence Memo No. 484.* Brookline, MA. (Eric Document Reproduction Service No. ED 207 799)

Papert, S. (1980). *Mindstorms: Children, computers, and powerful ideas*. New York: Basic Books.

Regional Technology in Education Consortia. (2002). *Network of regional technology in education consortia*. Retrieved April 1, 2002, from http://rtec.org

Ringstaff, C., Sandholtz, J., & Dwyer, D. (1991). *Trading places: When teachers utilize student expertise in technology-intensive classrooms* (No. ACOT report # 15). Cupertino, CA: Apple Computer Inc. Retrieved on July 5, 2002 from images.apple.com/education/k12/leadership/acot/pdf/rpt15.pdf

Ringstaff, C., Yocam, K., & Marsh, J. (1996). *Integrating technology into classroom instruction: An assessment of the impact of the ACOT teacher development center project*. (No. ACOT Report #22). Cupertino, CA: Apple Computer.

Sandholtz, J. H., Ringstaff, C., & Dwyer, D. (1997). *Teaching with technology: Creating student-centered classrooms*. New York: Teachers College Press.

Sells, B. L. (1959). The machine comes to math class. *Elementary School Journal, 60*(1), 14-17.

Skinner, B. F. (1961). Why we need teaching machines. *Harvard Educational Review, 31*, 377-398.

Solomon, G. (2002). Digital equity: It's not just about access anymore. *Technology and Learning, 22*(9), 18-26.

Wrigley, C. (1957). Data processing: Automation in calculation. *Review of Educational Research, 27*(5), 528-543.

CHAPTER 3

YOUNG LEARNERS

Constructing Social Studies With Technology

Linda Bennett

The use of technology in our lives has dramatically increased over the last 20 years. The latest cell phones are smart phones with applications being developed every day to expand the possibilities for using technology. These new technology tools are available but the development of a "communities of inquiry" is yet to come (Garrison, 2007).

While education has been slow to change, these tools are beginning to appear in schools. The U.S. Department of Education (2006) reported that 93% of public elementary school instructional rooms in the United States had Internet access. This increase in Internet availability in the classroom has brought quick and easy access to more information for students and teachers. In addition, newer networking technologies such as blogs or wikis have the potential to bring a greater change to classroom instruction than in the past (Reiser, 2002). Our education system is at a crossroad in how we choose to build a community of learners and embrace these tools to communicate, collaborate and produce information in new ways. The possibilities are limitless as we begin "leveraging

Technology in Retrospect: Social Studies in the Information Age 1984-2009, pp. 33–49
Copyright © 2010 by Information Age Publishing
All rights of reproduction in any form reserved.

collective intelligence in a community-building environment" (Solomon & Schrum, 2007, p. 24).

To address this challenge, the Partnership for 21st Century Skills and the National Council for the Social Studies (NCSS) developed an Information and Communication Technology (ICT) Literacy Map outlining the intersection between ICT Literacy and social studies. Beyond the traditional social studies curriculum, there needs to be a focus on skills such as creativity, critical thinking, communication and collaboration (Partnership for 21st Century Skills, 2007). Every day, students use information and communication technology, but teachers may not have information on how to integrate technology in social studies.

Understanding what has been published about the use of technology in schools can inform how technology is presented in the literature and possibly how technology is used in social studies. The National Council for the Social Studies Conference sessions and *Social Education* have been studied for the infusion of technology in social studies. VanFossen and Shiveley (2003) conducted a content analysis of the 1995-2002 technology sessions at the NCSS and Bolick, McGlinn, and Siko (2005) reviewed the 1983-2004 issues of *Social Education*. The findings from studies such as these indicate that teachers are discovering ways to use technology in the classroom and incorporate the tools in teaching. More research is needed to investigation of productive and efficient use of the Internet in K-12 social studies classrooms.

Since *Social Studies and the Young Learner (SSYL)* is the National Council for the Social Studies publication for elementary education and the only journal for elementary social studies, it is time to investigate the articles in the journal for the inclusion of technology. A review of articles from Volumes 1-21 can provide the historical perspective on technology in elementary social studies and add to the research on the use of technology in social studies education.

A copy of each issue of *SSYL* was collected for the study. Articles were read for the inclusion of technology in social studies, and 98 articles emerged. These articles were coded for the NCSS thematic strands, technology tools, grade levels, the instructional approach, technology themed issues, and the editor and author contributions.

From September 1988 to September 2009, there have been 85 issues of *Social Studies and the Young Learner*. There were four themed issues published each year. The following editors were responsible for the respective issues: Huber M. Walsh (September/October, 1988-March/April 1993), Gloria T. Alter (September/October 1993-March/April 1996), Sherry L. Field (September/October 1996-March/April 2006), and Linda Bennett (September/October 2006-September/October 2009).

The NCSS published 98 articles about technology and social studies in *Social Studies and the Young Learner*, with a range of 0 to 12 articles per year. From 1988 to 1996, there were 26 issues of *SSYL* that included technology in an article for the Media Corner, and there were 4 technology themed issues of *SSYL*.

TECHNOLOGY THEMED ISSUES

Since 1995, there were four themed issues on technology in elementary social studies. During that time, there has been a technology themed issue approximately every 5 years. "Technology and Social Studies," edited by Gloria Alter, was the first technology themed issue published in January/February 1995 (see Figure 3.1). The September/October 1999 issue was "Prospects, Possibilities, Realities: Technology and Elementary Social Studies." Richard A. Diem was the guest editor with Sherry Field (see Figure 3.2). Five years later, Phillip J. VanFossen joined Sherry Field in producing the March/April 2004 issue titled "Past Meets Future Social Studies on the Internet" (see Figure 3.3). In 2009, Linda Bennett and Michael J. Berson edited the latest issue "Welcome to the Digital Classroom" (see Figure 3.4).

The evolution of the technology themes is interesting because the focus for the four issues demonstrate the evolution of technology in elementary social studies education. The 1995 cover is a clip art image of a computer and the title is simply "Technology and Social Studies." The 1999 issue focuses on the future of technology, and on the cover is an image of outer space with a computer cord leading to the image of the earth. The connection to the learner and the Internet began in 2004 issue with a photo of student using a flat screen computer. The focus of the student looking at the computer screen in 2009 makes it appear that she is engaged in the digital classroom. The title for each thematic issue and the visual on the covers represent technology tools of the day.

In the editor's notes of the 1995 issue, Gloria Alter quotes, from *The Futurist*, that "by the year 2025, information technologies will be as ubiquitous and invisible as electricity" (Wagner, 1994, p. 39). In 2009, this dependence on technology is as valued and important as access to electricity. Another interesting component within the 1995 issue is the focus of the articles. The children's literature article, "Children, Technology and Social Studies," contains a review of books that explore the everyday use or operations of technology (Lombard, McGowan, & McGowan, 1995). In the "MayaQuest: A Student-Directed Expedition" (Hefte, 1995) and "Using Technology to Learn from Travelmates' Adventures" (Braun & Kraft, 1995) articles, students use the Internet to explore the world.

Figure 3.1.   "Technology and Social Studies," published January/February 1995.

Within this issue, there are several references to networking with others through conferencing and electronic mail such as AOL.

In the 1999 themed issue of *SSYL* on technology, there are eight articles related to technology. The opening article, "Learning about Climate: An Exploration in Geography and Mathematics," focuses on the use of graphic representations of information related to climate (Drier & Lee, 1999). Throughout this issue, the intent of the articles is to connect Internet sites and resources to social studies through historical documents, current events, service learning, literacy, and communication. Students and teachers use the Internet sites to gain new information related to social studies. In "The Garbers: Using Digital History to Recreate a 19th-Century Family," Mason and Carter (1999) describe how students engage in social studies curriculum projects such as "The Valley of the Shadow" to interact and use digital primary source materials. In addition, three of the

social studies & the young learner

A Quarterly for Creative Teaching in Grades K–6   September/October 1999 • Volume 12 Number 1

PROSPECTS,
POSSIBILITIES,
REALITIES
technology and elementary social studies

guest editor Richard A. Diem

Figure 3.2.   "Prospects, Possibilities, Realities: Technology and Elementary Social Studies," published September/October 1999.

technology related articles are linked to the NCSS Curriculum Standards for Social Studies.

The 2004 technology theme issue of *SSYL* is "Past Meets Future: Social Studies on the Internet." The five technology related articles in this issue focus on the use of Internet by elementary school students and teachers. This issue begins with an article by Berson and Berson about the need for students to learn responsible citizenship in cyberspace. Three articles emphasize elementary students and teachers using the Internet for higher order thinking. James M. Siveley presents multiple ways for teachers and students to evaluate websites. Phillip J. VanFossen describes how Web-Quests can be used for students to scaffold higher-order thinking skills. In "The Well-Constructed WebQuest," Shelly Kennedy describes the pedagogy and scholarship for the development of WebQuest. In "Colonial Williamsburg Electronic Field Trips," Roush (2004) describes how she used

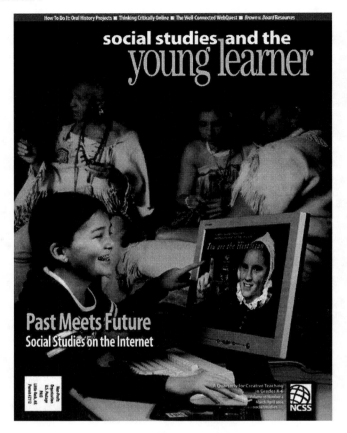

Figure 3.3.   "Past Meets Future Social Studies on the Internet," published March/
April 2004.

distant learning tools to take her students on field trips. This issue of *Social
Studies and the Young Learner* is a turning point in the journal's presentation
of technology and social studies. The interactivity of the learner and multimedia is the focal point for technology and elementary social studies.

The articles in the 2009 "Welcome to the Digital Classroom" invites the
learner to contribute to the digital world and become life long learners as
digital citizens. The eight articles begin to move technology and social
studies education into the Web 2.0 environment. From blogging and social
networking to publishing and producing work online, students are contributors to the vast amount of information that is distributed through technology. In "Students as Digital Citizens on Web 2.0" by Nebel, Jamison,
and Bennett (2009) and "Google Earth: A Virtual Globe for Elementary
Geography" by Britt and LaFontaine (2009), classroom teachers share how

Figure 3.4.   "Welcome to the Digital Classroom," published 2009.

to assist students with decisions making skills in Web 2.0. Online social environments are described in "Panwapa: Global Kids, Global Connections," "Here's What We Have to Say! Podcasting in the Early Childhood Classroom" (Berson & Berson, 2009) and "Exploring the Past with 21st Century Tools" (Schrum & Schrum, 2009). Other articles in this issue focus on historical thinking skills and student generated projects.

TECHNOLOGY AND THEMATIC STRANDS

Another way to look at technology in elementary school social studies is to determine to what extent the articles about technology and social studies are connected to the ten thematic strands in the NCSS Curriculum Standards. Articles were coded for inclusion of one or more of the ten thematic strands. Most articles focused on one strand. If the article included more than one, then the primary strand was recorded. If the article could apply to any or all strands, then it was recorded as all. Throughout the history of *SSYL*, there did not appear to be a difference in the inclusion or exclusion of strands.

The 10 thematic strands are:

1. Culture,
2. Time, Continuity, and Change,
3. People, Places, and Environment,
4. Individual Development and Identity,
5. Individuals, Groups, and Institutions,
6. Power, Authority, and Governance,
7. Production, Distribution, and Consumption,
8. Science, Technology, and Society,
9. Global Connections, and
10. Civic Ideals and Practices (see Figure 3.5).

If the article included all of the strands or the article could be used with any or all of the strands then the article was coded as such. The eleventh bar represents the frequency of occurrences that did not fit a strand (26). Throughout the years, there have been articles describing technology, but the type of technology that is described changes.

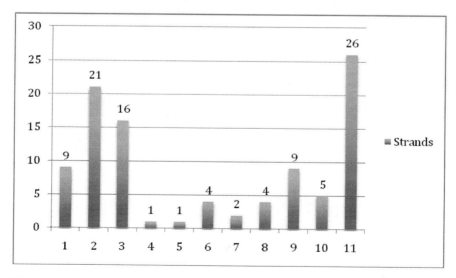

Figure 3.5.   NCSS 10 thematic strands and the number of articles related to each.

Thematic Strands 1, 2, 3, and 9, and 10 were discussed 9, 21, 16, and 9 times respectively. There were 21 instances of Strand 2: Time, Continuity, and Change and 16 for Strand 3: People, Places, and Environment in *SSYL*. For example, "Of time and trains" (Forsyth, 1990) includes both of these strands. The articles that include Strands 2 or 3 discuss different technologies such as filmstrips, CDROMs, lesson plans, and the Internet. Since Strands 2 and 3 contained the largest number of articles related to technology then the inclusion of technology in history and geography tended to be the content areas that predominates articles in *SSYL*.

Strand 1: Culture was included in nine articles. Some were related to global connections while others addressed specific cultures, such as a cultural group in the United States or people from a different country. The Global Connections: Strand 9 includes ways for students to communicate using tools, such as ePals, social networking tools, and podcasts. There were 1 to 5 articles about Strands 4, 5, 6, 7, 8 and 10.

Reviewing the technology and social studies articles by the 10 thematic strands shows that a range of social studies content is included in *SSYL* over time. There were 26 articles that focused on technology without explicit reference to a specific content area. A review of the technology would be useful for a teacher that does not have the knowledge, skill, or time to make the selection, without a review of the technology.

While social studies is the primary content for *SSYL*, there are other content areas, such as mathematics, music, art and literacy, that are integrated into articles. In 2001, J. Tunks wrote an interesting article: "Brazilian Music and Culture: An Internet Tour that includes Music, Culture, and the Internet." "Smart Books" by B. Coleman (1995) and "Literacy Resources for Teachers and Students who Compute" by S. L. Field and L. D. Labbo (1999) are two examples of integrating social studies and literacy.

The articles were reviewed for the use of technology to enhance teaching and learning. The elementary social studies curriculum and the developmental needs of students were factors in the types of instructional approaches that the authors included in the articles. There were unique lessons about topics such as toys or bicycles that were relevant to young students. There were a spectrum of strategies from games, simulations, databases, timelines, oral history, field trips, service-learning, map skills, and conflict solution. The classroom examples of how teachers used technology to enhance social studies instruction provided detailed information on how the lesson was implemented with students. In addition, there are examples of student-initiated projects.

A review for inclusion of technology in the elementary social studies classroom found that *SSYL* articles contained examples of technology that could be used in kindergarten through sixth grade. The overwhelming majority of the articles included technology that could be used at several grade levels. When specific software was described, the author provides the manufacturer's recommended grade levels. If the author was an elementary school teacher who taught the lesson, then the article focused on the grade level.

Throughout the years, there have been examples of educators writing about instruction that integrates technology into social studies. In Welton's (1998) article, "Using Technology to Integrate the Curriculum," he describes the removal of the Apple IIes and provides teachers with skills to use technology for writing, application of databases, presentations, and Internet. The administration and teachers of Ramirez Elementary School in Lubbock, Texas were exploring new tools and new skills during the late 90s. In "LeVieux Carre: A Field Trip to a New Orleans Parish," Howat (2007) wrote about how upper elementary students used tools such as MP3 players, digital cameras, GPS, and handhelds to discover landmarks and collect data.

Articles specific to the use of technology in kindergarten through second grade were rare. Since 2007, early childhood educators have contributed articles about how technology is used with young children. In "DeKalb County, Illinois: A Local History Project for Second Graders," Bell and Henning (2007) describe a local history project where students create a PowerPoint presentation about a historical figure from DeKalb County. Macken (2008) describes a lesson for first graders about Glover Cleveland, in "Artifacts bring Grover Cleveland's Presidency to Life for First Graders." A third example of young children engaged in using podcasting is Ilene Berson's (2009) article, "Here's what We have to Say! Podcasting in the Early Childhood Classroom." There are other articles throughout the years that are appropriate for technology to be used with young children, but the more recent examples above contain ideas specific to the developmental needs and interests of younger learners.

There are articles in *SSYL* that infused technology into social studies in unique ways, so it is useful to highlight examples. In the article, "The Price of Beanie Babies-and Other Web Wonders for K-6 Economics," Yoho (1998) takes a current topic of interest to students and building economics and the Internet. This approach to infusing technology into social studies could be used by students to learn about current topics and finding information on the Internet. The second example included technology in the title, but the text did not line up with a traditional example of technology in social studies. In "Bicycle Technology: Group Decision Making in the Classroom," Fertig (1997) describes how students engage in collaborative decision making related to the types of bikes that are ridden to school. The technology is related to the mechanics of the bicycle, which shows a creative lesson for students to learn how things work and why people select a type of bicycle for its technological assets. These examples demonstrate that elementary teachers or teacher educators have developed exciting ways to engage students in social studies and technology.

Several articles provided examples of technology use and higher order thinking skills while using technology in social studies. One such strategy is conflict resolution. *SSYL* has published at least three articles on this topic throughout the years. Braun (1992) wrote a piece for the Media Corner titled "Resolving Conflict: A Review of Selected Videotapes." In "Violence in Society, War in the World," Alter (1996) describes technology tools that were available for students to develop skills in conflict resolution and understand how violence can be prevented. The four steps to resolving conflicts were the focus of Burnett's (2000) article. Other higher order skills in *SSYL* articles were critical thinking, problem solving, mock trials, evaluating websites, and graphic interpretation.

Gallagher and Schott's (1991) article is a review of science, technology, and society in children's literature. As the first article related to technology beyond the Media Corner that was published in *Social Studies and the Young Learner*, it is interesting to see the need for technology literacy and using technology to improve life. The title of the article became Strand 8: "Science, Technology and Society in the National Council for the Social Studies Strands for Social Studies" (Gallagher& Schott, 1994; NCSS, 1994). The children's literature featured in the article focus on technological literacy and using technology to improve life. Within this article, the authors hit on numerous aspects of technology in education such as the development of new technologies and understanding how the household machines and appliances work. From the first article in 1988 to the last issue in September 2009, one of the principle goals of social studies education is to provide young learners with the opportunities to make informed decisions as a citizen.

TECHNOLOGY TOOLS IN *SSYL*

Each article was reviewed to determine what technology was included and the list of technology evolved into the groupings. These are the technology tools:

1. Filmstrips/video/audio/visual,
2. Software, games, simulations,
3. Perspectives/general,
4. Internet/WWW,

5. Databases/graphics,
6. Goggle Earth,
7. WebQuest,
8. Digital video, and
9. Networking/Web 2.0.

After several reviews of the articles and sorting of the technologies, the primary technological tool within each article was recorded. The range of technology related articles were a high of 30 for Internet/WWW to a low for digital video. From 1988-1996, each issue of *SSYL* contained the Media Corner section with a total of 33 articles about technology. The articles in the Media Corner were primarily about the first three technology tools, which include filmstrips, videos, audio, software, simulations, and games. There was a technology themed issue of *SSYL* in these 4 years with the following number of articles: 1995 (9), 1999 (8), 2004 (5) and 2009 (8), which totaled 30 articles. It appears that the Media Corner and the themed issues of *SSYL* constitute 64% of the technology and social studies articles.

While it is difficult to summarize the technology tools over time, the following information is useful for understanding how things changed. In Volumes 1-3, the articles were primarily a review of products. The focus for Volumes 4-6 was on how to use the tools (e.g., communication, conflict, uses, learning, connections, looking ahead, resources, and projects).

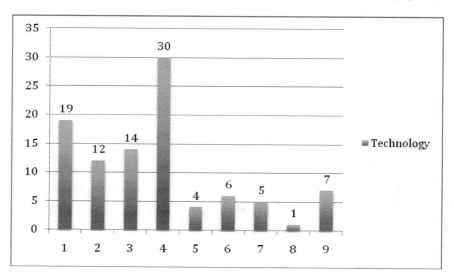

Figure 3.6.   Technology tools and the number of articles related to each.

For the most part, the early 90s were about products and how to use them. Then, *SSYL* published work that demonstrated how teachers and students were consumers of informational technology. Half of the articles during the 1996-1999 were about using the Internet or a list of websites. In Volumes 13-16, there were articles which included technology was approximately one-third the number of technology related articles as in Volumes 9-12 or 17-21. From 2000-2003, authors wrote about student use of technology for discovery and research. The Internet, in the context of specific social studies lessons, was the focus between 2004-2009. During the 1988-2009, *SSYL* published 30% of the articles related to the Internet/WWW. It is interesting to note that approximately half of the articles in *Social Education* from 1983-2004 were about the use of the Internet/WWW (Bolick, McGlinn, & Siko, 2005).

As time passed and more elementary schools had technology, the articles began to include how teachers and students were using the technology. With the influx of Web 2.0, the focus is on how to collaborate using technology in elementary social studies. This paradigm shift from consumers and producers to constructor is the current crossroad in the use of technology in elementary school social studies.

To draw upon this change, a brief summary of articles about WebQuest, Google Earth, and Web 2.0 is provided. In 1995, Bernie Dodge developed the WebQuest framework. There have been at least five articles about WebQuest; three of which appeared in the 2004 themed issue of *SSYL*. In this issue, Kennedy (2004) and VanFossen's (2004) articles are about how teachers can construct quality WebQuests and scaffold thinking skills, respectively. The articles, prior to this, were about how to use a quest or a social studies lesson using a quest. The inclusion of this tool and technique for learning social studies is one example of how the tool is introduced first, and then, teachers begin to design instruction using the technology. Over the last decade, WebQuest has been an example of how technology has been used in elementary social studies.

Google Earth is another technology tool that students use. Virtual maps and globes are online and interactive. Shin and Alibrandi (2007) and Britt and LaFontaine (2009) describe how students use Google Earth to learn geography. As the development of online tools abound, there will be more tools like Google Earth for elementary social studies.

With the introduction of Web 2.0 and the shift to using networking tools, young learners have more opportunities to construct social studies. Global connections or networking articles have appeared in *SSYL* since 1995, and until recently, the focus was on visiting other places or learning about a culture through tools such as ePals. The 2009 technology themed issue of *SSYL* is an introduction to the new networking tools that are available. Schrum and Schrum's (2009) article is about the use of twenty-first century tools, and Nebel, Jamison, and Bennett (2009) describe students as digital citizens in Web 2.0. The use of Web 2.0 and networking in elementary social studies brings limitless possibilities for teaching and learning.

REFLECTIONS AND RECOMMENDATIONS

Throughout the years, *Social Studies and the Young Learner* included articles about technology in elementary social studies. The inclusion of technology depended on the submission of authors who had an interest in technology or connection to the technology theme for an issue. The number of technology related articles seems to be due to the media corner, technology themed issues, and author submissions.

Future research into publications about technology and social studies could include online and print articles or books. *Social Studies and the Young Learner*, as well as publications such as *Leading & Learning with Technology, Digital Age: Technology-Based K-12 Lesson Plans for Social Studies* and *Contemporary Issues in Technology & Teacher Education*, can be included. A broader scope of work would provide additional depth to the use of technology in the field.

Further delving into the publications on technology in elementary social studies may connect to external influences such technology or social studies standards or the evolution of technology as a tool for teaching and learning. Since the late 90s, frameworks, position statements, and standards abound and provide guidance on using technology. A few of the standards are the "Technology Position Statement and Guidelines" (2006), "Media Literacy Position Statement" (2009), and "Powerful and Purposeful Teaching and Learning in Elementary School Social Studies" (Berson, Bennett, & Dodson, 2009) published by NCSS and the "National Educational Technology Standards for Students" published by International Society for Technology in Education (2007). Since these standards have been published in the last four years, the guidelines for social studies are only beginning to be referenced in the literature. Hopefully, these published standards can guide authors and educators in new directions for teaching and learning with technology in social studies.

Reviewing the publications on technology and social studies is informative, but understanding the learner's use of technology is also necessary. Young learners are using technology in their daily lives, and they are consumers, producers, and constructors of knowledge while using technology. Educators need to keep up with what young learners are doing with technology outside of the classroom, as well as the use of technology in the classroom. More articles in *SSYL* and other journals for elementary social studies educators need to include examples of student projects such as digital productions or networking for learning. Classroom teachers need to be authors so their exemplary work with young learners can be shared with others and, hopefully, used to promote technology and social studies innovations and practices.

CONCLUSION

By looking back at the last 22 years of *Social Studies and the Young Learner*, the articles published in *SSYL* represent a spectrum of ways technology has been included in elementary social studies. In retrospect, the question may not be which technology or social studies content is taught but what skills students need. Future articles about social studies and technology in *Social Studies and the Young Learner* need to be about the how students construct knowledge and apply skills as citizens in the twenty-first century. As we move forward with social studies and technology, there is a need for thoughtful and thorough reflection and a vision on how to make advancement in research and practice related to technology use in elementary school social studies.

REFERENCES

Alter, G. T. (1996). Violence in society, war in the world. *Social Studies & the Young Learner, 8*(4), 26-28.

Bell, D., & Henning, M. B. (2007). DeKalb County, Illinois: A local history project for second graders. *Social Studies & the Young Learner, 19*(3), 7-11.

Berson, I. R. (2009). Here's what we have to say! Podcasting in the early childhood classroom. *Social Studies & the Young Learner, 21*(4), 8-11.

Berson, I., Bennett, L., & Dodson, D. (2009). Powerful and purposeful teaching and learning in elementary school social studies. *Social Studies and the Young Learner, 22*(1), 31-33.

Berson, I. R., & Berson, M. J. (2009). Panwapa: Global kids, global connections. *Social Studies & the Young Learner, 21*(4), 28-31.

Berson, M. J., & Berson, I. R. (2004). Developing thoughtful "Cybercitizens." *Social Studies & the Young Learner, 16*(4), 5-8.

Bolick, C. M., McGlinn, M. M., & Siko, K. L. (2005). Twenty years of technology: A retrospective view of *Social Education*'s technology themed issues. *Social Education, 69*(3), 155-161.

Braun, J. A. (1992). Resolving conflict: A review of selected videotapes. *Social Studies & the Young Learner, 5*(2), 29-30.

Braun, J. A., & Kraft, C. (1995). Using technology to learn from travelmates' adventures. *Social Studies & the Young Learner, 7*(3), 8-9, 13.

Britt, J., & LaFontaine, G. (2009). Goggle Earth: A virtual globe for elementary geography. *Social Studies & the Young Learner, 21*(4), 20-23.

Burnett, E. M. G. (2000). Conflict resolution: Four steps worth taking. *Social Studies & the Young Learner, 12*(3), 20-23.

Coleman, B. (1995). Smart books. *Social Studies & the Young Learner, 8*(2), 27-28.

Drier, H. S., & Lee, J. K. (1999). Learning about climate: An exploration in geography and mathematics. *Social Studies & the Young Learner, 12*(1), 6-10.

Fertig, G. (1997). Bicycle technology: Group decision making in the classroom. *Social Studies & the Young Learner, 10*(1), 22-24.

Field, S. L., & Labbo, L. D. (1999). Literacy resources for teachers and students who compute. *Social Studies & the Young Learner, 12*(1), 29-31.

Field, S. L., Labbo, L. D., & Lu, C. (1996). Real people, real places: A powerful social studies exchange through technology. *Social Studies & the Young Learner, 9*(2), 16-18.

Forsyth, Jr., A. (1990). Of time and trains. *Social Studies & the Young Learner, 1*(2), 28-29.

Gallagher, A. F., & Schott, J. C. (1991). Science, technology and society in children's literature. *Social Studies & the Young Learner, 3*(4), 20-22.

Hefte, R. (1995). MayaQuest: A student-directed expedition. *Social Studies & the Young Learner, 7*(3), 4-7.

Gallagher, A. F., & Schott, J. C. (1991). Science, technology and society in children's literature. *Social Studies & the Young Learner, 3*(4), 20-22.

Garrison, D. (2007). Online community of inquiry review: Social, cognitive, and teaching presence issues. *Journal of Asynchronous Learning Networks, 11*(1), 61-72.

Howat, C. (2007). LeVieux Carre: A field trip to a New Orleans Parish. *Social Studies & the Young Learner, 20*(2), 24-29.

International Society of Technology in Education. (2007). *National educational technology standards for students* (2nd ed.). Washington DC: Author.

Kennedy, S. (2004). The well-constructed WebQuest. *Social Studies & the Young Learner, 16*(3), 17-19.

Lombard, R. H., McGowan, T., & McGowan, M J. (1995). Children, technology and social studies. *Social Studies & the Young Learner, 7*(3), 19-21.

Macken, C. (2008). Artifacts bring Grover Cleveland's presidency to life for first graders. *Social Studies & the Young Learner, 21*(2), 8-10.

Mason, C. L., & Carter, A. (1999). The Garbers: Using digital history to recreate a 19th-century family. *Social Studies & the Young Learner, 12*(1), 11-14.

National Council for the Social Studies Technology Select Subcommittee. (2006). Technology position statement and guidelines. *Social Education, 70*(5), 329-332.

Nebel, M., Jamison, B., & Bennett, L. (2009). Students as digital citizens on Web 2.0. *Social Studies & the Young Learner, 21*(4), 5-7.

Partnership for 21st Century Skills. (2007). *21st Century Skills Map ICT Literacy Map—Social Studies*. Retrieved January 11, 2010, from http://www.21stcenturyskills.org/index.php?option=com_content&task=view&id=31&Itemid=120

Reiser, R. A. (2002). A history of instructional design and technology. In R. A. Reiser & J. V. Dempsey (Eds.), *Trends and issues in instructional design and technology* (pp. 26-53). Upper Saddle River, NJ: Merrill Prentice Hall.

Roush, N. M. (2004). Colonial Williamsburg electronic field trips. *Social Studies & the Young Learner, 16*(4), 29-32.

Schrum, K., & Schrum, L. (2009). Exploring the past with 21st-Century tools. *Social Studies & the Young Learner, 21*(4), 24-27.

Shin, E., & Alibrandi, M. (2007). Online interactive mapping: Using Goggle Earth. *Social Studies & the Young Learner, 19*(3), P1-P4.

Shiveley, J. M (2004). Critical thinking and visiting websites: It must be elementary!. *Social Studies & the Young Learner, 16*(4), 9-12.

Solomon, G., & Schrum, L. (2007). *Web 2.0: new tools, new schools.* Washington DC: International Society of Technology in Education.

Technology Community for National Council for the Social Studies. (2009). Media literacy position statement. *Social Education, 73*(4), 97-99.

Tunks, J. (2001). Brazilian music and culture: An Internet tour. *Social Studies & the Young Learner, 14*(2), 29-32.

U.S. Department of Education, National Center for Education Statistics. (2006). Internet Access in U.S. Public Schools and Classrooms: 1994-2005 (NCES 2007-020).

VanFossen, P. J. (2004). Using WebQuests to scaffold higher-order thinking. *Social Studies & the Young Learner, 16*(4), 13-16.

VanFossen, P. J., & Shiveley, J. M. (2003). A content analysis of Internet sessions presented at the National Council for Social Studies annual meeting, 1995-2002. *Theory and Research in Social Education, 31*(4), 502-522.

Welton, D. A. (1998). Using technology to integrate the curriculum. *Social Studies & the Young Learner, 10*(4), 29-32.

Wagner, C. G. (1994). Toward the new millennium. *Futurist, 28*(6), 37-40.

Yoho, D. L. (1998). The price of Beanie Babies-and other web wonders for K-6 economics. *Social Studies & the Young Learner, 11*(2), 32-33

CHAPTER 4

THE INTERNET IN SOCIAL STUDIES CLASSROOMS

Lost Opportunity or Unexplored Frontier?

Adam Friedman and Phillip J. VanFossen

INTRODUCTION

The editors of this volume identify 1984 as the start of the "information age." If this is the case, then the World Wide Web or WWW (what is universally meant when people now discuss "the Internet"), is a relatively late comer to the party—Tim Berners-Lee "invented" the WWW in 1991 (with apologies to former Vice President Al Gore). However, one could argue that the information age did not really begin—or at least begin in earnest—*until* the WWW arrived. Indeed, it was only after the early and exponential growth of the so-called "information superhighway" that ordinary citizens were truly ushered into the information age. The WWW (hereafter, the Internet)[1] has indeed become ubiquitous, to the point that a vast majority of American citizens utilize the Internet in some way on a daily basis: for gathering information, for participating in government, for engaging in commerce and, more recently, for forming and participat-

Technology in Retrospect: Social Studies in the Information Age 1984-2009, pp. 51–74
Copyright © 2010 by Information Age Publishing

ing in online and virtual communities. The Internet has become so pervasive that the current generation of users—the so-called "digital natives"—are unable to imagine life without it.[2] For evidence of this ubiquity, one needs look no further than the fact that in 2006 the venerable Oxford English Dictionary added the word "Google" to its pages.

Another sign of this ubiquity is that American public school classroom access to the Internet has increased steadily since the late-1990s. In 1998, 89% of K-12 schools in the United States had Internet access, and 51% of K-12 classrooms were wired.[3] By 2005, 100% of all public schools in the United States reported having Internet access[4] and 94% of all K-12 public school *classrooms* in the United States reported having some type of Internet access, with 91% of *these* classrooms reporting broadband access. Most importantly, however, the ratio of public school students to instructional computers with access to the Internet fell from 12.2 students in 1998 to 3.8 students in 2005 (Wells & Lewis, 2006).

Shortly after its invention, the Internet was already being touted as the next great evolution in education generally, and in social studies education in particular. More accurately, the Internet was described as the next "revolution" in social studies teaching (Wilson & Marsh, 1995, p. 198). This chapter seeks to summarize the body of literature related to Internet use in the teaching and learning of social studies content in K-12 classrooms. In this, we try to focus primarily on literature that describes the study of *classroom* use of the Internet. We begin the chapter with an overview of the very early literature describing the Internet's potential for teaching social studies. We then move on to a review of the relatively scant research literature on the impact of the Internet on K-12 student learning and attitudes (including an overview of several interesting paths of recent research) and the inevitable call for additional research in this area. We then explore what has been written about the potential that Web 2.0 might hold for social studies teaching and learning, as well as social networking. Finally, we conclude the chapter by revisiting the question posed in our title. Has the use of the Internet in K-12 social studies classrooms been a "lost opportunity" or an "unexplored frontier?"

THE INTERNET'S POTENTIAL FOR SOCIAL STUDIES CLASSROOMS

Most of the earliest literature exploring K-12 classroom use of the Internet might best be described as attempts to convince classroom teachers and social studies educators of the tremendous value of the Internet; these might even be described as "cheerleading" pieces. Indeed, the first articles about Internet use trumpeted its potential to revolutionize classroom teaching. In summarizing the results of the first nationwide survey of classroom Internet use, Becker (1999) for example described the Internet as "the most valuable of the many computer technologies available to teachers and students" (p. 32). In "Social Studies and the Internet Revolution," the first article to appear in *Social Education* that described the Internet's potential, Wilson and Marsh (1995) went so far as to claim the such an "easily accessible means of electronic communication and research may not only enhance but *further revolutionize* ... these new approaches to teaching" (p. 198, emphasis added).

Early proponents of this "revolutionary" potential (Wilson & Marsh, 1995) pointed to the Internet's ability to take students beyond their classrooms and allow them to (virtually) experience cultures and peoples that they could not inside the "brick and mortar" of the school. Others described the Internet's potential for fostering inquiry and supporting student-based research (Braun, Fernlund, & White, 1998). Rose and Fernlund (1997), for example, noted that for "social studies, the Internet serves as a research tool of tremendous potential" (p. 163). Indeed, given the very nature of the social studies, the Internet was described as being "as well-suited to the social studies as for any other subject area" due primarily to "the interdisciplinary, media-rich structure of the Internet, which corresponds very well with the structure of the field of social studies" (VanFossen, 1999-2000, p. 88). White (1997) stated that "interactive multimedia projects and tools ... can show students in powerful ways how the content of the social studies draws upon many disciplines to achieve a broad understanding of our world and its history" (pp. 4-5). This early line of scholarship was developed by strong proponents of the potential of the Internet; those who might be described as "cheerleading" for the medium.

A second theme in the early literature on Internet use was the "how to" piece. These articles often began by briefly describing the Internet's potential but then went on to describe specific classroom uses of the medium. Between 1993 and 1997, two dozen articles (e.g., Foster & Hoge, 1997; Johnson & Clark, 1997; Wilson, 1997) appeared in *Social Education, The Social* Studies, or *Social Studies and the Young Learner* describing how to use Internet resources to teach geography, history, economics and/or civics. In addition, these articles discussed general "web strategies" (such as WebQuests) and provided suggestions for classroom application of Internet-based activities.

In one example of these "how to" pieces, VanFossen and Shiveley (1999) recognized that even as classroom Internet access was becoming more widespread, "social studies teachers (were) still exploring the many ways in which this powerful resource (could) be used" (p. 244). In response, VanFossen and Shiveley described how to use the vast array of primary source materials available from the Internet (e.g., the digital collections of the U.S. National Archives and Records Administration) to create online primary source packets—a sort of Internet "jackdaw."

The appearance in February 1996 of Fred Risinger's "Surfing the Net" column in *Social Education* was an institutionalized example of the "how to" piece. These popular columns have appeared in nearly every issue of *Social Education* since. These columns have covered a wide range of topics including the use of web resources for teaching about the U.S. Civil War, women, sub-Saharan Africa, privacy, population, energy policy, and political cartoons—to name but a few.

IMPACT OF INTERNET USE IN K-12 SOCIAL STUDIES CLASSROOMS

In spite of the rhetoric about the Internet's vast potential for impacting how social studies is taught and learned, however, very little research on the actual use of the Internet in K-12 social studies classrooms has been conducted. Evidence of this can be seen in the content analysis VanFossen and Shiveley (2003) conducted of paper sessions given at the annual meeting of the National Council for Social Studies (NCSS) from 1995 to 2002. They identified all sessions that focused on the Internet, and determined that the overwhelming majority of sessions devoted to the Internet (nearly 80%) were similar to the "how to" pieces described above. Less than 5% of the presentations were about research on Internet use in K-12 classrooms. Whitworth and Berson (2003) reached similar conclusions when they found that out of 325 journal articles about technology and the social studies published between 1996 and 2001, only eight were research studies.

Before researchers can examine the impact of classroom Internet use on K-12 student learning outcomes however, it is first necessary to investigate K-12 social studies teachers' beliefs and practices in terms of using the Internet within their instruction, as well as the factors that encourage —and barriers that impede—its use. Several studies have investigated the degree to which Internet use has been implemented in K-12 social studies classrooms, and the results failed to meet the expectations set by early proponents. Cuban, Kirkpatrick, and Peck (2001) studied two similar school districts, one with deep technology resources (including Internet access) and one without. They found that even when social studies teachers did implement technology such as the Internet, "more often than not their use sustained rather than altered existing patterns of teaching practice" (p. 813) and that "serious use of computers had no impact on established teaching practices" of the classroom social studies teachers in this study (p. 822).

Cuban, in his landmark study of computer use, concluded that computers were "oversold and underused" in America's schools and concluded, in a subsequent study, found that access to computer equipment and software (such as the Internet) seldom lead to widespread teacher and student use (Cuban, Kirkpatrick, & Peck, 2001). Other studies have explored Internet use in social studies classrooms and found that "technology is simply a more sophisticated and expensive way to meet the same learning outcomes as produced by more traditional methods" (Whitworth & Berson, 2003, "Conclusion," para. 1). Whitworth and Berson further concluded that social studies teachers continued to use the Internet primarily for accessing information for use in existing lesson plans. In other words, the Internet was a more efficient means of collecting resources for delivery of traditional, teacher-directed, lessons.

VanFossen (1999-2000) conducted a survey on classroom Internet use by secondary social studies teachers in Indiana and found that very few teachers were using the Internet in their classroom activities. Many reported significant barriers (e.g., lack of training and Internet access, lack of time, concerns over inappropriate surfing) that kept them from implementing Internet-based activities in their classrooms. Among those that were using the Internet in the classroom, however, few reported using the Internet for developing powerful social studies teaching and learning and most respondents were using it simply for "glorified information gathering" (VanFossen, 1999-2000, p. 104). VanFossen and Waterson (2008) replicated the Indiana study 6 years later. Despite reporting a significant decrease in the barriers to use (e.g., increased Internet access, more training) among Indiana social studies teachers, the vast majority of respondents still wanted to be using the Internet more than they currently were. In the first study, 80% of respondents wished to be using the Internet more often in their classrooms; in the second study (6 years later), 70% wished to be using it more often. Those teachers that were using the Internet were still engaging primarily in information seeking activities. As in the first study, Indiana social studies teachers were not using the Internet's "revolutionary" potential to develop powerful social studies teaching. Increases in classroom Internet access, computer hardware availability and significantly more Internet training among participants in the intervening 6 years resulted in "little impact on both the quantity and quality of [social studies] teachers' classroom Internet use" (VanFossen & Waterson, 2008, pp. 143-144). Finally, Friedman (2008) conducted a survey of North Carolina secondary social studies teachers using the same instrument and found similar results, concluding that "little has changed" in the past decade in terms of social studies teachers' Internet use in their classrooms (p. 191).

These few studies notwithstanding, very little research has examined the use of the Internet in actual K-12 classrooms and even less research has examined the impact of Internet use on student learning and/or attitudes. Indeed, rather than K-12 classrooms, such research has tended to focus on preservice teacher training programs that integrate and model Internet use in their social studies methods courses (e.g., Rock & Passe, 2004), but do not follow these new teachers into their own classrooms. Other studies have focused on Internet use by preservice social studies teachers. For example, Dutt-Donner and Powers (2000) reported using the Internet to enable preservice teachers to communicate about classroom management, course-related topics, and controversial issues; Doppen (2004) explored how preservice students utilized Internet-based primary sources to create lesson plans; and Bennett and Pyle, (2000) described pre-service students using the Internet for reflective journals.

Friedman and Hicks (2006) concluded that the remainder of the scant research literature on Internet use in classrooms fell into two categories: (1) personal accounts of what occurred in preservice social studies methods classes, and (2) small scale, qualitative studies of how K-12 teachers use the Internet. An example of the first is the Molebash (2002, 2004) study of technology integration (including Internet use) in an elementary social studies methods course. Molebash reported modeling the use of technology during two-thirds of the class meetings and that this modeling led preservice students to identify additional uses of technology in teaching, beyond simple Internet research.

Friedman (2006) represents an example of a small-scale qualitative study. He studied six world history teachers' use of online digital primary sources. The author concluded that, while training in technology use was important, the determining factor (the "tipping point" if you will) for teacher's Internet use and use of digital primary sources was access to an LCD projector for displaying web-based resources. A second example of such a small scale study can be seen in the pilot conducted by Shiveley and VanFossen (2009).

Shiveley and VanFossen (2009) used the NCSS Position Statement on Powerful Teaching and Learning (PTL) to develop an inventory of classroom Internet use—the Social Studies Internet Use Inventory (SSIUI)—that might be used to measure the various types of Internet use present in K-12 social studies classrooms. Shiveley and VanFossen (2009) noted that developing such an instrument was the first step to systematic study of the impact of classroom Internet use on student learning. The SSIUI was subsequently piloted in six social studies classrooms, and the results showed that it "differentiated Internet use among the six participants" (Shiveley & VanFossen, 2009, p. 22). In addition, Shiveley and VanFossen (2009) posited that this inventory could be used by both teachers and researchers to more systematically explore and reflect on classroom use of the Internet.

Swan and Hofer (2008) also reviewed the recent literature on technology and social studies education. While their review was not exhaustive and focused primarily on the use of the Internet in history education, their findings are nevertheless illuminating. They described a number of issues related to technology use generally, and Internet use specifically. One of their concluding remarks addressed the issue of limiting study to the preservice classroom:

> Studies of our own practice are useful and informative, but insufficient. If we are to develop a strong case for what constitutes "promising practice" .... Rather, researchers' next steps must be to test approaches in different settings with varied and larger populations, and to follow students and their teachers over time. (p. 321)

As Whitworth and Berson (2003) concluded, "there is still a need for research ... particularly how the use of new and innovative ways to integrate technology into the classroom impacts learning outcomes" (p. 478). Swan and Hofer (2008) went on to state that the "field would benefit from further exploration of ... how teachers navigate the different types of (technology) tools and resources in their own practice" (p. 322). In other words, social studies researchers should be looking in classrooms to see how and why teachers are implementing the Internet and, most importantly, what impact this implementation has on student learning and motivation.

Call for More Research on Internet Use in K-12 Classrooms

As the above quote implies, Swan and Hofer (2008) called for future directions of research in social studies education to include more focused study on how technology is being used in schools to support learning outcomes. The authors are not alone in this call for additional research on how K-12 teachers use technology in the classroom and the impact that use has on student learning and achievement. Indeed, in 2003 Whitworth and Berson determined that it was necessary to conduct research on "how technology use in the social studies impacts academic achievement and learning outcomes" (p. 484). This was echoed a year later, when Berson and Balyta (2004) deemed that the field of technology and social studies was in its "adolescence." They put forth that additional "empirical evidence" needed to be collected to determine the impact of technology on social studies instruction (p. 141, 148). Tracing the literature back 7 more years to 1997 (when the field was surely in its infancy, if it was in its "adolescence" in 2004), Martorella made note of the Internet, observing that it "continues to grow at a mind-boggling rate," and predicting (correctly) that "it will continue to grow and increase" (pp. 511-512). It should be noted however, that even at this relatively early stage (as we know it now) of technology in general and the Internet in particular, Martorella (1997) stated clearly that there was "a critical need for more research, reflection, and developmental efforts" (p. 512). Nearly a decade later, Friedman and Hicks (2006) continued this theme, arguing that the time had come to consider whether technology in social studies actually " 'work[s];' " in other words, research in social studies education "should take the next step in terms of studying what this technology actually does," as opposed to "continuing to imagine" its potential, and the next step forward should be for scholars to "examine the extent to which technology leads to improve[d] learning" (pp. 252-253).

As noted earlier in this chapter, the Internet in particular has been widely acclaimed as an incomparable and invaluable resource for teachers and students alike (Braun & Risinger, 1999; Cohen & Rosenszweig, 2006; Hicks & Ewing, 2003; VanFossen & Shiveley, 2000). Cohen and Rosenszweig captured the potential for teaching social studies with the Internet, noting that with a click of a mouse, everyone from a "high school student ... to senior historian" has equal access to primary historical sources (p. 4). Despite the repeated calls for research and investigation into Internet use in K-12 social studies and its impact on student achievement, however, the fact of the matter remains that empirical research on Internet use and its effectiveness on K-12 student learning has come about only relatively recently, with nearly all effectiveness studies focused on preservice students.

There are several reasons why this might be the case. Among the most apparent is that it can be a cumbersome process to engage in educational research (Berliner, 2002), as it can be difficult for a researcher to design studies and gain access to teachers, students, and requisite equipment in the K-12 environment. This is even more so where classroom Internet use is concerned, as it is often necessary for teachers to schedule a computer lab for such use, making naturalistic inquiry all the more difficult. Further, there can be logistical hurdles in the K-12 environment that are generally afterthoughts at the university level, such as access to computer labs and/or laptop carts, as well as LCD projectors. Despite these hurdles, there is an emerging literature base on student Internet use in the K-12 social studies classroom. Finally, and perhaps most importantly from a research standpoint, it was not until recently that researchers began to explore what "good" or "effective" Internet use might resemble. Saye and Brush (2002, 2004), for example, have conducted numerous studies on the type of Internet use in the social studies classroom that might best foster inquiry learning. However, their research has been on one Internet application in particular (PIHNet, described later in this chapter). Shiveley and VanFossen (2009), in their pilot study of the SSIUI (noted above) attempted to develop a tool to identify and assess "good" or "effective" Internet use within social studies classrooms.

The Use of the Internet in K-12 social studies

Scholars in the field of technology and social studies have attempted to define effective technology integration in the K-12 social studies classroom. Mason, Berson, Diem, Hicks, Lee, and Dralle (2000), in their *Guidelines for Using Technology to Prepare Social Studies Teachers,* advocated using technology (including the Internet) in ways that allow teachers or students to engage in learning activities that they otherwise would not be able to without the technology. The large-scale studies on classroom Internet use have demonstrated that, by and large, the Internet is used to support very low level learning tasks, and to augment—rather than supplant—traditional social studies teaching. For example, Friedman (2008), as well as VanFossen and Waterson (2008), in their replication study of Internet use by Indiana teachers, employed the Internet Use Scale (IUS) to differentiate higher-order Internet use from lower-order use. Results from both studies indicated that the two most popular uses of the Internet by secondary classroom teachers were "gather background information for lessons you teach" and "gather multimedia ... for use in lessons you teach" (p. 135). Not only are these both relatively low-order applications of the Internet, they both imply that teachers were using Internet resources to simply add to existing lessons already developed. In contrast, the two least popular uses were "have students complete an inquiry-oriented WebQuest" and "have students compare/contrast information from websites with different points of view"—both examples of relatively higher-order uses (VanFossen & Watterson, 2008, p. 136).

Swan and Hofer (2008) concluded that in order to understand how the Internet is used in particular classrooms by particular teachers and students, and its impact on learning, it was necessary to study individual classrooms. Among the first studies to ascertain the Internet's impact upon student achievement was Lee and Clarke's (2003) investigation of how 11th grade United States history students interacted with Internet-based primary source documents from the Cuban Missile Crisis. While some students described this as a successful experience, others encountered difficulties; but students in both groups declared the need for the inclusion of a "pedagogical interface" (p. 9) on these websites. Such an interface would be similar to the hard scaffolding recommended by Saye and Brush

(1999, 2006). Such a pedagogical interface might include "tools that would enable them [students] to find, comprehend, and interpret the documents," as well as contain "explanatory materials that they could use to make sense out of the content" (Lee & Clarke, 2003, p. 10). In other words, because the websites that the high school students utilized in this study did "nothing more than present the documents," results of this study showed that simply accessing documents online did not necessarily result in increased student learning and achievement (p. 9). As a result, Lee and Clarke recommended that prior to developing similar sites, "Web site designers should work with educators to construct such interfaces that facilitate students' uses of digital historical resources" (p. 11).

Lee and Clarke (2003) were not alone in stressing the need for more structured classroom Internet use. In 1995, Bernie Dodge and Tom March created the WebQuest instructional model with the intention of providing teachers with "an inquiry-oriented lesson format in which most or all the information that learners work with comes from the web" (Dodge, 2007). While the WebQuest model has become the predominant Internet-based curriculum model, McGlinn and McGlinn (2004), in their review of the literature on WebQuests and the social studies, concluded that "although educators increasingly recognize WebQuests as resources for teachers, little research has been conducted on their effectiveness" (p. 4836).

There have been a few studies of the use of WebQuests in the social studies classroom, notably Milson (2002) and Lipscomb (2003), who both conducted case studies of middle grades classes using WebQuests. In his use of WebQuests in a sixth grade classroom to study Ancient Egypt, Milson discovered that not all students desired to use Internet sources and that many attempted to find information as quickly as possible; however, he avers that WebQuests can be used by students of different academic ability. Lipscomb also reported a positive experience with eighth grade students using WebQuests to study the American Civil War, noting that student "journals showed a tremendous amount of creativity," and the teacher believed that the students "came away with a stronger understanding of the people who lived during the Civil War" (p. 153). In another study, Strickland (2005) compared learning outcomes between students who participated in a WebQuest about the Texas Revolution and students who where exposed to the same content by completing a project in which they created a poster. Strickland found that the WebQuest group scored significantly lower on the end-of-unit test than students who had participated in the traditional task. VanFossen (2009) studied the WebQuests developed and implemented by 32 social studies teachers (Grades 3-11) with their students ($n = 796$). Compared to a "traditional" lesson on the same content, a majority of students enjoyed the WebQuest model more, felt they learned more, and felt they had more control over their own learning using the WebQuest model. In addition, participating teachers had generally positive reactions to student use of the model. However, a number of students (and a few of the participating teachers) had less positive reactions. Data suggested that the model may not be effective with all students and called into question beliefs about the innate motivational benefit of the WebQuest model.

As these few studies demonstrate, the limited research that has been conducted has been undertaken with the emergence of new, innovative tools, and published when their impact has been tested and evaluated. It has been well documented that in the past decade and a half, the Internet itself has evolved in terms of types of applications, speed, and interactivity, and it has also changed in terms of teaching social studies. As new, innovative Internet tools and applications are developed for K-12 social studies, they are tested and reported upon more frequently than in the past. In the last few years, there have been several paths of research of Internet use in K-12 social studies classrooms, and the results of one study generally inform the research questions for the next.

Several Paths of Research

These recent research projects typically feature smaller-scale studies that detail Internet use by teachers and students in particular classrooms. Another characteristic of these studies is that they tend to use mixed methodologies, as quantitative data are used to measure specific learning outcomes, while researchers simultaneously collect qualitative data to chronicle the particulars of what took place in the classroom with teachers and students as they used the Internet. Additionally, these studies tend to take place in a series that are conducted by the same researchers in which the conclusions generally inform not only the research questions for the subsequent study in that particular series, but for other researchers studying student use of the Internet in the K-12 social studies classroom. Some of these include *Decision Point!*, *Student Websites and Historical Understandings*, the *Virtual Historian, PrimaryAccess*, and *Voicethread in Middle and High School Social Studies*.

The most longitudinal, and perhaps the most influential, of these is the work of Saye and Brush on PIHNet. Persistent Issues in History is an Internet-based multimedia tool in which historical sources are scaffolded so that teachers can design instruction so that they are "engaging their students in problem-based historical inquiry (PBHI)" (Saye & Brush, n.d.(a), online). Specifically, this project centers around *Decision Point!*, which is a "content database of over 1400 historical artifacts associated with the African-American civil rights movement" (Saye & Brush, n.d.(b), online). Among the goals of this research is for high school students to weigh the merits of various digital primary sources, and use them as a platform by which to draw their own conclusion about a historical problem; as such, they are necessarily engaging in higher order thinking. Saye and Brush (2004) argued that this skill set is necessary as students will soon be called upon to "make decisions about a wide variety of ill-structured social problems" as they become young adults (p. 349).

PIHNet has been an ongoing project, and the separate studies have clearly made a contribution to the literature of the Internet and social studies; the project's website (http://dp.crlt.indiana.edu/) lists 20 publications/conference presentations that have come about as a result of this research. It is critical to note that PIHNet leverages Internet-based resources to support inquiry learning for helping to address "the heavy cognitive demands of critical reasoning about ill-structured problems" (Saye & Brush, 2002, p. 77). In other words, PIHNet utilizes the Internet in such a way that the instructional focus is not on the Internet itself, but is instead on the historical processes inherent in the project. This is a strong endorsement of the recommendations of Mason et al. (2000), in that PIHNet is used in a way that both enhances content and allows teachers and students to engage in an activity that they otherwise would not be able to.

In *Student Websites and Historical Understandings*, Friedman and Heafner (2007, 2008a 2008b) have conducted a series of studies in 11th grade United States history classrooms that have attempted to engage high school students in higher order thinking as they analyze Internet-based primary source documents and create wikis to develop websites that demonstrate their understanding of specific content, which according to Mason et al.'s (2000) criteria, is an effective use of technology. In so doing, the researchers have used the results of their studies to inform subsequent research questions, particularly in terms of scaffolding learning tasks for students. These studies have used a quasi-experimental design in which two sections of the same course taught by the same teacher are compared; one section has engaged in this instruction while the other has been taught by the teacher's traditional means, and the two sections have been compared. As students undertake this project, they are learning social studies in a constructivist-oriented environment as they analyze primary source documents and synthesize their knowledge as they create a wiki. Results of these studies have indicated that, while students both experienced success in creating a wiki and reported enjoying the project, they did not score significantly higher than their counterparts on the end-of-unit test (Friedman & Heafner, 2007). However, these same students were tested on the same content 8 months later, and their breadth of knowledge was much greater than students who did not create wikis (Heafner & Friedman, 2008).

Another Internet-based tool that has been researched is the *Virtual Historian*. The *Virtual Historian* (http://virtualhistorian.ca) "is a web-based educational program for teaching Canadian history" (Virtual Historian, n.d.). Using this program, students assume the role of historian as they work with "cases" of particular historical events; within these cases they read and analyze primary source letters and images, and can complete activities within the context of the case. Research studies of the *Virtual Historian's* effectiveness have been conducted using a quasi-experimental design, and preliminary results have demonstrated that its use "can increase significantly students' understanding of the subject matter, their ability to write an essay with supporting evidence, and their critical thinking about the past" (Lévesque, 2008, p. 1).

Similar to the *Virtual Historian*, *PrimaryAccess* is a web-based tool designed by and for social studies educators in which the focal point is student analysis of primary source documents. Unlike the projects described above, however, *PrimaryAccess* allows users to create a narrated digital video of a particular time period from the images that they encounter. Similar to both the study of wikis and the work done on the *Virtual Historian*, *PrimaryAccess* involves students working on higher-order thinking, as they synthesize ideas and ultimately draw their own conclusions. Ferster, Hammond, and Bull, (2006) the developers of *PrimaryAccess*, partnered with several prominent copyright holders of digital primary sources, among them the Smithsonian Institution, the Library of Congress, and the Virginia Center for Digital History, in order to allow users to access the primary source documents in their collections. Research has shown that *PrimaryAccess* can be used in a number of ways; in case studies of middle and high school students. For example, Manfra and Hammond (2008) found that K-12 teachers could adapt their use *PrimaryAccess* in a manner that addressed their pedagogical goals.

Another web-based tool that has been researched in K-12 social studies is *Voicethread* (http://voicethread.com). Using *Voicethread*, it is possible to "talk about and share … images, documents, and videos" (Voicethread.com, 2007-2009). Similar to the *Virtual Historian* and *PrimaryAccess*, *Voicethread* can allow students to analyze primary source images and documents. As a result, this application has been noted as having potential to be a useful tool in the K-12 social studies environment, as it can "help students think through their ideas and share them with fellow students, collaboratively analyzing and commenting on primary sources using voice, text, or graphics" (Schrum & Schrum, 2009, p. 24). Friedman and Lee (2009) used a quasi-experimental design to study the utility of *Voicethread* for facilitating debate in both a middle and high school social studies classroom using a quasi-experimental design. While this study did not demonstrate a difference in the *Voicethread*-enhanced debate and traditional debate, the researchers nevertheless "would like to see additional studies that stretch the intended uses of Voicethread to engage students in dynamic and social ways" (p. 24).

The aforementioned studies of PIHNet, wikis, the *Virtual Historian*, *PrimaryAccess*, and *Voicethread*, while all are different types of Web 2.0 applications; there are several common underlying themes among them. The most prominent is that they allow teachers and students to engage in an activity that they otherwise would not be able to, as alluded to by Mason et al. (2000). Further, they also highlight some emerging trends on the Internet as a vehicle for delivery of social studies instruction in K-12 classrooms; each involves the scaffolding of primary source documents, and students engaging in higher-order activities as they create products, rather than passively listen or complete lower-order rote work. In terms of the literature, each of these studies explores the use of a specific Internet-based teaching and learning tool within the K-12 social studies classrooms by collecting data, as opposed to articles that merely described potential use. These studies also indicated that K-12 social studies teachers' and students' use of the Internet has evolved. For example, Lee and Clarke (2003) concluded that the Internet had been used as a one-way path of information, with students passively receiving information. However, the past half decade has produced studies that testify to increasing student interaction with and contribution to the Internet. This interactivity between the Internet and student users is the underlying premonition of Web 2.0 applications.

Web 2.0 in K-12 Social Studies

Although Web 2.0 is a relatively new term,[5] there already exists an emerging literature base on the potential as well as on the use of these applications in the K-12 social studies classroom. There are numerous examples of Web 2.0 applications, such as the aforementioned wikis, *PrimaryAccess*, and *Voicethread*, and other examples include weblogs (blogs) and podcasts. The potential for these sites to influence the teaching and learning of social studies has been noted. *Social Education*, the flagship practitioner journal for social studies teachers, has published a number of articles on specific ways in which Web 2.0 applications may be used to augment K-12 social studies instruction (e.g., Berson & Berson, 2006; Lipscomb, Guenther, & McLeod, 2007; Stoddard, Hofer, & Buchanan, 2008). Social studies scholars are beginning to explore Web 2.0 as evidenced by the theme of the Third Ackerman Colloquium on Technology and Citizenship, held in July 2009 at Purdue University. Among the goals of the Colloquium were to "engage participants in discussions related, but not limited to … the potential role of new media/Web 2.0 technology in the development of knowledge and skills required by citizens" (VanFossen & Berson, 2009).

The attention being paid by social studies scholars to Web 2.0 applications is well founded. Recent statistics reveal that "93% of teens use the Internet," and of those, 64% "have participated in one or more ... content-creating activities" (Lenhart, Madden, Macgill, & Smith, 2007, p. i). Creating content refers to those individuals "who have created or worked on a blog or webpage, shared original creative content, or remixed content they found online into a new creation" (p. 2). This statistic indicates that "59% of *all teens*" have developed Internet content (p. 2). Therefore, with the majority of adolescents not only accessing the Internet but generating knowledge on it, a parallel may be drawn to a decade ago. At the turn of the twenty-first century, the Internet was praised by social studies educators for making previously difficult-to-find or altogether unattainable materials available with a click of a mouse (VanFossen & Shiveley, 2000); the widespread and steadily increasing use of Web 2.0 applications has the potential to further alter social studies teaching and learning, as these tools may help move instruction from being teacher-centered and fact-based to an environment that is student-centered and open-ended.

In terms of research studies of the impact on Web 2.0 tools in K-12 social studies, research has tended to focus on the impact of a particular tool or application on the teaching and/or learning of specific social studies content, as opposed to the technology itself; an approach to technology in social studies advocated by Mason et al. (2000). The studies described above on wikis, *PrimaryAccess*, and *Voicethread* all used Web 2.0 applications, but in the support of social studies content.

Along the lines of interactivity, Massively Multiplayer Online Role-Playing Games (commonly referred to as MMORPGs), are another type of Web 2.0 application that has the potential to alter social studies instruction. In using a MMORPG, a player assumes a character (termed an *avatar*), and is responsible for all of the *avatar's* actions, including buying and selling products and communicating with other members of the online community. In terms of social studies, MMORPGs have tremendous potential, particularly in the areas of civics, citizenship, and economics. Not only are players part of a large community (some MMORPGs have hundreds of thousands of players), but players hail from all corners of the world, and they buy, sell, and trade property with one another highlighting the potential for making economic education come (literally) alive (VanFossen, Friedman, & Hartshorne, 2008). The impact of MMORPGs on K-12 social studies may not be felt for some time, however, as VanFossen, Friedman, and Hartshorne point out that acceptable use policies in school and the emphasis of standardized testing in schools might limit study in this area in the near term.

Finally, one of the most commonly used examples of Web 2.0 applications is social networking. This refers to "building online communities of people," and examples include *Facebook* and *Twitter*, and these sites allow users to update their status using text and images from anywhere that they have an Internet connection, including a mobile phone ("Social Network Service" 2009b). These sites play an important role in teenagers' lives as well; a recent study found that nearly two-thirds (65%) of teenagers who regularly use the Internet have a social networking account (Lenhart, 2009). Social networking sites hold tremendous potential for teaching and learning social studies at the K-12 level. This potential can be seen from the home page of *Facebook*, which states that it "helps you connect and share with the people in your life," and the notion of worldwide communication and global citizenship is apparent, as there is a prominent icon of individuals from around the world that are connected to one another ("Welcome to Facebook!," 2009).

These notions were recently carried out and literally displayed for the world to see through the use of Web 2.0 applications. During the disputed Iranian election of June 2009, it was well documented that while the Iranian government closed media outlets, through the use of *Twitter*, individuals shared real-time images of protests that would have otherwise been unattainable. The past 15 years have seen the Internet develop from a one-way to two-way path of information, and users around the world have exponentially increased; these trends lead to a likely conclusion that Web 2.0 applications could have an impact on K-12 social studies. The questions that social studies scholars should be exploring are those that ask when, and to what degree, such an impact will take place.

CONCLUSION

The title of this chapter poses a question. Has the Internet—specifically its use in social studies classrooms—been a lost opportunity or an unexplored frontier? After examining the research literature that has accumulated over the last dozen years, we feel very confident that the answer is both. Indeed, making the case that K-12 classroom use of the Internet has been underexplored is relatively easy as conclusions from the handful of studies that have actually explored K-12 Internet use in social studies classrooms all seem to sing the same refrain: there is a continued need for more research in this area. Whitworth and Berson (2003) are illustrative: "There is a need for research on the use of and effectiveness of technology in social studies classrooms that enhances social studies education (according to the NCSS standards) that goes beyond merely accessing information on the Internet" (p. 484).

Friedman and Hicks (2006) suggest that one explanation for this lack of systematic examination of classroom Internet use might lie in the way social studies scholars work. They stated that the number of researchers working in this field is quite small and that we often work in "splendid isolation" and we are content to spend our time working on "one-stop 'research'" as opposed to longer term "research and development" or replication studies (p. 249). In this, Friedman and Hicks speculated we have lost sight of the important objectives of classroom teaching and learning: "how many of us have developed an ongoing research agenda or program that has sought to connect with educational users, or even bothered to ask teachers what their questions and needs are?" (p. 249). Swan and Hofer (2008) echoed these calls for more meaningful study of classroom Internet use in their conclusion that, "It is focused inquiry with teachers in the classroom that we can more effectively understand how to best leverage technology to support a variety of pedagogical approaches in the social studies classroom" (p. 323).

Further explanation of this "lost opportunity" lies in Berson and Balyta's (2004) description of a field just emerging from an "adolescence" characterized by a dearth of "empirical evidence" exploring the impact of the Internet on student achievement in social studies content areas (p. 148). Put another way, Berson and Balyta's description implied that researchers are just now starting to consider more "grown-up" questions such as the value-added of technology (the Internet in particular) in the teaching and learning of social studies. Considering that we are approaching the 20th anniversary of the invention of the WWW, it is not a moment too soon. Moreover, as Freidman and Hicks (2006) have pointed out, social studies "can easily be criticized as being a field that is 'research light' which is not a strong place to be with calls for scientifically based research" (p. 251). Friedman and Hicks also argued that the relatively short history of this area of study provides researchers opportunities to "advocate for advancing the type of research that is conducted within social studies and technology" (p. 252).

Several studies have indicated that the time may indeed be ripe for moving this research out of its adolescence. Bolick, Berson, Friedman, and Porfeli (2007) reported the results of a survey of social studies methods professors and their use of technology, including the Internet, in their teaching. Results from this survey (the third such conducted since 1999) indicated that social studies methods professors were using technology much more frequently than previously reported. Indeed, findings indicated that, "technology beliefs and practices have changed over time and technology has been adopted by the field, as social studies teacher educators are using technology more frequently in 2006 than they were in 1999 (p. 186).

This implies that the now small field of researchers studying technology integration in social studies classrooms may be poised to grow—and grow to the point were classroom applications and use can and will be explored. If technology has indeed been accepted by the field of social studies educators, it follows that we might begin to see more research in on the impact of technology integration in the classroom.

If we accept the premise that the lack of systematic study of classroom Internet use represents a lost opportunity, what might seizing the opportunity look like? In other words, what should researchers working in this area focus on? Here we agree with Friedman and Hicks (2006) who wrote that "research should take an instructional design perspective, where the needs of teachers and students are analyzed, specific learning objectives are designed in which there is a 'seamless' integration of technology into social studies instruction" (p. 253). Swan and Hofer (2008) echoed this call when they concluded that some "of the most compelling research ... shares common attributes that may help guide future inquiry in the field" (p. 322). Among these attributes were: (1) spending the necessary time in classrooms to understand the complexity of teaching with the Internet, and (2) aligning the research with the "opportunities and constraints of the (social studies) classroom" which gives researchers "insight into how the intervention might play out in real classroom settings" (pp. 322-323).

VanFossen and Watterson (2008)—in their replication of the VanFossen (1999-2000) study of Indiana teachers Internet use—concluded that nearly all of the barriers to Internet use teachers reported in 1999 had disappeared or diminished greatly by 2005. In spite of this finding, respondents' classroom Internet use had failed to increase appreciably. VanFossen and Waterson (2008) concluded, therefore, that the teacher's pedagogical stance—their view of teaching and learning—might well be the most important indicator of classroom Internet use. One of the most important questions future researchers can explore, then, is whether Ertmer (2005) was correct in her conclusion that a teacher's pedagogical disposition is the prevailing factor in determining the success of classroom technology integration.

One final area worth investigating is the influx of the next generation of teachers, the vast majority of whom will be "digital natives." These new teachers will have grown up with ubiquitous digital computing. How will this impact their use of the Internet in their classrooms? Swan and Hofer (2008) recognized this issue when they concluded that it will become "increasingly important to examine the ways in which teachers experience these technologies, particularly those teachers without technological expertise" (p. 322). And what about those with such expertise?

The intuitive hypothesis, of course, is that the digital natives will be more comfortable using, and thus more likely to implement, technology—including the Internet—in their classrooms. Interestingly, there is some limited evidence that refutes this hypothesis. VanFossen (1999-2000) found a correlation between a teacher's experience (years teaching) and frequency of Internet use in their classroom. VanFossen and Jones (2006) found no difference between in-service and preservice teachers' beliefs about their preparation to use technology and their desire to use the Internet in their classrooms. These are very limited findings—all the more reason to engage in a systematic study of classroom Internet use. Such study should have the goal of discovering what factors most contribute to the use of the Internet in powerful and meaningful social studies teaching and learning. Something that, up until now, has been both an unexplored frontier and a lost opportunity.

NOTES

1. The Internet traces its origins back to the U.S. Department of Defense's ARPAnet of the 1970s. ARPAnet connected a series of computer networks that made sharing information between networks possible. The pre-WWW Internet consisted of file transfers, USENET, and very rudimentary electronic mail. It wasn't until the invention of the WWW and hypertext transfer protocol (HTTP) and hypertext mark-up language (HTML) in 1991—and the posting of the first web page on August 6 of that year—that the Internet became a tool teachers and students could actually use. For purposes of this chapter, the Internet will be defined as:

    the inter-linked hypertext documents of the World Wide Web (WWW) and the infrastructure to support electronic mail, in addition to popular services such as online chat, file transfer and file sharing, online gaming, and Voice over Internet Protocol (VoIP) person-to-person communication via voice and video. ("Internet," 2009)

2. Prensky (2001) terms this generation of Americans (those born in 1984 and after) as "digital natives," for whom computers and the Internet have always been part of their life, and he estimates that high school students today have spent twice as many hours engaged in video game play as reading books (p. 1).
3. Cattagni, A., & Farris, E. (2001). *Internet Access in U.S. Public Schools and Classrooms: 1994-2000*. Washington, DC: National Center for Educational Statistics. See http://nces.ed.gov/pubsearch/pubsinfo.asp?pubid=2001071
4. These figures represent computational estimates based on algorithmic calculations from raw data and, in the case of the secondary estimate, may have been rounded up (from 99.5% to 100%). See http://nces.ed.gov/programs/digest/d04/tables/dt04_424.asp

5. Wikipedia, itself a Web 2.0 site, states that the term was first noted in 1999, but it was 2004 before "the term began its rise in popularity" ("Web 2.0," 2009).

REFERENCES

Becker, H. J. (1999). *Internet use by teachers: Conditions of professional use and student-directed use.* Irvine, CA: Center for Research on Information Technology and Organizations. Retrieved on August 26, 2009 from http://crito.uci.edu/papers/TLC/findings/internet-use/

Bennett, L., & Pye, J. (2000). Using the Internet for reflective journals in elementary teacher preparation. *Journal of Social Studies Research, 24*(2), 21-30.

Berliner, D. C. (2002). Educational research: The hardest science of all. *Educational Researcher, 31*(8), 18-20.

Berson, M. J., & Balyta, P. (2004). Technological thinking and practice in the social studies: Transcending the tumultuous adolescence of reform. *Journal of Computing in Teacher Education 20*(4), 141-150.

Berson, I. R., & Berson, M. J. (2006). Privileges, privacy, and protection of youth bloggers in the social studies classroom. *Social Education, 70*(3), 124-128.

Bolick, C. M., Berson, M. J., Friedman, A. M., & Porfeli, E. J. (2007). Diffusion of technology innovation in the preservice social studies experience: Results of a national survey. *Theory and Research in Social Education, 35*(2), 174-195.

Braun, J., Fernlund, P., & White, C. (1998). *Technology tools in the social studies classroom.* Wilsonville, OR: Franklin, Beedle and Associates.

Braun, J. & Risinger, F. (Eds.) (1999). *Surfing social studies: The Internet book.* Washington, D.C.: National Council for the Social Studies.

Cohen, D. J., & Rosenzweig, R. (2006). *Digital history: A guide to gathering, preserving, and presenting the past on the web.* Philadelphia: University of Pennsylvania Press.

Cuban, L. (2001). *Oversold and underused: Computers in the classroom.* Cambridge, MA: Harvard University Press.

Cuban, L., Kirkpatrick, H., & Peck, C. (2001). High access and low use of technologies in high school classrooms: Explaining an apparent paradox. *American Educational Research Journal, 38*(4), 813-834.

Dodge, B. (2007). *What is a webquest?* Retrieved on July 28, 2009 from http://www.webquest.org/

Doppen, F. (2004). Beginning social studies teachers' integration of technology in the history classroom. *Theory and Research in Social Education, 32*(2), 248-279.

Dutt-Doner, K. M., & Powers, S. M. (2000). The use of electronic communication to develop alternative avenues for classroom discussion. *Journal of Technology and Teacher Education, 8*(2), 153-172.

Ertmer, P. A. (2005). Teacher pedagogical beliefs: The final frontier in our quest for technology integration? *ETR&D, 53*(4), 25-39.

Ferster, B., Hammond, T., & Bull, G. (2006). PrimaryAccess: Creating digital documentaries in the social studies classroom. *Social Education, 70*(3), 147-150.

Foster, S. J., & Hoge, J. (1997). Surfing for social studies software: A practical guide to locating and selecting resources on the Internet. *Social Studies and the Young Learner, 9*(4), 28-32.

Friedman, A. (2006). World history teachers' use of digital primary sources: The effect of training. *Theory and Research in Social Education, 34*(1), 124-141.

Friedman, A. M. (2008). Social studies teachers' use of the Internet to foster democratic citizenship. In P. J. VanFossen & M. J. Berson (Eds.), *The electronic republic? The impact of technology on education for citizenship* (pp. 173-195). West Lafayette, IN: Purdue University Press.

Friedman, A. M., & Heafner, T. L. (2007). You think for me, so I don't have to. *Contemporary Issues in Technology and Teacher Education* [Online serial], 7(3). Retrieved from http://www.citejournal.org/vol7/iss3/socialstudies/article1.cfm

Friedman, A. M., & Heafner, T. L. (2008a). Finding and contextualizing resources: A digital literacy tool's impact in ninth grade world history. *The Clearing House, 82*(2), 82-86.

Heafner, T. L., & Friedman, A. M. (2008b). Wikis and constructivism in social studies: Fostering a deeper understanding. *Computers in the Schools, 25*(3-4), 288-302.

Friedman, A. M., & Hicks, D. (2006). The state of the field: Technology, social studies, and teacher education. *Contemporary Issues in Technology and Teacher Education, 6*(2), 246-258.

Friedman, A. M., & Lee, J. K. (2009, June). *Using Voicethread as a debate tool.* Paper presented at the third James F. Ackerman Colloquium on Technology and Citizenship Education: "Citizenship Education 2.0: Digital Media in a Networked World," West Lafayette, IN.

Heafner, T. L., & Friedman, A. M. (2008). Wikis and constructivism in social studies: Fostering a deeper understanding. *Computers in the Schools, 25*(3-4), 288-302.

Hicks, D., & Ewing, E. (2003). Bringing the world into the classroom with online-global newspapers. *Social Education, 67*(3), 134-139.

Internet. (2009, June 16). In *Wikipedia, the free encyclopedia.* Retrieved June 16, 2009, from http://en.wikipedia.org/wiki/Internet

Johnson, C., & Rector, J. (1997). The Internet ten. *Social Education, 61*(3), 167-169.

Lee, J. K., & Clarke, W. G. (2003). High school social studies students' uses of online historical documents related to the Cuban Missile Crisis. *The Journal of Interactive Online Learning, 2*(1), 1-15.

Lenhart, A. (2009). *It's personal: Similarities and differences in online social network use between teens and adults.* Retrieved on August 21, 2009 from http://www.pewinternet.org/Presentations/2009/19-Similarities-and-Differences-in-Online-Social-Network-Use.aspx

Lenhart, A., Madden, M., Macgill, A. R., & Smith, A. (2007). *Teens and social media. Pew Internet & American Life Project.* Retrieved on August 21, 2009 from http://www.pewinternet.org/~/media//Files/Reports/2007/PIP_Teens_Social_Media_Final.pdf.pdf

Lévesque, S. (2008). *Preliminary results of study on historical literacy with the Virtual Historian.* Retrieved on August 18, 2009 from http://www.virtualhistorian.ca/Research/Executive_Summary_VH.pdf

Lipscomb, G. (2003). "I guess it was pretty fun": Using webquests in the middle school classroom. *The Clearing House, 76,* 152-155.

Lipscomb, G. B., Guenther, L, M., & McLeod, P. (2007). Sounds good to me: Using digital audio in the social studies classroom. *Social Education, 71*(3), 120-124.

Manfra, M. M., & Hammond, T. C. (2008). Teachers' instructional choices with student-created digital documentaries: Case studies. *Journal of Research on Technology in Education, 41*(2), 223-245.

Martorella, P. (1997). Technology and social studies: Which way to the sleeping giant? *Theory and Research in Social Education, 25*(4), 511-514.

Mason, C., Berson, M., Diem, R., Hicks, D., Lee, J., & Dralle, T. (2000). Guidelines for using technology to prepare social studies teachers. *Contemporary Issues in Technology and Teacher Education* [Online serial], *1* (1). Retrieved from http://www.citejournal.org/vol1/iss1/currentissues/socialstudies/article1.htm

McGlinn, M., & McGlinn, J. (2004). The effects of WebQuests in the social studies classroom: A review of research. *Society for Information Technology and Teacher Education International Conference, 2004*(1), 4833-4839.

Milson, A. (2002). The Internet and inquiry learning: Integrating medium and method in a sixth grade social studies classroom. *Theory and Research in Social Education, 30*(3), 330-353.

Molebash, P. E. (2002). Constructivism meets technology integration: The CUFA technology guidelines in an elementary social studies methods course. *Theory and Research in Social Education, 30*(3), 429-455.

Molebash, P. E. (2004). Preservice teacher perceptions of a technology-enriched methods course. *Contemporary Issues in Technology and Teacher Education* [Online serial], *3*(4).

Prensky, M. (2001). Digital natives, digital immigrants. *On the Horizon, 9*(5), 1-6.

Rock, T., & Passe, J. (2004). Technology integration at the university level: An analysis of an elementary social studies methods course. *Contemporary Issues in Technology and Teacher Education* [Online serial], *4*(3).

Rose, S., & Fernlund, P. (1997). Using technology for powerful social studies learning. *Social Education, 61*(3), 160-166.

Saye, J., & Brush, T. (n.d.(a)). *Persistent Issues in History Network.* Retrieved on July 30, 2009 from http://dp.crlt.indiana.edu/index.html

Saye, J., & Brush, T. (n.d.(b)). *Persistent Issues in History Network.* Retrieved on July 30, 2009 from http://dp.crlt.indiana.edu/new_member.html

Saye, J. W., & Brush, T. (1999). Student engagement with social issues in a multimedia supported learning environment. *Theory and Research in Social Education, 27*(4), 472-504.

Saye, J. W., & Brush, T. (2002). Scaffolding critical reasoning about history and social issues in multimedia-supported learning environments. *Educational Technology Research and Development, 50*(3), 77-96.

Saye, J. W., & Brush, T. (2004). Scaffolding problem-based teaching in a traditional social studies classroom. *Theory and Research in Social Education, 32*(3), 349-378.

Saye, J. W., & Brush, T. (2006). Comparing teachers' strategies for supporting student inquiry in a problem-based multimedia-enhanced history unit. *Theory and Research in Social Education, 34*(2), 183-212.

Schrum, K., & Schrum, D. (2009). Exploring the past with 21st century tools. *Social Studies and the Young Learner, 21*(4), 24-27.

Shiveley, J. M., & VanFossen, P. J. (2009). Toward assessing Internet use in the social studies classroom: Developing an inventory based on a review of relevant literature. *Journal of Social Studies Research, 33*(1), 1-32.

Social network service. (2009). *Wikipedia.* Social network service. Retrieved on August 21, 2009 from http://en.wikipedia.org/wiki/Social-networking

Stoddard, J. D., Hofer, M. J., & Buchanan, M. (2008). The "starving time" wikinquiry: Using a wiki to foster historical inquiry. *Social Education, 72*(3), 144-146, 158-160.

Strickland, J. (2005). Using webquests to teach content: Comparing instructional strategies. *Contemporary Issues in Technology and Teacher Education, 5*(2), 138-148.

Swan, K. O., & Hofer, M. (2008). Technology and social studies. In L. S. Levstik & C. A. Tyson (Eds.), *Handbook of Research in Social Studies Education* (pp. 307-326). New York: Routledge.

VanFossen, P. (1999-2000). An analysis of the use of the Internet and World Wide Web by secondary social studies teachers in Indiana. *The International Journal of Social Education, 14*(2), 87-109.

VanFossen, P. J. (2009). Student and teacher perceptions of the WebQuest model in social studies: A preliminary study. In J. K. Lee & A. M. Friedman (Eds.), *Research on Technology in Social Studies Education* (pp. 101-126). Charlotte, NC: Information Age.

VanFossen, P. J., & Berson, M. J. (2009). *About the colloquium.* Retrieved on August 20, 2009 from http://www.edci.purdue.edu/vanfossen/colloquium/About.htm

VanFossen, P. J., Friedman, A. M., & Hartshorne, R. (2008). The emerging role of synthetic worlds and massively-multiplayer online role-playing games (MMORPGs) in social studies and citizenship education. In R. Ferdig, (Ed.), *Handbook of research on effective electronic gaming in education* (pp. 235-250). Hershey, PA: IGI.

VanFossen, P. J., & Jones, D. (2006). *Indiana social studies teachers interest in receiving professional development by podcast.* A technical report to the Indiana Department of Education, Indianapolis, IN. Submitted for the James F. Ackerman Center for Democratic Citizenship.

VanFossen P. J., & Shiveley, J. M. (1999). Using the Internet to create primary source teaching packets. *The Social Studies, 91*(6), 244-252.

VanFossen, P. J., & Shiveley, J. (2003). A content analysis of Internet sessions presented at the National Council for the Social Studies Annual Meeting, 1995-2002. *Theory and Research in Social Education, 31*(4), 502-522.

VanFossen, P. J., & Waterson, R. A. (2008). "It is just easier to do what you did before...": An update on Internet use in secondary social studies classrooms in Indiana. *Theory and Research in Social Education, 36*(2), 124-152.

Virtual Historian. (n.d.). *What about the Virtual Historian?* Retrieved on August 18, 2009 from http://www.virtualhistorian.ca/About_Us_e.html

Voicethread.com. (2007-2009a). *Voicethread.* Retrieved on August 19, 2009 from http://voicethread.com/

Web 2.0. (2009). In *Wikipedia, the free encyclopedia*. Retreived on August 19, 2009 from http://en.wikipedia.org/wiki/Web_2.0.

Welcome to facebook! (2009). *Facebook.* Retrieved on August 21, 2009 from http://www.facebook.com

Wells, J., & Lewis, L. (2006). *Internet Access in U.S. Public Schools and Classrooms: 1994–2005* (NCES 2007-020). U.S. Department of Education. Washington, DC: National Center for Education Statistics.

White, C. (1997). Civic participation and the Internet: Prospects for civic deliberation in the information age. *The Social Studies, 88*(1), 30-39.

Whitworth, S. A., & Berson, M. J. (2003). Computer technology in the social studies: An examination of the effectiveness literature (1996-2001). *Contemporary Issues in Technology and Teacher Education* [Online serial], *2*(4). Retrieved from http://www.citejournal.org/vol2/iss4/socialstudies/article1.cfm

Wilson, E. K. (1997). A trip to historic Philadelphia on the web. *Social Education, 61*(3), 170-175.

Wilson, E. K., & Marsh, G. E., II. (1995). Social studies and the Internet revolution. *Social Education, 59*(4), 198-202.

CHAPTER 5

DIGITAL HISTORY AND THE EMERGENCE OF DIGITAL HISTORICAL LITERACIES

John Lee

March 6, 1993, Dr. Lynn H. Nelson, a history professor at the University of Kansas, posted the first link on a new web-based index of historical resources called HN Source: The Central Information Server For Historians. Renamed and organized 6 months later as WWW-VL History, the project was part of the World Wide Web Virtual Library, a larger effort aimed at cataloging web resources. The WWW-Virtual Library, created by the inventor of the web, Tim Berners-Lee, came along as scholars and academicians were increasingly using the web to share information and ideas. Today, hundreds of millions of pages of historical information is available online; from the high profile collections of American Memory (http://memory.loc.gov) and the National Archives and Records Administration (http://archives.gov) to small-scale publications such as The Diary of Samuel Pepys (http://www.pepysdiary.com/) and even smaller scale projects such as my own production, The Story of Asaph Perry (http://www.dhpp.org/Cherokee/narrative/index.html).

The wide availability of digital historical resources has shifted how these historical resources are used (Ayers, 1999; Rosenzweig, 2001) with

Technology in Retrospect: Social Studies in the Information Age 1984-2009, pp. 75–90
Copyright © 2010 by Information Age Publishing
All rights of reproduction in any form reserved.

more people now able to engage the raw materials of the past. Beyond being able read or view historical resources, the web now enables users to create, analyze, interpret, and communicate about historical ideas and issues. Fueling these new uses are collaborative technologies commonly termed Web 2.0 that enable not just information sharing but collaborative content generation using a wide range of continually evolving, primarily web-based tools (Boggs, 2007). Daniel Cohen and Roy Rosensweig (2004) argued that the discipline of history is primed to move into the world of Web 2.0, which he describes as the "interaction between historians and their subjects, interoperation of dispersed historical archives, and the analysis of online resources using computational methods" (p. 293). In the few years since Cohen's premonition, the field of history has indeed gone 2.0. This chapter explores the emergence of this 2.0 version of digital history given the unique needs of teachers and students in K-12 environments and explores some of the unique digital historical literacies needed in this age of Web 2.0.

What does it mean to teach and learn digital history? And perhaps more importantly, what are the literacies that support work in digital history? Consider the following vignettes from two teachers teaching the same subject matter, but influenced by their environment in very different ways.

Antony Capella began the lecture to his eighth grade class as he began all his lectures, with a story. This one was particularly interesting to his students. The story was about Mary Church Terrell, an African American woman and civil rights leader who was the first president of National Association of Colored Women and the first African-American female member of the District of Columbia Board of Education. Mr. Capella started the lecture by reading the words from Terrell's 1940 autobiography, A Colored Woman In A White World. He bought the book after learning about Terrell in a graduate history class he took several years ago and has been using it in his class ever sense. The passage from Terrell that Mr. Capella read was as follows. "When I was only six years old my mother decided to send me from Memphis, where I was born, and where my parents were living at the time to Yellow Springs, Ohio, so that I might go to school. My mother did not want me to remain in Memphis and attend school there, for right after the Civil War the educational facilities for colored children were very meager indeed. My mother was one of the most ambitious and progressive women I have ever know. Although she was a slave she could read and write and had actually studied French, in spite of the fact it was strictly against the law in Tennessee to teach slaves to read. Mother was determined to give me a thorough education." Mr. Capella followed this reading with a brief, but compelling account of Mary Church Terrell's career as a civil rights leader emphasizing the her commitment to her own education and the education of all children in the United States. He encouraged his students, through his enthusiastic portrayal of Terrell's story, to learn more about how women such as Mary Church

Terrell defied limitations, took advantage of opportunities, and ultimately suc-
ceeded in life. Mr. Capella's hope was that his students would read the accounts
and be interested in the stories while learning life lessons from his instruction and
being inspired to greatness themselves.

Simone Bere understands the power of a good story and has always tried to help
her students understand not only the story, but also how the story was put together.
Ms. Bere wanted to apply this approach to a recent lesson on Mary Church Terrell
and her autobiography "A Colored Woman In A White World." In preparation for
the lesson, Ms. Bere found a presentation on the Library of Congress website of one
page of a draft of Terrell's book. The draft was typed and included several correc-
tions and notations. Ms. Bere thought the draft version would be a nice addition to
her lesson. She started to look for additional resources and found a number of use-
ful online materials, including a map-based presentation of the places mentioned
in Terrell's autobiography, a presentation from the Library of Congress of multiple
drafts from Terrell's book, a collection of letters and other materials relating to Ter-
rell's pursuit of an appointment to the Children's Bureau in the Department of
Labor in the Coolidge presidential administration, and several online versions of
her famous 1898 speech to the National Association Of Colored Women titled "The
Progress Of Colored Women." With these resources in mind, Ms. Bere designed an
activity that involved her students engaging a variety of sources around a series of
questions about the way Terrell chose to tell her story. While emphasizing the uplift-
ing characteristics of the story, Ms. Bere wanted students to dig behind it and find
the human struggle that played out in Terrell's struggles, both in writing her story
and her ultimately unsuccessful effort to obtain a position in the federal govern-
ment. The work required students to engage digital historical resources and con-
struct interpretations using real-life contexts.

Important similarities and distinctions are evident in these descriptions. Mr. Capella and Ms. Bere actively sought out information and
knowledge. They were both open to new ideas and were constantly on the
lookout for materials they could use in class. The difference in these
vignettes comes in the way they found new information and developed
new knowledge. Mr. Capella received information in a formal class setting, his college history course, and incorporated what he learned into a
presentation on women and civil rights. Ms. Bere discovered new information while trying to find resources for another activity. Although the
distinctions may seem trivial—a simple difference in process—the implications are enormous. Mr. Capella lives in a world of received historical
knowledge where experts construct fully formed ideas and hand them
over to novices. Ms. Bere lives in a world of co-constructed historical
knowledge, where the raw materials of the past are available for negotia-
tion and interpretation. Both Mr. Capella and Ms. Bere are historically literate and both have the abilities to understand the past using specific
strategies and tools, but the differences are important. In this chapter, I

attempt to describe what it means to be historically literate in the twenty-first century and the implications for such literacy in teaching and learning history. First, I present some background on the notion of historical literacy in teaching and learning history as well as background on the emergence of digital history as a field or genre within the larger discipline of history.

HISTORICAL LITERACY

On a basic level, historical literacy, like the notion of literacy itself might be thought of as simply the ability to read works of history. But, for most scholars historical literacy entails much more than just reading. Perfetti, Britt, and Georgi (1995) offered a comprehensive description of historical literacy in their introduction to an edited volume of research on historical thinking.

> To be able to engage in discourse on history is to be able to do more than tell the story. One must be able to indicate, through speaking or writing, some awareness of what we call the "methods" of history. By this we do not mean specifically the tools and methods of historians, although the idea is in that direction. Rather, we mean developing awareness that, for example, the received story is simple and distorting and that the story had to be recorded in documents of various kinds, which serve as the evidence for the story. Historical literacy also implies an appreciation that evidence counts and some sense of where evidence comes from. Without knowing the sources of evidence, students cannot evaluate the story. (p. 4)

Perfetti, Britt, and Georgi's connotation of historical literacy places active engagement and interpretation above received knowledge.

Although history has long been a standard part of official school curricula in western countries, most of that instruction is patterned after the university lecture model, with teachers delivering information for learners to make sense of and often memorize. With some notable exceptions (e.g., the New Social Studies of the 1960s), history instruction has focused on students learning to recognize patterns and recall people, events, and dates. The focus of these history courses was, and for some continues to be, the teacher. In such contexts, teachers typically know what they want students to learn and then proceeded to convey these understandings using a limited range of didactic instructional approaches. Among these approaches is lecture, but didactic instruction is certainly not limited to lecture. The most important premise of didactic instruction is that the teacher knows precisely what the student is to know. Students may or may not be actively engaged, although high quality didactic instruction should result in active engagement though questioning and the mutual consideration of information (both teacher and students). Didactic instruction might be thought of more broadly as a form of classical teaching. There are other forms of classical teaching (e.g., dialectical or Socratic methods), which, in spite of different approaches to student engagement, all begin with the premise that there is some agreed upon knowledge that a teacher understands and desires to help students know.

Much of the rationale for teaching history using classical, teacher-centered methods rests in the metaphorical belief that students are empty vessels into which information can be "poured." This approach suggests that students must first collect or memorize factual historical information and over time may begin to engage in more complex interpretative activities. This notion that knowledge can be differentiated among levels of difficulty, in part, emerged from the work of Piaget and later Bloom who suggested that children learn and think in progressively complex ways. Through the 1970s most of the teaching and learning in history reflected this hierarchal and linear structure. Younger children were deemed unable to think in the complex ways demanded by the study of history (Hallam, 1967), and thus history was restricted in most primary and even secondary school settings to low-level knowledge acquisition.

Research and curricular reform in the United States and Britain called into question this traditional approach to learning history. In the early 1970s, the British government implemented the Schools Council History Project, which re-envisioned school history as facts and generalizations to be understand as well as a disciplined approach to thinking. After 2 decades of research, a similar approach was put forward by the National History Center in the United States through its National History Standards project, which similarly cleaved the teaching and learning of history into historical understanding and historical thinking. Historical thinking includes the processes that result in historical understandings.

These changes in the way history was taught in Britain and the United States were in large part supported by and based on research—particularly, research by cognitive scientists that challenged conventional thinking about learning and suggested that humans learn by doing and making associations. Within this cognitive science context, research on historical thinking accelerated in the 1980s and 1990s, with the corpus of findings laying a foundation for a new type of history instruction focused on inquiry, the use of authentic historical sources, and interpretation. Several more recent milestone research projects defined this new approach to history learning. Among these were research projects conducted by Sam Wineburg (1991), Bruce Vansledright (1995), and Keith Barton (1997). The cumulative idea emerging from this research was that children can learn history using disciplinary structures or ways of thinking in history.

Moreover, such learning experiences require active engagement with historical source material with teachers serving to support the work.

These findings suggested a transition from traditional instructional approaches to more constructivist approaches. At root, this transition reflected a larger philosophical and scientific move toward a form of education that does not privilege "fixed" knowledge. Instead, systems for learning can be understood, but the forms of that knowledge are always constructed in social settings given cogitative conditions such as the abilities of a learner to form particular understandings. In history, this meant a move away from teaching and learning a story with specific and known facts toward disciplinary work focus on using historical materials as evidence and the student construction of historical interpretations. The area of digital history has perhaps been the most forward thinking area in the discipline of history regarding students' work with historical resources.

THE EMERGENCE OF DIGITAL HISTORY

A steady pace of change and innovation has defined the field of digital history, and much of this change has focused on how history is learned. Change is a powerful motivator, but also a stimulant for creativity. In many ways the discipline of history needed digital environments such as the web to continue and progress what was already underway. Throughout the twentieth century, the discipline of history expanded and, in some ways, transformed, encompassing a wide range of perspectives and incorporating a widening body of information as evidence. The emergence of new perspectives within and alongside standard historical scholarship such as Marxism, feminism, social history, environmental history, sensory history, and most recently digital history have brought to the forefront of the discipline voices and ideas that were previously, at best, studied through the prism of political or military history. In 1976, when the journal *Social History* published its first edition, the editors wrote in the inaugural issue that social history "must be at once iconoclastic, corrosive of received explanations; creative in producing new concepts and devising new methods; and aggressive, encouraging incursions into all fields of historical analysis" ("Editorial," 1976, p. 1). Much like the emerging social history of 30 years ago, digital history today offers something decidedly new.

Beyond the additive value of online historical resources, digital history offers a new way of thinking about, doing, and communicating about history. Professor William Thomas describes these conditions in his working definition of digital history.

Digital history is an approach to examining and representing the past that works with the new communication technologies of the computer, the Internet network, and software systems. On one level, digital history is an open arena of scholarly production and communication, encompassing the development of new course materials and scholarly data collections. On another, it is a methodological approach framed by the hypertextual power of these technologies to make, define, query, and annotate associations in the human record of the past. To do digital history, then, is to create a framework, an ontology, through the technology for people to experience, read, and follow an argument about a historical problem. ("Interchange," 2008, p. 454)

One of the most unique characteristics of digital history is accessibility. In fact, the emergence of digital history was hailed as a democratizing move in the discipline. Edward Ayers, one of the first historians to embrace digital history, saw potential in the use of computer technology to extend the field of history. Describing that potential in the context of recent moves in the field, Ayers (1999) argued that the

great democratization of history over the last few decades has not been accompanied by a democraticization of audience. Innovation in the field seems to have slowed, the heady days of the new political history, the new social history, the new women's history, and the new cultural history eclipsed or absorbed into a general eclectic practice. A budding interest in new narrative techniques seems to have faded. Perhaps the tools of the digital world can help us out of this lull. (para. 5)

Likewise, Cohan and Rosenzweig (2005) have suggested that historical information online is democratizing the profession and extending the reach of scholars to new audiences. In discussing their own work Cohan and Rosenzweig argue, much like other digital historians, that work in the field of digital history has "a basis in a broader democratic aspiration to make the History Web a place where ordinary historians can practice their craft in new and innovative ways" (p. 14).

As a part of a progression in the discipline of history, digital history also has progressed over time. Steven Mintz describes the progression of digital history in four stages ("Interchange," 2008). Stage 1 is a static form of archiving, bringing to mind the first large scale efforts to present historical information online through online historical archives such as the Valley of the Shadow at http://valley.lib.virginia.edu/ and American Memory at http://memory.loc.gov/. Stage 2 involves the doing of history. Mintz (n.d.) cites his work on a project called eXplorations at http://www.digitalhistory.uh.edu/learning_history/ as an example of an environment where students can interact with historical information toward creating new knowledge. Other resources offer more nuanced and complex environments for doing digital history such as Picturing Modern America at http://cct2.edc.org/PMA/ (Tally & Goldenberg, 2005), Historical Thinking Matters at http://historicalthinkingmatters.org/ (Martin & Wineburg, 2008), and SCIM-C at http://historicalinquiry.com (Hicks, Doolittle, & Ewing, 2004). Next, stage 3 incorporates social media and collaborative work. Stage 4 involves the virtual representation of historical space. Mintz's suggests that digital history has undergone substantial change in the short time that field has been in existence.

Even with these proclamations of newness and change, several questions linger. The first of these deals with differences—how does digital history differ from historical work done in traditional or nondigital environments, specifically with regard to resource use, presentation, and structure? Most importantly, digital historical resources are more accessible. In addition, their use encourages increased archival activity and promotes the development of social networks. Digital historical resources are easier to manipulate and search as well as being more flexible with collections often including an organizational strategy that mirrors the content of the collection (Lee, 2002a).

A second question concerns distinctions—namely, what does it mean to do digital history and how are such activities distinct from the regular doing of history? The act of historical inquiry in digital environments (using digital resources and/or with the intent of reporting digitally) involves some important and unique elements. Perhaps the most distinctive component is the experiential nature of digital history. William Thomas calls this "history in the digital," going on to argue that digital history is an "experience for users—a process, an active, spatial, virtual-reality encounter with the past" ("Interchange," 2008, p. 460). One that Thomas argues enables historians and history students to "take advantage of the multiple media forms" (p. 460).

A third question concerns limitations. Access to digital historical resources among novices is perhaps the most important barrier for digital history. There seems to be little systematic concern for how students access historical resources. Most digital historical resources use highly idiosyncratic presentational forms. In part, this results from the nature of the web—programmers and digital historians are able to present historical materials in an almost infinitely configurable forms and formats. For example, an historical image can easily be presented in various sizes, resolutions, presentational frames, and even in altered forms. Each of these forms can serve important purposes. Smaller versions may be arrayed on a web page to aid users as they browse a collection. For novices and students, this can be particularly important. Often, students have a limited amount of time to locate resources so any mechanism that improves the efficiency with which they can locate materials would be beneficial. The format of a presentation is equally important. Again, novice and student users need more support in their work with historical information, so a presentation of historical information that includes levels of detail that can be accessed according to the user's level of prior knowledge can be an important feature.

Beyond these questions of differences, distinctions, and limitations are other issues related to the nature of digital historical resources. Understanding the nature of digital historical resources is an important prerequisite to their use. One issue concerns the organizational nature of digital historical resources. In organizational terms, digital historical resources can be archival and/or interpretative (Lee, 2002b). Archival digital historical resources are aimed at the preservation of historical records. Interpretative resources seek to preserve, but go a step further to suggest some interpretation about the past. The key factor in these two organizational approaches is intent or the manner in which the resource is presented.

Another issue concerns the retrieval of information. By considering the organizational nature of digital historical sources, we can begin to understand how students might retrieve or access the historical materials on these websites. Digital archival historical collections are often very difficult for students to use and often do not include pedagogical structures that might otherwise aid information retrieval. Roy Rosenzweig (2001) suggested that archival sites take shape as either virtual versions of existing archives or completely new, but similarly structured archives. Many of these new archives are personal enthusiast collections, while others are very high quality professional collections. Interpretive digital history websites, on the other hand, often contain description, explanation, analysis, and/or evaluation of historical primary sources. They may also include original digital historical narrative or analytical works as well as the actual primary source documents used to conduct historical inquiry. In fact, some of the best interpretative digital history sites include significant numbers of primary sources materials, but interpretative sites do not necessarily include all the documents that would be in an archival collection. Websites which function primarily or solely to preserve historical resources should reflect considerations which relate to access, retrieval, use, and protection of the resources. Whether a site directly or indirectly aims to achieve particular interpretive goals, the design of the site should reflect broad sensibilities related to the most robust use of the materials as possible.

DIGITAL HISTORICAL LITERACY

Work in digital history demands much from students. In addition to what we might call traditional historical skills such as the abilities to summarize and contextualizing historical resources, digital history requires skills or understandings related to accessing historical information and construct-ing that information in various forms. Certainly, this digital historical lit-eracy shares much with traditional conceptualizations of historical literacy. Although no single agreed upon view of historical literacy exists, a common shape for the concept of historical literacy is evident. Histori-cal literacy is typically thought of as the range of skills and dispositions that enable communication in the discipline of history. The Bradley Com-mission (1995) offered one clear view of historical literacy or what they referred to as "History's Habits of Mind" as "the perspectives and modes of thoughtful judgment derived from the study of history" (p. 9).

These ways of thinking in the discipline of history can be thought of as literacies for history and serve as a useful way of organizing possible approaches to learning history. Peter Lee (2005) suggests that historical literacy demands an "understanding of the discipline of history, and a usable framework of the past" (p. 9) He worries that "students who never get beyond common-sense conceptions of history will find it easy to accept ready-made versions of the past, or alternatively to reject the whole enterprise as inherently fraudulent" (p. 9). Other more focused efforts to consider what historical literacy is can be found in the work of Robert Bain (2004), Samuel Wineburg (2001), and David Hicks and Peter Doolit-tle (2009).

Digital historical literacy builds off these notions, but adds new con-texts, dispositions, and ways of understanding and thinking about history. These ideas collectively give shape and structure to a pedagogy for digital history. Using existing scholarly work on digital history, this digital historical pedagogy takes into consideration the unique needs and con-siderations of students as novices in historical work as well as the needs of teachers in preparing to teach using digital historical resources. Below are some initial thoughts about the new contexts, dispositions, and ways of thinking that are emerging in digital history, specifically as they related to the idea of finding information, itself one of the most unique and initially problematic dimensions of digital historical work. These ideas emerged from my work with middle grades teachers and students over a one semester period as they engaged in historical work using online resources.

The first consideration for giving shape to a digital historical pedagogy relates to context. Such a context takes into consideration where students do their work in history and why they engage in the activities. The location of students' work in digital history is multidimensional. Untethered to a physical place such as a classroom, students are able to engage digital historical resources in places and at times that meet their needs. Students can access digital historical resources virtually in place at any time, but more importantly they can access resources when and where their interests are piqued. This condition is ultimately one of context. Consider the number of times you have found yourself interested in a particular topic. The fact that digital historical resources are online means that students can engage historical work when the time is right. For most, this condition takes shape with the search for information, often for discrete ideas that are sometimes even trivial. But, these quests for information serve an important purpose, by conditioning the mind to expect learning opportunities in all sorts of contexts. Students may start by using the web to simply answer a question that emerges in a classroom or a conversation with a friend, but with support from teachers, students can extend these experiences to conduct more substantive inquiries on historical questions. In contrast, work with print-based historical materials is limited in terms of when and where the work is done, and also constrained by the systems of support in place to work with the physical resources. If students need a resource online they can access the information and support from a teacher in various contexts. Students can also access historical information in online social spaces that evolve over time to meet the needs of these novice users.

A second consideration for using digital historical resources relates to the reasons why students engage digital historical materials. While curriculum and teacher planning play as important a role in digital history as in traditional history, the ease of access and flexible nature of digital resources provide new pathways into historical work for students. Most importantly, access allows students to experiment and play with historical material.

In my work with middle grades students, I examined how they went about selecting images from a collection of *Life* magazine photographs that are available through Google at http://images.google.com/hosted/life. Students used the collection (which at the time had over 2 million images) to find images that were interesting and to use these images as a springboard for learning about some a curriculum topic. This work was lightly structured and intended to provide a sort of free-range experience for students. The idea was to create a sense of wonder and curiosity among students and then monitor how they navigated through the collection. Students' work with the historical photographs was intended to reflect an authentic rational for studying about the past. Linda Levstik and Keith Barton (2005) have written about why students study history arguing that it can help children be informed on the past, present, and future. Specifically, Levstik and Barton describe students' interest in history as related to questions about who we are, possible futures, and significant themes and questions in history (pp. 1-3). Likewise, Peter Stearns (1998) describes the study of history as important for understanding human change, morality, and identity given that history is "essential to individuals and to society, and because it harbors beauty" (para. 5).

As students navigated through the *Life* online collection they used resources that they found to be interesting and evocative. The open-ended task involved students using keywords from the state curriculum to conduct searches on the *Life* photograph website. Students were asked to talk about why they chose the word(s) for their search, why the selected certain images from the search results list, and to describe the images selected. The activity was designed to be broad enough to capture some of the more authentic reasons for studying history posed by Levstik and Barton (2005) and Stearns (1998). Student responses often reflected their personal interest. For example, one student searched on "1970s." She said she picked the term because she "liked things that are not so easy these days. Like, my parents they would talk about their days with all that stuff." She located an image of a woman, commenting that she was "dressed all weird in these bellbottoms and weird heel thingies." This student continued her work, later searching on the word "economy." Unlike the previous experience where she focused on images that resonated with her given some personal connection, the student rapidly scrolled through a series of photos commenting that they were "confusing." In the end, this student was not able to land on an image that she found particularly compelling. Her actions illustrated the role of personal interests in these sorts of open-ended activities. When asked why she was spending more time on certain pictures this student said that the she enjoyed pictures in color, "things that I usually don't see," and "something that relates to me."

Contexts for digital history feed off and in turn help inform student dispositions. Students immersed in digital contexts will come to expect information to be readily available. Of course, such a condition is as much a blessing as a curse. An uncritical use of information about the past from online sources that may not be particularly reliable or even forthright is problematic. Student dispositions related to online information access should be critical and aimed at the corroboration and confirmation of information. Such a stance about work in history is not unique for digital environments. Wineburg (1991) and Hicks, Doolittle, and Ewing (2004) describe corroboration as central to historical thinking. What is unique in the digital environment is the idea that not only do ideas (i.e., historical interpretations) need confirmation from additional sources, but each source must pass a test of worthiness. Donald Leu and colleagues describes this process as "critical evaluation."

> Whereas critical evaluation is important when reading offline information, it is perhaps more important online, where anyone can publish anything; knowing the stance and bias of an author become paramount to compre-

hension and learning. Determining this in online contexts requires new comprehension skills and strategies. For example, knowing which links take you to information about who created the information at a site (and actually choosing to follow these links) becomes important. So too, is knowing how to check the reliability of information with other information at other sites. Students do not always possess these skills. (Leu, Coiro, Castek, Hartman, Henry, & Reinking, 2008, p. 327)

Corio and Dobler (2007) describe a process of self-direction as also being critically important for students as they encounter online information and navigate specific web-based presentations. Managing each interaction with new information while also managing the larger process being engaged requires a considerable cognitive load. As students work with digital historical resources they are balancing a critical evaluation processes with more specific disciplinary processes. The net effect should enable dispositions among students to be more critical and disciplined in all their work.

These contexts and dispositions support specific ways of thinking and understanding that are central to working with historical resources in online environments. This emphasis on understanding reflects Chris Dede's (2007) work where he uses the phrases understandings and performances in place of knowledge and skills.

Categorizing what students need for the 21st century as *understandings* based on interwoven content knowledge and process skills is a more accurate depiction of how the mind works than the separation between these that current frameworks typically impose, and how students actualize those understandings in practice are *performances*. (p. 5)

One particular understanding that is central to students' work with digital historical resources relates to accessing online historical information. An understanding about how to access information is multiple faceted. On its simplest level, access involves being able to browse and search collections as well as the ability to use organizational information (e.g., finding aids). But, beyond simple search and browse access, students need to understand the shape of historical presentations, collections, and even archives. Such an understanding requires an ability to both analyze and synthesize information. Students need to pull together materials in larger settings and need to see how these pieces of historical information fit together.

In my work, I asked students to locate information in two online digital historical collections. One collection was the Digital Vaults from the National Archives and Records Administration at http://www.digitalvaults.org an online presentation of a small set of historical resources using a highly visual and intertextual interface. Students were asked to complete a structured activity from Digital Vaults that was focused on the Lincoln Monument. The activity, titled Men and Monuments, posed questions that require users to locate information from an array of small thumbnail images. The activity was highly structured and required few critical decisions of students as they accessed information. In another activity, students were asked to search a collection of 2,000 Works Progress Administration (WPA) posters from the 1930s highlighting WPA cultural activities, online at http://memory.loc.gov/ammem/wpaposters. Unlike the Digital Vaults activity, this work was lightly structured and focused on students' interest. Much like students' work with the *Life* magazine collection, students were free to locate posters that they found compelling. One distinction between the WPA poster activity and the *Life* magazine activity concerned the processes students used to search. Students were provided with search terms from the state curriculum in the *Life* magazine activity. In the WPA poster activity, students were simply asked to follow their interest.

The contrasts between the Digital Vaults and WPA poster activities were interesting. When asked, students were unable to describe the scope or intent of the Digital Vaults collection. Most students focused their descriptions on the activity arguing that the collection was about Abraham Lincoln or was focused on monuments. In contrast, students saw the larger shape of the WPA poster collection. Most were able to describe the resource as a collection of materials that was designed to advertise cultural programs offered by the WPA. Students' ability to synthesize across the multiple items they located in the WPA collection and to make an argument about the purposes and functions of the collection was productive and in keeping with what a teacher might want to accomplish in a more direct presentation of information about the New Deal.

CONCLUSION

Digital history represents, in some ways, a frontier. Work in digital history is emergent, seemingly boundless and typically marked by creative and passionate energy. As historians and history enthusiasts continue to work and produce in online environments, students will need to likewise develop more comprehensive understandings about how to use the resources that are being creating. This online environment affords much for teachers and students in history. Most importantly, digital history offers a laboratory for ideas and experimentation. For example, we might ask how students might decipher interpretative stances that are taken in an online collections and how these affect the presentation of information in the collection.

There are several issues to consider going forward. What are the social dimensions of digital history environments? What are some design principles that can guide the development of structured digital historical interfaces? How can digital historical resources directly address expectations emerging from curriculum, high stakes tests, and disciplinary expectations? What are the central digital historical literacies that should be emphasized in K-12 classrooms? Work on these questions and others will drive digital history forward. In all this work, digital history should be about active collaborative engagement in dynamic environments. With teachers and students as consistent participants in these digital historical environments much can be gained from digital history.

REFERENCES

Ayers, E. L. (1999b). *The pasts and futures of digital history.* Retrieved February 20, 2009, from http://jefferson.village.virginia.edu/vcdh/PastsFutures.html

Bain, R. B. (2005). "They thought the world was flat?": Applying the principles of *how people learn* in teaching high school history. In J. Bransford & S. Donovan (Eds.), *How students learn: History, mathematics, and science in the classroom* (pp. 179-214). Washington, DC: The National Academies Press.

Barton, K. (1997). "I just kinda know": Elementary students' ideas about historical evidence. *Theory and Research in Social Education, 25*(4), 407-430.

Boggs, J. (2007). Web 2.0 for historians: An introduction. *Journal of the Association for History and Computing, 10*(2). Retrieved September 20, 2007, from http://mcel.pacificu.edu/jahc/jahcx2/boggs.html

Bradley Commission on History in Schools. (1995). *Building a history curriculum: Guidelines for teaching history in schools.* Westlake, OH: National Council for History Education.

Cohen, D. & Rosensweig, R. (2005). *Doing digital history: A guide to presenting, preserving, and gathering the past on the Web.* Philadelphia: University of Pennsylvania Press.

Coiro, J., & Dobler, E. (2007). Exploring the comprehension strategies used by sixth-grade skilled readers as they search for and locate information on the Internet. *Research Quarterly, 42*, 214-257.

Dede, C. (2007). *Transforming education for the 21st Century: New pedagogies that help all students attain sophisticated learning outcomes.* Retrieved from, http://www.gse.harvard.edu/~dedech/Dede_21stC-skills_semi-final.pdf

Editorial. (1976). *Social History, 1*(1), 1-3.

Hallam, R. N. (1967). Logical thinking in history. *Educational Review, 19*, 183-202.

Hicks D., & Doolittle, P. (2009). Multimedia-based historical inquiry strategy instruction: Do size and form really matter? In J. K. Lee & A. Friedman. (Eds.), *Research on technology in social studies education* (pp. 127-154). Charlotte: NC: Information Age.

Hicks, D., Doolittle, P. E., & Ewing, T. (2004). The SCIM-C strategy: Fostering historical inquiry in a multimedia environment. *Social Education, 68(3)*, 221-225.

Interchange: The promise of digital history. (2008). *Journal of American History,* *95*(2), 452-491.

Lee, J. K. (2002a). Digital history in the history/social studies classroom. *The History Teacher, 43*(4), 503-518.

Lee, J. K. (2002b). Principles for interpretative digital history web design. *Journal of the Association of History and Computing 5*(3), Retrieved from http://mcel.pacificu.edu/jahc/2002/issue3/k-12/lee.php

Lee, P. (2005). Historical literacy. *International Journal of Historical Learning, Teaching and Research, 5*(1). Retrieved from http://www.centres.ex.ac.uk/historyresource/journal9/9contents.htm

Leu, D. J., Coiro, J., Castek, J., Hartman, D., Henry, L. A., & Reinking, D. (2008). Research on instruction and assessment in the new literacies of online reading comprehension. In C. C. Block & S. Parris, (Eds.). *Comprehension instruction: Research-based best practices* (2nd ed., pp. 321-346). New York: Guilford Press.

Levstik, L., & Barton. K. (2005). *Doing history: Investigating with children in elementary and middle schools* (Ver. 3). Hillsdale, NJ: Erlbaum.

Martin, D., & Wineburg, S. (2008). Seeing thinking on the web. *History Teacher, 41*(3), 305-319.

Mintz, S. (n.d). "eXplorations," *Digital History: Using new technologies to enhance teaching and research.* Retrieved from http://www.digitalhistory.uh.edu/learning_history/

Perfetti, C. A., Britt, M. A., & Georgi, M. C. (1995). *Text-based learning and reasoning: Studies in history.* Hillsdale, NJ: Erlbaum.

Rosenzweig, R. (2001). The road to Xanadu: Public and private pathways on the history web. *The Journal of American History, 88*(2), 548-579.

Stearns, P. (1998). Why study history. *American Historical Association.* Retrieved from http://www.historians.org/pubs/Free/WhyStudyHistory.htm

Tally, B., & Goldenberg, L. B. (2005). Fostering hstorical thinking with digitized primary sources. *Journal of Research on Technology in Education, 38*(1), 1-21.

VanSledright, B. (1995). "I don't remember—the ideas are all jumbled in my head." Eighth graders' reconstructions of colonial American history. *Journal of Curriculum and Supervision 10*(4), 317-345.

Wineburg, S. (1991). Historical problem solving: A study of the cognitive processes used in the evaluation of documentary and pictorial evidence. *Journal of Educational Psychology, 83*(1), 73-87.

Wineburg, S. (2001). *Historical thinking and other unnatural acts.* Philadelphia: Temple University Press.

CHAPTER 6

FROM PERSONAL PASTIME TO CURRICULAR RESOURCE

The Case of Digital Documentaries in the Social Studies

Meghan McGlinn Manfra and Thomas C. Hammond

INTRODUCTION

The history curriculum often reflects the larger social discourse (Evans, 2006; Nelson, 2001; Ross, 2001). As new events unfold, such as the collapse of Eastern bloc communism or terrorist attacks on the United States, they are integrated into mandated history curricula (e.g., Virginia Department of Education, 2008). As new political trends develop, such as shifts in campaign financing or court resolutions of disputed elections, they become fodder for teacher-designed activities addressing political history and campaign tactics ("Teaching About the Presidency," 2008). Since the dawn of American K-12 history instruction, a classroom practitioner is in a constant process of selection and absorption as today's

Technology in Retrospect: Social Studies in the Information Age 1984-2009, pp. 91–107

current event becomes tomorrow's curricular content (Hess, 2009; Knight, 1902).

An important component of the distillation of social issues into history content instruction is the choice of technology. Starting with the advent of motion pictures in the early 1900s (Saettler, 1990), technologies from commercial enterprises or personal entertainment have been integrated into history classrooms: television sets, videos, personal computers, Internet-based resources, and more (Cuban, 1986). In some cases, these resources were developed with K-12 instructional contexts in mind: the online exhibits at the Library of Congress' American Memory project (loc.gov/ammem), for example, were designed to be useful to students and teachers, and come bundled with lesson plans, suggested connections to curricular themes, and professional development materials. However, many technological resources used by history educators were developed for other purposes—these include professional archives such as the Avalon Project (avalon.law.yale.edu) or general purpose tools such as web-blogs or digital cameras. These tools have become classroom resources through individual teachers' decisions to adopt them and integrate them into their practice.

The digital video editor is a particularly rich example of a home-use application that has emerged to become a robust curricular tool in the social studies classroom. With the advent of iMovie and Movie Maker, self-produced digital videos or digital documentaries have proliferated in social studies classrooms. The adoption of the digital video editor into the classroom presents tremendous opportunities for enhancing student learning and even transforming the curriculum. At the same time, the use of this tool within the classroom context leads to new questions regarding student and teacher efficacy with technology, curricular structure and pacing, purposes of social studies education, and historical thinking.

In this chapter we trace the adaptation of digital video editing for home use into the classroom. We explore the current literature and research base related to the integration of digital documentaries in the social studies classroom, drawing attention to its affordances and limitations. Ultimately we propose a taxonomy of digital documentaries based on the desired learning outcomes.

HISTORY OF PERSONAL FILM

Motion picture cameras date from the late 1800s. The first cameras were bulky—Thomas Edison's camera weighed more than 1,000 pounds—and truly priceless in the sense that they were not commodities available for sale. Early film stock was nitrate-based and therefore dangerously incendiary; a reel could be ignited by a projector's bulb. Given the inflexibility and danger involved, the first films were contrived—even Edison's 1893 *Blacksmith Scene* (http://www.youtube.com/watch?v=5qZa-RLtCU0) was a staged event before a black background (Barnouw, 1974). The Lumiere brothers resolved the problem of immobility by devising a brief case-sized camera that could be carried anywhere and set up to capture scenes of daily life (e.g., *Snowball Fight,* http://www.youtube.com/watch?v=KL0th6vWe-8, and *The Arrival of a Train at La Ciotat Station,* http://www.youtube.com/watch?v=2cUEANKv964) that typifies personal use of video (Barnouw, 1974). These early Lumiere films were known as "actualities"—records of life as it actually happened. "Safety" film, using an acetate base, replaced nitrate film and cleared another hurdle toward the home market by making movies safer to project. Edison's 1912 Home Kinetoscope brought compact projection equipment and the safety film into the consumer market, albeit for displaying already-printed films, not recording new footage.

Movie cameras for amateur use were produced and marketed as early as the 1920s. Eastman Kodak's standard 8 mm camera dates back to 1932, and the proliferation of handheld, home-use movie cameras became woven into the American pop-cultural record. The 1939 World's Fair events in San Francisco and New York City were captured in home movies (www.archive.org/details/GoldenGa1939_2; www.archive.org/details/Medicusc 1939); the Kennedy assassination in 1963 was filmed by hobbyist Abraham Zapruder using an 8 mm camera. While these cameras could easily capture, store, and replay moving images, editing required significantly more effort. Accordingly, most home movies remained un-edited, becoming part of the amateur video, straight-to-the-screen aesthetic. In the early 1980s, Sony and other electronics companies introduced consumer-market film cameras recording to Betamax and VHS tapes. Home movies shot on tape could be edited more easily than film by using a dual player system.

These early camcorders recorded analog data, but manufacturers experimented with recording the audio and then the video as digital data. Binary data captured on miniDV and Digital8 tapes could be transferred to a computer for viewing and editing far more fluidly than was possible in a dual-deck or on-camera system. Early versions of digital video editors cost thousands of dollars and required specialized hardware, such as video cards. In 1999, the Apple Computer company transformed the casual-use market by bundling a powerful video editor, iMovie, with its operating system. In 2000, Microsoft released a competing free, bundled editor, Windows Movie Maker.

With the availability of iMovie and Movie Maker, the home user possessed a complete toolbox for filming, editing, and storing digital video. YouTube.com, founded in 2005, made it far easier to share and distribute digital video. Previous to YouTube, digital video could be posted to Internet repositories, but file sizes and text-only browsing structures limited the dissemination. On YouTube—and equivalent sites that sprang up soon thereafter—creators could upload short video clips for public display. Browsers could search the collection, see thumbnails, and subscribe to user or group video lists. YouTube was an instant phenomenon, serving millions of videos per day within its first month of its official launch (Graham, 2005). By 2009, YouTube was serving hundreds of millions of videos and receiving hundreds of thousands per day (YouTube, 2009). Users could post replies to videos, write text comments, and create on-screen annotations within videos. The advent of Web 2.0 applications like YouTube facilitated the emergence of video-sharing as a conversational medium, similar to verbal or textual dialog.

INTEGRATION IN THE SOCIAL STUDIES CLASSROOM

Historical Context

From the advent of motion pictures, the social studies classroom has appeared to be a natural venue for film. Motion picture pioneer Thomas Edison frequently singled out educational uses of his invention, and saw the social studies classroom as a point of entry into the school market. In 1912, Edison had two assistants display his new Home Kinetoscope to a group of reporters. The *New York Times'* article ("Edison shows," 1912) on the event relates that, "the children in Public School 155 are saving up to buy one of the new machines for their own edification." In the 1920s, Yale University sponsored a set of *Chronicles of America Photoplays* covering topics such as the settling of Jamestown and the Lewis and Clark expedition (Knowlton & Tilton, 1929). The Historical Society of Great Britain published its own statement on *The Value of Films in History Teaching* (Consitt, 1931). By the 1960s, the National Council for the Social Studies (NCSS) formulated guidelines regarding the appropriate classroom use of film (Hartley, 1965).

The vision for these early uses of film in social studies education was primarily didactic—delivering predetermined content to learners, but in a more engaging, emotional format than previous media. Educators believed students would be more interested in watching a film about Jamestown, for example, than in reading textual accounts (Knowlton & Tilton, 1929). This pattern persisted up until The New Social Studies of the 1960s when films were used to spark student inquiry.

Film featured prominently in the elementary curriculum, *Man: A Course of Study* (MACOS, "Education: Teaching Man," 1970). For example, a series of lessons about baboons offered students "the opportunity to look at their own experience" and "see man as a member of the animal kingdom" (Education Development Center, 1969, p. 4; see also http://www.macosonline.org/course/). To this end, the unit included several films. These films, often without narration, were used to spark inquiry and teach the skills of the social science disciplines. For example, students were encouraged to observe the baboons in their natural habitat via the films and ponder questions such as, "What is distinctive about the human species?" (p. 4). This approach to integrating film to challenge students' epistemological positioning—instead of receiving information from the film, students were to construct meaning from it—was typical across the New Social Studies projects. For instance, Lord (1969) wrote about an American history unit on slavery that

> began with the filmstrip on the slave trade but instead of the usual state-
> ment by the teacher of "we see here," which is usually followed by an expla-
> nation of what is before the students, the teacher asked, "What do you see?"
> and "What do you know about slavery from what you see?" (p. 27)

Contemporary Integration of Film and Student Created Digital Video

Today film is still commonplace in social studies classrooms, but often for didactic purposes (cf. Marcus & Stoddard, 2007). After the decline of the New Social Studies (see Fenton, 1991), the critical uses of film became less grounded in history education, and shifted to the fields of film studies and media literacy (e.g., Amelio, 1971; Buckingham, 1998; Kellner, 1995). More frequently, teachers use film in social studies classrooms to enrich the curriculum. For instance, a survey of United States history teachers in two states reported that 90% used feature films in their classes at least once a week (Marcus & Stoddard, 2007). Some history educators use film as a text, a primary source document of the era of the film's pro-duction or the director's viewpoint—studying *Stagecoach*, for example, to teach, not about the Wild West, but cultural mores of 1939 (Dobbs, 1987; Percoco, 1998—see also Hess, 2007).

While these uses of film in the classroom can enhance the curriculum, we are most interested in the transformative potential of student created digital videos or documentaries. We believe that digital video editors have enabled students to become curriculum creators. The earliest examples we have found of students creating digital documentaries originated in technology or media literacy classes as students experimented with *creat-ing* film, not just studying it (Burn et al., 2001). However, a unique conflu-ence of traditional documentary and digital documentary-making came in a 1995 report from an Australian history class. After viewing Ken Burns' popular and acclaimed documentary series, *The Civil War*, high school students conducted local history projects on the experiences of young people during World War I. The tools used by the students included analog video cameras, multitrack tape recorders, an Amiga 2000 computer (employing multiple software packages), and a VCR to capture students' final products (Brown, 1995). This project was an early example of digital documentary-making in the classroom, where the process required significant instructional time and technological expertise on the part of the teacher and students.

Aside from these early adopters, the most consistent integration of student created digital documentaries has occurred outside of the social studies classroom. A well-known extracurricular activity, the National History Day competition, has included a "media" project category almost from its inception. In the early years, these projects often consisted of slide shows and video recordings. Marking the transition to digital formats, in 2001 the category was renamed "documentary." Today groups of students submit digital documentary entries for History Day competitions at the local, state, and national levels. These projects are assessed based on their historical scholarship and aesthetic qualities, including music, transitions, and cinematography. According to Joann Williford (personal communication, August 11, 2009), the director of the National History Day competition in North Carolina, teachers either approach the history day competition as a culminating take-home project or as an extra credit assignment.

Although student created digital documentaries are often viewed as an enrichment activities, there are some classroom-level efforts to integrate these projects into the daily curriculum (Hofer & Owings-Swan, 2005; Hofer & Swan, 2008; Manfra & Hammond, 2008). For example, Jon Carl, a teacher at Francis Joseph Reitz High School of Evansville, Indiana was eager to "get students passionate about history by turning them into historians," so he created a digital documentary-making class ("Making History," 2008, para. 2). His students are responsible for the entire production process including researching, scripting, filming, and editing. The documentaries are edited by local historians and technology specialists and aired on the local public television station.

To make the integration of student created digital documentaries more seamless for teachers, new Web 2.0 tools have been developed. PrimaryAccess (www.primaryaccess.org) is a free, web-based application that includes a variety of scaffolds to support students (Ferster, Hammond, & Bull, 2006). These scaffolds guide students through the process of creating a digital documentary. First students are provided with a list of teacher-selected images from which they assemble a storyboard. The students then engage in an iterative process of writing their scripts, associating images with the scripts, and adding motion and titles. At each step, teachers can review students' files and provide feedback in the form of text or audio notes. Because the application and data are online, students and teachers can work from any Internet-connected computer, beginning a project in class and continuing it at home or in the library.

The Digital Director's Guild (http://www.ddguild.org/, Swan, Hofer, & Levstik, 2007) provides a community for teachers interested in integrating digital documentary-making into their classrooms. Resources available at the site include handouts for teachers and students and strategies for scaffolding student work. They use high-end, commercial video editing tools (e.g., Final Cut Pro) or bundled products such as iMovie and MovieMaker.

REVIEW OF THE RESEARCH LITERATURE

Research on the integration of digital moviemaking into the curriculum is not unique to the social studies. Educators from a variety of disciplines have studied its effectiveness for teaching content knowledge and discipline specific skills (e.g., Burn et al., 2001; Emme, Kirova, Kamau, & Kosanovich, 2006). The majority of the current literature is situated within instructional technology research, not the social studies.

The research literature on digital documentaries in the field of the social studies has primarily focused on teacher case studies and reports of single classrooms. Several studies have used Technological Pedagogical Content Knowledge (TPCK, or TPACK; Mishra & Koehler, 2006) to discuss the integration of digital documentary projects into classroom practice (e.g., Hofer & Owings-Swan, 2005; Hofer & Swan, 2008; Manfra & Hammond, 2008). Below we provide an overview of recent research related to digital moviemaking or digital documentary making.

According to Hofer and Swan (2005),

> Digital moviemaking can broadly be defined as the use of a variety of media (images, sound, text, video, and narration) to convey understanding. In practice, digital directors utilize user-friendly nonlinear video editing software (i.e., Windows MovieMaker, Apple's iMovie) to create videos to communicate information. (p. 104)

Our own research has focused extensively on the use of PrimaryAccess (Bull, Ferster, & Hammond, 2008; Ferster, Hammond, & Bull, 2006; Hammond & Manfra, 2009; Hammond, 2010; Manfra & Hammond, 2008). A pattern across the literature reveals that the choice of tool can be significant—an application can empower teachers' pedagogical content knowledge by providing scaffolds for structuring student work (Manfra & Hammond, 2008) or it can frustrate the instructor and subvert the teaching process (Yow & Swan, 2009).

We prefer the term "digital documentary" because it connotes a historical purposing and most of the practical integration and research related to moviemaking within the social studies falls within the definition of digital history (Lee, 2002). Regardless of the terminology used, student created digital documentaries are generally short and use still images or video. They incorporate student voice through narration. Within the social studies, digital documentaries differ from digital storytelling (see Lambert, 2002) since they do not always follow a traditional narrative arc but can be used for historical inquiry (Bull, Hammond, & Ferster, 2008). Digital documentaries also differ from digitized oral history projects. Oral history projects (e.g., Levin, 2003) seek to capture and record a primary source historical account, whereas digital documentaries are constructed historical accounts, drawing upon primary sources—which could include digitized oral histories—as *evidence* (see Lee, 2005). Student-created digital documentaries provide an authentic product (i.e., one that has meaning beyond the academic context in which it was produced) through which students can demonstrate content knowledge, historical thinking skills, and civic understanding. We have found that student outcomes from the digital documentary-creation process are largely contingent on teachers' pedagogical aims. Furthermore, the process itself introduces constraints, whether from the technology used (Norman, 1998) or the internalized models held by teachers and students (Buckingham, 1998; Hess, 2007). Below we discuss these outcomes and limitations and provide suggestions for further study.

To Teach Discipline-Specific Content and Skills

The bulk of research on student-created digital documentaries in the social studies classroom has examined student outcomes related to content knowledge instruction. Similar to writing a research paper, students are asked to research a particular event or person from the past and create a short movie (Ferster, Hammond, & Bull, 2006; Hofer & Owings-Swan, 2005; Swan, Hofer, & Levstik, 2007; Manfra & Hammond, 2008). Our research (Manfra & Hammond, 2008; Hammond & Manfra, 2009) has demonstrated students often produce movies that are fairly accurate; there are few or no statements that stand out as a misconception or misconstruction of accepted versions of historical events. Furthermore, these projects often closely approximate information and even the wording found in the standard curriculum (Manfra & Hammond, 2008). Similarly

Swan, Hofer, and Levstik (2007) found "Movies where students made more use of archival resources tended to be more interesting, but also more historically sound" (p. 18).

In addition to focusing on content knowledge, digital documentary making also seems to provide students an opportunity to develop discipline-specific skills. To create a digital documentary, students conduct historical research, consulting primary and secondary sources. They rely on historical skills such as chronological understanding, historical empathy, and analysis of perspective when writing a movie script. According to Swan, Hofer, and Levstik (2007), through the digital documentary making process "We can engage students as digital directors. Students can not only develop historical questions and select and evaluate sources relevant to those questions, but can frame (literally and figuratively) and present historical interpretations" (p. 17). We found similar evidence in a study we conducted in two history classrooms (Manfra & Hammond, 2008). One of the teachers, an 11th grade, U.S. history teacher asked his students to take on a historical identity and relate the past through a fictionalized first person account. As a result of this assignment, students went beyond the standard curriculum and added more depth to their narratives. They approached the past from the perspective of someone living at the time, which forced them to confront thorny issues of the antebellum period, including slavery, tensions between the north and the south, and the relationship between yeoman farmers and plantation owners. Similarly, Hofer and Swan (2005) assigned students in a social studies methods course to create a 3-5 minute documentary film on an aspect of the Civil Rights movements. In their follow-up study they found evidence of engagement in historical thinking, as delineated by the National Center for History in Schools (1996), including understanding chronology and engaging in historical interpretation. Apparently younger students can also flex their historical skills through digital documentary making. Hofer and Swan (2006) studied a classroom in which fifth grade students were asked to engage in "myth busting" about the past. They wrote,

> We designed the historical documentary project to accomplish two parallel goals: expanding students' understanding of how history is constructed as well as engaging them deeply in the process of research and development of a digital narrative on a chosen historical figure. (p. 124)

To Teach Civic Ideals

The aims of the social studies are not limited to content knowledge and skill instruction. There is also a long tradition in the field related to civic education (Barton & Levstik, 2004; NCSS, 1994). Digital documentaries can be an integral part of civic education; creating documentaries encourages students to develop knowledge, skills, and attitudes necessary for citizenship (Manfra, 2008). Even in a history curriculum, the pedagogy of a digital documentary project can be used to engage students in powerful themes of civics education (Hammond, in press).

The Telling their Stories Oral Archives Project (www.tellingstories.org) is an example of a digital history project that engages students in authentic intellectual work and civic meaning making (Manfra & Stoddard, 2008). The project was conceived by high school students at the Urban School of San Francisco, but has developed affiliates in southern Mississippi (Herndon, 2008). The students conducted and filmed interviews with Holocaust survivors, concentration camp liberators, Japanese-American internees, and others. The videos and transcripts are then posted on a public website. This project has grown to include dozens of students, teachers, and community members with the goal of preserving the past and teaching civic lessons. Through the process of collecting, editing, and producing documentaries of the oral histories, the students become not only historians but also activists, bringing once marginalized voices to the center of the discourse.

TPACK: Focus on the Teacher

Learning outcomes for students, the extent to which digital documentary making contributes to content, skill, and civic knowledge acquisition, largely depends on the pedagogical aims of the teachers who integrate these projects in the classroom. The interplay between teacher pedagogical aims and technological tools with content knowledge has been summarized as technological pedagogical content knowledge (TPACK, Mishra & Koehler, 2006). This framework has proven useful in analyzing data and articulating findings in studies about the integration of digital documentary making in the social studies classroom and its effects on instruction and student learning outcomes. For instance, when Hofer and Swan (2008) asked their methods students to create a 3-5 minute documentary film on an aspect of the Civil Rights movement, they hoped to model for their students the intersection of pedagogy with technological content knowledge. Our research has demonstrated that although students have agency in the classroom, the teachers' TPACK contributes significantly to the extent to which digital documentary making is integrated successfully for constructivist learning.

According to Hofer and Swan (2005) "Digital moviemaking offers an opportunity to harmonize the use of technology to support student-centered pedagogy and unique disciplinary approaches rooted in discipline-specific pedagogy" (p. 104). However the opportunity for a more student-centered pedagogy in contingent on teachers' willingness to shift pedagogy from mimetic to more constructivist aims (Drake & Nelson, 2009). The technology on its own cannot be described as constructivist, rather it is digital documentary making paired with student-centered pedagogical aims (such as collaborative learning) and authentic intellectual work (teaching historical thinking and civic values) that has the potential to improve social studies instruction. In our experience, in classrooms where the teacher uses digital documentary making as a strategy to teach fact-based, content knowledge the student movies tend to mimic class notes and the textbook. On the other hand, when the teacher allows for greater latitude and the classroom is more student-centered, the final products go beyond the curriculum and, in some cases, reveal deeper content understandings (Hammond & Manfra, 2009; Manfra & Hammond, 2008).

Limitations and Areas for Further Study

The interrelationship between the various elements that make up the TPACK model illustrate the extent to which positive student outcomes related to learning are contingent on teacher pedagogy. For some teachers, especially those who embrace a more traditional, teacher-centered approach to teaching, it is difficult to integrate student created digital documentaries into the classroom (Hofer & Swan, 2006). In all of the research studies reviewed for this chapter it does not seem to be the technology that it is the major issue for teachers and students. Rather, projects tend to fall short of their potential to make social studies learning more authentic due to reluctance on the teacher's part to pursue student-centered instruction. Despite new tools and increased accessibility to the Internet, teachers tend to still assign student-created digital documentaries as add-on assignment in the curriculum, usually placed at the end of a unit of study to serve as review. High stakes testing and strict curricular standards at the state and district level have limited the time teachers are willing to spend on these projects with their students and the license they give students to explore authentic social studies issues (Hofer & Swan, 2006; Manfra & Hammond, 2008). The school use of digital documentaries seems to continue to privilege content knowledge learning over other potential student outcomes, including historical thinking, creativity, and self-direction. This factual focus has further exacerbated the divide between in-school and at-home digital moviemaking. At the same time research suggests that teachers find historical thinking difficult to teach and support (e.g., Barton & Levstik, 2003), which also contributes to teacher reluctance to integrate digital documentary making for more complex outcomes.

Since the Center for Technology and Teacher Education at the University of Virginia developed PrimaryAccess in 2005, more than 5,000 movies have been produced and posted by students and teachers. The collection is the single largest repository of digital documentaries to date. Other sources exist, such as the Digital Directors Guild (ddguild.org) or the postings of individual classrooms or research efforts (e.g., http://www.springfield.k12.il.us/movie/?mod=4201), but the samples of exhibited student work are much smaller, typically less than 100. Our review of a sample of the movies in the PrimaryAccess database revealed that a majority relate historical facts without interpretation or historical perspective. For instance, the primary source images used in these digital documentaries function as signifiers, standing in for previously integrated concepts, rather than texts for scrutiny and interpretation. A photograph of Rose Parks or Martin Luther King, Jr., is a shorthand for "the Civil Rights Movement," "African-Americans," or "the 1950s" rather than evidence of a place, a person, or a time period. This pattern is similar to the findings of Swan, Hofer, and Levstik (2007) in their work with elementary students: "Rather than developing their own interpretive lens through which to view the Great Depression, World War II, or the Civil Rights Movement, for instance, some of the documentaries operated like expository reports of facts, names and chronologies of events" (p. 19). In these cases, digital documentaries can re-capitulate existing history education practices and share the flaws of existing practices rather than move the social studies curriculum forward (Martorella, 1997; Crocco, 2001).

A PROPOSED TAXONOMY

Despite these negative trends, we are convinced that student-created digital documentaries have the potential to engage students in authentic intellectual work (Newmann & Wehlage, 1993) that goes beyond mere factual recall. Based on our review of student-created digital documentaries we are eager to move their integration towards more a more seamless and intellectually meaningful pedagogical tool by proposing a taxonomy of digital documentaries. According to Popham (2009) a taxonomy or "classification scheme" is "useful both in describing instructional objectives under consideration and in generating new objectives" (p. 102). Our taxonomy proposes five objectives for digital documentaries: to provide a historical narrative, to offer a historical interpretation, to dramatize the historical past, to engage the audience in historical inquiry, and to reflect on the past. We describe each of these objectives in Table 6.1. We propose this taxonomy as a tool for social studies teachers and teacher educators to more thoughtfully integrate student created digital documentaries in the classroom to accomplish learning objectives that go beyond merely recalling the past. Rather than being prescriptive, our taxonomy illustrates various, perhaps overlapping,

Table 6.1.   Proposed Taxonomy of Digital Documentaries

Digital Documentary Category	Description	Congruent Intended Learning Outcomes
Historical narrative or exposition	Follows a traditional narrative arc—beginning, middle, and end. Traces the chronology of an event or idea, or a biography of a historic character. Provides a survey of the historical topic. Uses historical images and artifacts (texts, photographs, illustrations, maps, oral history interviews, etc.) but without differentiating between primary and secondary sources. Primary sources are used as illustrations of events, not historical evidence.	Factual knowledge and larger historical understandings
Historical interpretation	Provides a historical interpretation of a defined—although not always explicitly stated—historical question. Uses primary and secondary sources and treats the primary sources as evidence, not illustrations.	Primary source analysis, perspective-taking as an act of historical thinking, historiography; factual knowledge and larger historical understandings
Historical dramatization	Provides a historical interpretation through historical fiction. Focus on aesthetics and dramatic story-line. May use primary source images or derivations of primary source images, but visuals serve as dramatic devices, not evidence.	Empathy / understanding of perspectives of historical actors; factual knowledge and larger historical understandings
Historical inquiry invitation	Poses questions rather than delivers information. Can be used to introduce a topic or to mark unknown or unknowable topics at the end of a unit.	Engagement, introduction to an inquiry process, eliciting prior knowledge
Historical reflection	Explores the author's reactions to selected primary sources or to historical figures, events, or ideas. Primary sources images may be used, but idiosyncratically, situated within a personally-constructed context.	Engagement, integration of larger historical understandings

objectives for the integration of student-created digital documentaries in the classroom. This taxonomy can be used to not only design but also to assess digital documentary projects, by first clarifying the intentions of the project (e.g., perspective-taking or close analysis of primary sources) and then articulating the components required to reach these aims.

CONCLUSION

The relatively recent interest in digital documentaries is the latest iteration of a longer historical trend of integrating film into the social studies curriculum. It also represents the repurposing of home and commercial-based technology for learning. Although students are often now the creators of historical documentaries, the pedagogical aim continues to focus on the linear retelling of past events. This usage ignores the potential for student created digital documentaries to make learning more authentic and meaningful for students by engaging them in historical inquiry and civic meaning making. Our taxonomy proposes alternatives to the commonplace use of digital documentaries and a new framework for evaluating their effectiveness for learning.

REFERENCES

Amelio, R. J. (1971). *Film in the classroom: Why to use it, how to use it.* Dayton, OH: Pflaum/Standard.

Barnouw, E. (1974). *Documentary: A history of the non-fiction film.* New York: Oxford University Press.

Barton, K. C., & Levstik, L. S. (2003). Why don't history teachers engage students in interpretation? *Social Education 67,* 358-361.

Barton, K., & Levstik, L. (2004). *Teaching history for the common good.* Mahwah, NJ: Erlbaum.

Brown, A. (1995). History, digital imaging, and desktop video. *Learning and Leading with Technology, 22*(8), 19-21.

Buckingham, D. (1998). Media education in the UK: Moving beyond protectionism. *Journal of Communication, 48*(1), 33-43.

Bull, G., Hammond, T., & Ferster, B. (2008). Developing Web 2.0 tools for support of historical inquiry in social studies. *Computers in the Schools, 25*(3-4), 275-287.

Burn, A., Brindley, S., Durran, J., Kelsall, C., Sweetlove, J., & Tuohey, C. (2001). The rush of images: A research report into digital editing and the moving image. *English in Education, 35*(2), 34–47.

Consitt, F. (1931). *The value of films in history teaching.* London: G. Bell & Sons.

Crocco, M. S. (2001), Leveraging constructivist learning in the social studies class-room: A response to Mason, Berson, Diem, Hicks, Lee, and Dralle. *Contemporary Issues in Technology and Teacher Education, 1*(3), 386-394.

Cuban, L. (1986). *Teachers and machines: The classroom use of technology Since 1920.* New York: Teachers College Press.

Dobbs, C. M. (1987). Hollywood movies from the Golden Age: An important resource for the classroom. *Teaching history: A journal of methods, 12*(1), 10-16.

Drake, F. D., & Nelson, L. R. (2009). *Engagement in teaching history: Theory and practice for middle and secondary teachers* (2nd ed.). Upper Saddle River, NJ: Pearson.

Edison shows the home kinetoscope. (1912, March). *New York Times.* Retrieved August 26, 2009, from http://query.nytimes.com/mem/archive-free/pdf?res=9A05E5D81231E233A2575BC2A9659C946396D6CF

Education Development Center. (1969). *Baboons. Man: A Course of Study.* Cambridge, MA: Education Development Center. Retrieved January 15, 2010 from http://www.macosonline.org/course/guides/Five-Baboons.pdf

Education: Teaching man to children. (1970, January). *TIME Magazine.* Retrieved August 31, 2009, from http://www.time.com/time/magazine/article/0,9171,878677,00.html

Emme, M. J., Kirova, A., Kamau, O., & Kosanovich, S. (2006). Ensemble research: A means for immigrant children to explore peer relationships through fotonovela. *Alberta Journal of Educational Research, 52*(3), 160-181.

Evans, R. W. (2006). The social studies wards, now and then. *Social Education, 70*(5), 317-321.

Fenton, E. (1991). Reflections on the "New Social Studies." *The Social Studies, 82*(3), 84-90.

Ferster, B., Hammond, T., & Bull, G. (2006). PrimaryAccess: Creating digital documentaries in the social studies classroom. *Social Education, 70*(3), 147-150.

Graham, J. (2005, November). Video websites pop up, invite postings. *USA Today.* Retrieved August 26, 2009, from http://www.usatoday.com/tech/news/techinnovations/2005-11-21-video-websites_x.htm

Hammond, T. C. (2010). "So what?" Students' articulation of civic themes in middle-school digital documentary projects. *The Social Studies, 101*(2), 54-59.

Hammond, T. C., & Manfra, M. M. (2009). Digital history with student-created multimedia: Understanding student perceptions. *Social Studies Research & Practice, 4*(3), 139-150.

Hartley, W. H. (1965). *How to use a motion picture.* Washington, DC: National Council for the Social Studies.

Herndon, E. (2008, November 15). Students from McComb High participate in civil rights video. *Enterprise-Journal.* Retrieved January 14, 2010 from http://www.enterprise-journal.com/articles/2008/11/16/news/03.txt

Hess, D. (2007). From *Banished* to *Brother Outsider, Miss Navajo* to *An Inconvenient Truth*: Documentary films as perspective-laden narratives. *Social Education, 71*(4), 194-199.

Hess, D. (2009). *Controversy in the classroom: The democratic power of discussion.* New York: Routledge

Hofer, M., & Owings-Swan, K. (2005). Digital moviemaking—the harmonization of technology, pedagogy and content. *International Journal of Technology in Teaching and Learning, 1*(2), 102-110.

Hofer, M., & Swan, K. O. (2006). Standards, firewalls, and general classroom mayhem: Implementing student-centered technology projects in the elementary classroom. *Social Studies Research and Practice, 1*(1), 120-144. Retrieved February 15, 2009, from http://www.socstrp.org/issues/PDF/1.1.13.pdf

Hofer, M., & Swan, K. (2008). Technological pedagogical content knowledge in action: A case study of a middle school digital documentary project. *Journal of Research on Technology in Education, 41*(2), 179-200.

Kellner, D. (1995). *Media culture: Cultural studies, identity and politics between the modern and the post-modern.* London: Routledge.

Knight, G. W. (1902). What an American History teacher must be and do. *The School Review, 10*(3), 208-216.

Knowlton, D. C., & Tilton, J. W. (1929). *Motion pictures in history teaching: A study of the Chronicles of America Photoplays as an aid in seventh grade instruction.* New Haven, CT: Yale University Press.

Lambert, J. (2002). *Digital storytelling: Capturing lives, creating community.* Berkeley, CA: Digital Diner.

Lee, J. (2002). Digital history in the history/social studies classroom. *The History Teacher, 35*(4), 503-518.

Lee, P. (2005). Putting principles into practice: Understanding history. In M. S. Donovan & J. D. Bransford (Eds.), *How students learn: History, mathematics, and science in the classroom* (pp. 31-77). Washington, DC: National Academies Press.

Levin, H. (2003). Making history come alive. *Learning and Leading with Technology, 31*(3), 22-27.

Lord, D. C. (1969). Teacher training and the inquiry method: The program at Texas Women's University. *The History Teacher, 2*(2), 24-32.

Making history: An Indiana teacher uses technology to feel the history. (2008, February 15). *Technology & Learning, 28*(7), 26. Retrieved September 1, 2009 from, http://www.techlearning.com/article/8482

Manfra, M. M. (2008). Digital history and citizenship education. In P. J. VanFossen & M. J. Berson (Eds.), *The electronic republic? The impact of technology on education for citizenship* (pp. 196-213). West Lafayette, IN: Purdue University Press.

Manfra, M. M., & Hammond, T. C. (2008). Teachers' instructional choices with student-created digital documentaries: Case studies. *Journal of Research on Technology in Education, 41*(2), 37-59.

Manfra, M. M., & Stoddard, J. (2008). Powerful and authentic digital media strategies for teaching about genocide and the Holocaust. *The Social Studies, 99*(6), 260-264.

Marcus, A. S., & Stoddard, J. D. (2007). Tinsel Town as teacher: Hollywood films in the high school classroom. *The History Teacher, 40*(3), 303-330.

Martorella, P. (1997). Technology and the social studies—or: Which way to the sleeping giant? *Theory and Research in Social Education, 25*(4), 511-514.

Mishra, P., & Koehler, M.J. (2006). Technological pedagogical content knowledge: A framework for teacher knowledge. *Teacher's College Record, 108*(6), 1017-1054.

National Council for the Social Studies. (1994). *Expectations of excellence: Curriculum standards for social studies.* Washington, DC: Author.

National Center for History in the Schools. (1996). *National standards for history* (Basic edition). Los Angeles, CA: Author.

Nelson, J. (2001). Defining social studies. In W. B. Stanley (Ed.), *Critical issues in social studies research for the 21st century* (pp. 15-37). Greenwhich, CT: Information Age.

Newmann, F. M., & Wehlage, G. G. (1993). Five standards of authentic instruction. *Educational leadership, 50*(7), 8-12.

Norman, D. A. (1988). *The design of everyday things.* New York: Doubleday.

Percoco, J. A. (1998). *A passion for the past: Creative teaching of U.S. history.* Portsmouth, NH: Heinemann.

Popham, W. J. (2009). Objectives. In D. J. Fliders & S. J. Thornton (Eds.), *The curriculum studies reader* (3rd ed, pp. 93-106). New York: Routledge.

Ross, E. W. (2001). *The social studies curriculum: Purposes, problems, and possibilities.* Albany, NY: State University of New York Press.

Saettler, P. (1990). *The evolution of American educational technology.* Greenwich, CT: Information Age.

Swan, K., Hofer, M., & Levstik, L. (2007). And Action! Students collaborating in the digital directors guild. *Social Studies and the Young Learner, 19*(4), 17-20.

Teaching about the presidency and the 2008 election—What are the problems? (2008, Winter/Spring). *Social Science Docket, 8*(1), 7-14.

YouTube. (2009). *YouTube fact sheet.* Retrieved August 26, 2009 from http://www.youtube.com/t/fact_sheet

Virginia Department of Education. (2008). *United States history: 1865 to the present.* Retrieved January 14, 2008 from http://www.doe.virginia.gov/testing/sol/frameworks/history_socialscience_framewks/2008/2008_strikethrough/framewks_ushist1865-present.pdf

Yow, S., & Swan, K. (2009). If you built it, should I run?: A teacher's perspective on implementing a student-centered, digital technology project in his ninth-grade geography classroom. In J. Lee & A. Friedman (Eds.), *Research on technology and social studies education* (pp. 155-172). Charlotte, NC: Information Age.

CHAPTER 7

WHERE WE'VE BEEN; WHERE WE ARE; WHERE WE'RE GOING

Geospatial Technologies and Social Studies

Marsha Alibrandi, Andrew Milson, and Eui-Kyung Shin

For its 2008 annual meeting, the American Education Research Association (AERA) theme, titled: Research on Schools, Neighborhoods, and Communities: Toward Civic Responsibility, was aimed at discussions that were geospatial in nature:

> the geography of opportunity has become a local, national, and global challenge. Cities and metropolitan regions are experiencing intensified city/suburban fiscal disparities. The trend toward increased class- and race-based *geospatial* polarization has implications for schools, neighborhoods, and related social institutions and groups. The resulting local, state, and federal government responses often create new problems.
>
> Civic responsibility in education requires that multiple sectors of the community—individuals, governments, and nongovernment organizations—accept the charge of creating high-quality educational opportunities irre-

Technology in Retrospect: Social Studies in the Information Age 1984-2009, pp. 109–131

spective of neighborhood or other *geospatial* considerations. [emphasis ours] (AERA 2008 Conference Theme: http://www.aera.net/meetings /Default.aspx?menu_id=342&id=2898)

In his 2008 AERA presidential address, Dr. William F. Tate selected the topic, "The Geography of Opportunity: Poverty, Place and Educational Outcomes," a paper that used several GIS maps of "opportunity" that completely ignored the regions where job development was needed, thus giving "opportunity" to wealthy elites while urban poor would remain in complete isolation from such opportunities (Tate, 2008).

The skills required to perform complex analyses on data based information is rarely experienced by a student in social studies. Thus, students' abilities to ask *why* and *how* historic conditions exist *where* are difficult for them to ask or perform inquiry to uncover. Geographer Joseph Kerski (2008a) describes these as "the whys of where."

Helping students visualize the world as interconnected and interdependent and to expand their understandings of distribution and demographics, geospatial technologies can become effective tools for improving citizenship education. Student understandings or constructions of each of the National Council for Social Studies (NCSS) 10 themes (Table 7.1) can be enhanced with an introduction of its spatial dimensions. Through the use of geospatial technologies (or GSTs), students can inquire about local or global issues and solve problems from a spatial perspective in our society. Thus, the use of GSTs can help students improve their critical thinking, problem-solving and decision-making skills to make informed decisions (Kerski, 2008a); necessary skills for active citizenship (Milson & Alibrandi, 2008b).

WHERE WE ARE, WHERE WE'VE BEEN, WHERE WE'RE GOING

Recently, GSTs such as Internet-based mapping (or web-mapping), Geographic Information Systems (GIS), digital globes such as Google Earth, Bing Maps 3D (formerly MS Virtual Earth), and Global Positioning Systems (GPS), have been incorporated into K-12 classrooms to promote students' spatial thinking and problem solving (Shin & Alibrandi, 2007; Alibrandi, 2003; Bednarz & Bednarz, 2008; Kerski, 2008b; National Research Council, 2006).

Access to geospatial data via Internet-based mapping allows users to manipulate geospatial data in GIS environments over any Internet-accessible application (aka "App") from desktops to hand-helds (Milson & Earle, 2007). Google Earth and Google Maps allow users to explore any region in the world in 3-D format (Doering & Veltsianos, 2007). Geospatial

Table 7.1.   National Council for Social Studies (NCSS) 10 Themes

	NCSS Theme	Spatial Dimensions
I.	Culture & Cultural Diversity	Cultural Diffusion, Migration, Language Regions
II.	Time, Continuity & Change	Political History & Change, Population, Migration, Human Evolution
III .	People, Places & Environments	Environmental History, (see I. above), Energy/resource distribution
IV.	Individual Development & Identity	(See I.) Cultural, Linguistic, Religious, National identities
V.	Individuals, Groups & Institutions	(See I.) Social Networks, Diffusion of Innovations, EU, OPEC, NATO, UN, &c.
VI.	Power, Authority & Governance	Political Geography, Economic Geography (also see V. above), the "State"
VII.	Production, Distribution & Consumption	Resource Distribution (Natural, Human, Capital), Transportation, Manufacturing, Trade, Development, Imperialism, Colonialism
VIII.	Science, Technology & Society	Diffusion of Innovations, (see VII above), Social Movements
IX.	Global Connections	Environmental, Economic, Political, Cultural networks; Trade, War & Peace
X.	Civic Ideals & Practices	Social & Political Equity, Representation, Diffusion of Forms of Governance

hand-held equipment, such as GPS units and even cell phone technologies, have become more accurate and affordable, so schools and districts can integrate their use with relatively small budgets. GPS combined with GIS allow users to collect geospatial data and share it through "cloud computing" on the Internet (Merchant, 2007).

A BRIEF GLOSSARY OF
GEOSPATIAL INFORMATION TECHNOLOGIES (GSTS)

As an aid to this discussion, some definitions might help readers to distinguish some of the available geospatial information technologies. A teacher-friendly description of these technologies and their classroom utility were described by Todd Kenreich in 2008 at: http://www.socstrp.org/ issues/PDF/3.3.11.pdf . In his review, Kenreich provides examples of the types of digital mapping tools listed below. (GSTs):

Global Positioning System (GPS): A system of satellites orbiting the globe that facilitate location and communication devices such as GPS receivers and cell phones.

Geographic Information Systems (GIS): Data based systems that integrate features, attributes, events, still and streamed video images, symbols and other information to a location on a digital map. For example, think of the many layers on a TV weather map—political boundaries, satellite imagery, streamed video of clouds and precipitation. The digital map is a grid of locations onto and from which the other layers of information can be projected. Analyses between the data layers can reveal new relationships and information.

Online map servers: Mapquest and *Google Maps* are online map servers based on single layers of GIS maps. Through "mash up" capacity, information from existing web services such as hotel, restaurant and real estate information from other online sources may be projected onto the map using street addresses. No "behind the map" analyses are available.

Online mapping: In addition, there are online GIS map servers from state and federal agencies and industries that allow users to manipulate data layers provided by the agency server. Generally speaking, these are not equipped with "mash up" services. An example would be Social Explorer, (http://www.socialexplorer.com/pub/maps/map3.aspx?g=0) that serves US Demographic data including historic census data, or MassGIS (http://www.mass.gov/mgis/) that serves Massachusetts state and municipal data.

Digital Globes: Digital globes such as *Google Earth* and ESRI's *ArcGIS Explorer (AGX)* project data in 2D and 3D, are capable of projecting GPS and GIS data, aerial, satellite and remotely sensed images, video, sound clips and other content.

In the IAP International Social Studies Forum's *Digital Geography: Geospatial Technologies in the Social Studies Classroom* (Milson & Alibrandi, 2008a), contributors Alibrandi, Shin and Milson described some of the horizons met by innovative educators working to integrate new geospatial technologies into the social studies. Each presented unique perspectives; one a retrospective time line; another a lay of the land of state standards that either support or ignore their impact; and a third the microcosm of a classroom teacher working closely with students to construct new spatial understandings using digital mapping with a Geographic Information System (GIS).

In this retrospective, the authors return to present a three-part discussion that weaves pre-Internet applications such as *Oregon Trail* and *Carmen Sandiego,* with some of the spatially-based tools and more recent incremental changes in a timeline that includes new communication and geospatial tools that shaped the final quarter of the twentieth century.

It seems a remote past to recall a classroom of students without cell phones. How rapidly those tools and such teaching tools as interactive white boards change the sociocultural communication norms, learning activities and even content accessible in social studies classrooms. Facebook, Skype and ever-changing communication tools are even integrating geospatial capability with GPS and Google maps. The following discussion will include "where we've been; where we are; and where we're going" in terms of the use of geospatial technologies in social studies education.

As geospatial tools such as GPS, GIS and digital globes such as Google Earth bring the Earth's places and problems closer to "home," how will social studies classrooms respond? Within hours of the Haitian earthquake, aerial images, maps, and satellite imagery of the event are being made available.

The younger our K-12 students (or "digital natives"), the more likely their encounters and social networks are technology-enabled—and dependent. The tools that capture the interest and attention of digital natives are increasingly spatially-enabled. The common question of social networking—"what are you doing?"—may begin to morph into "where are you?" as new software such as Google's *Latitude* enables people to share their whereabouts with family and friends through wireless devices. Will these spatially-enabled tools become components of social studies teaching and learning and inquiry in the coming decades?

This chapter locates the "prologue" of geospatial technologies in the last quarter of the twentieth century, describes the processes of change at the start of the twenty-first century, and attempts to lay a path toward geospatial inquiry might enrich social studies education. In June 2009, the Partnership for the 21st Century unveiled its "Skills Map for Geography" in collaboration with the National Council for Geographic Education (NCGE) which joins the existing social studies skills map (see: http://www.21stcenturyskills.org/documents/21stcskillsmap_geog.pdf and http://www.21stcenturyskills.org/images/stories/matrices/ICTmap_ss.pdf).

Says David Nagel (2009) in *THE Journal:*

The Partnership for 21st Century Skills has teamed with the National Science Teachers Association and the National Council for Geographic Education to launch the latest in its series of 21st century roadmaps for core academic subjects, in this case K-12 science and geography. The maps were introduced at the National Education Computing Conference (NECC) being held this week in Washington, DC.

The 21st Century Skills and Science Map and the 21st Century Skills and Geography Map are the third and fourth in a series of maps aimed at core academic subjects in K-12 education. The purpose of the maps in general is to provide a framework and resources for integrating technology and other 21st century skills into core subject areas. The maps are targeted toward educators, administrators, and policymakers and include lesson plans for integrating 21st century skills into existing curricula, as well as specific student outcomes, along with models designed to help enhance student achievement at specific grade levels. (http://thejournal.com/articles/2009/06/30/partnership-releases-21st-century-skills-maps-for-science-geography.aspx)

With so many emerging geospatial technologies, alignment with the Partnership for the 21st Century furthers the impetus for schools to integrate these technologies and facilitates the alignment with existing standards. This is further discussed in the "where we're going" section.

WHERE WE'VE BEEN: A TIMELINE OF GST ANTECEDENTS AND DEVELOPMENTS

Looking back to the 1980s seems difficult now with the exponential growth of technological innovations we daily take for granted. But none of the current applications would have developed without their precursors. It may be dim in memory, but such innovations as the *Oregon Trail* game and *Where in the World is Carmen Sandiego?* were actually used by the preservice teacher candidates of today. Scholastic's Tom Snyder software for the single-computer classroom was where many social studies educators began integrating technology into social studies classrooms. Yet the game-like simulations designed for student engagement then still continue to engage and many of the products have transitioned across media to television and Internet applications.

With hundreds of thousands of time lines and timeline entries, it is presumptuous to add yet another—the ultimate social studies educator's dilemma—"what to leave in; what to leave out" becomes dangerous territory. This timeline is revised and adapted from Alibrandi and Baker's (2008) version from *Digital Geography* (see Figure 7.1). The attempt was to highlight some of the landmarks along the way, the enabling technological and media developments that spurned the rapid growth of applications.

During the 1980s, federal legislation began making technology grants available to schools. Thus began the changing landscapes of learning and teaching. But no one could call the change an earthquake. Although there was much ado about the potential for change, fear of change and competition for resources, the change itself crept slowly into classrooms during that decade. Those of us using computer labs or actively using the one-computer classroom were in the minority. The use of e-mail was promoted

A Time Line of events, publications, and innovations related to Geospatial Integration in K12 schools

	-1990	1990-95	1996-2000	2001-05	2006-2010
National Level Initiatives & Events	1985: The GENIP The Geographic Education National Implementation Project (GENIP), a consortium of geographic associations committed to improving the status and quality of geography education in the United States launched (now at http://genip.tamu.edu/) 1986-1991 (http://www.nsdc.org/library/publications/jsd/jsd11-97brko.cfm) **National Geographic Society's (NGS) Summer Institutes and State Geographic Alliances** **Geographic Awareness Week** is launched	1992: Direct ESRI support for K-12 GIS. Charlie Fitzpatrick, formerly of the NGS Summer Institutes, hired by ESRI (Environmental Systems Research Institute), GIS software industry leader. 1994: *Geography for Life*, National Geography Standards released: (http://www.nationalgeographic.com/xpeditions/standards/matrix.html) 1994: Global Learning and Observations to Benefit the Environment (GLOBE) program launched. Educational environmental data collection program using digital probes is made compatible with ESRI's ArcVoyager 1994: ESRI hires George Dailey (formerly of US Census Bureau) and Angela Lee 1995: The *NatureMapping* Program whose vision is to create a national network linking natural resource agencies, academia and land planners with local communities primarily through schools, wins the national RENEW America Award (http://depts.washington.edu/natmap/) 1995-1999 Pennsylvania State /TERC project using NASA-sponsored EarthKam (see Barstow et al, 1999)	1997: April 27. National Council for Social Studies Standards introduced 1998 & 1999: ESRI sponsors Authorized Teaching Program summer institutes at SW TX University. Many participants became leaders in GIS in Education, with 3 teaming as authors of *Mapping Our World* (ESRI Press, 2002).[1] 1999: First GIS Day, national initiative by ESRI, NGS and Association of American Geographers (AAG) surpassed its goal of reaching 1 million as more than two million participated in events worldwide. 1997-2005: KanCRN Kansas Collaborative Research Network for student research and collaboration with online mapping of student-entered data. (http://kancrn.org/index.cfm) 1999 Roger Williams University (Hosted by Dr. Richard Audet) invited university faculty of education to a 1-week institute on GIS. C. Fitzpatrick introduced ArcVoyager and RI state and US GIS agents from the Census Bureau and other agencies described GIS integration initiatives.\ 1999 First International Symposium on Digital Earth, held in China (see: http://www.fotr5.org/)	2001: NSF funds what becomes the KanGIS web portal, designed by Tom Baker 2002: No Child Left Behind Act (NCLB) passed, January 2003: 4-H Adoption of GIS in its programs – See www.esri.com/4-H	2006 My Wonderful World www.mywonderfulworld.org/ Multi-partner 5-year geographic education initiative hosted by National Geographic Society, sponsored by several media, federal agency and industry partners 2009: Teachers Teaching Teachers GIS (T2G) Institute 2009: Jan 30, 2009 ... *The Partnership for 21st Century Skills Map: Science and Geography* 2009: GeoMentor initiative launched at ESRI EdUC
State of Technology	1978: US Air Force launches Boeing satellite GPS² 1980s Federal Educational Technology Funding: Chapter 1, formerly Title I of the Elementary and Secondary Education Act, supports compensatory education services (including the purchase of necessary equipment) for educationally disadvantaged student at schools serving children from low-income families. Its fiscal year (FY) 1985 appropriation was $3.7 billion. Nearly 90% of the 16,000 school districts in the country participate. (National Advisory Council on the Education of Disadvantaged Children, "Title I, Today: A Factbook," Department of Education, Spring 1981, p. 23.) Chapter 2 is a block grant authority that replaced more than a score of categorical programs, most of which had been authorized by the Elementary and Secondary Education Act of 1965. Among the authorized uses of Chapter 2 funds is the purchase of "instructional equipment and materials suitable for use in providing education in academic subjects for use by children and teachers in elementary and secondary schools..." (Section 577(1)(b) of ECA). The FY 1985 appropriation for Chapter 2 was $531.9 million. Potentially all school districts in the country were eligible to receive Chapter 2 funds. 1983: Census Bureau introduces TIGER, its Topologically Integrated Geographic Encoding and Referencing system 1986: First SPOT satellite launched by Centre National d'Etudes Spatiales (CNES), France	2/5/95 Mapquest launches its www.mapquest.com website 8/9/95 Netscape goes public. For an historic document, see: www.nsf.gov/od/lpa/news/03/pr0343.htm 1997: The Library of Congress releases the first of the Panoramic Maps Collection: (http://memory.loc.gov/ammem/pmhtml/panhome.html) as reported in: http://scout.wisc.edu/Reports/ScoutReport/1997/scout-970613.html)	Google founders, Larry Page and Sergey Brin as Stanford grad students begin collaborating on 'BackRub'—a process for tracing back links from websites 2000: www.davidrumsey.com launched with now over 14,800 historic maps served online. One major collection features unique overlays of the original maps from the Lewis & Clark expedition. 	2002: Google acquires Picasa, a digital photo management company (http://picasa.google.com/)and publicly offers stock options 2004: Google acquires Keyhole Corp, a digital and satellite imaging company 2005 *Google Maps and API launch* *Google Earth -* Google launches Google Maps (http://maps.google.com/) Google launches Google Earth (http://earth.google.com/) Google Maps are connected to mobile phones	2006 Microsoft release Virtual Earth 3D (browser-based virtual globe) – http://local.live.com 2007: Emergence of Cloud computing 2008: Google Chrome web browser released 2008, 09ESRI releases its online digital globe software: *ArcGISExplorer*. (AGX) comparable to GoogleEarth, AGX has increased capability for integrating databased GIS layers, images, video and GPS.

Figure 7.1 SS Tech Retro Time Line. *Figure continues on next page.*

Figure 7.1 continued. SS Tech Retro Time Line.

Row categories (left margin, reading bottom-to-top): **Academic & Industry Publications & Products** / **State of GSTs:**

1980-1990	1990-95	1996-2000	2001-05	2005-2010
1962: CGIS Canadian Geographic Information System coined and founded by Dr. Roger Tomlinson	1995: ESRI's ArcView 2.1 released, for both Power Macintosh and pc platforms	1997: Alibrandi: Thinking Spatially, Acting Locally. Green Teacher.	2001: ESRI launches MapObjects 2.1.	2006-ESRI releases ArcWeb Explorer (GIS is in a browser) (http://www.esri.com/software/arcgis/explorer/index.html)
1970s-1980s Harvard's Laboratory for Computer graphics and spatial analysis	1995: Bernie Dodge introduces WebQuests adopted by thousands of SocialStudies educators	1997: Audet & Paris: GIS Implementation model for schools: Assessing the critical concerns, Journal of Geography.	2002: AAG launches www.aag.org/sustainable MyCOE Launch My Community, Our Earth	2006, NRC, Learning to think spatially
1974: Oregon Trail released, MECC; also 1978, 1980, 1985, 1992, 1996, 2001, 2008, 2009 (various publishers)	1996: Berkley Geo-Research Group releases their Geodesy project, now at: http://www.bcrg.com/geodesy/page3.htm	2000: Geography Network launched (www.geographynetwork.com), a collaborative and multi-participant system for publishing, sharing, and using digital geographic information on the Internet. ESRI ArcLessons launched: http://edcommunity.esri.com/arclessons/arclessons.cfm	2003: ESRI.com launched the Lewis and Clark Web site to commemorate 200 years of geographic exploration and mapping. to support redevelopment efforts.	2006, NRC, Beyond Mapping
1982: Tom Snyder Productions: Decisions, Decisions released. See: http://www.tomsnyder.com/products/products.asp?Subject=SocialStudies	1997: ESRI's ArcView 3.0 released Map Objects and ArcExplorer released ESRI's GIS Store for maps, software & publications is launched –ESRI's Virtual Campus is launched	ArcGIS 8.1 released	2003: ESRI launches ArcLessons (now located at: http://gis2.esri.com/industries/education/arclessons/arclessons.cfm)	2006 Christman, N. Charting the Unknown: How computer mapping at Harvard became GIS
1982: GRASS (open source) GIS introduced by US Army Corps of Engineers	1998: ESRI launches GeoChallenge in conjunction with National Geographic Society	ArcExplorer 3.1 Java Edition released.	2001 Green (ed), GIS: A sourcebook for schools	2007 Baker & Keroski launch new http://edcommunity.esri.com new products that are Mac accessible are accessible. ArcWebExplorer (http://www.arcwebservices.com/aw/index.isp) and a new edition of ArcExplorer JavaEdition for Educators (AEJEE): http://edcommunity.esri.com/software/aejee/) with increased functionality for both Windows and Mac introduced. Also see: http://edcommunity.esri.com/apps/wedge/s/
1985: Where in the World is Carmen Sandiego? Released, Pharos Books; also: 1990, 1995, 1996, 2001 (various publishers and PBS)	1995: TERC: First National Conference on the Educational Application of Geographic Information Systems (EdGIS) Report. TERC.	ESRI hosted its first Education User Conference immediately preceding the 21st Annual International User Conference in San Diego, California. More than 400 K812 teachers, college and university instructors, school administrators, librarians, and museum professionals shared their experiences using GIS in the classroom for research and public access.	2002 Malone, Palmer & Voigt: Mapping Our World. ESRI Press	2007 Sinton, D. & Lund, J., (Eds.) Understanding Place: GIS and Mapping Across the Curriculum
1986: ESRI's Arcinfo released		2000: Ludwig & Audet, Eds. GIS in Schools. ESRI Press.	2003 Alibrandi: GIS in the Classroom. Heinemann	2007: Google Educator and Sightseer newsletter launched (see: http://bbs.keyhole.com/ubb/z0320a1700/june07.htm) and http://www.google.com/educators/community.html
1986: MapInfo founded		2002: Leap Frog introduces its first Talking Globe	2003 Zannelli-English: Community Mapping. ESRI Press	2008: Milson, A. & Alibrandi, M. (Eds.). (2008). Digital Geography: Geo-Spatial Technologies in the Social Studies Classroom. Information Age Press.
1987: IDRISI project, early GIS Clark University			2003 Bednarz & Baker, Eds. Research on GIS in Education (special issue), Journal of Geography.	First-Ever 21st Century Skills Map Released: Social Studies
1988: National Center for Geographic Information and Analysis (NCGIA) founded. A consortium of universities with a mission of advancing geographic information research, developed a Core Curriculum in 1990 (1998 and 200 versions now at: http://www.ncgia.ucsb.edu/pubs/core.html)			2005 Baker: Internet-Based GIS Mapping in support of K-12 education. Professional Geographer.	2009 21st Century Partnership launches its Geography Skills Map
1989: KIDSNET launched (now at: http://www.kidsnet.org/)				

Figure 7.1 continued.   SS Tech Retro Time Line.

as a means of collaboration, but teachers' home computers and access to ISPs (Internet service providers) were limited, and how else would teachers become comfortable with the new tools?

Viewing the rate of technology adoption from Rogers' (2003) diffusion of innovations theory, the need for social acceptance of the innovation must be acknowledged. Not all innovations are "good," nor necessary or useful. The value of adopting the innovation must outweigh the friction of shifting from traditional methods. But the rate of acceptance of teachers as technology adopters or models had a slow uptake curve. Not until curriculum-based software applications hit the education market would social studies teachers incorporate them. As teachers saw students' research and collaboration skills and content knowledge enhanced by using early successful software products, those "early adopters" came to trust the value of certain technologies in their classrooms.

It may be argued that the opening of the Internet to the public has revolutionized content delivery and expectations. Certainly the window on the world has opened ever wider as a result of web accessibility—of images, maps, data, search engines, applications, and mash ups. School access was almost immediate, and Internet access overcame many of the barriers previously experienced. Using diffusion theory, Shannon White (2008) compared school Internet adoption to GIS adoption and found very different uptake curves.

For many of what Rogers calls "early adopter" teachers back in the mid-1990s, it meant opening the box and sharing the application (and the power) with students who had much more time—and the age appropriate propensity—to explore the dimensions of new applications. Teachers discovered that new strategies and pedagogies were both facilitated and required to integrate technology. These reflected the strategies of "information age" work places, where problem solving and collaboration are required in constructing or accessing data bases, generating data, and plotting and presenting the data in new ways. The teachers integrating these technologies were truly innovators in education and "early adopters" of geospatial technologies (Alibrandi, 2003).

As many have found, the transmission of teaching and learning with technology was also slow in teacher preparation programs in which professors who had never taught with technology faced the challenge of how, why and whether technology integration was "worth it" in terms of student learning. Studies trying to bridge that gap became confounded by the demand for data based in test results, wholly inadequate to measure the *types* of learning, such as problem-solving, analysis, creativity and presentation. What was able to be measured with standardized testing was content, so a classic mismatch in research and "outcomes" has slowed the response to those concerns. Yet, those innovations that began on two-toned screens with little imagery piqued student interest in the 1980s and the imagery, mapping, content and applications available today continue to do so.

Allan Paivio's (1986) dual coding theory is useful in providing a framework for understanding how we learn both visually and linguistically. Recognized for opening conceptual spaces for designers and developers to create new "intuitive" applications to digital media, Paivio's theory bridged the gap for designers, cartographers and map developers of the early 1960s and 1970s. Dual coding theory describes the relationship of image-based memory ("imagens") and language-based memory ("logogens") that have been discussed in subsequent treatises on literacy and "visualization" in learning. During the 1970s studies of students' learning from (albeit static, noninteractive) maps had proliferated (Golledge & Stimson, 1997). Once the landscape of learning switched to learning with interactive maps, it became more difficult to research, since students could now access interactive maps independently.

WHERE WE ARE: CURRENT USES OF GEOSPATIAL TECHNOLOGIES TO ENHANCE K-12 EDUCATION

In the volume *Digital Geography* (Milson & Alibrandi, 2008a) we presented research on impacts on geospatial technology integration up to that year. In his 2008 review, Zafer Unal (2008) describes the volume this way:

> *Digital Geography* presents a comprehensive guide to history of GIS, discusses what future might bring regarding GIS, provides examples of the use of different GIS tools that are currently available, and the integration of GIS in education.
>
> The book begins with the history of geospatial technologies in education, the influence of the standards movement, and the growth of an international geospatial education community are explored. While authors of this section provides definitions, background information, the history and present status of GIS, they also tried to answer what most educators agree about the future of GIS in K-12 by providing the results of their interview with educators.
>
> The discussion then turns to the range and applicability of GIS in education, providing examples of the use of geospatial technologies for teaching and learning history, geography, civics, economics, and environmental science. The authors of this section introduce the development stages of different applications that apply GIS in education and experiences of students/teachers and their use of these applications for education including but not limited to My World GIS Software, GIS for History, Internet-based GIS, Mapstats for Kids, and GoogleEarth.

Next, the book turns to a detailed section-by-section analysis of the reviews and critiques of recent research relevant to geospatial technologies in education. The theoretical perspectives are proposed that could guide research and practice in this field.

The book concludes with an in-depth discussion on the theory, research, and practice associated with teacher preparation for using geospatial technologies in education. The authors of this section explore the importance of preparing teachers for GST expeditions with their students and makes recommendations for teacher education based on their research results.

Digital Geography presents a comprehensive guide to history of GIS, discusses what future might bring regarding GIS, provides examples of the use of different GIS tools that are currently available, and the integration of GIS in education. (http://edrev.asu.edu/reviews/rev681.htm)

Since April 2000, with Charlie Fitzpatrick's introduction in *Social Education* "Navigating a New Information Landscape," an increasing number of articles and entire issues on spatial thinking, geography and GIS have appeared in NCSS publications *Social Education, Social Studies and the Young Learner, Contemporary Issues in Technology and Teacher Education, Social Studies* and *Social Studies Research and Practice*. The presence of these contributions reflects the increasing presence of Internet-based geospatial tools available to and in use by hundreds of thousands, if not millions of users.

In addition to these specifically in social studies journals, numerous articles in the *Journal of Geography, The Geography Teacher* and trade publications have also increased. For an online bibliography of geospatial education related publications, see: http://edcommunity.esri.com/research/index.cfm?fa=home.bib. The list is maintained by members of the GISEdCommunity, comprised of educators involved in integrating geospatial technologies through in-service, grant and outreach programs, preservice course work, research and publications. Current research is being generated on student learning with GIS, GPS and digital globes by an emerging group of researchers on geospatial technologies in K-12 and related settings. The group has met since the 2007 at ESRI Education User and NCGE conferences.

Certainly the splash of Google Earth on the Internet has had an immense impact and a more immediate uptake for educators in both English and social studies. Google's monthly *Sightseer Newsletter* and GElessons.com link Google Keyhole group's web search engines with web-based projects that connect historic, social, and political phenomena that augment social studies curricula from history to global studies. Collaborating with UNESCO Heritage, the David Rumsey Map Collection, Google Earth's community provides a gateway for collaboration between teachers, students and schools. On the *gelessons.com* website, "Student-controlled lessons" (an inquiry-based model) such as British geography teacher Noel Jenkins' "The Diamond Trade," combine aerial and remotely sensed images of diamond mining in Africa and other locations, combining these with links to articles, book and films about the hazards of the trade.

Google Earth's Google Lit Trips provide an excellent connection between reading and spatial thinking by adding the spatial dimension to young adult and adult literature. Titles such as Elie Weisel's *Night*, Khaled Hosseini's *Kite Runner*, Steibeck's *Grapes of Wrath* and many more can now be seen in GoogleEarth (at: http://www.googlelittrips.org/). Jerome Burg's site is organized by grade level, so popular titles as diverse as *Make Way for Ducklings* and *Brothers in Hope: Lost Boys of Sudan* can be found among Burg's Google Lit Trips. Teachers and students are encouraged to add Lit Trip versions of their favorite titles.

The value of the Lit Trip concept is its ability to assist readers to visualize images to make concrete the text as they read. This use of Paivio's dual coding theory is inherent in the Lit Trip genre, and is particularly important for linking geospatial thinking and reading comprehension. Elizabeth Hinde of the University of Arizona has contributed immensely to the dimensions of geoliteracy and integrated curriculum. Hinde has published numerous articles demonstrating results from studies in Arizona, where ESL and ELL students are a significant segment of the student population. Dr. Hinde has recently constructed a webspace specifically for ELL geoliteracy at the Arizona Geographic Alliance website at: http://alliance.la.asu.edu/azga/. Hinde's work is an important resource for elementary social studies in demonstrating the combined improvements in both geospatial literacy and reading comprehension (see especially Dr. Hinde's most recent publications at: https://sites.google.com/a/asu.edu/hinde/publications).

Another development in 2009 allows Google Earth's older imagery to be available using a time slider bar that can demonstrate change in a particular location over time. (see Figure 7.2). The images aren't yet that old, but the utility of this feature for demonstrating environmental history and change has great potential (see: http://google-latlong.blogspot.com/2009/02/new-in-google-earth-50-historical.html). The United Nations Environmental Programme's *Atlas of Our Changing Environment* is available on Google Earth at: http://na.unep.net/OnePlanetManyPeople/index.php

HOW AND WHY INTEGRATE GSTS INTO SOCIAL STUDIES?

By helping students visualize the world as an interconnected and interdependent place and expand their sense of place and affiliation, GSTs have

Figure 7.2.   Google Earth with Historical Imagery Slider visible. Slider icon is highlighted in toolbar.

been effective tools for improving K-12 education. The use of GSTs helps students improve their critical thinking, problem-solving and decision making skills to make informed decisions for the Earth and its people (Kerski, 2008a), necessary skills for active citizenship.

Internet-based maps for viewing and exploring archived or real-time geospatial data and are especially powerful tools for inquiry (Baker, 2005). The use of collaborative Internet-based mapping that utilizes data submitted by geographically dispersed participants can be used by a large number of student contributors, from across the world. Students participate in such projects by submitting the data they have gathered or generated on a web-mapping site, such as the GLOBE Project (http://www.globe.gov). The data is then projected in an IGIS map via the web along with data submitted by other students who may live on the other side of the world (Baker, 2005). This type of project affords unique and powerful opportunities for students to experience environmental participation and citizenship at the global level.

Using the Internet-based GIS, *Globalis* application (http://globalis.gvu.unu.edu/), Milson, Gilbert, and Earle (2007) worked with high school students in their world geography classes to explore issues that

African countries face and guided students to find possible solutions. The researchers found that

> emerging IGIS environments, such as *Globalis*, allow students information as they visualize data in various formats, make hypotheses about what they are seeing, test their thinking by exploring additional evidence, and ultimately draw connections that they can formulate into generalizations about the topic. (p. 141)

As a result, students who participated in the study gained "greater cultural awareness and empathy for the complexity of the problems facing the people and countries of the African continent" (Milson & Earle, 2007, p. 234). Thus, Milson and Earle asserted that the use of IGIS facilitated the students' inductive learning, which includes discovery, problem-based, project-based, and inquiry learning important to educate active citizenry in decision making for the Earth and its people.

DeMers and Vincent (2007) used *ArcView* (GIS software) and *ArcAtlas: Our Earth* (a collection of digital thematic maps) to help students examine questions related to the nature, causes, and possible consequences of the distributional patterns. In their spatial inquiry that examined the difference between historical range and present range of the lions in Africa, the high school students determined the factors that might have affected the changes in the distribution, predicted future distribution and planned for the preservation of these animals. DeMers and Vincent further advocate the ample potential for the type of exploration that *ArcAtlas* can provide for students.

Using Google Earth combined with *ArcExplorer* (a GIS software), Doering and Veletsianos (2007) provided middle school students with opportunities to work with "real-time" data to learn about Team GoNorth!'s travel to the Arctic (GoNorth!: Arctic National Wildlife Refuge (ANWR), http://www.polarhusky.com). According to Doering and Veletsianos, the middle school students developed a sense of place through the real-time data they either acquired or created. The findings imply that students can develop their sense of belonging by visually comparing and examining their own and other places using "real" data can provide authentic learning experiences about nonfamiliar places.

ESRI provides space for sharing lesson plans using geospatial technology on its websites (http://edcommunity.esri.com/arclessons/arclessons.cfm). The lesson plans posted and shared with teachers are becoming more diverse in the topics and requiring more sophisticated thinking from students during the inquiry process. For example, looking closely at a lesson titled "Analyzing Fossil Fuel Production and Consumption," that asks students to examine the relationships of fossil fuel production and consumption and its effect on Earth.

These examples demonstrate GSTs as effective tools to help students think about real-world problems and solutions using spatial frameworks and applications (Kerski, 2008a). When students are using geospatial technology, "they are not just learning about natural hazards or demographics but are rethinking their role in society, rethinking lifelong learning, and rethinking their own career path" (Kerski, 2008a, p. 65). They are developing high-level critical thinking skills in spatial terms, rather than meaninglessly looking and browsing through maps. These types of projects can enhance students' geographic perspectives, their examination of real-world problems, and their active participation in addressing critical sociopolitical, economic, environmental and historical issues.

RENEWED COMMITMENT TO
PROFESSIONAL DEVELOPMENT: THE T3G INSTITUTES

In the opening chapter of *Digital Geography* (Alibrandi & Baker, 2008), stakeholders in geospatial education were interviewed about the state of the technology and what was needed and on the horizon. All interviewed stated that a renewal of the training institutes of the previous decade was needed to increase the footprint of competent educators to disseminate the integration of geospatial technologies. Dubbed "T3G," the Teachers Teaching Teachers GIS institute was an opportunity for "learning new strategies to facilitate the integration of GIS in K-12 instruction as well as focusing on teaching *with* GIS rather than teaching *about* GIS" (Smith, 2009, personal communication,)

Participation in the institute required an application demonstrating GIS competence. Thirty participants were instructed by the stakeholders who had, when interviewed in 2007, underscored the need to resume the training venue after a decade.

Participants described the highlights of the training as an excellent opportunity to become familiar with ESRI resources—particularly the instructors as well as to engage with the variety of expertise of their fellow participants. Among the activities was a preview of the new AGX digital globe (free download available at: http://resources.esri.com/arcgisexplorer/900/index.cfm?fa=whatsnew).

Utilization of "Gallery walks" at ESRI headquarters and among the participants who developed GIS products and shared their individual projects to one another enhanced both learning and community. Field work on a historic farm with GPS, and digital photos, GPS to GIS demonstrated both water issues and technology application. The participants will develop lessons for the *ArcLessons* online collection, and each developed an Action Plan for Professional Development and/or instruction (Alvarez & Smith, 2009, personal communication).

A NEW PARADIGM OF PARTNERSHIP IN SOCIAL STUDIES?

At the 2009 ESRI User Conference, K-12 Schools Manager, Charlie Fitzpatrick introduced another new initiative to encourage "GeoMentors" to become involved in schools. With GIS Day an annual international event falling on the Wednesday before Thanksgiving during Geography Awareness Week, GeoMentors would volunteer to work with schools as technical partners. The concept has been described and recommended since Ludwig and Audet's (2000) original *GIS in Schools*, but remains a new concept in social studies teaching. The practice of collaboration in geospatial technologies is both inherent and necessary, but remains a novelty in social studies practice. GIS Day would be an opportunity for any social studies teacher to request that a GeoMentor visit a school (see: http://edcommunity.esri.com/geomentor/ or http://edcommunity.esri.com/geomentor/). Schools hosting an event can be matched with a GeoMentor though registering a GIS Day event or by searching the Events tab for nearby GIS Day events.

As we enter the new decade, findings from a study by Palm Beach County GIS specialist Donna Goldstein (2010) in Florida link GIS instruction to improved FCAT scores for students including ESL students in reading as well as improved scores in science. While increases in social studies scores did not reach statistical significance in the sample, the benefits across the board support Hinde and Ekiss' (2005) findings of mutual benefits in literacy and geoliteracy. These findings signify a new platform for future studies, and provide a platform for renewal and revival of geographic content to improve reading comprehension. These findings are important in reclaiming lost Social Studies ground in elementary classrooms.

WHERE ARE WE GOING? GST IN THE CLOUD

It is a hazardous endeavor to attempt to predict the future of any technology. It is even more hazardous to attempt to predict how that technology might be adopted in the K-12 environment. Rather than venture into making predictions about the unpredictable, we will speculate about how emerging geospatial technologies might intersect with trends in educational technology and consider how these developments might transform the geography classroom.

In their *2009 Horizon Report: K-12 Edition*, the New Media Consortium (Johnson, Levine, Smith, & Smythe, 2009) profiled six emerging technologies that are likely to become mainstream within the K-12 environment within the next 5 years. The identified technologies are collaborative environments, online communication tools, mobiles, cloud computing, smart objects, and the personal web. Both collaborative environments and online communication tools are expected to become mainstream in K-12 settings within the next year. Mobiles and cloud computing are predicted to see more widespread K-12 adoption within the next two to three years. The final two technologies, smart objects and the personal web, are likely to be several years from mainstream use for K-12 education. Although each of these technologies has relevance for the emergence of GIT in K-12 classrooms, we will focus on cloud computing as the emerging technology that is most likely to increase the rate of adoption of GIT for geography teachers.

DEVELOPING 21ST CENTURY SKILLS?

In the Partnershiopo for the 21st Century Geography Skills Map, student use of many sources identified in this chapter are recommended. Using web-based mapping resources such as www.worldmapper.org the UN, and www.nationmaster.com open-ended student problems are posed, and analysis using the resources is suggested. Interestingly, the direct use of such web-based resources is pushed down to the elementary level. This is somewhat problematic vis-à-vis current trends in elementary classrooms whose focus is on reading usin g more traditional methods and texts. That said, if 21st Century skills are to be addressed, students' early use of these tools provides the foundation for the more critical applications listed in the 9-12 categories of the Map, such as locating urban restoration and environmental cleanup using aerial and satellite imagery.

Unfortunately the assumptions about familiarity with such sites as www.historical.maptech.com among elementary teachers is a major one. Unless teachers have specific training on how to use such maps with elementary students, it is unlikely that the assumed 21st Century goals will be met. There are also strong critics such as geographer and teacher educator David Sobel and Richard Louv who maintain that elementary school children need "hands-on" engagement in the physical environment as central to their development.

While the 9-12 expectations of students using GIS to create choropleth maps (i.e., thematic maps showing classified data such as per capita GDP by state) and providing critical discussions of different classification schemes, Middle school recommendations are for GPS and GIS use which are age-appropriate and currently in use in select school systems. In the 9-12 map, students are to use "Google Earth, ArcExplorer Java Edition (ESRI)-free GIS software for schools, Terra Server, GIS" in presentations defending site selections for the next Olympics.

What is disappointing about the 21st Century Geography Skills Map is that these recommendations have been echoed by the geospatial education community for the past 15 years with only incremental progress seen. The document relies upon only those technologies extant in 2009, when it was published, but leave little to the imagination of what the next 90 years of the century might require in terms of geospatial understandings and skills.

Among the barriers to teaching and learning with GSTs, the technical issues of geographic data acquisition, software licensing, storage of large data files, and the need for substantial processing power have been persistent (e.g., Baker, 2005; Gatrell, 2001; Bednarz & Bednarz, 2008). The collection of geographic data for use in GIS, such as digital remote sensing images, digital aerial photographs, and survey measurements, is typically cost-prohibitive or beyond the technical expertise of a geography teacher (Shin, 2008; Milson & Earle, 2007). It is possible to collect geographic data through Global Positioning System (GPS) measurements, but this method also involves equipment, time, and technical skills that are not often available. Numerous online resources have become available for acquiring geographic data for use in GIS, but technical skills are often required to format the data correctly and the data are not always available free of charge. Once data are acquired, they must be organized and stored in a geographic database in order to be used for visualization and analysis. This has typically meant purchasing and installing software, such as ESRI's *ArcView*, on school computers. The most common geographic data formats result in relatively large file sizes and the software needed to perform queries on these data require robust processing power. Some of these barriers have been disintegrating with the advent of Internet-based GIS (Milson & Earle, 2007) and the development of GIS software intended for use in school settings (Edelson, Smith, & Brown, 2008; Milson & Curtis, 2009), but the intersection of GIS and cloud computing may offer the best solution yet to these perennial technical issues.

One primary purpose of cloud computing is to move data and software applications off of local computers and onto a large network of computers that can share storage and processing capacity. Multiple users can have access to data and applications through the web browser on their local computer without needing to store large datasets or run software applications on that computer. Each user can also communicate and collaborate with others in a shared space that leverages the resources of the cloud without taxing the capacity of the local computer. Google has become well-known for harnessing the concept of cloud computing for a variety of web-based applications. The launch of Google's Chrome OS provides a browser-based operating system that is intended to challenge the dominance of Microsoft's Windows ("Breaking Windows," 2009). The advantages of cloud-based applications for school settings is that they are often free or low-cost, require little to no installation or maintenance, and can often run efficiently on older computers with lower processing power and memory. The challenges associated with cloud computing for teachers include negotiating school district Internet filters and network availability, as well as the need to trust in a company or service provider to continue maintenance of the application and storage of the data and student work products.

The intersection of GIS and cloud computing has been called *Web GIS* (*ArcGIS Online* Services—The Foundation of Web GIS, 2008). ESRI, the leading GIS software company, has developed both *ArcGIS Online* and *ArcGIS Explorer* as web GIS applications. *ArcGIS Online* is a repository of maps, layers, and GIS services. The process of data acquisition and storage is simplified through *ArcGIS Online* since one can search for maps and open them easily without needing to download or store the data on a local machine. It is possible for a registered user to share maps, add tags for easy searching, store collected maps and tools in a "My Content" folder, and join groups to share content and to receive updates about new postings to *ArcGIS Online*.

ArcGIS Explorer (AGX) is a web-based GIS application that is available for free download (http://resources.esri.com/arcgisexplorer/). After locating relevant maps and layers in *ArcGIS Online,* one can open the map in AGX. AGX can be referred to as a *GeoBrowser* since it enables novice GIS users to engage in geo-visualization and geo-analysis through a web browser interface. Consistent with cloud-based applications, one does not need to store large digital geographic data files on the local computer to view and analyze those data. When using an industrial strength GIS, such as *ArcGIS Desktop*, one must understand map projections and various file formats before maps can be rendered properly. GeoBrowsers, such as AGX, are designed to project maps "on-the-fly." Maps can be viewed in 2D or 3D in a format that resembles *GoogleEarth's* digital globe. Additionally, AGX supports dynamic links to websites, photos, live webcams, Flash animations, and graphs and can be used to generate presentations that are similar to Microsoft PowerPoint. It is also much easier to import GPS data in the form of waypoints, tracks, and routes through the GPS Exchange Format (GPX), an XML data format that allows transfer and display into AGX.

Beyond the easing of barriers related to data acquisition, software licensing, data storage, and processing power, web GIS and similar cloud-based applications offer teachers and students a tool for producing and publishing user-generated geographic content. The value of designing lessons in which students produce work for an authentic audience has been documented frequently by educators (e.g., Lindquist, 2002). Those promoting the use of GIS in education have repeatedly called for opportunities for students to engage in authentic, local investigations in which they conduct social studies and do geography (Alibrandi, 2003; English & Feaster, 2002; Hill & Natoli, 1996; Shin, 2006; Milson & Alibrandi, 2008a; Milson & Alibrandi, 2008b). Through web GIS applications such as AGX, these goals may finally be realized to a much broader degree than has been the case to date. Perhaps a future *Horizon Report K-12* will note the potential for GSTs to become mainstream instructional technologies in K-12 classrooms.

IMPLICATIONS AND CONCLUSIONS

In the National Research Council's conclusions from their 2006 report on spatial thinking, the interdisciplinary nature of spatial thinking and problem-solving was acknowledged. While this should be good news, it is really just common sense and would return us to an integrated program of reading for content in social studies, geography and science, just as many of the readers of this volume might recall. The Scientific Reading Association still produces its SRA Reading Laboratory kits used 50 years ago. Many of us learned science and geography content through this reading system.

We are encouraged by the research (Goldstein, 2010; Hinde & Ekiss, 2005) that demonstrates increased performance by students using geospatial technologies on standardized tests in reading and science. Since measurement of student achievement using technology has been difficult, we also anticipate the development and findings from more closely-aligned instruments. Because the use of technology in classrooms is still considered innovative, and because those relevant skills and understandings may or may not appear as traditional gains in content mastery, the instruments and measures we design, develop and test in the next decade must consider a wider range of skills, abilities and applications.

With the rapid development of hand-held communications technologies using web-based content, it is likely that users will become more familiar with geospatial applications and developments at the industry end. There are of course both advantage and disadvantages to the industry leading the curve of spatial thinking and problem solving. Along with access must be taught the basic understandings of *actual*, grounded in physical reality geospatial phenomena; *virtual* or digital skills and understandings; *critical* thinking skills sufficient to detect gaps, unrepresented or underrepresented information that presents biased perspectives; and *ethical* reasoning skills to be able to use, retrieve, develop, and apply skills, information and knowledge for a just and sustainable planet.

ACKNOWLEDGMENT

The authors wish to thank our series editors, reviewers, and Dr. Thomas R. Baker and Dr. Joseph Kerski for their suggestions.

REFERENCES

Alibrandi, M. (2003). *GIS in the classroom*. Portsmouth, NH: Heinemann.

Alibrandi, M., & Baker, T. (2008). A brief social history of GIS in education, 1994-2006. In A. J. Milson & M. Alibrandi (Eds.), *Digital Geography: Geo-Spatial Technologies in the Social Studies Classroom. International Social Studies Forum* (pp. 249-270). Information Age.

ArcGIS Online Services—The Foundation of Web GIS. (2008, Fall). *ArcNews Online*. Retrieved August 4, 2009, from http://www.esri.com/news/arcnews/fall08articles/arcgis-online-services.htm

Baker, T. R. (2005). Internet-based GIS mapping in support of K-12 education. *The Professional Geographer, 57*(1), 44-50.

Bednarz, S. W., & Bednarz, R. S. (2008). Spatial thinking: The key to success in using geospatial technologies in the social studies classroom. In A. J. Milson & M. Alibrandi (Eds.), *Digital Geography: Geo-Spatial Technologies In The Social Studies Classroom. International Social Studies Forum* (pp. 249-270). Information Age.

Breaking Windows; Google v Microsoft. (2009, July). *The Economist, 392*(8639), 64. Retrieved August 4, 2009, from ABI/INFORM Global. (Document ID: 1781420791).

Dodge, B. J. (1995). WebQuests: A structure for active learning on the World Wide Web. *The Distance Educator, 1*(2), 10-13.

Doering, A., & Veletsianos, G. (2007). An investigation of the use of real-time, authentic geospatial data in the K-12 classroom. *Journal of Geography. 106*(6), 217-225.

DeMers, M. N., & Vincent, J. S. (2007). ArcAtlas in the classroom: Pattern Identification, description, and explanation. *Journal of Geography. 106*(6), 267-284.

Edelson, D., Smith, D., & Brown, M. (2008). Beyond interactive mapping: Bringing data analysis with GIS int the social studies classroom. In A. J. Milson & M. Alibrandi (Eds.), *Digital Geography: Geo-Spatial Technologies In The Social Studies Classroom. International Social Studies Forum* (pp. 249-270). Information Age.

English, K. Z., & Feaster, L. S. (2002). *Community geography: GIS in action*. Redlands, CA: ESRI.

Environmental Systems Research Institute (n.d.). *ArcLessons* Retrieved September 2, 2009, from http://edcommunity.esri.com/arclessons/lesson.cfm?id=450

Gatrell, J. D. (2001). Structural, technical, and definitional issues: The case of geography, GIS, and K-12 classrooms in the United States. *Journal of Educational Technology Systems, 29*(3), 237-249.

Goldstein, D. (2010). *Integration of geospatial technologies into K-12 curriculum: An investigation of teacher and student perceptions and student academic achievement.* Unpublished dissertation, Florida Atlantic University.

Golledge, R., & Stimson, R. (1997). *Spatial behavior: A geographic perspective.* New York, NY: Guilford Press.

Hill, A. D., & Natoli, S. J. (1996). Issues-centered approaches to teaching geography courses. In R. W. Evans & D. W. Saxe (Eds.), *Handbook on teaching social issues* (pp. 167-176). Washington, DC: National Council for the Social Studies.

Hinde, E., & Ekiss, G. (2005). *No Child Left Behind ... Except in Geography? GeoMath in Arizona answers a need, 18*(2), 27-29.

Johnson, L., Levine, A., Smith, R., & Smythe, T. (2009). *The 2009 Horizon Report: K-12 Edition.* Austin, TX: The New Media Consortium.

Kenreich, T. (2008). Technology integration: "Zoom, Pan, and Think": The Interactivity of Digital Maps. *Social Studies Research and Practice.* Retrieved January 14, 2010 from http://www.socstrp.org/issues/showissue.cfm?volID=3&IssueID=9

Kerski, J. J. (2008a). The world at the student's fingertips: Internet-based GIS education opportunities. In A. J. Milson & M. Alibrandi (Eds.), *Digital Geography: Geo-Spatial Technologies In The Social Studies Classroom* (pp. 119-134). Charlotte, NC: Information Age.

Kerski, J. J. (2008b). Toward an international geospatial education community. In A. J. Milson & M. Alibrandi (Eds.), *Digital Geography: Geo-Spatial Technologies in the Social Studies Classroom. International Social Studies Forum* (pp. 61-74). Information Age.

Lindquist, T. (2002). *Seeing the whole through social studies* (2nd ed.). Portsmouth, NH: Heinemann.

Ludwig, G., & Audet, R. (Eds.). (2000). GIS in schools. Redlands, CA: ESRI.

Milson, A. J., & Alibrandi, M. (Eds.). (2008a). *Digital geography: Geospatial technologies in the social studies classroom.* Charlotte, NC: Information Age.

Milson, A. J., & Alibrandi, M. (2008b). Critical map literacy and Geographic Information Systems: The spatial dimension of civic decision making. In P. J. VanFossen & M. J. Berson (Eds.), *The electronic republic? The impact of technology on education for citizenship* (pp. 110-128). West Lafayette, IN: Purdue University Press.

Milson, A. J., & Curtis, M. (2009). Where and why there? Spatial thinking with Geographic Information Systems. *Social Education 73*(3), 113-118.

Milson, A. J., & Earle, B. D. (2007). Internet-based GIS in an inductive learning environment: A case study of ninth grade geography students. *Journal of Geography, 106*(6), 227-237.

Milson, A., Gilbert, K., & Earle, B. D. (2007). Discovering Africa through Internet-based Geographic Information System: A Pan-Africa summit simulation. *Social Education, 71*(3),140-145.

Merchant, J. (2007). Using geospatial data in geographic education. *Journal of Geography, 106*(1), 215

Nagel, D. (2009, June 30). Partnership Releases 21st Century Skills Maps for Science, Geography. *THE Journal.* Retrieved July 15, 2009, from http://thejournal.com/articles/2009/06/30/partnership-releases-21st-century-skills-maps-for-science-geography.aspx

National Research Council, Committee on Support for Thinking Spatially. (2006). *Learning to think spatially.* Washington DC: National Academies Press.

Paivio, A. (1986). *Mental representations: A dual coding approach.* New York, NY: Oxford.

Rogers, E. (2003). *Diffusion of innovations.* New York, NY: Free Press.

Shin, E. (2006). Using Geographic Information System (GIS) to improve fourth graders' geographic content knowledge and map skills. *Journal of Geography, 105*(3), 109-120.

Shin, E. (2008). Examining the teacher's role when teaching with Geographic Information Systems (GIS). In A. J. Milson & M. Alibrandi (Eds.), *Digital geography: Geospatial technologies in the social studies classroom* (pp. 271-290). Charlotte, NC: Information Age.

Shin, E., & & Alibrandi, M. (2007). How to do it: Online Interactive mapping: Using Google Earth. *Social Studies and the Young Learner, 19*(3), P1-P4.

Tate, W. F. (2008, April). *The geography of opportunity: Poverty, place and educational outcomes.* Presidential Address presented at the annual meeting of the American Educational Research Association, New York, NY.

Unal, Z. (2008). Review of *Digital Geography: Geospatial Technologies in the Social Studies Classroom* (A. Milson & M. ALibrandi, Eds.). Retrieved January 14, 2010, from http://edrev.asu.edu/reviews/rev681.htm

White, S. (2008). Diffusion of innovations theory: Framing IT and GIS adoption In A. J. Milson & M. Alibrandi (Eds.), *Digital geography: Geospatial technologies in the social studies classroom* (pp. 169-196). Charlotte, NC: Information Age.

CHAPTER 8

FRAMING CHILDREN AS CITIZENS

A Journey From the Real World to Digital Spaces

Ilene R. Berson

Information and communication technology has an increasing influence in children's lives and is changing how they interact with their peers, families, and teachers. The infusion of information and communication technologies can be exciting and enlightening as well as confusing and overwhelming. In the world today where technological innovations are continually shifting the way we interact with others and access information, change is a never ending dynamic. As we try to make sense of events in the world, we draw on prior experience to guide our understanding, and the media plays a critical role in influencing the public agenda on issues. This chapter explores early conceptualizations of children and their place in the digital world by tracing the frames of children as objects in need of protection to current conceptualizations of children as autonomous agents engaged in civic participation within digital spaces.

Technology in Retrospect: Social Studies in the Information Age 1984-2009, pp. 133–142

INTRODUCTION TO FRAMING

Framing is a communication process that assists people in quickly making sense of the world. Shared cultural cues are used to trigger deeply held values and subsequently influence perceptions and opinions about issues affecting children. Effective communicators strategically select words and images so that intended messages are conveyed through a lens that directs the viewer's judgments about social issues. Understanding these frames provides important insight into a powerful communication element that is used to influence opinions by connecting with deeply held beliefs about principles and ideals. These frames are used by news media, political movements, and organizations for information dissemination.

However, communication is a complex process because ideas are expressed through both verbal and nonverbal cues that activate preconceived notions about the world. As people try to process overwhelming amounts of visual and auditory information, they will ignore some cues and infer meaning from relevant frames based on their own life experience. People rely on these established frames as mental shortcuts to integrate and digest the vast information that bombards them everyday. This process occurs automatically unless there is incongruity in the message (which creates a shift in the frame) or purposeful study of frames reveals the meaning that is attributed to the constructed communication. Although frames are intended to direct people to a predetermined understanding, some frames may be confusing or subject to misinterpretation. The importance of frames in communication has led to intensive study and analysis of these mental shortcuts. Research (FrameWorks Institute, 2002; Tannen, 1993) has revealed that frames can be triggered by purposeful use of words, messengers, or visual images that promote issues or influence the public toward a political cause or candidate. Subsequently, these communication elements may attract attention amid the din of excess information and sway decision outcomes regarding policy and practice.

FRAMING CHILDREN IN DIGITAL SPACES

The visual imagery of children can serve as metaphors for many concepts, such as fear, innocence, and hope for the future. These are contrasted with alternative frames of children as active, empowered citizens, especially within digitally-mediated environments. These frames have implications for the social studies classroom, particularly since these organizing principles can galvanize public support for a focused educational agenda that highlights issues related to cybersafety/cybercitizenship.

Choices in the way we frame topics associated with children in digital spaces must be made carefully and consistently in order to optimize powerful communications necessary to ensure that the public will engage in these issues. The way that a story is told in the news can influence the thinking of parents and educators and undermine constructive directions. Horrifying stories that highlight tragic consequences of technology and statistics of abuse and adverse events lead to damaging consequences for public understanding and engagement. These tactics may have initially gotten the attention of the public, but they have subsequently stagnated people's thinking and diminished opportunities for young people in a digitally connected world.

An analysis of children as symbols provides a concrete visual of the role that young people play through their civic participation in both indirect and direct ways. It is important for educators and caregivers to pay attention to how messages on technology can contribute to practices that foster positive and constructive roles for media in a child's life or lead to policies that emphasize protection and security.

THE IMPERILED CHILD

All too often, children in digital spaces are portrayed in the media in conjunction with stories involving criminal atrocities and sexual predators. News media is attracted to child cyberexploitation for its sensationalism, including personal stories of unseen predators who seek out vulnerable children online. These stories fit within a well-established news emphasis on crime – the best covered news topic in America. It is, therefore, an easy story to tell with commonly entrenched conventions. The dominant news frames reinforce and exaggerate concerns for stranger dangers online and cyber risks for youth. This contributes to initiatives that heighten distrust of others and a focus on safety measures to protect against stranger dangers rather than fostering global connections and understanding. The message of prevention and constructive engagement is lost.

While the establishment of a certain degree of public horror relative to the issue of cybervictimization was probably necessary in the early years to create public awareness of the issue, the resulting conceptual model adopted by the public has created a barrier to advancing the issue further in terms of individual behavior change, societal solutions, and policy priorities. Solutions emphasize personal safety and individual behaviors that can keep children far removed from harmful outsiders so as to prevent tragic consequences. As a result trust in online communities or the benefits of technology are eroded, and distrust of online acquaintances is perpetuated. Outsiders are demonized, and the perceived fragility and vulnerability of young people necessitates that they be protected from online communities, thereby supporting policies in schools that filter or limit access to social networks.

Another associated view of the imperiled child is that young people espouse declining values and are driven by selfishness and materialism (Amundson, Lichter, & Lichter, 2000). This popular frame diminishes the idea of children assuming a positive community role in digital spaces. Instead young people are viewed as an endangerment to one another and contribute to the risks found in cyberspace. This focus on ever-present hazards has led to a public discourse and policies that emphasize safety. The public holds negative perceptions of teens and children as "rude," "wild," or "irresponsible." In digital spaces, they have been framed as the perpetrators of cyberbullying and peer harassment.

The implications of the imperiled child news frame are clear for public policy—heightened support for more punitive and regulatory youth policies. Parents and educators will continue to spend more time worrying about controlling access to cell phones and content on the Internet, and policies focused on enrichment and development are absent from the public agenda. Consequently, policy directives related to quality learning experiences that optimize the potential of internet and communication technologies are irrelevant, given the core definition of safety as the main concern.

Genderfication Frame

A subtheme of the imperiled child frame is found in news stories and cybersafety resources that feature girls as the primary victims. Images of young girls in suburban neighborhoods whose safe homes are invaded by terrible dangers from online predators pervade public service announcements and educational internet safety resources. The stranger danger campaigns of the past portrayed stereotypes of men luring children on the playgrounds with candy and lost puppies. However, the modern day threat is from an online friend who sounds just like any other youth, using interactive digital media to form relationships with girls. Extensive media coverage portrays the Internet as the new neighborhood for child predators, which provides a cloak for those who prey on children. Parents and child professionals have become increasingly aware of child abductions and sexual exploitation which were initiated through the Internet, and in the United States computer facilitated child sexual exploitation has been acknowledged as a pervasive crime, even when statistics on youth risk suggest that the actual prevalence of online single offender crimes against girls has been exaggerated (Finkelhor, Ormrod, Turner, & Hamby, 2005).

Nonetheless, girls are portrayed as accessible, vulnerable, and unprotected. Cassell and Cramer (2007) suggest that

> the panic over young girls at risk from communication technologies is not new rhetoric in America. There has been a recurring moral panic throughout history, not just over real threats of technological danger, but also over the compromised virtue of young girls, parental loss of control in the face of a seductive machine, and the debate over whether women can ever be high-tech without being in jeopardy.

The social and cultural communities of the Internet have unique perspectives on power, identity, and gender. Identity is confounded in a virtual venue where the self is socially constructed and changing. Children may feel that they can better represent their authentic self online where social roles and personalities are formulated from more limited cues. The inner self is dynamic in a virtual venue, and multiple presentations of one's identity may enhance the positive and negative development of the individual.

Berson, Berson, and Ferron (2002) found that online dialogue is used by girls as a mechanism to empower themselves and find a voice. In face to face interactions young women may perceive that body size, facial features, and other superficial characteristics are judged as more important than personality. Conversely, online exchanges take place in a context that often is devoid of these visual cues. In cyberspace, the pressures to fit in and act a certain way are moderated by the perceived anonymity and false security of being protected behind the computer screen, often in the comfort and safety of one's home. Cyberspace provides girls a context where they can shed society's traditional expectations and explore alternative aspects of themselves (Cassell, Huffaker, Tversky, & Ferriman, 2006).

However, in many public service announcements it is common for young female users of technology to have no agency in the response to cybervictimization. Moreover, parents are portrayed as technologically deficient adults whose vulnerable teen girls have appropriated the technologies and created dangerous networks outside the family. These images transform the discourse away from the promise of technology and emphasize its misuse. The positive benefits of digital resources are obscured by the threat of harm.

FRAME OF EMPOWERMENT

While children are ascribed roles of naiveté, innocence or delinquency in the news media, in actuality, they turn out to be active and informed consumers and producers of mediated conversations and texts. Students are immersed in a world of interactive media and social networking.

Advertisers have made headway with the public and raised the volume on messages that highlight children as digital natives. Young people consume huge amounts of information through various media outlets and simultaneously create and distribute their own messages via digital technologies. In television commercials even babies and toddlers are depicted with computer skills and adult-like intentionality when interacting on the web.

The important identity construction, self-efficacy, and social network production work that children do online is not only largely ignored, but too often condemned by educators. When we view children's engagement with technology as an opportunity for fostering 21st century skills we shift toward a frame of empowerment.

When children are depicted exploring their technological prowess, they project a stronger sense of agency, and the public comes to recognize children as more likely to be empowered by technology than damaged by it. The internet allows for a tremendous potential of creative expression—expression that was not initially vetted by adults in the early images of children as victims.

CONCLUSION

The strategies employed so successfully by child advocates to generate media coverage and public awareness on cybervictimization has resulted in a vicious cycle in which new communications on the issue tend to conform to, and reinforce, the entrenched frames of fear, danger, and child protection. Images of cyberpredators have overshadowed coverage of empowered children constructively engaged with technology.

It is not surprising, then, that the public's frame of reference has perpetuated boundaries that have restricted technological affordances within educational contexts. By understanding frames and the influence of news media in reinforcing patterns of thinking with sensational events, educators can be strategic about choosing which narratives to emphasize, which to challenge, and which to downplay. A close examination of news coverage also gives advocates a window into what they are up against as they try to increase public support for student engagement with technology. The dominant child protection frame does not shift the public towards constructive thinking or rethinking of the larger policy issues.

Media coverage has presented a skewed frame of the lives of American children. The emergence of the imperiled child news frame has negative consequences and perpetuates a mischaracterization of American youth.

It paints a portrait of children in grave danger and need of protection. The challenge for advocates is to invigorate alternative frames that are more likely to set up constructive policy options. This is the challenge we accept when we "reframe"—not more of the same news, but substituting a different way of looking at the challenges and opportunities children face in order to prompt a reconsideration of our policy priorities for children.

> Making further headway in engaging the public on the issue will have to involve more than raising the volume on awareness campaigns…. Advocates have relied on the power of tragic stories and statistics to move public opinion. These tactics have been effective, but may now have reached the limits of their ability, in themselves, to change people's thinking. If they are reinforced by explanations that help people understand the problem and its solutions more clearly, communications stand a chance of having a much greater impact. (Aubrun & Grady, 2003)

A compelling role for the social studies emerges from this awareness of how to balance perceived vulnerabilities due to our reliance on technology with the opportunities for educational enhancement.

Simple and concrete models help people understand approaches and solutions. Effective frames may be composed of metaphors that help organize meaning and help define a social issue. They also may guide adults' behaviors with children and lead to policies that nurture, ignore, punish, or empower youth. For example, the National Research Council (2002) of the National Academy of Sciences created a compelling metaphor to explain why education was the most important tool on which parents and policymakers should rely when fostering safety for children in digital spaces.

> Technology–in the form of fences around pools, pool alarms, and locks—can help protect children from drowning in swimming pools. However, teaching a child to swim—and when to avoid pools—is a far safer approach than relying on locks, fences, and alarms to prevent him or her from drowning. Does this mean that parents should not buy fences, alarms, or locks? Of course not—because they do provide some benefit. But parents cannot rely exclusively on those devices to keep their children safe from drowning, and most parents recognize that a child who knows how to swim is less likely to be harmed than one who does not. Furthermore, teaching a child to swim and to exercise good judgment about bodies of water to avoid has applicability and relevance far beyond swimming pools—as any parent who takes a child to the beach can testify. (NRC, 2002, p. 187)

Regrettably, we often fail to teach our children how to swim in the new media waters. Indeed, to extend the metaphor, it is as if we are generally adopting an approach that is more akin to just throwing kids in the deep end and waiting to see what happens. To rectify this situation, a serious digital literacy agenda is needed in America. Digital literacy programs teach children and adults alike to think critically about media to better analyze and understand the messages conveyed through information and communication technologies.

The frame not only encourages schools to highlight digital literacy efforts at every level of the education process, but also the metaphor opens opportunities for other community stakeholders and government policymakers to play a role in the solution. The efforts of schools should be accompanied by widespread public awareness campaigns to better inform parents and other child serving professionals about the potential for technology to foster children's skills as citizens in the 21st century.

Digital communication is integrally connected with global understanding, multicultural respect, diversity, and tolerance. Literacy efforts empower youth to analyze, interpret, and create images and information which are disseminated in digital environments. They provide skills so youth can decipher complex messages in an informed and knowledgeable way and, thereby, counteract the temptation to react without forethought to the influence of powerful words, images, and sounds.

Within education, debate ensues as to whether current attempts to refine teaching and learning with hands-on, inquiry-based applications of technology effectively prepare students for participation in a global participatory medium. While some educators are promoting cutting edge developments in technology integration into social studies, there has been a parallel movement guiding educators to shield children and youth from a range of threats associated with digital technologies. Delving into this discourse and the range of issues being considered often reveals a confusing array of opinions and recommendations for action.

In particular, the rhetoric of the cybersafety movement initially highlighted the urgency of action through accounts of violence and victimization. Yet this focus on events often lacked unifying goals and purposes, resulting in a movement that has been less instructive and more alarmist. This chapter has explored the evolving frames of digital awareness and safety that have shifted from a focus on child protection to child empowerment.

Since schools are at the forefront of immersing young people into the digital world, educators play an integral role in preparing students for the adoption of communication technologies. This key role also comes with responsibilities and challenges to enhance the benefits of technology while minimizing risks. One of the challenges associated with digital awareness is facilitating the inclusion of these issues into the existing social studies curriculum.

However, digital literacy is not a novel area for exploration in the social studies, and several skills which are essential for cyberliteracy are already an integral component of the content area. These include competencies in understanding perspective or point of view, critical thinking skills to analyze and evaluate the validity and credibility of information, experience in accessing diverse forms of information, and exposure to digital environments.

Despite the presence of elements of digital education within curricular frameworks, many teachers continue to feel ill-prepared to assist students in understanding digital technology and the intensified flow of information through various forms of media. This is exacerbated by the fact that youth are well acclimated to the digital medium and have adjusted rapidly to it. Today's students spend more time immersed in an image-laden culture of television, movies, and video games than with static, printed text. Given the digital environment in which youth are immersed, becoming "a successful student, responsible citizen, productive worker, or competent and conscientious consumer, individuals need to develop expertise with the increasingly sophisticated information and entertainment media that address us on a multi-sensory level, affecting the way we think, feel and behave" (Alliance for a Media Literate America, 2003).

REFERENCES

Alliance for a Media Literate America. (2003). *What is Media Literacy?* Denver, CO: AMLA.

Amundson, D., Lichter, L. S., & Lichter, S. R. (2000). *What's the matter with kids today? Television coverage of adolescents in America. Reframing Youth Issues.* Washington, DC: FrameWorks Institute.

Aubrun, A., & Grady, J. (2003). *Two cognitive obstacles to preventing child abuse: The "other mind" mistake and the "family bubble."* Retrieved from http://www.issuelab.org/research/two_cognitive_obstacles_to_preventing_child_abuse_the_other_mind_mistake_and_the_family_bubble

Berson, I. R., Berson, M. J., & Ferron, J. (2002). Emerging risks of violence in the digital age: lessons for educators from an online study of adolescent girls in the United States. *Journal of School Violence, 1*(2), 51-72.

Cassell, J., & Cramer, M. (2007). Hi tech or high risk? Moral panics about girls online. In T. MacPherson (Ed.), *Digital Youth, innovation, and the unexpected: The MacArthur Foundation Series on Digital Media and Learning* (pp. 53-75). Cambridge, MA: MIT Press.

Cassell, J., Huffaker, D., Tversky, D., & Ferriman, K. (2006). The language of online leadership: Gender and youth engagement on the Internet. *Developmental Psychology 42*(3), 436-449.

Finkelhor, D., Ormrod, R., Turner, H., & Hamby, S. L. (2005). The victimization of children & youth: A comprehensive, national survey. *Child Maltreatment, 10*(1), 5-23.

FrameWorks Institute. (2002). *Framing public issues.* Washington, DC: Author.

National Research Council. (2002). *Tools and strategies for protecting kids from pornography and their applicability to other inappropriate Internet content.* Washington, DC: Author.

Tannen, D. (Ed.). (1993). *Framing in discourse.* New York: Oxford University Press.

CHAPTER 9

WIRED TO ACT

Black Youth's Civic Engagement and Technology Use in Twenty-First Century Elections

Patrice Preston-Grimes

As we enter a new century, an informed, active citizenry remains essential to a sound democracy (Parker, 2005). Educating students to become competent and responsible citizens in the United States continues to be an established theme of interest and study in many schools, after-school programs and community organizations (Arthur, Davies, & Hahn, 2008). As educators, scholars, and parents debate the meanings and most effective approaches to teach civic knowledge, skills, and attitudes, a myriad of political, economic, and social changes during this same period has altered the climate in which students are oriented, or socialized, to participate in the democratic process (Owen, 2008). These changes can impact young adults, in particular, as they enter the civic arena for the first time and begin to identify and carve their own levels of civic participation and engagement.

Technology in Retrospect: Social Studies in the Information Age 1984-2009, pp. 143–156
Copyright © 2010 by Information Age Publishing
All rights of reproduction in any form reserved.

Youth interest and involvement in the political process, for example, has shifted in recent years. Following the landmark National Voting Rights Act of 1965, youth voter turnout declined over the next 2 decades (Levine & Lopez, 2002). Black youth, in particular, were less likely than White youth to state that they could make a difference by voting or solving community problems and expressed distrust of government (Lopez, 2002). Since 2002, however, this trend has reversed (Riemer, 2006; Young Voter Strategies, 2007). Civic engagement patterns among Black, Hispanic, and Asian American youth have changed, with the most significant gains in civic participation among Black youth as evidenced in their voting in elections, their memberships in politically-oriented groups, their donations to party candidates and causes, and their contact with the media (Marcelo, Lopez, & Kirby, 2007).

At the same time, the use of technology to promote civic knowledge and action, especially via the Internet, has received increased attention. Although VanFossen (2006) has questioned the actual effectiveness of the use of websites and web logs (or "blogs") to impact voting behavior and advocacy, his conclusions may have been premature. Palfrey and Gasser (2008) also acknowledge the lack of empirical data to support the idea that new technologies have increased civic activism; however they remain cautiously optimistic that change is at hand. In their view,

> New technologies are transforming certain aspects of politics. The fundamental rules still apply, but the way the game is played is changing. Digital natives (i.e., people born after 1980 who share similar patterns of interaction with information technologies and each other) are, in many cases, leading the way. (p. 258)

Likewise, Owen (2008) cautions that survey research in political socialization is often based on white, middle class participants and does not capture contextual factors that can affect research outcomes. An increased research focus on cross-national and cross-cultural studies, Owen notes, has the "potential to identify differences in political values and orientations that are linked to particular conditions, such as those associated with stable verses newly emerging democracies" (p. 5). Wilkenfeld's (2009) emerging research on the role of multiple contexts in the development of youth's civic engagement also begins to address this gap. In that study, data analyses of the 1999 U.S. sample of the IEA Civic Education Study merged with 2000 U.S. Census data determined that there is a "civic engagement gap" among U.S. youth associated with one's individual demographic characteristics. In other words, one's family, friends, school, and neighborhood community can play a key role in shaping youth civic identify and development.

The remainder of this chapter examines the efforts for one such con-stituency, African American youth, and the ways in which technology has played a role in disseminating information to support their civic and political participation. Although there are many characteristics that can elucidate variations of civic engagement within any identified group (i.e. class, gender or economic level), the ways in which race has factored into past and present concepts of civic engagement in the United States is remains a fundamental, and often ignored area of study, especially in social studies classrooms (Howard, 2003). Therefore, I begin this chapter by examining historical and current trends in civic engagement among Black youth. Next, I describe the role of technology to support civic engagement and dialogue, with a description of the unique convergence of these factors in the 2008 election of the nation's first Black President, Barack Obama. I conclude the chapter with suggestions for further study, specifically as they relate to promoting civic literacy and sustained demo-cratic action among Black youth and other underrepresented groups.

PAST CIVIC ENGAGEMENT IN BLACK COMMUNITIES

Prior to the Civil Rights movement of the 1950s and 1960s, teaching and practicing education for citizenship was an established practice in many African American segregated schools, especially in the South (Preston-Grimes, 2007). Black educators and their leaders taught and modeled democratic principles to students in many ways, in spite of the racial and social discrimination that existed in the larger society.

With the advent of school desegregation, however, key institutional and community structures that supported Black students' civic learning and practice were dismantled, due in part, to the closure of many racially sep-arate schools (Irvine & Irvine, 1983). Consequently, many Black students were relocated to formerly all-White schools with White teachers and administrative staffs. This change in school context and the subsequent massive reduction of the Black public school teaching force (related to school consolidations) suggest that it was difficult for Black students to receive the "politically relevant teaching" that accompanied their civic education in segregated schools (Beauboeuf-Lafontant, 1999; Preston-Grimes, 2010). Without that support, Black students (and their families) had to navigate on their own how to make sense of teaching civic ideals in a racially charged and transitional climate.

By the early 1970s, civic engagement, as measured by the attitudes of Black adolescents in selected U.S. cities, reached an unprecedented low. Studies of political socialization processes among Black youth, for exam-ple, identified variables that contributed to the students' low levels of political efficacy and high levels of political cynicism (Dennis, 1969; Greenberg, 1970; Lyons, 1970). Consistent with these findings, Rodgers (1974) distinguished "trust in mankind" as a key variable to explain Black public school students' negative beliefs that they could not influence the political process, which included (but was not limited to) the election of public officials. Even through Rodgers identified increases in students' political knowledge with civic education, he concluded "only through alternations in the political fortunes of blacks can their feelings of political efficacy and political cynicism be shifted toward more supportive political attitudes" (p. 279). Of note, the findings did not support feelings of Blacks' personal inadequacy, but attributed their negative beliefs to feeling excluded from the larger political decision-making processes in their communities.

In recent years, measures of youth civic engagement indicate disparities remain between Black adolescents and other groups (Beaumont, 2004; Gimpel & Lay, as cited Levine & Youniss, 2006; Rubin, 2007). However, current data suggest that among minority youth, African Americans are the most politically engaged racial/ethnic group (Marcelo, Lopez, & Kirby, 2007). Although some researchers now define engagement to consist of voting, membership in mainstream political organizations, and working for political campaigns, others measure youth engagement more broadly to include participation in community service efforts and individual acts of volunteerism for civic and social causes (Levine & Youniss, 2006). The 2006 Civic and Political Health of the Nation (CPHN) survey, for example, cites 19 "core indicators of civic engagement [to describe] civic, electoral and political voice activity" and youth attitudes about government and current events (Lopez et al., 2006, p. 7). Nevertheless, the CPHN study concluded that although the trends in civic engagement are rising, majority of youth between ages 15 to 25 are not involved in civic efforts.

It is important to note that the definition of civic engagement continues to evolve, as twenty-first century youth move beyond prescribed agendas of past eras to define and participate in their own causes. At a 2003 higher education conference, one black student activist described his generation's actions as "new student politics" that can be expressed in various ways like writing, rapping, or making flyers for a cause (Hamilton, 2003, p. 20) Longo, Battistoni, and Drury (2006) concur that in the millennium, students often target civic efforts toward causes in which they believe that they can make a difference as an individual. Volunteering at community service agencies and participating in nonpartisan activities, such as fundraising for health and environmental causes, are ways that today's youth think one person can tackle large and often complex social issues—and be effective. Central to this growing trend is the idea that becoming a "good citizen" does not begin with allegiance to a group identity or political party, but can start with a solo effort, then link to others who share the same point-of-view (Hamilton, 2003). Taken together, these factors set the stage for youth to seek new ways to acquire civic knowledge and skills, and to act on their beliefs outside of traditional structures and organizations. With access and support, technology can become the younger generation's tool of choice to develop political voice.

THE ROLE OF TECHNOLOGY

At the start of the twenty-first century, the creation of Web 2.0 on the World Wide Web marked a new era of communications. This technology enabled computer users to share information and change website content. Unlike noninteractive websites (e.g., Web 1.0), where site managers posted information for passive viewing, Web 2.0 enabled users to collaborate, modify, and retrieve specific online information. Often called "the participatory web," examples of Web 2.0 websites include applications like social networking services, video-sharing sites, Wikis and blogs (short for "web blog"). Owen (2008) aptly states that Web 2.0 has "allowed people, especially younger citizens, to form their own groups that meet and act both digitally and offline" (p. 16).

One example of the rising popularity of Web 2.0, especially among minority youth, is the use of social networking services, that is, online groups of people who "join a community" to share similar interests and ideas. Community Connect, Inc (CCI) is the parent company of three such sites—AsianAvenue, BlackPlanet, and MiGente—that record sizeable membership. Byrne (2008) describes their growth,

> AsianAvenue was introduced in 1997, and in less than two years, it became the leading Asian American Web site, garnering more than 2.2 million members by March 2002. As a result of this success, BlackPlanet was launched in September 1999. In the first year, more than 1 million members joined BlackPlanet, and by April 2002, its community expanded to 5.3 million members. Both AsianAvenue and BlackPlanet have consistently ranked among the highest trafficked sites for their respective ethnic markets.... MiGente was launched in October 2000, and is considered the most popular English-language community for Latinos. More than 500,000 members registered within the first two years. (p. 16)

The success of these specialized sites, as compared to more mainstream social networks, such as MySpace and Facebook, is their direct appeal to racial and ethnic minority teens and young adults, and their stable membership numbers over time (Byrne, 2008).

Given their communication capacity and potential, social networking sites are a logical avenue to promote civic engagement and "online activism." By definition, this new type of involvement is "done with the assistance of the Internet and other information and communication technologies (ICTs) as an *intentional* [emphasis added] means of political action" (Adler & Goggin, as cited in Remtulla, 2008, p. 278). Remtulla further identifies three types of online activism: (1) awareness/advocacy, in which information from alternative sources is posted online, (2) community oriented sites that "seek to build relationships and share dialogue" (p. 269), and (3) action groups that rally for specific social causes online. Deliberate online acts include members signing e-mail petitions and contacting local media/officials, via site links, to express points-of-view.

Two websites in particular—Rock the Vote (http://www.rockthevote.com) and Hip-Hop Summit Action Network (http://hsan.org)—promote social networking features with information geared towards political advocacy for youth. As its name implies, Rock the Vote (RTV) has a primary purpose: to engage youth for democratic participation through voting and voter registration efforts. Headquartered in Washington, DC, this nonprofit organization is run by a paid staff that supervises a nationwide field organization. From its beginnings in 1990, RTV has enlisted entertainment artists to spread its message to English and Spanish language speakers via personal appearances, concerts, and media public service announcements. Its website touts its accomplishments, citing that RTV "ran the largest youth voter registration drive in history in 2008," enlisting 2.6 million voters via direct mail, phoning, online, and in-the-field canvassing. In addition to voter registration efforts and issue advocacy, RTV encourages youth to investigate social issues and voice their opinions at public forums.

On a broader scale, the *Hip-Hop Summit Action Network* (HSAN, n.d.) is another website that is dedicated to "social, political and economic development and empowerment" with a wide ranging agenda that spans civic, environmental, and public health issues. Music mogul and millionaire Russell Simmons founded HSAN in 2001, believing that the music artistry and youth culture that emerged from the streets of Bronx, New York were ripe to capture and channel their attention towards socially relevant causes. Its board of directors is a virtual "who's who" of key music and entertainment industry decision makers who wield enormous influence beyond the music industry. Annually, HSAN hosts open dialogue programs in major U.S. cites to register voters and conducts youth leadership forums. One of its featured online sites is titled, "Get Your Money Right," to encourage youth, especially in financially hard-hit communities, to develop economic literacy skills needed in the current domestic and global climates.

Although Rock-the-Vote and Hip-Hop Summit Action Network do not claim subscription membership numbers of other social networks (e.g., Facebook, MySpace), they are two of a growing number of interactive websites designed to provide a path in the digital milieu for new and underrepresented voices. Their potential to widen that critical public space merits further study. Interestingly, it was the savvy foresight of a young, ambitious politician at the center of the political mainstream who harnessed social networking's capabilities to craft one of the most unpredicted intersections of civic engagement, youth participation, and technology in U.S. history.

THE AGE OF ELECTRONIC ENGAGEMENT

The November 2008 history-making election of freshman U.S. Senator Barack Obama to the nation's presidency "usher[ed] in an era of profound political and social realignment in America" (Helman & Kranish, 2008, p. 1). From the moment of announcing his 2007 candidacy via YouTube, to his election night acceptance speech seen and heard by millions around the world, the skillful use of communications media and technology launched his campaign message (and political brand) to victory. A blogger on Mathoda.com summed up the impact of Obama's plan,

> Thomas Jefferson used newspapers to win the presidency, F. D. R[oosevelt] used radio to change the way he governed, J. F. K[ennedy] was the first president to understand television, and [2004 U.S. presidential hopeful] Howard Dean saw the value of the Web for raising money.... But Senator Barack Obama understood that you could use the Web to lower the cost of building a political brand, create a sense of connection and engagement and dispense with the command and control method of governing to allow people to self-organize to do the work. (Carr, 2008, p. 2)

Hence, Obama's consistent delivery of a clear, invitational political message and his effective technology use to reach diverse audiences were crucial elements that produced a successful get-out-the-vote campaign that won the election.

The Obama campaign's communications plan was threefold: (1) use the Internet as a portal to campaign, fundraise, and deliver his campaign positions, (2) craft campaign messages—written and visual—to post (and update regularly) via social networking sites, and (3) diversify media and technology outlets to include the traditional (e.g., radio, television, and newspapers) and the novel (e.g., cell phone ring tones, text messaging). In the process, the Obama organization created virtual, grassroots civic space for thousands of Americans, especially voters ages 18-29, to engage in political dialogue in ways that they had never experienced on such a magnified scale (Ogilvy CEO, 2008, pp. 2-3).

Obama's Internet (media) plan was the brainchild of Facebook founder Chris Hughes, who worked without pay throughout the campaign to oversee the social networking organization. As a key advisor and consultant, Hughes was instrumental in launching the mybarackobama.com website during the crucial, early months of the 2007-2008 Democratic primary campaign season. The site contained position statements, campaign news updates, photos, videos, blogs, and chat rooms. The campaign joined many social networks, including the CCI group, Facebook, Faithbase, and MySpace; within days, thousands of people began "friending" Obama on the campaign trail. As the campaign progressed, Obama's materials were updated and uploaded. Those who did not have Web access or preferred to be contacted in traditional ways received phone calls, direct mail solicitation and/or face-to-face canvassing calls (Ogilvy CEO, 2008, pp. 4-5)

By Summer 2008, mybarackobama.com morphed into the Obama for America website; in January 2009, it evolved into Organizing for America, continuing the grassroots website's mission to lobby for legislation reflecting party positions on the economy, energy, health care, and education. Key Obama campaign strategist Mitch Stewart manages the site that is updated regularly.

From its first appearance on the 1996 political campaign trail to its current implementation through the Internet/websites, social networks, and media/tech strategists, technology has secured a place in American political organizing and advocacy. For some participants in this Web 2.0 age, digital tools will aid their entry into a civic community; for others, it may hinder it. Palfrey and Gasser (2008) conclude,

> They [youth] didn't get involved in politics because of the technology, but the technology became the medium that drew them together. The Internet became the common network, both literally and figuratively, of a new generation of activists who came of age in 2004, 2006 and 2008 election cycles. (p. 260)

Although some aspects of twenty-first century campaigning have changed from past eras, the fundamental reasons for civic education and participation—to acquire and demonstrate the knowledge, skills, and attitudes to be a contributing community member—remain constant. The last section examines how Black youth responded to the 2008 civic call and presents implications for their future engagement and participation.

VOICES OF YOUTH—2008 AND BEYOND

America's youth participated actively in the history-making 2008 U.S. presidential election. Voting 2 to 1 in favor of Barack Obama, their voter turnout as a group registered 11 percentage points higher than voting youth in 1996. To their credit, African American youth posted the highest voter turnout for any racial or ethnic group in a national election since 1972; Obama received 95% of the Black youth vote and nearly 100% of the African American female vote (Todd & Gawiser, 2009; Youth Vote, 2009, pp. 1-2). Of the District of Columbia and 11 states with the highest proportion of African Americans, Obama won in seven (Delaware, District of Columbia, Illinois, New York, Maryland, North Carolina, and Virginia).

If voter turnout remains a key indicator of civic engagement, the findings suggest that Obama received an overwhelming vote of confidence from two constituent groups—youth and African American women (Todd & Gawiser, 2009; Youth Vote, 2009, p. 5). As national youth voter registration numbers may inch upward from 2006 and 2008 benchmarks, it is important for educators, as well as future candidates, to consider ways to harness this momentum and the newly identified capacity of technology to support younger constituents of underrepresented groups in their civic engagement efforts.

In spite of the euphoria that accompanied Obama's election night victory, concerns remain. Many eligible young people neither registered nor voted, even with unprecedented efforts to reach them via technology and grass roots campaign strategies. A newly released CIRCLE and Spencer Foundation study provides insight into this issue. Findings indicate that some youth who are not college educated are less likely to vote than their college-educated peers (Youth Vote, 2009, pp. 4-5). This is consistent with Kirby, Marcelo, and Kawashima-Ginsberg's (2009) findings that young people who lack higher education are not as involved as their college peers in other civic acts, including volunteering. Differences in civic participation between college and noncollege educated youth raise another layer of issues regarding equity, access, and use of social capital within segments of the youth population. However, the history of African American's civic participation indicates that youth can develop positive civic efficacy, in spite of adverse conditions, especially when they are approached personally to become involved, are taught their rights and responsibilities in a trusting environment, and can practice decision-making skills related to those rights (Preston-Grimes, 2007).

To be sure, the resurgence of Black youth's civic engagement, and especially voting strength, holds promise for their future civic life and our nation's political health. As a targeted constituency, Black youth rallied and demonstrated the power of technology as a political tool through their savvy Internet use and extensive social networking. By receiving and exchanging unfiltered electronic (political) messages in "real time," they communicated ideas and implemented action with a breadth and speed never before achieved and built coalitions to influence the larger electorate. In the same manner that massive public, nonviolent, organized demonstrations symbolized empowerment during the Civil Rights movement of the 1960s, the "virtual communities" that Black youth created during the 2008 U.S. presidential campaign became a springboard for students' political voice and agency. As a result, established civil rights organizations, such as the National Association for the Advancement of Colored People (NAACP) have recognized this potential and are incorporating similar new technology tools and strategies into their operations to reach wider (youth) audiences (Bromley, 2009).

Educators can also learn to improve their instruction by studying the ways in which youth implemented technology in their 2008 election participation. To begin, teachers, like their students, must become proficient with specific technology tools and applications that support civic teaching (Nebel, Jamison, & Bennett, 2009). It is no longer practical for some teachers to ignore the impact or potential influence of technology, relegating it to "the younger generation." Competent teachers seek professional development and independent learning opportunities to prepare themselves, and their students, to maximize the communication tools at hand. At the same time, teachers must continue to promote students' responsible decision-making, as students research and review online content, participate in blogs and social network forums, and publish their political and social opinions in the increasingly expanding cyberspace.

Equally important, educators should reconsider their own definitions of what constitutes meaningful citizenship education, in light of the influences of race, gender and status on our nation's founding and governance. As Tyson (2003) notes,

> we must look at schools in the context of a society governed by class, caste, and entitlement and examine the role race plays in inculcating and endorsing the values of a dominant society. We must examine in depth the social reality for many Americans who in our not so distant past were denied basic civic (citizen) rights. (p. 19)

Tyson concludes that teachers who consider the historical and social conditions that have shaped the Black youth's civic engagement are more likely to create relevant teaching strategies to promote their critical thinking, quality dialogue, and thoughtful decision making, particularly when they present topics, through different lenses ... different properties than the ones deeply established in the consciousness of American society. These different perspectives engender many possibilities, particularly opportunities to transform an ideology of enslavement and oppression, to one of economic, political and social equality. (p. 21)

From the events of the 2008 presidential election, an active, Black youth constituency emerged to redefine what it means to be an engaged citizen. Clearly, they demonstrated that targeted technology use provided entry into a democratic (voting) process that had not always welcomed their participation.

Comprehensive, critical instruction of civic knowledge and skills, coupled with thoughtful technology application, has the potential to help all youth develop attitudes that will promote long-term civic participation, both inside and outside of the classroom. Ideally, our learning environments, like the world-at-large, will reflect the multiplicity of ideas and expressions to help youth make wise choices as they navigate their life experiences and public spaces.

REFERENCES

Alder, R. P., & Goggin, J. (2005). What do we mean by "civic engagement?" *Journal of Transformative Education, 3*(3), 236-253.

Arthur, J., Davies, I., & Hahn, C. (Eds.). (2008). Education for citizenship and democracy in the United States (pp. 263-278). *The SAGE Handbook of Education for Citizenship and Democracy.* Los Angeles: SAGE

AsianAvenue [social networking site]. (n.d.). Retrieved January 10, 2010, from http://www.asianave.com/

Beauboeuf-Lafontant, T. (1999). A movement against and beyond boundaries: Politically relevant teaching among African American teachers. *Teachers College Record, 100*(4), 702-723.

Beaumont, E. (2004). *Engaging students politically goes beyond the voting booth. Carnegie perspectives.* Stanford, CA: Carnegie Foundation for the Advancement of Teaching.

BlackPlanet [social networking site]. (n.d.). Retrieved January 10, 2010, from http://www.blackplanet.com/

Bromley, A. (2009). *Civil rights pioneer presents new face: Young president of the 100-year-old NAACP.* Retrieved November 3, 2009, from http://www.virginia.edu/uvatoday/newslease.php?print=1&id=10210

Byrne, D. N. (2008). The future of the race: Identity, discourse, and the rise of computer-mediated public spheres. In A. Everett (Ed.). *Learning race and ethnicity: Youth and digital media* (pp. 15-38), Cambridge, MA: MIT Press.

Carr, D. (2008). *How Obama tapped into social network's power.* Retrieved December, 31, 2008 from The New York Times.com website: http://www.nytimes.com/ 2008/11/10/business/media/10carr.html?pagewanted=print

Dennis, J. (1969). *Political learning in childhood and adolescence: A study of fifth, eighth, and eleventh graders in Milwaukee, Wisconsin.* Madison, WI: Wisconsin Research and Development Center for Cognitive Learning

Greenberg, E. S. (1970). Children and government: A comparison across racial lines. *Midwest Journal of Political Science, 14,* 267-273.

Hamilton, K. (2003). Activists for the new millennium. *Black Issues in Higher Education, 20(5),* 16-21.

Helman, S., & Kranish, M. (2008, November 5). Historic victory: Obama elected nation's first African-American president in a romp. *The Boston Globe,* pp. A1, A12.

Hip-Hop Summit Action Network. (n.d.). Retrieved January 10, 2010, from http://hsan.org

Howard, T. (2003). The dis(g)race of the social studies. In G. Ladson-Billings (Ed.), Critical race theory perspectives on social studies: The profession, policies, and *curriculum* (pp. 27-43). Greenwich, CT: Information Age.

Irvine, R. W., & Irvine, J. J. (1983). The impact of the desegregation process on the Education of Black students: Key variables. *The Journal of Negro Education, 52(4),* 410-422.

Kirby, E. H., Marcelo, K. B., & Kawashima-Ginsberg, K. (2009). *Volunteering and the college experience.* Retrieved January 3, 2010, from University of Maryland, Center for Information and Research on Civic Learning and Engagement (CIRCLE) website: http://www.civicyouth.org/PopUps/ FactSheets/College_Volunteering.pdf

Levine, P., & Lopez, M. H. (2002) *Youth voter turnout has declined by any measure.* Retrieved January 28, 2004 from University of Maryland, Center for Information and Research on Civic Learning and Engagement (CIRCLE) website: http://www.civicyouth.org/research/products/fact_sheets_outside.htm

Levine, P., & Youniss, J. (2006). *Youth civic engagement: An institutional turn.* CIRCLE Working Paper 45 from University of Maryland, Center for Information and Research on Civic Learning and Engagement (CIRCLE).

Longo, N., Battisoini, R., & Drury, C. (2006). Catalyzing political engagement: Lessons From civic educators from the voices of students. *Journal of Political Science Education, 2(3),* 313-329.

Lopez, M. H. (2002). *Civic engagement among minority youth.* Retrieved January 28, 2004, from University of Maryland, Center for Information and Research on Civic Learning and Engagement (CIRCLE) website: http://www.civicyouth.org/ research/areas/race_gender_outside2.htm

Lopez, M. H., Levine, P., Both, D., Kiesa, A., Kirby, E., & Marcelo, K. (2006). *The 2006* Civic and political health of the nation: A detailed look at how youth participate *in politics and communities.* College Park, MD: Center for Information and Research on Civic Learning and Engagement (CIRCLE).

Lyons, S. R. (1970). The political socialization of ghetto children: Efficacy and cynicism. *Journal of Politics, 32,* 288-302.

Marcelo, K. B., Lopez, M. H, & Kirby, E. H. (2007). *Civic engagement among minority youth.* Retrieved January 22, 2009, from University of Maryland, Center for Information and Research on Civic Learning and Engagement (CIRCLE). website: http://www.civicyouth.org/PopUps/FactSheets/FS_07_minority_ce.pdf

MiGente: The power of Latinos [social networking site]. (n.d.). Retrieved January 10, 2010, from http://www.migente.com/

Nebel, M., Jamison, B., & Bennett, L. (2009). Students as digital citizens on Web 2.0. *Social Studies and the Young Learner, 21*(4), 5-7.

Ogilvy CEO: New media key to Obama campaign. (2008, December 31). EurActive.com, 1-5. Retrieved December 31, 2008, from http://www.euractiv.com/en/pa/ogilvy-ceo-new-media-key-obama-campaign/article-1768

Owen, D. (2008, September). *Political socialization in the twenty-first century: Recommendations for readers.* Paper presented at a meeting of the Center for Civic Education and the Bundeszentrale fur politische Bildung, James Madison's Montpelier. Orange, VA.

Palfrey, J., & Gasser, U. (2008). *Born digital: Understanding the first generation of digital Natives.* New York: Basic Books.

Parker, W. C. (2005). *Social Studies in elementary education* (12th ed). Upper Saddle River, NJ: Pearson Prentice Hall.

Preston-Grimes, P. (2007). Teaching democracy before *Brown*: Civic education in Georgia's African American schools 1930-1954. *Theory and Research in Social Education, 35*(1), 9-31.

Preston-Grimes, P. (2010). Fulfilling the promise: African American educators teach for democracy in Jim Crow's South. *Teacher Education Quarterly, 37*(1), 35-52.

Riemer, H. (2006). *Young voter turnout surges in 2006.* Retrieved March 23, 2007 from, http://rockthevote.com

Remtulla, K. A. (2008). Democracy or digital divide?: The pedagogical paradoxes of online activism. In D. E. Lund & P. R. Carr (Eds.), *Doing democracy: Striving for political literacy and social justice* (pp. 267-280). New York: Peter Lang.

Rock the Vote: Building political power for young people. (n.d.). Retrieved January 10, 2010, from http://rockthevote.com

Rodgers, H. R. Jr. (1974). Toward explanation of the political efficacy and political cynicism of Black adolescents: An exploratory study. *American Journal of Political Science, 18*(2), 257-282.

Rubin, B. C. (2007). There's still not justice: Youth civic identity development amid distinct school and community contexts. *Teachers College Record, 109*(2), 449-481.

Todd, C., & Gawiser, S. (2009). *How Barack Obama won: A state-by-state guide to the historic 2008 Presidential election.* New York: Vintage Books.

Tyson, C. A. (2003). A bridge over troubled water: Social studies, civic education, and critical race theory. In G. Ladson-Billings (Ed.), *Critical race theory perspectives on social studies: The profession, policies, and curriculum* (pp. 15-25). Greenwich, CT: Information Age.

VanFossen, P. J. (2006). The electronic republic? Evidence on the impact of the Interneton citizenship and civic engagement in the U.S. *International Journal of Social Education, 21*(1), 18-43.

Wilkenfeld, B. (2009, May). *Does context matter? How the family, peer, school, and Neighborhood contexts relate to adolescents' civic engagement.* (CIRCLE Working paper #64). Boston: Tufts University.

Young Voter Strategies. (2007). *Young voters by the numbers: A large, growing, diverse, and increasingly active electorate.* Retrieved March 5, 2009 from http://www.rockthevote.com/assets/publications/research/rtv_young_voters_by_the_numbers-2007.pdf

The youth vote. (2009, September). *The CIRCLE research and practice roundup, 6*(2), 1-3.

CHAPTER 10

AN EXAMINATION OF TECHNOLOGY USE IN MIDDLE SCHOOL SOCIAL STUDIES CLASSROOMS DURING THE 2008 U.S. PRESIDENTIAL ELECTION CYCLE

A Case Study

June Byng

"It is true that in teaching these additional [technology] skills, we lose class time, but this does not mean that students are learning less. They are learning differently."

—O'Hara (2000, p. 80)

OVERVIEW

As new information technologies have evolved many school districts across the United States, fearing they would be left behind in the tech

Technology in Retrospect: Social Studies in the Information Age 1984-2009, pp. 157–178
Copyright © 2010 by Information Age Publishing
All rights of reproduction in any form reserved.

race, have endeavored to integrate these tools into their school curriculum. While some educators still cringe at the mere mention of the words
(technology or computer), social studies teachers are among the myriad
educators who have found significance in daily technology use in their
classrooms (Bennett, 2005; Buchholtz & Helming, 2005; Stang & Street,
2007). One reason may be that the ability to connect easily with diverse
individuals and obtain information regarding other cultures through
technology has the power to dispel stereotypical perspectives regarding
various cultural groups (Baek & Schwen, 2006; Carano & Berson, 2007);
one of the precepts that is at the heart of the social studies.

As technology use in schools and classrooms continues to be a priority,
societies around the world have also been impacted by its use (Becker,
2001; Priest & Sterling, 2001; Rodrigues, 1997) and although many
researchers have explored student use of technology in the classroom, the
teacher's role in supporting technology use is seldom studied (Kim & Rissel, 2008). Rodrigues argues,

> Technological literacy, and its application to communications and produc-
> tivity, has become as fundamental to functioning in society as traditional
> skills like reading, writing, and arithmetic, and their application to commu-
> nications and productivity.... Yet most students don't spend enough time on
> computers daily to learn how to use them as powerful education tools.
> (p. 375)

From the study of physical geography (Carano & Berson, 2007), to
helping students with disabilities (Hasselbring & Williams Glaser, 2000;
Steele, 2007), technology use has assumed a vital role in our daily rou-
tines (DeGennaro, 2008; Rodrigues, 1997). However, can technology use
help students become more civic-minded?

Factors Influencing Technology Use in the Classroom

Franklin (2007) found that teacher preparation, teacher philosophy,
and grade level are three factors that significantly influence the use of
computers. Park and Ertmer (2007/2008) agree with Franklin and add
that teachers' philosophies regarding technology use in their classrooms
are influenced by their experiences during teacher preparation and their
initial classroom teaching assignment. Becker (2001) notes several factors
that determine whether or not a teacher will use computers often with students that include: (1) access to computers inside the classroom, (2) daily
class schedules, (3) pressures to cover all of the objectives set forth by the
curriculum, (4) lack of computer knowledge and proficiency, and (5) level

of technical ability. Other factors include leadership, access and availability, incentives, personnel support, and external constraints.

Barriers

Regardless of the subject area being taught, there are many barriers to technology use in the classroom (Franklin, 2007; Hasselbring & Williams Glaser, 2000; Oncu, Delialioglu, & Brown, 2007; Park & Ertmer, 2007/2008; Priest & Sterling, 2001). These barriers include, but are not limited to, *too much curriculum to cover, lack of time, and high stakes testing* (Franklin, 2007), *inadequate teacher training* (Hasselbring & Williams Glaser, 2000; Priest & Sterling, 2001), *high cost for technology* (Hasselbring & Williams Glaser, 2000), *accessibility* (Oncu et al., 2007; Park & Ertmer, 2007/2008), *availability or insufficient number of technological resources including hardware and software* (Oncu et al., 2007; Priest & Sterling, 2001; Whitworth & Berson, 2003), *applicability, influence of colleagues, teachers' skills/knowledge, and students' skills/knowledge* (Oncu et al., 2007), *teachers' beliefs about instructional technology, preferred teaching methodologies, and willingness to make changes to classroom practices* (Park & Ertmer, 2007/2008), and *immature software and lack of proper maintenance and support* (Priest & Sterling, 2001). However, despite these barriers, several positive gains have been reported, some as a result of the integration of technology in many teacher preparation programs and social studies classrooms (Whitworth & Berson, 2003).

Positive Gains

Today, many educators and students have both access and training to support their technology infusion goals. However, the "computer continues to serve the primary function of facilitating students' access to content and remain somewhat relegated to being an appendage to traditional classroom materials" (Whitworth & Berson, 2003, p. 483). The National Center for Education Statistics (NCES) (2008a) reports that nearly 10 years ago the ratio of students per instructional computer in public schools was approximately 6 and the ratio of students per instructional computer with Internet access was 9. Since that time the NCES (2008b), utilizing its Fast Response Survey System (FRSS) to track access to information technology in schools and classrooms, found many noteworthy improvements particularly in the area of Internet access.

Key findings from the most current FRSS survey on Internet access, conducted in the fall 2003, revealed that overall U.S. public schools have made steady advancements in increasing Internet access in their class-rooms. Nearly 100% of public schools in the United States had Internet access with 95% utilizing broadband connections. Thirty-seven percent of schools have a full-time paid technology director or coordinator on their campus and 88% of public schools with access to the Internet had a website. Additionally, 82% of public schools with Internet access reported that their school or district provided teacher professional development regarding integration of the Internet into the curriculum. Only 1% per-cent of schools reported not having any teachers attending such profes-sional development during the time the survey was administered.

STUDENTS LEARN DIFFERENTLY

Over the years, American youth have proven that they are extremely knowledgeable and skilled at using technology especially the Internet and synchronous and asynchronous communication. Technology has become a part of their daily lives both at home and at school. DeGennaro (2008) believes that this revelation has serious implications for the ways in which educators approach their students. When students are allowed to use technology they become more actively engaged in their classroom assign-ments. DeGennaro argues that teachers can fully engage their students by integrating successful technological approaches along with efficient peda-gogical practices. Ultimately, as students become actively engaged in interactive technological practices they will learn to function as members of a larger community of learners and their education will be well grounded in a worldwide societal context.

BENEFITS OF TECHNOLOGY USE IN THE CLASSROOM

Technology use in the classroom not only benefits students but also teach-ers. There are many tangible benefits that are derived from its use includ-ing higher student participation and improved student academic performance (Heafner, 2004; Peck, Cuban, & Kirkpatrick, 2002; Rodri-gues, 1997). Additionally, the U.S. Department of Education (2008) reported several benefits of technology use in the classroom including increased student motivation to complete assignments, increased self-esteem, increased technical skills proficiency, higher rates of completion of complex assignments, increased teamwork among students, greater utilization of external sources, and enhanced ability to make design deci-sions based on the needs of their audience. Heafner posits that utilizing technology in the classroom adds a natural ingredient which has the potential to alter the very composition of any assignment. Prior research has found that technology use in the classroom may directly impact student learning because as student self-efficacy, self-worth, and self-motivation increase, their academic performance also improves significantly. There are other tangible benefits of exposing students to technology. Peck et al. (2002) reported that technology use in the classroom can (1) guide students towards becoming more technologically literate which can result in them obtaining jobs in the future, (2) provide avenues and access to modernized pedagogical resources that may ultimately lead to enhanced student educational attainment, and (3) help school leaders move from a teacher-centered approach to a student-centered one thereby allowing students to take ownership of their own learning through engagement in multiple real-life learning activities. Rodrigues agrees with Peck et al. and adds,

> It [technology] makes our nation's businesses more productive, it makes out homes safer and more energy efficient, it makes our transportation run more smoothly, and it entertains and informs us. The promise of technology is for education includes better test scores, better student performance, and better instruction. (p. 375)

THE CURRENT STUDY

The purpose of this study was to examine the use of technology in middle school social studies classrooms during the 2008 U.S. presidential election cycle. The general research questions were: (1) How are middle school social studies educators utilizing technology in the classroom during the 2008 U.S. presidential election cycle and (2) What strategies can be identified in middle school social studies classrooms to inform future needs and forecasts for technology use in social studies classrooms?

PARTICIPANTS

Selection for study participation was based on two criteria: (1) current social studies classroom teacher, social studies department coordinator, academic dean, or principal and (2) currently serving in a middle school in the area of social studies. The three female participants in this study included two middle school social studies classroom teachers and one middle school social studies department coordinator (serving Grades 6, 7, and 8) on the same campus. One teacher serves both seventh and eighth grade students and the other is a sixth grade teacher. The department coordinator, who also doubles as a sixth grade social studies teacher, is responsible to oversee campus-wide implementation of social studies policies and practices. One teacher has been a social studies teacher at this school for almost 10 years, while the other classroom teacher has served for 4 years. All participants were previously known by the researcher as all had served on the faculty of the campus for two years prior to this study.

THE CAMPUS

The campus where all participants serve is located in a suburban school district in South Texas. The school is located in the middle class neighborhood although over 80% of the students have been identified as disadvantaged and 56% have been labeled at-risk.

Regardless of their financial standing, most students own a cell phone, iPod, digital camera, or other electronic devices which are often confiscated when they are observed using them on campus. Student use of personal technologies such as cell phones, iPods, cameras, hand-held games, and other communication devices, are prohibited on the grounds of the campus. If a student caught using such technology more than three times within the current school year, the item is seized and kept in a secure location on campus until the end school year at which time it is returned to the parent of the student.

During the 2008 school year, the campus instituted a new "no camera phone use on campus" policy to discourage students from taking pictures and recording videos of serious offenses. Regardless of this threat, many students continue to find creative ways to communicate with each other.

The Academic Excellence Indicator System (AEIS) data published by the Texas Education Agency (TEA, 2008) revealed that for the 2007-2008 school year this campus educated over 1,000 students. The ethnic makeup of the campus was as follows: 92% Hispanic, 4.4% African American, 2.9% White, 0.1% Native American, and 0.6% Pacific Islander. 48% of the teachers on this campus are of Hispanic descent, 2.9% are of African American, 47.7% White, and 1.4% Pacific Islander. 7.1% have been identified as Limited English Proficient (LEP) and 20.5% are high mobility.

Although all students are required to take social studies classes, only eighth graders are assessed on the yearly Texas Assessment of Knowledge and Skills (TAKS) test. The average years of teaching on this campus is 9.3 years with the average years of teaching service within the school district at 5.9 years. 5.7% of the teacher workforce are beginning teachers, 31.5% have 1-5 years of teaching experience, 27.7% have 6-10 years experience, 23.2% have 11-20 years of teaching experience, and 12% have over 20 years of experience. For the 2006-2007 school year, the campus spent only $9,197 (or 0.2%) on career and technology education which equates to approximately $9.00 per student. The campus group (similar campuses) spent approximately $1,815,399 (1.1%) or $59 per student on career and technology education.

DATA COLLECTION AND DATA ANALYSIS

The two principal means by which data were collected for this qualitative case study included interviews and review of secondary source documents such as district websites, instructional web pages, worksheets, and hand-outs. Data analysis consisted of first identifying participants who met the criteria related to the purpose of the study, reviewing interview transcripts several times for clarity, and reviewing secondary sources including AEIS data and classroom/school/district data. Once the data were collected they were coded and placed into similar or dissimilar categories. Finally, using cross-analysis and constant comparative data analysis (Creswell, 2005), the categories were connected in order to uncover relationships. By utilizing the constant comparative technique, the researcher continually examined and compared themes generated from the various interviews and documents. The researcher served as the chief apparatus for collecting and analyzing data and two structured interviews were conducted with the teacher participants simultaneously. The interview examined several areas including participants' knowledge, training, and experiences in technology use. After sharing the coding process and initial emerging themes with other researchers acquainted with this study, recommendations were made regarding the integration of categories. As a result, modifications to the final analysis were completed based on these suggestions.

Data was gathered via interviews that attempted to understand the following areas as they related to social studies classroom teachers: Training, Communication and Collaboration, Obstacles, Rewards, Influences, and Effectiveness. To ensure confidentiality, the identities of the subjects were kept confidential and pseudonyms were used. Participants' responses were independently analyzed and a cross-analysis was utilized in order to uncover similar or dissimilar themes between cases (Creswell, 2005).

In order to assess, elucidate, and corroborate the data, both classroom teacher participants were provided an electronic copy of the interview transcripts along with preliminary interpretations. The teachers confirmed the accuracy of the transcripts, the interpretation of the data, and the plausibility of the results. All of the data presented in this study, audiotaped or otherwise, were completely transcribed and fully scrutinized, and although the perimeters of this study did not allow the researcher to observe any classroom lessons, rich data was derived from the interview with the teachers that gave clear insight into students' response to technology use in the classroom.

While the interviews of both classroom teachers were audiotaped, due to time constraints, the department coordinator was e-mailed a copy of interview questions which was completed and e-mailed back to the researcher. As with the classroom teachers, the interview document with responder answers along with the researcher's preliminary interpretations were returned to the department coordinator for review. The department coordinator assessed, confirmed, and corroborated the data and subsequent interpretation. Additionally, a second face-to-face meeting was held with each participant during which time they were invited to ask questions about the study and thanked for their participation in the study.

Since the district where all of the participants are located has removed computer literacy as a course, classroom teachers are now responsible to integrate the use of technology into their lessons. However, the teachers on this campus have always attempted to integrate some type of technology into their lessons. The new technology integration policy requires each department to include technology lessons or projects. The eighth graders are the only students who are required to take the social studies state assessment, and in 2008 the percentage of students who met the passing standard for social studies was 89%, a 3% decline from the previous school year. However, for all participants, integrating technology into their social studies lessons is more than merely doing their job and more than fulfilling a requirement. In their responses to the interview questions, teachers reported collaborating often with their colleagues and building relationships with their students. Above preparing their students for the state assessment, all participants see their role as critical to preparing students for life.

TRAINING AND PREPARATION

Although participants reported that they did not receive any specific formal training in use of social studies technology, they acknowledged receiving basic technology training provided by their Campus Instructional Technologist (CIT), a full-time paid faculty position. In order for an individual to assume the position of CIT, he/she must have at least 3 years of classroom teaching experience and must undergo several hours of district level technology training. Additionally, all participants reported spending a great deal of their own personal time learning various systems and software products. As such, all have found creative ways to enhance the value of the technology support and equipment they receive. One teacher noted, "We make our own little games up with technology use, but besides using that, no specific programs in general." The department coordinator believes that training and preparation is driven significantly by the internal motivation and dedication of the educators and added that she often uses her own personal time "playing around with the new technology until I figure it out!"

Communication and collaboration

There is a tremendous amount of communication and collaboration among social studies teachers within the social studies department. They have also developed good working relationships with colleagues in other departments and grade levels. This is confirmed by the department coordinator who noted, "Each grade level works well to make sure each other knows how to use the technology available." During the current school year, teachers have engaged in new collaborative initiatives. For example, the teachers stated,

> This year we're going to attempt to incorporate some math concepts into social studies. 8th grade is going to do something with distance on charts and graphs. We are going to try to collaborate. Because a lot of the stuff ... I know charts and graphs overlap. I mean, we teach graphs and charts, they teach graphs and charts. Social studies teaches a lot of things that other subjects do, like science. They [science teachers] do landforms and earth processes and things like that. And we use the reading strategies. Mr. R gave me a bunch of little sheets and most of our kids use that when we do our social studies reading, so that helps.

Curriculum and Instruction

Although all district curricula are developed by district office professionals, social studies teachers have broad discretion in determining how the curriculum will be implemented. As with all other subject areas on this campus and within the district, teachers work with their department coordinators to integrate technology into their lesson plans which must be based on the district curriculum. The role of the department coordinator in supporting technology use is to "purchase all department technology." As such, the coordinator feels a sense of responsibility to ensure that the technology is "put to good use."

Obstacles

All participants agree that time is the biggest obstacle to the implementation of technology-based lessons. One teacher remarked,

I would like to do more. Sometimes you just can't because of what curriculum dictates. You can't spend a whole lot of time on it. Because I would love to spend a lot of time doing, you know, playing Jeopardy, PowerPoint and stuff with the kids, but I can't get it out as much. It's fast pace.

The other teacher added, "I think for me the obstacle is having time to learn how to use, because I use Qwizdom quite often but I have to go through the process of learning it. You need to make time for that." Qwizdom (2008) is an interactive online system that combines response system interactively, customized presentations, formative assessments, and online reporting into one complete solution. With this technology tool, students use a wireless remote to provide answers to questions. The company maintains that this technology engages, motivates, and empowers each student.

The department coordinator agreed with both teachers that time was the biggest obstacle to the implementation of technology-based lessons. However, one additional obstacle noted by the coordinator is "when you have the technology, but people [teachers] in the department won't take the time to play with it and use it." According to the coordinator, this obstacle is overcome by modeling the use of technology. The coordinator adds, "I take it [new technology] home or stay late to figure out how to use it, then show them how easy it really is. I've also offered department staff development on the technology we currently possess."

The obstacle of time, however, does not keep these teachers from making every effort to incorporate technology use into their lessons. One of the ways they deal with the time factor is to work together. One teacher stated,

I think the great thing about our sixth grade teachers is that we work together. And so, if we know there's something we want to do, we all talk about it and we say "What can you do? What can you do?" to make it happen.

The other teacher quickly added,

You know I can say that about our whole department. We all plan together. We do the same lessons, same class. We all do the same thing. So we collaborate all the time about everything. Like if you walk into my room, we're doing the same thing. We're doing the exact same thing.

Rewards

All participants cited higher student participation in classroom activities as a reward of using technology. It is important to note that passing the TAKS test was not mentioned as a reward of technology integration. One teacher noted, "[...] I have kids who have speech impediments.

Whenever I use this projector {points to the projector} or even Power-Point I have their total attention." The other teacher joined in, "For them, this is part of their life now {pointing to the newly installed overhead projector in the ceiling and the laptop}. This is everyday. This is up every-day." The department coordinator adds, "The kids love it [Qwizdom]. When we use Qwizdom, they don't even know they are learning!" All of these educators have found that their students are more engaged when they infuse their lessons with technology. One teacher noted,

> When we do the Qwizdom [...] we just started this year, so we used it the first time for geography test that we're doing, and the kids loved it. They say, "This is fun. This is fun. I love this. I love this" because they have the remotes in their hand. I told them it was a game, and when you say game {playful laughter} [...] anything that's a game [...]

Factors That Influence Technology Use

Apart from the time constraints, all participants agreed that it was up to the classroom teacher to take the initiative and learn the various systems and software that they needed to integrate into their lessons. These educators are not motivated to use technology in order to meet a district requirement. They understood the inherent value of technology integration and have seen student academic performance increase as a direct result of technology use. Moreover, the idea of technology "fit" was important to the department coordinator who stated, "I will only use technology if it fits. I won't force a lesson to fit the technology.... It makes me more aware of technology when I'm planning. I try to incorporate it as much as possible."

Effectiveness

The department coordinator believes that she is effective, "To a certain degree." She uses technology weekly in lesson presentations and also as an assessment (Qwizdom, PowerPoint, and Word." However, the lack of sufficient time is reported as the one thing that is needed in order to become more effective. She notes, "Time, time, time. It always takes time to learn new software and hardware." If she were given more time, she believes that technology could be utilized much more effectively. One example cited is "Students using a PowerPoint to create a fictional island government (End of unit assessment)." An example of an ineffective use of technology reported by the department coordinator is "teacher reading notes off of PowerPoint slides each day."

Both teachers believe that they are also being effective in their integration of technology in their classrooms. One teacher remarks, "I think that we enjoy using it … since last year each of us have had a presentation with the laptop and so we're very comfortable … we're very comfortable." When asked what they would need in order to become more effective, the teachers first applaud their district and campus for providing new projectors and technology for each classroom on their campus. However, they believe that the new equipment should be used to develop higher order thinking skills in their students. If money was not a concern, both teachers wholeheartedly agree that, "The kids would have their own laptops." They were excited about the possibilities that would open up for their students if this were to happen. They also mentioned other resources that might be beneficial for their students. One teacher explained,

> I think that [laptops for each student] would be great. I heard of something called Kendall and you download books. You buy them online and you…in 5 minutes or 10 minutes you download it on computer. You can do all sorts of things on it. I saw it when I was watching Oprah. I want one because if they are able to do that in school you can download all the assignments, they can take it home…since we're phasing out computer lit. [Computer Literacy] in the district and the teachers we would like to have higher order thinking and integrate technology in that. Because a lot of times we use it for instruction, but it's harder to apply it to the higher order thinking where the kids are more involved but, I would like a whole day on learning how to incorporate one computer to have the kids use it, not just for instruction like teaching but how can we use it where they can go up it … besides pointing … how do you use one computer.

The other teacher added that an effective use of technology would be, "Like a civic lesson even something … [like in] … government. [For example] You can pop the CD in [the computer], the kid could go through the [lesson] … that would be something. I was thinking about."

Overall, both teachers strongly believe that an effective use of technology would be to integrate various aspects into their daily lessons as appropriate. However, using technology to develop collaboration among students would depend on the goals and objectives of the lesson which is driving by the district curriculum.

Leadership Style

The department coordinator reported that she attempts to "lead by example" and makes every attempt to be "sympathetic to the struggles of teachers both in the classroom and in their personal life." This similar leadership style is evident in the teachers' approach to teaching. Both teachers adhere to a Teacher-Student Negotiated approach (Zhao, 2007) to utilizing technology in their social studies classrooms. As such, their goal is never to control everything but instead use various strategies to guide their students towards become independent thinkers and learners. One teacher described a regular day in her classroom,

> When they [students] walk in, they know exactly what they're supposed to do. Like the focus [warm-up activity] in right there [points to the focus which is written on the board]. They know the grab bag. They know … everything's on the board. They're independent. I mean, I guide them. When they walk into the classroom and I close that door, I can see everyone working. They know they're going to have a test [all students take the district social studies assessment, however, only 8th grade students are required to take the social studies state assessment]. They know what they have to do.

Although these teachers are flexibility in their approach to technology use and integration, there are classroom organizational structures in place that facilitate the smooth functioning of their lessons. One other teacher added,

> I think for me, there are some things that are very structured for me in middle school and that's the major thing they need to learn. They need the structure. Well, when they walk in, every single teacher on campus has an agenda and a focus. They have to copy the agenda and do their focus. That structure. I think every department has something else that's structured.

In response to this comment, the other teacher responded, "we cannot do that [technology integration in 7th and 8th grade] without structure [the structure provided by 6th grade teachers]. It's hard." Again, these educators viewed their roles beyond that of the classroom teacher. They believed that their role is to prepare their students for real life experiences including moral values. The teacher continued,

> sometimes they [students] work in groups and sometimes they don't. It just depends. I know I'm very strict. The kids say, "She's mean. She's mean." But it's just because you're trying to teach them right from wrong and you're trying to teach them how to grow and be responsible … I do try to do fun things that the kids are gonna like doing. [The other teacher nodded in agreement.]

It was evident throughout this interview that these two teachers were extremely supportive of teach other both as professionals and also supportive of the goals and objectives of the department as a whole. For example, one teacher reported, "I do try to do fun things because that's what the kids are gonna like doing." "She does," replied the other teacher, "In her defense she's very fun. She's very fun.... You do a lot projects. She does awesome projects." During the interview the teachers also made connections to their own school experiences and how they have shaped the way in which they approach their craft. It is apparent that reflecting on their prior experiences has allowed them to be sympathetic to the needs of their students who mostly come from low socioeconomic backgrounds. One teacher offers a possible explanation:

> mostly that's because [that's] the way I am. I remember when I was in school and when we only did book work I just had a hard time. And, so I know some kids need projects and they need to move and they need different things.

Preparing Future Teachers

Both teachers encourage future teachers to become fully acquainted with popular social studies software and other products such as Qwizdom and Thinking Maps (graphic organizers). Additionally, since the only technical support that teachers receive comes from their CIT, they must be willing to invest personal time in order to learn these software and equipment. A strong motivating factor that helps to ensure that teachers integrate some type of technology into their lessons is the school district's technology integration requirement. However, since the district does not specify the extent or depth to which technology must be incorporated many teachers only accomplish the minimum requirement. The district technology integration policy does not appear to be an agonizing task for these social studies teachers who understand the value of technology and have found creative ways to utilize technology on a daily basis. Finally, in order to adequately prepare future middle school social studies teachers and coordinators, the department coordinator recommends that future preparation courses demonstrate to new teachers "Ways of using various forms of technology as assessment [because].... When our students graduate, they will not take pencil and paper tests in their jobs!"

Priority

A priority for social studies agreed upon by all participants is the procurement of laptops for each student. As one teacher noted, "If I had laptops I could move mountains with some of these kids. Some of the kids

who have a hard time focusing on the board [even though] they have it right in front of them." The department coordinator believes that assessment is a priority for technology use in middle school social studies classrooms and notes, "I think teachers need to let the kids show their knowledge through pod casts, wikis, blogs, websites, etc."

Relationship With Students

The participants in this study believe that the teacher-student relationship is the backbone of academic achievement. Each year teachers are expected to spend the first 2 weeks of school engaged in "Getting to know you" activities. As a result of this campus culture, both teachers' believe that their relationship with their students is one of the most, if not the most, important part of their job. This may explain why none of the participants mentioned student discipline as a barrier to integrating technology tools in their daily classroom instruction. One teacher shared an impromptu story which demonstrates the strong relationship being developed between the teachers and students on this campus. Excitedly, this teacher reported that on the day of the interview she became upset at her first period class because they did not complete their focus. As such, she informed them, "you're getting a zero because you didn't do your focus." After her students pleaded with her to give them another chance, she agreed, but added, "I'll give you a chance, [but] when I call you, you better know the answers." After about 10 minutes, during which time there was a campus-wide fire drill, she expected that some of the students did not have time to meet the challenge. What happened next surprised her. She notes, "They answered every last question *without looking* ... I actually spoke the question, they knew the answer and they were hard questions to do it just from memory." She was pleased that her students were able to rise to the occasion. They had showed her that they were able to do the work and added, "Okay, you don't get the zero...I was so mad at first." She jokingly told them, "Okay, you were lucky this time." Later, when the class reviewed the material in preparation for the quiz, the teacher reported that, "They knew every answer to every question. [The students answered, "This is J this is K."

This teacher also made a clear connection to her prior experiences, the use of technology, and her relationship with her students. Sharing her experience on the other campus, she mentioned the added value of technology on her current campus and compares it to the lack thereof on the previous campus. She reports,

"I did my student teaching in other schools. It's difficult. I felt so bad for the challenges they [students] have to go through. I mean nothing like this [pointing to the presentation system]. [The students would say] That was so boring. I would lose them." Although she had the same type of relationship with these current students as she did with the other students, she realized that students in her previous school still were at a disadvantage because they did not have access to many of the technology that she has come to attribute increasingly to improved student participation and engagement.

It was also apparent that both teachers felt a sense of duty, responsibility, and pride in their work with the students within their campus community. They view their school and classroom as a place where students can accomplish their goals, a place where they can learn, grow, and be successful. One teacher reports,

> that's why I'm so proud of working here at this school is because no matter what a child is going through at home if they come here they can learn. They can learn here. Put aside their problems for a little bit. They may not have paper but we give them every opportunity to learn and we don't put obstacles, we try to [encourage them].

TECHNOLOGY USE DURING
THE 2008 PRESIDENTIAL ELECTION CYCLE

In the month of October, 2008, this middle school campus, and all campuses within the district held mock online elections during the 2008 presidential election cycle. The campus utilized a website, Quia, which displayed the two nominees and their respective platforms and "the kids went on there and they clicked for the person they wanted to vote for" explains one teacher. The election was open to every student on campus who voted during his or her social studies period. Although each student was able to cast a secret ballot, the ways in which they received information about the candidates varied. On this campus, social studies teachers used a single laptop, located in a secure area of the classroom. Prior to voting, they presented the issues as they related to each candidate's position. Some social studies teachers provided written information about each candidate and where they stood on the issues. As one of the teachers walked over to the area where the laptop is located, she proudly pointed to the laptop and remarked, "This was our voting booth. I sat my kids right here and they voted in the corner in private. They had to stand in line. If I had a curtain I would have used that." This entire process took about 10 to 15 minutes.

The other teacher explained how she and others took a different approach to providing information to the students regarding the candidates' positions. As such the process took a full day to complete. These teachers presented the issues, without revealing the name of the candidate. The teacher reported,

> it did take a long time because we had a paper and we didn't have the names of the nominees and their platforms were there. So we took the whole day because we went over each platform and the kids really didn't understand every single thing. Like they had questions about some of the vocabulary, so we explained them as unbiased as we can possibly do it.

The teacher proceeded to explain the rationale behind the decision to withhold the candidates' names from the platform handout:

> It [the student handout] didn't have which candidate was for which platform and they asked us "Why won't you tell us?" We said because we want you to vote based on what your true feelings, what you really think. If you vote for who you think it may be your parents or maybe ... it should be based on what you like. So, and when we told them later, some of them said, "Oh, but I wanted to vote for McCain and I voted for Barack. Oh, but I wanted Barack and I voted for McCain.

During the discussion of the 2008 mock presidential election, one teacher suggested, "You know maybe we can do that [mock election] when we have district" Immediately, the other teacher finished her sentence, "Yeah, local elections" The other teacher added, "Right, local elections. They [the students] can understand the difference between local government and [national government] ... and federal government and state government." This was a very exciting moment as the teachers appeared to see the possibilities for extending the students' experiences voting in the mock presidential elections to other areas of civic participation. During a brief follow-up meeting with the department coordinator, she again mentioned that their campus would welcome actual voting machines that could be used campus-wide for mock elections including local elections. By using real, live machines, students would also be exposed to the various ballot initiatives that have the potential to impact their school, community, city, state, or nation. "I don't see why we can't have that on our campus," exclaims the department coordinator. Overall, both teachers are pleased with the way in which their classes have progressed so far this year and they believe that their students have learned a great deal in a short space of time.

IMPACT OF STATE ASSESSMENT

While both teachers and the department coordinator see the value in technology integration, it was evident that their perspectives regarding its use were somewhat different. Classroom teachers were more concerned with student learning, personal growth, and ability to function outside of the classroom. The department coordinator, while just as concerned with aspects of students' personal growth and development mentioned by the teachers, also advocates using technology to assess student performance. For example, she stated that an effective use of technology would be "Students using a PowerPoint to create a fictional island government" as part of an end of unit assessment. Additionally, her own technology use is mostly limited to preparing weekly lesson presentations and assessment on Qwizdom, PowerPoint, and Word. Early assessments are vital as they provide a glimpse into a student's future performance on the state assessment and school leaders must make decisions regarding additional tutorials, staffing, and resources in order to provide supplemental services to students who are in jeopardy of failing the state test.

One area that did not receive significant attention during the interview but was briefly discussed was the impact of state assessment on the use of technology in the classroom. Regarding the use of technology projects, the 7th/8th grade teacher reported, "The 7th graders are like that [like the 6th grade classes] because we do a lot of projects. [In] 8th grade, we can't do as much. The stakes are too high and they have so much information [to learn in order to prepare for the test]." It is important to note that although the impact of state testing could have been be named as an obstacle to the integration of technology, specifically for the eighth graders, this teacher did not mention this when asked the question earlier. This may be attributed to the fact that while there is less integration of technology in the eighth grade, all students are exposed to some form of technology in their social studies classroom on a daily basis.

Concluding Thoughts

This qualitative case study examined technology use in social studies classrooms during the 2008 U.S. presidential election cycle and sought to identify strategies that can be used to inform future needs and forecasts for technology use in middle school social studies classrooms. Findings revealed that technology use in the social studies classroom did not increase significantly during the 2008 presidential election cycle; however, technology use in general produces higher student participation and improved academic performance. Strategies that can inform future needs and forecasts for technology use in social studies classrooms include: (1) daily use of technology tools, (2) formal training for educators, and (3) additional time for teachers to learn new technology. The factors which

influence the use of technology in the classroom included lack of time, preparation for standardized tests, and lack of training.

Based on prior research findings, Zhao (2007) developed a Continuum of Technology Use in the Social Studies Classroom (Table 2). According to Zhao the characteristics of a Teacher-Student Negotiated classroom are as follows: (1) the teacher sets specific requirements and assigns topics, (2) the students explore a variety of information using teacher provided resources, (3) the role of technology is as a tool for accessing content information, organizing information and/or presenting findings, (4) technology tools include Internet & web-based resources, PowerPoint, Timeline, and (5) the classroom is organized around both individual and collaborative learning. The findings of this study placed these social studies classrooms squarely in the "Teacher-Student Negotiated" column. These findings provide encouragement for the teachers in this study who believe that technology should be used to guide students towards developing higher order thinking skills. Students become active participants in their own learning as a result of exposure to technology in the classroom. As the social studies teachers and school leaders on this campus continue to provide multiple technological tools in a variety of arenas, including civic participation, these teachers and this campus will be well on course to becoming student-centered

Although the social studies department in this study continues to receive the tools necessary to integrate technology and although they are provided on-site support from their department coordinator and CIT, some teachers remain unmotivated or apprehensive to incorporate technology in their daily lessons. The department coordinator acknowledges, "Sadly, many teachers are still afraid of technology. We need more teachers, who are compassionate to older learners [veteran teachers], to show those scared of technology just how easy it really is!

The participants held similar views regarding technology integration in their classrooms. They believed that technology use allowed them to be efficient, supported their instruction, and enhanced student learning. The benefits of technology extended to both teachers and students. Findings suggest that these teachers because they valued the technology tools, did not consider the district technology integration policy a burden but an advantage.

These teachers needed additional time and means of utilizing technology to provide support to students who are required to take the state assessment. These educators demonstrated that when teachers witness tangible benefits of technology integration, they are more willing to modify their instructional strategies. For social studies teachers who are responsible for grade that are not tested on TAKS, this is somewhat easier to accomplish.

The participants in this study were also willing to take a risk by introducing new technology unfamiliar to them. Teachers of the future must know that while they should understand the technology they introduce to their students, they do not necessarily have to be experts.

According to Zhao (2007) in order for students to reap all of the benefits that technology offers, teachers must be willing to assume the role of facilitator and collaborator, student must led instruction and self-decided inquiry, technology must provide a combination of tools necessary for inquiry and presentation including Internet, overhead projector, Power-Point, Microsoft Publisher, Inspiration, Timeline, digital/video camera, and pedagogy must be both individual and collaborative. Preparation programs must instill within teachers that they do not have to be the source of all technology knowledge but instead assume their role in the classroom community of learners. However, social studies classroom teachers remain the most influential person in the implementation of technology-related classroom lessons. Additionally, as new teachers enter the workforce they must observe veteran teachers modeling appropriate integration of technology in their classrooms on a regular basis. This will ensure that they too begin their educational journey with good practices. As was noted by the department coordinator in this study, modeling the effective use of technology helps teachers to feel more comfortable with the tools and is an effective way to address the lack of technology use in the classroom.

There are several implications for technology use in both the preparation and practice of social studies educators and classroom teachers in general that can be drawn from this study. These include:

1. Teacher preparation programs and district professional development training must focus on using technology to augment instructional practices.

2. Technology use and integration must be modeled by campus and district leaders continuously.

3. District curriculum and resources must incorporate technology use.

4. Social studies teachers must be allowed a reasonable amount of time to practice with new technology tools.

It was evident throughout this study that teachers are thrilled with their access to the new presentation systems. They believe that this has made an enormous difference since they have students who have trouble taking notes from oral lectures. One teacher noted, "I have kids who can't write that fast, but just by me putting my notes up [on the projector] there,

using my camera and them copying it, just looking at it … it's perfect."
The teachers believed that the majority of their students are visual learners. As such, the use of technology benefits them significantly. The other
teacher reflected on how lucky they were to have access to all of the various technologies,

> Just having the ability to use the presentation systems and now we have pro-
> jectors, and we have computer labs. We're very lucky. We're very lucky that
> we have that because not all teachers have the ability to use that or have
> access to that.

NOTE

[…] indicates inaudible material
{ } indicates participant actions
Underlined text indicates word(s) emphasized

REFERENCES

Baek, E., & Schwen, T. M. (2006). How to build a better online community: Cultural
    perspectives. *Performance Improvement Quarterly, 19*(2), 51.
Becker, H. J. (2001). *How are teachers using technology in instruction?* Paper presented
    at the meeting of the American Educational Research Association. Retrieved
    November 12, 2008 from http://www.crito.uci.edu/tlc/findings/conferences-
    pdf/how_are_teachers_using.pdf
Bennett, L. (2005). Guidelines for using technology in the social studies class-
    room. *The Social Studies, 96*(1), 38.
Buchholtz, K., & Helming, M. (2005). Making history come alive through technol-
    ogy. *Phi Delta Kappan, 87*(2), 174.
Carano, K. T., & Berson, M. J. (2007). Breaking stereotypes: Constructing geo-
    graphic literacy and cultural awareness through technology. *The Social Studies,
    98*(2), 65.
Creswell, J. W. (2005). *Educational research: Planning, conducting, and evaluating
    quantitative and qualitative research.* Thousand Oaks, CA: SAGE.
DeGennaro, D. (2008). Learning designs: An analysis of youth-initiated technol-
    ogy use. *Journal of Research on Technology in Education, 41*(1), 1-20.
Franklin, C. (2007). Factors that influence elementary teachers use of computers.
    Journal of Technology and Teacher Education, 15(2), 267.
Hasselbring, T. S., & Williams Glaser, C. H. (2000). Use of computer technology to
    help students with special needs. *The Future of Children, 10*(2), 102.
Heafner, T. (2004). Using technology to motivate students to learn social studies.
    Contemporary Issues in Technology and Teacher Education [Online serial], 4(1).

Retrieved November 12, 2008, from http://www.citejournal.org/vol4/iss1/socialstudies/article1.cfm

Kim, H. K., & Rissel, D. (2008). Instructors' integration of computer technology: Examining the role of interaction. *Foreign Language Annals, 41*(1), 61.

National Center for Education Statistics (2008a). *Internet access in U.S. public schools and classrooms: 1994-1999.* Retrieved November 25, 2008, from http://nces.ed.gov/surveys/frss/publications/2000086/index.asp?sectionid=4

National Center for Education Statistics (2008b). *Internet access in U.S. public schools and classroom: 1994-2003.* Retrieved November 25, 2008, from http://nces.ed.gov/surveys/frss/publications/2005015/index.asp?sectionid=2

O'Hara, S. (2000). The last word: Teaching in the world that is (Instead of the world that should be). *Black Issues in Higher Education, 17*(12), 80.

Oncu, S., Delialioglu, O., & Brown, C.A. (2008). Critical components for technology integration: How do instructors make decisions? *The Journal of Computers in Mathematics and Science Teaching, 27*(1), 19.

Park, S. H., & Ertmer, P. A. (2008). Impact of problem-based learning (PBL) on teacher's beliefs regarding technology use. *Journal of Research on Technology in Education, 40*(2), 247. (Original work published 2007)

Peck, C., Cuban, L., & Kirkpatrick, H. (2002). Techno-promoter dreams, student realities. *Phi Delta Kappan, 83*(6), 472.

Priest, R. H., & Sterling, D. R. (2001). Integrating technology. *The Science Teacher, 68*(3), 61.

Qwizdom Education. (2008). *Product overview.* Retrieved December 10, 2008, from http://www.qwizdom.com

Rodrigues, W.E. (1997). Raising the bar, lowering the barriers: Improving learning with technology. *Vital Speeches of the Day, 63*(12), 375.

Stang, K., & Street, C. (2007, May/June). Tech talk for social studies teachers: The Jamestown Colony: Access and Technology. *The Social Studies, 98*(3), 88.

Steele, M.M. (2007). Teaching calculator skills to elementary students who have learning problems. *Preventing School Failure, 52*(1), 59.

Texas Education Agency. (2008). *Academic Excellence Indicator System.* Retrieved December 10, 2008, from http://www.tea.state.tx.us/perfreport/aeis/index.html

U.S. Department of Education (2008). *Effects of technology on classrooms and students.* Retrieved November 25, 2008, from http://www.ed.gov/pubs/EdReformStudies/EdTech/effectsstudents.html

Whitworth, S. A., & Berson, M. J. (2003). Computer technology in the social studies: An examination of the effectiveness literature (1996-2001). *Contemporary Issues in Technology and Teacher Education, 2*(4), 472-509.

Zhao, Y. (2007). Social studies teachers' perspectives of technology integration. *Journal of Teacher Education, 15*(3), 311.

CHAPTER 11

HIGH SCHOOL UTILIZATION OF TECHNOLOGY AS A SOURCE OF INFORMATION FOR THE 2008 U.S. PRESIDENTIAL ELECTION

A Case Study

Vanessa Hammler Kenon

OVERVIEW

This case study sought to gain a clearer understanding surrounding the use of technology in social studies classrooms during the 2008 U.S. Presidential Election. As a part of this effort its focus was to observe the connection and disconnection of information, as well as the truths and mistruths surrounding data found on the Internet pertaining to the election. This concern looked at access from both a student and teacher perspective. This research also attempted to look at how the school

Technology in Retrospect: Social Studies in the Information Age 1984-2009, pp. 179–194
Copyright © 2010 by Information Age Publishing
All rights of reproduction in any form reserved.

community that was part of this study obtained and used "facts" gleaned through the Internet.

In this case study the distinct topic matter was the 2008 presidential candidates and their bid for the role as the country's highest-ranking official. As this election directly affected the future of the high school participants and their community it also looked the ways in which they made decisions that might affect their movement into the world of higher education and the global workplace.

The study was conducted at a South Texas High School Campus of 1,400 students in a large urban area. The campus academic indicator is classified by the Texas Education Agency (2007-2008) as "Academically Acceptable," and is inclusive of a large number of disadvantaged socioeconomic status Latino students. The campus culture is reflective of the urban community as a whole and a good site to conduct research reflective of the majority of the community it represents.

Background

Sharpe (2006) reports that when the World Wide Web appeared in our lives, it was as if a seed crystal had been dropped into a supersaturated solution.

> In just a few years a whole new structure came into place, linking up our desktop computers and the world of information into a new level of order. The computers were all there; what was needed was a simple, uniform way to link them. Suddenly everything was possible, as millions of people began to communicate with information servers everywhere. We are now at a similar threshold: the re-organisation of all our "smart"' things as they join the connected world. (p. 16)

The Internet and the tools it provides for learning has opened a new world of information access for students. Students are no longer limited to outdated text and information, which is often obsolete before the ink is dry.

Diem (2008) tells us the ways technology is practiced in our democracy and the consequences of these practices is important as students are prepared to take their place in this environment. Those practices are at the heart of what he calls "techno-cultural stamping," which he defines as the imprinting of the classified norms of society on its individual members (Diem, 2008). To that end, the world becomes a Global Learning Community (GLC) when a student logs online and that "techno-cultural" stamping takes on global societal implications.

The concept of global learning networks originated in rural Southern France in the early 1920s by a teacher named Celestin Freinet (Rogers, 1999). Freinet and a colleague in Brittany began an interschool collaboration which is said to have revolutionized education of the time (Rogers, 1999) and led to the *Mouvement de l'Ecole Moderne* (Modern School Movement). By 1966 at the time of Freinet's death, his network had grown to over 10, 000 schools in 33 countries.

Web based learning where students' study and work together globally by way of the World Wide Web offers many opportunities to utilize more on line versions of Freinet's learning community ideas. This mode of learning offer students a high school college bridge as well as a global one. Web based learning bridges many of these gaps in an attempt to make education programs more interesting to the technology savvy youth population of today. These digital technologies and expanding new international communities are closing spatial and temporal gaps while opening the doors to many socioeconomically disadvantaged students to new technology and cultures (Buzzetto-More, 2006).

Economics, Culture, and Access

Technology has made the educative process easier for those who know how to navigate it, but it poses a barrier for those who fear it, do not have the knowledge to utilize it fully, or do not have readily available access to the high-speed resources needed to become an active participant. Many schools trying to enter the web based learning arena either have no access to web based learning networks or do not have the technology or resources (Gragert, 2008). Quite often the importance technology plays at the campus has a lot to do with the school's cultural environment and how much emphasis of importance is put toward technology.

Hoy and Miskel (2005) have conducted numerous studies on school culture and climate, and they define organizational culture as "a system of shared orientations that hold the unit together and give it a distinctive identity" (p. 165). They argue that there is a large amount of disagreement about the definition of shared norms values, philosophies, perspectives, beliefs, expectations, attitudes, myths, and the ceremonial aspects. Organization culture, Hoy and Miskel found, has become a fashionable construct in analyzing school culture, yet it remains analytical, philosophical, and rhetorical rather than empirical. The question also arises whether an organization has one culture or many cultures (pp. 165-171). As part of this study the cultural environment of the campus played a major role in both data collection and pursuant analytic framework.

Alston (2004) states there is much more to access than just getting into colleges and institutions of higher education, especially for those who are crossing the physical borders of nations and languages. The community and global awareness component is vitally important in all aspects of preparation for college academically, financially, and culturally. Web based learning programs helped students to excel and expand their experiences in all three areas. Lu, Diggs, and Wedman (2004) researched the efficiency of a web based learning in an attempt to examine what works and what does not, as well as evaluate the role of the supporting artifacts in inhibiting or developing global classroom partnerships. Like most of the other literature from researchers, they stressed the importance of the greater issues of cross-cultural and interpersonal relations and greater awareness of other cultures over the vastness of the technology (Lu, Diggs, & Wedman, 2004).

This study utilized the Halverson (2003) qualitative design cycle analysis model (DCAM) as part of this process. Halverson reported this model allows leaders of education to evaluate how those guiding students use the identified artifacts during the process of program integration and utilization. Technology artifacts are crucial in web based learning systems and projects, however, no matter what type of technology educators use they must remember it is the people and the content that matter (Gragert, 2008).

Web based global learning communities like iEARN allow educators to analyze how the participant leaders of students in the project identify, develop, and utilize artifacts and allow the educators to design and track a system which is utilized by the students to achieve their goal of broader global experience while preparing for and gaining access to higher education programs. While assessing work projects for their students using technology, educators must remember Web2 tools exclude 90% of the world, so educators must be careful about technology choice within their classroom.(Gragert, 2008). Some of the Web2 technology may be what Halverson (2004) calls "inherited artifacts." Halverson's definition would designate designed artifacts as a web page or individual project created specifically for the web based learning module.

Received artifacts would be identified as the more official documents from campus administration. This could include school technology policies which might block access to certain more creative election sites addressing the 2008 presidential campaign. Inherited artifacts are those which institutionalize practice (Halverson, 2004). Examples of these artifacts may be consistent items like the grading system structure, report cards, and curriculum requirements in the areas addressing the U.S. political system as they relate to the election and state or national mandates which guide where issues relating to the election should be covered. In the area of technology, these artifacts could include certain web logs, eBay access, Skype, social websites, and log in links that a partnering or Internet host partner may have access to but the rest, or a portion of the community may not.

Halverson (2003) also stated that once the artifacts are identified, the data gathered must be evaluated once again to understand how those artifacts shape the practice educational leaders decide to put into practice. The next step of the model is designed to trace the development of the artifacts as outcomes to evaluate the leaders' problem identifying and problem solving practices (Halverson, 2003). From this step the leaders would move to change or revise artifacts or the practice of their utilization of the internet to assist the students. This study used the Halverson (2003) methods to approach finding an answer to the research question: The study triangulated data from the artifacts, observations, and interviews collected as a part of this case study.

Design

Artifacts

Research for this project began with collection of the curriculum artifacts and documents. This included collection of documents throughout the campus relating to the 2008 U.S. Presidential Election. Classroom papers in the form of posters and notices posted by the staff were also captured through digital photography and analyzed along with the other curriculum documents. They served as visual learning material to direct the student's choice of Internet searches. Discussion in this section will focus on postings, curriculum related to the election, campus political materials, and campus and student handouts.

Observations

This study was of comprised of six campus visits with a total of eleven documented observations of the participants. The documented notations highlighted the discoveries related to research efforts targeting the 2008 U.S. Presidential Election and website usage. Observations were both scheduled and unscheduled. Both faculty and staff were open, receptive, and inviting when the researcher appeared on campus and in each individual classroom. Those observations were conducted in the main campus areas, classrooms, labs, libraries, technology rooms, offices, and campus hallways. The researcher was granted full access of the facilities.

Interviews

The study design included faculty and staff participants. The participants were asked fifteen questions related to campus technology usage and the 2008 U.S. Presidential Election. Supporting questions for the interview protocol to answer the overarching question as proposed to the faculty and staff were as follows:

1.   Please describe the programs or courses on your campus which provides regular internet usage and or interaction education modules for the student population?
2.   Would you describe these experiences or projects as hands on, individual or group?
3.   Which types of websites are blocked on your campus?
4.   Are students allowed access to personal e-mail through school computers?
5.   Are students allowed to use their cell phones for internet access and if so do they utilize this technology?
6.   Is streaming video allowed in your classrooms?
7.   Are students allowed to share their political views in class?
8.   Which websites do you most often utilize in your classroom?
9.   Which internet browser do you utilize with your class?
10. Please describe the programs or courses on your campus including student participation in educational modules which encourage participation in the 2008 U.S. Presidential Election?
11. Is technology readily available on campus for your students to track election information through the web?
12. Describe some of the obstacles you face in obtaining access to technology for your students?
13. What types of websites are utilized by your students to obtain information about the 2008 U.S. Presidential Election?
14. How would you describe your campus staff and faculty experience with technology to obtain information about the 2008 U.S. Presidential Election?
15. Has your school utilized or investigated the utilization of global learning communities to expand student knowledge in the election or appointment of heads of nations in other countries?

Follow-up questions and prompts resulting from answers to these questions were also evaluated. Also, an additional comment from the first interviewee was substantial enough in content substance to turn it into a question. To make sure each participant had the same protocol, that question was added to each of the interviews. That question was as follows: What percentage of the students on your campus would you estimate have internet access in their homes?

Procedures for the interviews were clearly defined with the participants. The interview time, date, and place was confirmed with subjects a week ahead and again the day before. The purpose of study was explained and confirmed with subjects when they agreed to participate and again before the question session. The participants all agreed to the digital recording of their conversations and the digital recorder was then turned on. Confidentiality of comments were confirmed with subjects and paperwork signed at the time of the interview. Initial interview questions were conducted and follow-up questions conducted as prompted by initial questions. Participants were encouraged to make any final comments they would like. The interview process was concluded and the interviewee was assured once again of confidentiality. The tape recorded was turned off at that time.

Limitations

Limitations of the study included a single campus case study and the time element surrounding the election. A multicampus, district wide case study would have given a wider range of information on how the district as a whole utilized the Internet to collect data on the 2008 U.S. Presidential Election. There is a good chance each campus could have learned from the broad range of creative efforts and opportunities the World Wide Web provides. Also, the time element from the point of the school year starting in August, access to the schools granted by administrators in September, and the Institutional Review Board approval in October, the time element was really tight. The positive element was the willingness of the teachers and quick access to complete the data collection process before the election. The interviews were held after the election, and this was a good strategy because the interviews were far richer with details provided on student and staff reaction to the results.

Study Findings and Discussion

Document (Artifact) Collection

The first artifacts collected included documents from the student assignments that tasked them to search for data on the Internet as well as follow up with surveys based on their findings throughout the campus. They used information on data collected over the Internet to poll students and staff on selected issues. Students were also asked to utilize collected information to stage a campus debate session and mock election. One student served as Obama and another student served as McCain. The students then held a campus wide debate and election. Even though the main focus of the campus election focused on the Democratic and

Republican candidates, the curriculum artifacts clearly showed data from both Ralph Nader and Bob Barr were also utilized as a part of the classroom discussions. Curriculum artifacts included websites such as SelectSmart.com, npr.com, cnn.com, TeachersCurriculumInstititute.com, mysanantionio.com, slate.com, politico.com, nationalreviewonline.com, and foxnews.com, washingtonpost.com, newyorktimes.com. These were all used extensively, but not exclusively to collect data during the course of the election. These sites were utilized by both students collecting data and faculty when accessed for students was limited. Many of these sites were accessed through the library's Elton B Stephens Company (EBSCO) database system when computers were available.

Participants

A total of 14 subjects were interviewed as possible participants who had the potential to add depth and data to this study. The subjects included four technology teachers, two head administrators, the career lab coordinator, a government staffer assigned to campus, a business teacher, an advanced placement economics teacher, the library resource administrator, an advanced placement government teacher, a counselor, and the monitoring teacher. All were interested in participating. The study participants were narrowed down to the advanced placement economics teacher, the monitoring teacher, the advanced placement government teacher, and the library resource administrator. These four were scheduled for interviews over a 2-week time period just after the events of the presidential election.

Campus Visits and Observations

The monitoring teacher who worked throughout the campus introduced me to the classrooms where the bulk of technology was utilized. From this group we narrowed the study to those actively participating in research surrounding the 2008 U.S. Presidential Election. From this group the research moved into the participant selection.

Observations included student searches for data to support their stand on the candidate and the issues. A part of this observation session included the faculty putting together teams to support on campus campaigns which included mock presidential advisors and members of the campaign staff. Cross curriculum work included integration of courses and faculty to include government, economics and advertising to produce a campus campaign.

Researcher Participant Observations

Once the participants were selected, a minimum of two observations was conducted as they worked with fellow faculty, staff, and students.

Some of the observations were random visits when the researcher showed up to the site without notification. Other observations included scheduled visits to meet with the participants during class, library, or lab times. All four participants were highly active with students and constantly on the move.

Early observations included a large amount of transitioning between classrooms, the library and rooms containing technology to access the materials needed to conduct student research. There was little to nonexistent technology readily available in individual classrooms. Observations included watching the faculty interact with students to utilize limited technology resources for online searches both in the classroom and in the library.

The most serious technology issue occurred in the classrooms trying to conduct research when the library was not available. In one class students huddled around two laptops. One of those laptops appeared to be a private one brought in by a student. Students often stayed behind after class time to work on the projects to access the few computers available. Special sessions for discussion of the recent information retrieved concerning the election was also discussed during lunch time meeting for both the democratic and the republican groups. The meetings were open campus wide and held in the government class.

Observations also noted students coming into the library to research information for their election survey only to find another class there utilizing all of the available computers. A visit to the Go Center produced a surprise as a place which at one time was used for students to come in and out to work on college preparation materials and find a computer for research. This center was filled with what appeared to be a class in lecture at the computer stations. Each station was filled.

Participant Interviews

Monitoring Teacher Mr. A

Monitoring Teacher Mr. A. served as an excellent source for campus wide practices. He was able to provide a information on Internet usage campus wide, including students using their telephones as an Internet source in an environment where computers were limited. Mr. A stated:

> I've never seen a student get on the Internet on their phone. It may be just because at this age they don't have enough money to pay for it, for that service. I guess they if they were allowed to for those projects allowed to get on the internet I imagine the teacher would allow them to use the phone also for that. But I can't imagine that has actually happened yet. Again, I've never seen a student do it with that kind of technology.

Mr. A also reported that the government class, where this study found most of the active work for the 2008 Presidential Election was conducted, was one of the most creative on campus for utilizing web based research. He reported that the class not only used the Internet to research the candidates but also took the class to hear President-Elect Obama speak when he appeared not far from campus. He did have some concerns about student apathy, disengagement, and lack of concern about the election after all of the work conducted on campus concerning student awareness of the candidates and the issues. Mr. A reported:

> Each candidate had a team and as a group they would go online and collect information cause students are a lot more disengaged from politics than we are. And really it was possible that the elections was held November 3rd ... whatever date that was ... uh two weeks prior to that you would have a lot of students who just had a vague idea that there was even going to be an election and had no idea what the candidates stood for. Even students who saw Obama, when it was all over when we talk about it in class, we could tell they didn't really understand what he was talking about because they had no background knowledge. Uh, they liked him but, when he would get specific, they just ... he lost them. Yeah.

Mr. A reported that the classes who conducted the most internet research on the election were history and economics.

Library Resource Staff Mrs. B

Mrs. B was new to the campus staff, but experienced. She was very passionate about students learning research skills and stressed a concern about the lack of computers and computer labs on campus for research. Because of the lack of computers, she found more word processing going on in the library rather than research. Mrs B stated:

> So we have a little bit of research going on but most of it is word processing due to the lack of computers in our school and the lack of computers at home these students do not have. It's limited ... because I have the library booked to the end of the year teachers have pretty much signed up ... we're limited we have 20 computers. And most of the time if two teachers want to sign up they want to use the computers we don't have enough. And I have teachers coming in constantly every day they're asking to come in to use the computers and I have to turn them away or ask them ... we have print materials but of course it's good too, but a lot of them want to get on to the internet and I have to turn them away because I don't have room for them. I try fit as many classes as I can here and maybe depending on the project we can double up students on the computers but that's pretty much the situation right now.

Mrs. B noted that many of the students conducting research in the library surrounding the 2008 U.S. Presidential Election utilized the periodicals through the district's EBSCO system. She also acknowledged that because of the lack of computers on campus and at home for the student population, many students show up before school to get their work completed. Mrs. B declared:

> A small amount a lot of students come in here and I hear them tell the teachers "I don't have a computer at home" and we open at 7:30 so we're open an hour before school every day so I have students in here every day and that's exciting. I am not excited they don't have computers at home but I'm excited that they are in here and using the library.

The concern that was most prevalent in this interview was for the other students who could not or did not get in to complete work. Mrs. B had a very strong compassion for her students and was quite concerned about them falling behind due to the lack of technology availability for research there on campus during the regular school day.

AP Government Teacher Mr. C

Mr. C's government class was the most involved in the 2008 U.S. Presidential Election and his class use of technology clearly went well beyond the current election. His classes appeared to use the internet in many creative was and for many other assignments. Like the other participants, his main problem was access to technology on the school campus. He also admitted that very few of his students had computers at home to utilize the many capabilities available in the text associated with his class. Mr. C stated:

> Starting with my advanced class my textbook is online. If I had access to internet for more kids I would be able to access a lot more stuff for them which would enable more of them to pass the AP test. I teach basically freshman college government, AP. Their textbook is online ... a lot of the material they could access online if they had computer capabilities of doing so. I assign stuff ... I give them ... I give them ... extra time because a lot of time they can't get to the computer. So I give them a week usually to do something. I would be able to use it much more quickly, use my time expectations, writing letters to the editor, writing letters to Congress stuff like that on opinions and in my regular class and all my classes.

Mr. C also reported that access to the library for on line research was very limited.

> We can go to the library but the competition to get in there is pretty tough. She takes it like every other day and she takes it like every other day.... (He

is pointing to the classes next door while speaking) … you can't get in there. You have to do like three months in advance and I can't remember that far in advance to sign up for it so I forget. (He laughs) You go in and it's like you're not supposed to be in here.

They sign up in January for April, you know. I don't blame them for signing up. They sign up for once a week for all year and three teachers do that and there's only two days left for everybody else, all the other 50 teachers."

Economics, the number one answer. They have laptop.org and all these things for third world countries and we're close to being a third world country right here.

Because Mr. C teachers college level classes on a high school campus internet access is important and he also found block sites a problem when researching with his students for information on the presidential election. He declared:

CSpan was blocked at one time. (He laughs) … like I had to call and get that unblocked … the district has to cover themselves, but I … the technology I just have to call them up whenever that happens. There was one called Campaign Circus.com or org, I can't remember it had a lot of good stuff for the campaign but since it had circus in it I guess it had humor it had the commercials it had a little bit of everything so you could watch the funny stuff and you could watch like a speech, but it was called campaign circus so that was blocked. I was like come on man, how do you even know about that. Who knows about campaigncircus.com

To keep information on the election timely, Mr. C's class listened to the news daily on npr.org. and critiqued other political websites as well as wrote their own political cartoons. Mr C stated:

Npr.org … we listen to news everyday on … I can't think of what they call it … daily, hourly, news thing … that they have every hour. It's a five minute summary of the news. They will write about it and then we discuss it. And then we do political cartoons off that. Washington Post.com … New York Times, NPR, politico.com, that's probably the top ones.

Mr. C also had a strong interest in global governments and comparative studies for his students, but the state curriculum is not designed to foster this. He declared:

I wish we had comparative government more though. I think laws and stuff in government class and U.S. History and World History other than that we tend to focus on us we don't look at other stuff it's all about us, we don't look outside, we're very inward looking. So I would say we are lacking in that. I mean yeah, we do, I do talk about other parts, but it's not part of the curriculum. It's all about the United States Congress, yeah I try to connect it to other places, but do we do an investigation in depth of other governments, but no not at this time.

AP Economics Teacher Ms. D

Ms D utilized the Internet for student research quite often because her classes use curriculum from the Ford Partnership for Advanced Studies national program. The program required online interaction for the majority of its modules which are downloaded directly from the programs national website. The program is offered to high school and middle school students at no cost. It is aligned to the national and Texas state curriculum standards. Ms D stated:

> We definitely use the internet for research. We use it for the research because we use uh Ford PAS program that calls for a lot of current statistics on different countries. So we constantly are using the internet to research. You know like the economic indicators, the social standard indicators ... any laws regulating uses of resources for those countries, my students also play the stock market, so we do that also online. So that's what we do in my class-room. We also occasionally listen to NPR and we do that through npr.com

> We definitely use Ford PAS, NPR CIA.gov, the kids will use various websites, the UNICEF uhm ... goodness ... there's several websites where they go and look up statistics of countries, laws regulating the use of resources in countries.

Ms. D reported in her interview that her class investigated economic issues related to the 2008 U.S. Presidential Election using the Internet and participated in the mock elections and surveys conducted by the students.

> Our participation was more when we participated as an audience with the government class. And there was ... my students are his students ... so it was a lot of my students that were participating and we were more, played more of the audience part. We had a mock election. A two day mock election.
> McCain did ... no ... I'm gonna take that back. He won the presentation they did the best job, but Obama won the election. The kids voted on who had the better presentation and McCain won as far as presentation went, but Obama won the election. And of course the kids came with their surveys to our class so my students got to participate. Then we brought up discussions in our room which were great. It was neat because if they had a question I was "Don't ask me, ask the candidates."

Ms D also had trouble accessing technology when her students attempted to research information related to the economic issues surrounding the election. Since these issues played a major part in the discussion, her economics classes conducted extensive research, strictly in the economics, area throughout the election. She stated:

> My class we didn't do anything other than follow the economic things like ... and like I said we could only have access to the computers every two weeks. It's kind of frustrating because like I said we don't, we don't get the newspaper a couple of years ago we would get the newspaper every day and we don't anymore. Everything is online.

Ms D echoed a recurring trend in this study concerning the quality of access for her students to technology on her campus. She said she has to print many of the articles from her computer and this limits the research rigor and enrichment of her class. For the election she stated she mainly used cnn.com and npr.com to pull and print information for her students.

> Yes. I was pretty much printing the information ... cnn.com, NPR.
>
> What I would have to do ... I would have to print articles that I thought were important and then the kids would read the articles and come up with questions and then we would discuss the articles. I would have preferred to let them go online and bring up, print an article that they thought was important and then share it. But I couldn't do it that way. So I would have to pick the articles because of lack of access to technology. So yeah, I mean it still worked out great but I still think we would have had it would have been more rich, more from the students perspective if they had say I found this article and I want to discuss this article. Versus heres the article guys now come up with questions and let's discuss it. That's more teacher led.

Ms D stated this really limited her students when there was a rich amount of economic campaign information. She stated that lack of access was a critical issue for teaching her class and other classes in the core curriculum areas.

> Enough access ... every two weeks and then I am done for the year. The library is booked. It's interesting because the library has about sixteen computers which is wonderful, but it's almost booked everyday by different teachers so it's the library ... you have a whole full class, which is wonderful using them, but that's our access to computers we go to the library. And you've seen that when we're in the library. We don't have a computer lab. Now we do have labs. There are labs for classes ... the business classes. The computer classes BCIS. They have their own labs, but we don't have access to those. We don't have a computer lab, per se.

The issue of lack of access to technology continually appeared as a concern throughout all methods of data collection in this study.

Common Elements in the Data

Common concepts in the triangulation of data between the artifacts, participant observations, and interviews once coded included the access to technology and the common choices of websites utilized to gain information on the 2008 U.S. Presidential Election. Access issues included the ability to utilize computers on campus. The school did not have a designated computer lab where students could go to conduct research and the library stations are regularly booked. Space and rooms were available in the library for lap top carts but laptops carts for students are non-existent at the campus. The economic status of this school played a major role in the issue of technology access at this campus and the students' ability to retrieve rich data through the World Wide Web on the 2008 U.S. Presidential Election. This lack of access limited a lot of the creativity and depth students were able to put into their online research and projects. Rather than student based research the teachers were forced to use more faculty based research. Students were able to engage in a limited amount of student based research.

Part of the access issue also focused on the matter of blocked websites as an access component. Several of the blocked sites served as valid resources for research. This included the presidential candidates MySpace accounts online. These sites produced rich, daily responses from the candidates on current issues. Campus technology blocked this access. Data from the interviews and observations by the researcher showed that student access to the internet outside of school ran close to 55%.

Most importantly to note is that despite the difficulties noted above faculty and staff still managed to assist students in investigating data on the election from a rich source of websites. The study also revealed that a large portion of the information collected to support classroom studies related to the 2008 U.S. Presidential Election was collected from data resources online. This data included reports, streaming video data, personal statements form the candidates, as well as streaming audio data.

SUMMARY AND CONCLUSION

The issue of access to technology noted in the in the observations, artifact collection, and interviews with the faculty still plagues this school environment. To their credit, the faculty and research staff creatively put together assignments to promote efforts of research in relation to the 2008 U.S. Presidential Election despite this problem. This included handouts and video clips presented in class when internet access was limited or relevant streaming video data was blocked. It was also clear that the faculty and staff held the students to well respected sources to gather information and stayed away from places such as blogs and Wikipedia to obtain data.

Access, lack of computers, and lack of onsite technology staff seemed to be the biggest obstacles for the faculty and staff appeared to be the major hurdle for classroom technological use on this campus. These same issues have haunted a continuing segment of school populations since the first time computers began to appear in school settings. Despite this the faculty and staff of this school did not let this deter their efforts to insure that their inner city high school students shared a role in on the most historic presidential elections in this nation's history.

REFERENCES

Alston, J. A. (2004). The many faces of American schooling: Effective schools research and border-crossing in the 21st century. *American Secondary Education, 32*(2), 79-93.

Buzzetto-More, N. A. (2006). Navigating the virtual forest: How networked digital technologies can foster transgeographic learning. *Issues in informing science and information technology, 3,* 103-112.

Diem, R. (2008). Prologue. In P. VanFossen & M. Berson (Eds.), *The electronic republic: The impact of technology on education for citizenship* (pp. xi-xxii). West Lafayette, IN: Purdue University Press.

Gragert, E. (2008, February). *Internationalizing classes: Web2 tools in a Web1 world.* ISSA conference.

Gragert, E. (n.d.). *iEARN-USA: Our mission.* Retrieved November 30, 2008, from http://www.us.iearn.org/about/iearn_usa_mission.php

Halverson, R. (2003) Systems of practice: How leaders use artifacts to create professional community in schools. *Education Policy Analysis Archives, 11*(37), 1-35.

Halverson, R. (2004). Accessing, documenting, and communicating practical wisdom: The phronesis of school leadership practice. *American Journal of Education, 111*(1), 9122.

Halverson, R. (2004). Accessing, documenting, and communicating practical wisdom: The phronesis of school leadership practice. *American Journal of Education, 111(1),* 90.

Hoy, W. K., & Miskel, C. G. (2005). *Educational administration: Theory, research, and practice* (7th ed.). New York: McGraw Hill.

Lu, W., Diggs, L., & Wedman, J. (2004). Building cross cultural partnerships through the Internet: What works and what doesn't. In L. Cantoni & C. McLoughlin (Eds.), *Proceedings of world conference on educational multimedia, hypermedia and telecommunications 2004,* 4782-4786. Norfolk, VA: AACE.

Rogers, A. (1999). The origins of a global learning network. Retrieved November 19, 2008, from http://gsh.lightspan.com/gsh/teach/articles/origins.htm

Sharpe, B. (2006). *Emerging technologies for learning: The ambient web.* Science Park, Coventry, England: British Educational Communications and Technology Agency.

Texas Education Agency (2007-2008). *Campus AEIS Report.* Retrieved December 9, 2008, from http://www.tea.state.tx.us/cgi/sas/broker

CHAPTER 12

CONSUMERS OR PRODUCERS OF DEMOCRACY

Moving Civic Education From the Information to the Empowerment Age

Joe O'Brien

"In the 21st century, participatory media education & civic education are inextricable"
—Rheingold (2008, p. 103)

"A central opposition within the curricular
[approaches to citizenship education] is participation versus transmission"
—Parker (2001, p. 9)

INTRODUCTION

"Once upon a time" represents my first memory of what now characterizes participatory media—sharing, socializing, content generation, and user agency, all used to describe participatory media, aptly describe storytelling. A storyteller or medium addresses a group, sharing stories that

Technology in Retrospect: Social Studies in the Information Age 1984-2009, pp. 195–237
Copyright © 2010 by Information Age Publishing

provide insight into the group's history and traditions. Each speaker uses techniques that serve to personalize the story, while maintaining its overall integrity. In turn, each person in the group while listening to the story is creating mental images and thus making the story their own. Storytelling builds a sense of community since the tales that are passed on remind each person of their shared legacy. In this sense participatory media is as old as the first storyteller, whose very anonymous nature illustrates how anyone can become a storyteller. Technologies, such as the telephone came to redefine an essential aspect of storytelling, that is, communication, while the advent of radio redefined another element, that is, information. Later, technologies, such as movies and television gradually separated participation from the media. However, this changed when the Apple Company caught the world by surprise with the 1984 Super Bowl commercial for the Macintosh (Mac) computer.

A new age was born, one where the emphasis began to shift from consumers to producers of information. What was important about the Mac personal computer was not simply what it was, but also the potential it represented, the democratization of information and knowledge. On the other hand, the name though highlighted a limitation of the Mac, that is, a *personal* computer. While now one was better able to "produce" information and ideas, the audience for these products was limited. Almost 25 years before the first Mac, Licklider published *Man Computer Symbiosis* in 1961,[1] one of the first steps in the creation of an integrated system of networked computers. The advent of the Internet and then the World Wide Web opened up much larger audiences for individuals. Still, most users were dependent upon others to access these audiences since a software "language" barrier existed. Once online authoring tools became readily available and more intuitive, the potential first glimpsed in 1984 began to bear fruit. The emergence of social network sites and content sharing sites such as YouTube opened up an online democratic commons area, which meant that the Internet no longer was simply a means to communicate with friends and colleagues and to interact with information, but was a place to gather and act with others and to create and "publish" ideas. Since youth are some of the most avid users of online participatory media an opportunity exists to enable students not to simply learn about civic action, but to become civically engaged throughout their citizenship education experience.

This chapter's purposes are: to explore the Internet's evolution from an information source to a means for the collective generation and online publication of knowledge and a place for civic and social interaction; to analyze the changing patterns of young people's academic and social use of the Internet; to trace the relation between these changes and social studies' mission of citizenship education during past 25 years within the context of Parker's (2001) transmission and participatory curricular approaches and Morrisett's 1984 suggestion that computers potentially were a "strong catalyst ... to shake education out of its rut" (p. 514); and, to analyze challenges and potential both of youth's use of participatory media for civic purposes and of the preparation of young people for civic action in an online setting, which serves as the basis for recommendations for future research and policy. In addressing these purposes, I seek to address issues such as: whether online civic and commercial activity will become so intertwined for youth as to raise concerns about their ability to separate the two; how to reconcile an expert or representative model of government with the direct democracy features of many online places; how schools and civic groups with an online presence will address how "Web sites and online communities aimed at promoting civic engagement, activism, or community involvement among youth are generally facilitators of the civic engagement that occurs in the offline world, but not necessarily the places where that engagement occurs" (Raynes-Goldie & Walker, 2008, p. 161); and, how educators link participatory media and citizenship education so as to empower youth.

ONLINE PARTICIPATORY MEDIA: ESTABLISHING A CONTEXT

Online participatory media's history is very short. As illustrated by the reference to storytelling though, what characterizes participatory media is almost as old as humanity itself since participation in human interaction is critical to communication. Early forms of information and communications technology (ICT), such as the printing press, focused on increasing the generation and transmission of ideas or content, as opposed to human interaction. Later, communications technologies, such as the telegraph and the telephone, emerged and enabled people to communicate with each other across distances unimagined by prior generations. Movies, and later television, are technologies that became the basis for twentieth century "old media" or content generators, which slowly took the "participatory" element out of the medium. Movies, though watched in a collective setting, shifted the emphasis from the group to the individual. While individuals were aware of and influenced by how the audience responded, a movie's visual nature caused audience members to stay focused on the screen and this diminished the sense of the collective. In silent movies storytelling shifted from words to images, this meant that an audience member no longer needed to create mental images of the story being weaved by a teller, but to simply imagine the words being spoken. Sensitive to this fact, actors and actresses relied upon nonverbal language to communicate with each other and therefore with the audience. The addition of sound meant even less was required of the audience. Finally, the introduction of television took storytelling out of the collective or community setting and placed it in the home. The nature of television resulted in short, episodic stories, ones devoid of the components associated with storytelling or of today's participatory media.

In all fairness this is a simplistic overview. On occasion television has brought the nation together and forged new roads in culture. Masterpiece Theater challenged us to contemplate reproductions of some of the Western world's greatest cultural works. National and global audiences have witnessed epic historical events, such as the 1969 moon landing and the 1986 *Challenger* crash. Also, audiences have observed people of other lands, though typically presented from the cultural perspective of the producers. In this sense, television offered people a window on the world, forging an unparalleled sense of the human collective. While television represents the stereotypical old or traditional media technology, a brief examination of television's evolution during the past 15 years reveals similarities now associated with online participatory media and will serve as a segue to online participatory media's history.

Within the communications field, the 1990s and early 2000s witnessed a democratization of content and greater involvement of the audience, a process largely driven by a market economy. Television programs illustrate this point in several ways. First, there is the ultimate oxymoron in televised entertainment, reality shows. Reality shows such as *Big Brother* represent the ultimate egalitarian approach to television, that is, anyone can become a celebrity, and added a voyeuristic quality to the viewer's passive role. There also was a market-driven quality to such shows on two levels. On one level, since everyday people, as opposed to market-proven stars, populated the shows and since such shows were typically shot in ordinary places, production costs were low when compared to a drama or comedy show. On another level, almost all reality shows depend upon an element of competition, be it the social tensions that arise among people as they live in close quarters under the constant eye of the camera or shows where contestants compete against each other in long term, "real life" adventures, such as *Survivor* or *Amazing Race*. What distinguished the latter shows from their predecessor, the game show, is that with game shows the game and not the contestants is the star, while in a show like *Survivor* the contestants and the setting are the stars. One's "15 minutes of fame" could now extended to an entire season resulting in the democratization of celebrity-hood.

Second, shows became more interactive and began to change how we define audience. *Who Wants to be a Millionaire*, first aired in 1999, offered the audience several means to participate such as Phone-a-Friend and Ask the Audience. Shows like *American Idol* and *Dances with the Stars* offer viewers multiple chances to vote. Voting was not limited to adults since cartoon shows routinely offered children a chance to vote for their favorite episodes and would broadcast the "winners" the following week. Beginning in 2000, Cartoon Network even let fans vote on which cartoon shorts would become a series. Voting, the ultimate democratic act and expression of personal autonomy, became a routine feature of commercial television.

Third, reality shows and early twenty-first century game shows perpetuated the Horatio Alger myth, that is, work hard and you shall succeed in a democratic, capitalist society. Stop and consider, for example, the world reaction to Susan Boyle and her rendition of "I've Dreamed a Dream" on *Britain's Got Talent*. Virtually everyone was touched by her performance, particularly when placed within the context of her home life and physical appearance. More importantly, consider how this episode illustrated the convergence of information and communication technologies, given how her video performance became viral and reached a global audience. She benefited from the "indefinite and infinite … [and] instantaneously accessible" nature of the Internet (Greenhill & Fletcher, 2003, para. 2).

Fourth, television show producers moved from the gradual merging of more participatory techniques within shows themselves to breaking the episodic nature of such shows to more directly involve the audience on an ongoing basis, typified by the online site for *Dancing With the Stars* (http:// abc.go.com/primetime/dancingwiththestarsindex?pn=index). Here. audience members can: use a message board and participate in a blog in the Community section; vote during an upcoming show in the Vote section; and provide input during the season about different dances and costumes in Design the Dance, which is used to select the dance, costumes, and dancers for a special show. The site illustrates both how producers use online participatory media to build a social-audience network for a show as well as the blurring of the line between producer and audience. The site also is a means to market the show's merchandise and the products of other companies.

These changes represent quite a leap from watching *Miami Vice* or *The Cosby Show* in 1984 when participation meant waiting for a commercial to get a snack to today watching *Dancing With the Stars* on a 55" LCD, while cruising the show's online site and using your mobile phone to send text messages both to the show and to friends that are watching across the community where you live. While online technologies have transformed television entertainment, participatory media is most closely associated with online technologies such as: "blogs, wikis, RSS tagging and social bookmarking, music-photo-video sharing, mashups, podcasts, digital storytelling, virtual communities, social network services, virtual environments, and videoblogs" (Rheingold, 2008, p. 100). Today, participatory media technologies share these characteristics and raise several issues for civic educators:

1. Overall, "participatory media are social media" (Rheingold, 2008, p. 100). Whereas with Web 1.0 the Internet primarily was a global repository of information, which meant the focus was on information technologies, with the advent of Web 2.0 communications technologies began to mature, making e-mail the new "snail mail," and to merge with information technologies. Citizenship education needs to come to terms with digital participatory media, which is mobile, personal, social, and ubiquitous.

2. Democratizing effect, particularly of content and content generation that "challenges traditional definitions of information gatekeepers and authoritative voices" (Delli Carpini, 2000, p. 347) and best illustrated by the distinction between Encyclopedia Britannica and Wikipedia. This has implications both for a transmission approach to citizenship education and a representative model of democracy.

3. Expansion of choices about what to convey and who is part of a user's audience or network. "Many-to-many media now make it possible for every person connected to the network to broadcast as well as receive" digital content so that the "asymmetry between broadcaster and audience ... has changed radically" (Rheingold, 2008, p. 100). With young people facing a diverse array of choices online, ranging from whether to electronically "sign" a user agreement to determining what personal information to post, and interacting in an environment where roles are relatively fluid roles makes learning how to make informed decisions all the more critical.

4. Increased personal and group autonomy in negotiating personal identity and creating or reinforcing interpersonal networks—just as desktop publishing helped to enable niche marketing, so too online authoring tools and networking sites enable any group to create an online presence and to act upon its interest. One result is to "shift the nature of community from geographic to interest based" (Delli Carpini, 2000, p. 347). Online places such as "social network sites are providing teens with a space to work out identity and status, make sense of cultural cues, and negotiate public life" (boyd, 2008, p. 120) and "allow for a degree of freedom and autonomy for youth that is less apparent in a classroom setting" (Ito, Horst, Matteo, & boyd, 2008, p. 2).

5. Ability to network and increased autonomy have resulted in new online spaces, particularly game and socially oriented spaces. S. Coleman (2008) contends though since "entry into the virtual public sphere is cheaper and less burdensome than making one's presence felt in the conventional public sphere, it is particularly attractive to young people whose experiences and aspirations might otherwise be marginalized or forgotten" (p. 202), making them ideal places to cultivate civic engagement.

6. Commercialization of the Internet resulting in more regulation and sense of order—originally online behavior was guided by an informal code of ethics known as netiquette, now a growing body of user/service provider policies guide more and more of online behavior. As indicated by the situation with FaceBook discussed later, the Internet's commercialization blurs the line between users as online citizens and consumers.

As noted by Cliff, O'Malley, and Taylor (2008), digital participatory media has resulted in the ever-increasing fluid nature of the online environment, which is distinguished by:

> the blurring of distinctions between boundaries, at multiple levels: blurring between the personal/private and the public; between the individual identity and group identity, and therefore between individual output and group output; between what is part of the digital landscape and what is "reality"; between formal and informal learning; between work, play and education. (p. 18)

How did we get to this point and what might it mean for youth's ability to become civically engaged and the mission of social studies education?

A BRIEF HISTORY OF THE INTERNET'S EARLY YEARS

During the 1960s Licklider and other research scientists, such as Leonard Kleinrock, Donald Davies, Paul Baran, and Lawrence Robert, worked on the creation of an interconnected system of computers, which resulted in the Advanced Projects Research Agency Network (ARPANET) in 1969. Robert Kahn demonstrated ARPANET at the 1972 International Conference on Computer Communication, the same year that Ray Tomlinson introduced electronic or e-mail. The following year Kahn introduced Transmission Control Protocol (TCP) and Internet Protocol (IP), which served as the basis for an open-architecture network and permitted: "each distinct network ... to connect to the Internet" (Leiner et al., 2003). Since "communications would be on best effort basis" so that if information was not received the source automatically would resend it, there was no need for "global control at the operations level" (Leiner et al., 2003, "The Initial Internetting Concepts" section, bullet 2). The potential for the Internet's participatory capacity began to emerge in 1979 when the first electronic "bulletin board" was created and the first modem went on the market. As traffic on the Internet increased with the use of TCP/IP, Domain Name System (DNS) replaced the long string of numbers with names for host sites. By 1985 though, Internet use was still largely limited to research by scientists and universities. According to Gerodimos (2004) an online or cyberculture was evolving that was characterized by "cyberspace's key elements: decentralised network structure, virtuality, transcendence of geographical boundaries and time, opportunities created by the nature of the new ICTs, equality amongst users, netiquette" (p. 2).

Until 1985 the national government had funded the Internet, but during the next decade the government enabled the private sector to assume control and sought to broaden the Internet's user base. Such efforts included: the privatization of the National Science Foundation's (NSF) computer "backbone"; NSF's requirement that any university that received NSF funding for an Internet connection had to provide access to all "qualified users" and to use TCP/IP on its network; the establishment of "peer to peer" model for exchanging information online; and, the elimination of NSF's Acceptable Use Policy that prohibited using the National Science Foundation Network (NSFNET) for "commercial purposes." The transition was completed by 1995 as exemplified by four events. First, NSF turned over its four major Network Access Points to Sprint, Ameritech, MSF (Metropolitan Fiber Systems) Inc., and Pacific Bell, leading to the development of Internet service providers (ISPs). Second, the initial stock offering of Netscape, a browser application first launched as Mosaic in 1992 that made the World Wide Web (WWW) more possible, set the stage for the commercialization of Internet content and the development of e-commerce. In 1996 there were 1.8 times more .com and .net domains than .edu domains. By 2000 there were six times as many commercial sites as educational ones. Third, in 1991 Yahoo (Yet Another Hierarchical Officious Oracle) was launched, aided by the development of Hyper-Text Markup Language (html) and Hyper-Text Transfer Protocol (http) in 1991, which permitted use of multimedia and use of certain words to serve as "links" and enabled the WWW to serve as a repository of multimedia documents. Finally, Bezos launched Amazon.com and Omiydar started AuctionWeb, later known as eBay, which became two of the most commercially successful sites.

THE INTERNET GOES COMMERCIAL & SOCIAL: 1995-2004

Between 1985 and 1995 personal computers became widely available and by the end of the 1990s Digital Subscriber Lines (DSL), which drew upon an upgraded telecommunications infrastructure, became popular. The broadening and easing of access to the Internet and the popularization of personal computers created fertile ground for the dot.com revolution in the late 1990s. However, the Internet's growth as a marketplace raised questions:

> how can the Internet's efficiency and information collection capabilities be balanced against genuine concerns about consumer privacy; how should the Internet be regulated to make it a safe and reliable transaction medium for consumers; and, how should existing regulations be adapted, and new ones designed, to ensure the health and competitiveness of on-line markets? (Peterson, Balasubramanian, & Bronnenberg, 1997, p. 344)

For many early Internet adopters such questions represented more serious problems with the Internet's growing commercialization.

In 1985, early Internet adopters founded the Free Software Foundation, which promoted autonomy to distribute and revise computer software. The Free Software Movement grew out of the hacker culture, which dated to the 1960's. Supporters promoted ideals, several of which have come to characterize participatory media, such as sharing, openness and collaboration. For them, given the origins of the Internet as a forum for collaborative scholarly endeavors, online intellectual property was an oxymoron. How was any one person or group able to claim ownership of the articulation and application of an idea that arose from an approach to knowledge generation that was much larger than one individual or group? When Netscape released its source code in 1998, leaders of open source projects started the Open Source Initiative, an organization that advocated for open source software."Open source is a development method for software that harnesses the power of distributed peer review and transparency of process," a process that results in software of "better quality, higher reliability, more flexibility, lower cost, and an end to predatory vendor lock-in" (Open Source Initiative, 2007). They purposefully did not use free software since they desired to distance the Initiative from the Free Software Movement and considered the movement's history as too confrontational. In that same year Rich Skrenta and several colleagues also started the Open Directory Project (n.d.). According to the site: "The Open Directory Project is the largest, most comprehensive human-edited directory of the Web. It is constructed and maintained by a vast, global community of volunteer editors" ("About" section). The Linux operating system and Mozilla browser represent the most prominent examples of FLOSS (free/libre/open source software).

FLOSS has served as counterweights to the growing commercialization of parts of the Internet, illustrating the societal nature of cyberspace. In promoting an open source, as opposed to a commercial approach to software development, for example, open source supporters argue that since "communities of developers [are] contributing to the development of particular source applications" that "one can expect open source software projects to progress at least as quickly and efficiently as commercial software applications" (Taney, 2008, p. 4). The free software movement in general and Peer-to-Peer file sharing in particular, best known by the Napster affair, gave Pedersen (2004) cause to argue: "[t]he Free Software experiment successfully undermines the private property rights based form of ownership" (p. 11). Today, the tension between the hacker and online commercial cultures manifests itself in issues such as: whether online intellectual property is owned by individuals or belongs to the collective; whether to have open or fee-based access to sites; the value and use of online personal information; and, the appropriateness of censoring online content.

A more competitive relation during this time was between old and new media businesses. Beginning in the late 1990s, new media was "dominated by the extraordinary growth of the Internet and the World Wide Web" (Gorman & McLean, 2009, p. 232). During the late 1990s and first part of the twenty-first century, new media businesses such as online service providers sought ways to supplant old media businesses, such as movie and television companies. In turn, as new media businesses became more commercially viable, they competed with each other "for content and market share in verticals outside of the core algorithmic search product" such as "to become the default video platform" (Searchenginehistory, "Virtual Search" section, para 1) and as they sought "to sell targeted traffic to advertisers on a cost per click basis" (Searchenginehistory, n.d., "Pay Per Click" section, para. 1). The dot.com explosion in the late 1990s and the subsequent crash in 2000 helped to differentiate those businesses that were most capable of realizing the shift from content to service providers and the potential of emerging Web 2.0 technologies. The emergence of better browser applications, growth in e-mail services, and development of search engines were but several of a growing number of online applications. By the late 1990s bulletin boards had morphed into chat rooms, such as those popularized by AOL (America Online). Until the late 1990s, most people used the Internet to gather information and to communicate with others via e-mail, but as services like chat rooms became more popular, online technologies began to serve social purposes. Just as the Internet itself went through a decade long incubation period before the public began to widely use the net's information services, the same was true of the more socially oriented digital technologies. The three early participatory media technologies, blogs, wikis, and social network sites (SNS), illustrate this point.

In 1992, Tim Berners-Lee, who was instrumental in the establishment of the World Wide Web, created a "What's New" website which contained hot links and is considered one of the first examples of a blog. In 1994, Claudio Pinhanez published "Open Diary," an online journal and Justin Hall created a "personal home page." In 1996, Microsoft purchased Vermeer Technologies to obtain FrontPage, one of the first web authoring tools, and bundled the program with Microsoft Office and its browser, Internet Explorer. In late 1997, Jorn Berger created the name "weblog" which was followed a year later by the launch of Open Diary and Pitas and Blogger were established in 1999 which simplified making a weblog. RSS or Really Simple Syndication further made subscription to blog posts easier. As bloggers began to need fewer and fewer skills, their numbers increased, as well as their visibility and influence as demonstrated by their "coverage" of a speech by U.S. Senate Majority Leader Trent Lott in 2002. The senator stated the nation would have avoided a lot of problems if voters had elected Senator Thurmond, who had run for president on a segregationist platform. While old media businesses failed to cover the story, several bloggers brought it to the public's attention. After the bloggers generated public interest in the story, the mainstream media finally covered it, which caused Lott to resign. Bloggers' political clout was reinforced in 2004 when several reported that Dan Rather used forged documents in a story about President Bush, leading to the credentialing of blogger Garrett Graff for daily White House briefings. That same year video blogs came into fashion and Flickr, a photo-sharing program, popularized photo blogging.

The emergence of the World Wide Web and the launch of the Netscape browser also helped to make wikis possible. Marc Cunningham launched WikiWikiWeb in 1995. According to his home page:

> This site's primary focus is people projects and patterns in software development. However, it is more than just an informal history of programming ideas. It started there, but the theme has created a culture and dramatic identity all its own. All Wiki content is work in progress. Most of all, this is a forum where people share ideas! It changes as people come and go. Much of the information here is subjective. (para. 2)

As implied by the description, wikis sought to create a communal means to exchange ideas and to create and revise content. While e-mail permitted one-to-many communication, each recipient had to review the sender's message, make revisions, and send to the group again, resulting in a stilted form of collaboration. By permitting many-to-many communication, wikis made the collaboration more immediate and intimate. Wiki-WikiWeb's history though illustrated a problem of online communities, one of governance. For example, once a wiki community's size reached a critical mass, how was the community to ensure the integrity of what the group developed? Wikipedia, which helped to popularize wikis when launched by Jimmy Wales in 2001, has adopted a governance or management system where individuals take on roles, such as editors, and have access to the site's technical features. While such sites lost some of the immediacy and intimacy that served as the initial basis for the wiki community, the governance system allowed the sites to better accommodate larger numbers of users, a situation akin to moving from a direct to a representative democracy.

According to boyd and Ellison (2008) social network sites (SNS) enable users to "(1) construct a public or semi-public profile, (2) articulate a list of other users with whom they share a connection, and (3) view and transverse their list of connections and those made by others within the system" (p. 211). The first major SNS, which contained all these features was SixDegrees.com which "opened" in 1997, followed by LiveJournal and BlackPlanet in 1999 and then MySpace in 2003 and Ning, Bebo, and Facebook (beyond Harvard) in 2005. Sites, such as Ryze.com opened in 2001, focused on business, as opposed to social networks. The rapid growth of Friendster, launched in beta form in 2002, illustrated how online communities were subject to the ills found in organic communities. The site lacked the servers and storage space to handle both the increasing number of new users and the amount of their usage. When Friendster tried to manage the growth by limiting how much members used the site, the most committed members became angry and exercised their public voice as they complained in online forums. Blogs, wikis, and SNS represent examples of Web 2.0 applications and illustrate the shift from Web 1.0 technology where the focus was on information to Web 2.0 where the focus now was on communications or, more appropriately, participation. Now online users were able to generate their own content, exercise their public voice, address a variety of audiences, and create networks around a common interest within the context of a growing online democratic culture.

SOCIAL STUDIES & TECHNOLOGY: AN AMBIVALENT RELATIONSHIP—1984-2003

In K-12 public education the advent of each new technology has resulted in demands by its advocates for a corresponding dramatic change in how teachers instruct and young people learn, though such a change has yet to occur. Sharples Graber, Harrison, and Logan (2009) claimed that since the publication of a 1953 United Nations Educational, Scientific and Cultural Organization report on the effects of movies and radio on children, "adults have sought to protect children from the perceived dangers of the new media" (p. 71),[2] which offers a possible explanation for the limited impact of each technology on K-12 teaching and learning. Forty years ago Lunstrum and Scheider (1969) offered several reasons why television "did not bring the revolution that some had predicted and many had hoped for" (p. 155): "the difficulty of making common 'homework' assignments ... [since] some students may not have access to a television set for the assigned program"; the prospect of "turning students into a captive audience for the advertising sponsors of the assigned programs"; and, "the great difficulty facing teachers in attempting to incorporate future unpreviewed television programs into their planning" (p. 156). While television failed to make an impact in the classroom, educators realized that young people in 1969 were spending "more time watching movies and television than any other endeavor" (Valenti, 1969, p. 146).[3] Valenti's and Lunstrum and Scheider's corresponding claims suggested a pattern that those in social studies would encounter time and again during the next 40 years. The advent of each new major technology, while influencing youth's personal lives, had little impact on their school lives. A decade later Ingraham (1980) captured social studies educators' response to yet another new technology, in his case videodiscs:

> The 1980's are sounding a clarion call for more teaching aids. We have heard it all before. In earlier decades, supportive services to social studies teaching were to be found in motion pictures, both silent and sound; filmstrips, with and without sound; overhead projectors and transparencies; recorders; slides and posters; radio and television, inside and outside the classroom, with videotape cassette players and recorders (VJRS); 8mm and super-8mm films and projectors with and without sound; single concept and nonverbal films; simulations and programmed instruction; and computer-assisted instruction-truly a mixed media menu for social studies teachers. But was that enough? (p. 641)

Ingraham's (1980) question continued to echo in the field for this entire time period. Rather than address technology in a holistic manner, social studies parceled it into discrete parts. First, as noted by Berson, Lee, and Stuckart (2001) social studies educators tended to take an instructional "tools" approach to technology. Second, students needed to learn certain knowledge and skills to use the technology. For computers this meant students learning keyboarding and word processing skills, while with the Internet this meant learning about sourcing sites. Third, there was the study of the technology within a societal context, as represented by science, technology, and society, which became a theme in the National Council for the Social Studies (NCSS) curriculum standards. Finally, there was student use of technology outside of school, which was often used to justify technology as an instructional tool.

Throughout the 1980s and 1990s much of the discussion about ICT focused on its use with instruction, a fact that inhibited discussion about the relation between advances in ICT and citizenship education. Consider the matter from this perspective. In essence each form of technology on one level is a tool, ranging from a pencil to the space shuttle's booster rockets. At the same time though certain technologies are such an integral part of our lives that we hardly consider them mere tools. When was the last time that you thought of your car or central air conditioning as a tool? Contrast this with your thinking about the screwdriver that is in a kitchen drawer or toolbox. At some point certain "tools" or technologies become so such a part of our daily lives that life without them is difficult to imagine. At the same time, incorporating such tools into our lives requires a change in our lifestyle. Not surprisingly then, advocates of each particular instructional technology took great pains to reassure possible users, as illustrated by Kendall and Budin (1987) who edited the first issue of *Social Education* devoted to the use of computers:

> It will be a long time in the future, if ever, that the computer will replace the social studies professional. At present, the computer cannot replace the uncanny ability and wit of a teacher.... Some things can be done more effectively using a computer, others cannot. The computer and other technologies will not and should not create a new social studies curriculum. They will not change the goals and traditional content of social education, but they may eventually reshape how things are taught and even make teachers' lives a little easier. For now and in the future, the computer offers the teacher an exciting new tool or resource—no more, no less. (pp. 32-33)

Ironically in the same issue in an interview with Robert Taylor, a former research director for the Department of Defense's Advanced Research Projects Agency (DARPA), the editors reported Taylor suggesting that with the integration of computers into curriculum and instruction " 'the teacher will become' more often a coach" and "may move from being the master of the classroom to coach of information, navigators, teaching students how to navigate all the information and form judgments based on it" (Kendall & Budin, 1987, p. 35). He went on to place student use of computers in a civic context:

> One would hope that if we have the much broader access to information that computers can provide, and people learn how to use the information as they're going through school, they'll be in a better position to judge policies

and actions that are increasingly going to be a part of everybody's life, as long as this nation remains a democracy. (p. 36)

Taylor's vision of computer use paralleled that of Morrissett who in 1984 presented four possible futures for social studies. The first three were: "the inertia of the past will prevail"; "education will move slowly but surely—and maybe not so surely—toward agreed upon ideal states"; and, "the new social studies is not dead, but only sleeping" (pp. 512-514). Interestingly, his fourth prediction was that "a revolution requires a strong catalyst; computers may be it" (p. 514). According to Morrissett, "computers offer solutions to so many educational problems" (p. 514).

> Individualized instruction, interactive learning, manipulative learning, visual learning, reduced paper work for teachers and administrators, and access to tremendous banks of data and programs offer prospects for unprecedented changes in teaching and learning methods and the organization of educational institutions. (p. 514)

What makes his thinking particularly prescient is that he was writing toward the end of the "back to basics" movement, a time when minimum competency testing ruled the day. In the same issue, on behalf of NCSS, Rose, Brandhurst, Glenn, Hodges, and White (1984) presented the "Social Studies Microcomputer Courseware Evaluation Guidelines" (pp. 573-576). Interestingly, these guidelines, coupled with a position statement on the use of microcomputers, represented NCSS's last official statements about the use of technology for over 20 years.[4]

A 1988 issue of *Social Education* devoted to television hinted at the potential convergence of information and communication technologies and the emergence of participatory media. In an introduction Fontana (1988) noted:

> The future ... holds new promise in the marriage of television with other technologies to create what is now termed a 'hypermedia' environment— one in which the teachers and students can gain access to the information they need to introduce, explain, support, or otherwise explicate a concept. (p. 349)

In the same issue Pelton (1988) indicated that tele-education meant the

> use of the media for remote teaching of information, whether by one-way systems that use data, voice, compressed video, full motion video, or by an interactive systems that allows students to interact, typically with one-way video and a return audio link. (p. 368)

Martorella (1997) captured the state of the field well when he wrote "technology is a sleeping giant in the social studies curriculum" (p. 511) and how the giant would be "struck by how little the social studies curriculum has been affected by the technology changes sweeping the nation" (p. 511). He noted that the field not only needed to consider the instructional use of technology, but also to engage in "a dialogue centered around the profound social consequences of technology trends both for the nation and the world" (p. 512). His voice was one of the few of the time that argued: "effective citizenship involves mastery of computer technologies" (p. 513).[5]

On one level, the disconnect between technology and citizenship education in the late 1990s is particularly puzzling given the widespread presence of computers and the Internet in the nation's schools. On another level though, the overriding concern in K-12 public education was addressing the digital divide, a national concern expressed by President Clinton (2000) in his final State of the Union Address:

> Opportunity for all requires something new: having access to a computer and knowing how to use it. That means we must close the digital divide between those who have the tools and those who do not. Connecting classrooms and libraries to the Internet is crucial.

In this endeavor the nation was highly successful. In 1981 one or more computers were available for instructional use in only 18% of schools, but by 1994, 98% of schools had at least one (National Center for Educational Statistics, 2003). By 1999, nearly 98% of the schools had access to the Internet. Not surprisingly, "Internet use and accessing information on the Web" was "the most common use of technology in the social studies" (Whitworth & Berson, 2003). Mehlinger (1996) recognized problems, which were addressed several years later, such as the need for teachers to receive training, particularly since teachers seemed to use technology as "a more sophisticated and expensive way to meet the same learning outcomes as produced by more traditional methods" (Whitworth & Berson, 2003, p. 12), and to conduct research to determine the technology's effectiveness. With the former, pressure was placed upon educators to use computers and Internet access to help justify the public expenditure to place them in schools.

With the latter, Mason, Berson, Diem, Hicks, Lee, and Dralle (2000), several of the authors representing the vanguard of a new generation of social studies scholars interested in technology, articulated the following principles that captured well much of what had been missing in discussions about the relation between technology and social studies: extend learning beyond what could be done without technology; introduce technology in context; include opportunities for students to study relationships among science, technology, and society; foster the development of the skills, knowledge, and participation as good citizens in a democratic society; and, contribute to the research and evaluation of social studies and technology. Such principles represented a more holistic approach to technology within social studies and citizenship education, an approach much needed given the field's failure to connect technology and citizenship education. Berson, Lee, and Stuckart (2001) couched their review of the literature in some of these principles by considering how "technology facilitates social studies practices … such as civic responsibility, global understanding, and historical awareness" (p. 210), how "technological agency" might further the "broader purposes of social studies [such] as economic production, human interaction, democracy, and critical thinking" (p. 213), the interaction between technology and society and the effects of technology on individuals and the community. In looking ahead they called for "meaningful reform which does not trivialize human interaction, community consciousness, or collaboration in the context of global connectivity" (p. 224). Crocco's call for the field to "adopt and promote a powerful, research-based theory of learning [so as] to leverage technology for real change in social studies teacher education and, by extension, in our nation's schools" (p. 392) complemented Berson, Lee, and Stuckart's appeal for meaningful reform.

At the turn of the millennium though, connecting technology to social studies larger mission of citizenship education was still a work in progress, as illustrated by two issues of *Theory & Research in Social Education*, the fall 2000 issue, the first one devoted exclusively to articles on technology and social studies, and the summer 2001 issue devoted to citizenship. The former never mentioned citizen or citizenship and the latter never mentioned technology! While a couple of the authors in the technology-related issue did address matters such as computers and privacy, it was done primarily within a school context, which again might illustrate the limiting nature of conceiving and acting upon technology primarily as an instructional tool. Diem (2000), though, suggested that the field's future lay with participatory media: "As a conglomeration of a number of network tools within an integrated software package with a common user interface, web-based learning environments provide incredibly fertile ground for the development of creative learning environments" (p. 496).

VanFossen and Shiveley (2003) studied the Internet sessions presented at the NCSS annual conference from 1995 to 2002 and concluded that while the number of such sessions dramatically increased between 1995 and 1999, they declined by over 50% from 1999 to 2002. They raised several questions as to why this might have occurred, but two possible explanations that were not explored were the impact of Diem serving as NCSS president in 1998, who had authored technology related articles for almost 20 years, and the effects of the U.S. government's "Preparing Tomorrow's Teachers to Use Technology" (PT3) grant program on the research interests and professional affiliation of social studies faculty that were interested in technology. Established in 1999, the PT3 grant program provided funding to teacher education programs that sought to integrate the use of technology to enhance prospective teachers' ability to make the use of technology an integral part of their teaching. As a result, many social studies scholars gravitated toward the Society for Information Technology in Teacher Education, which consisted of faculty members across different disciplines with an interest in technology. This might explain why the "Guidelines for Using Technology to Prepare Social Studies Educators" was first published in *Contemporary Issues in Technology and Teacher Education* journal (CITE) as opposed to the NCSS publication, *Theory & Research in Social Education* (TRSE). As noted by Friedman and Hicks (2006) though, while PT3 "elevated technology to the forefront of educational arena," they wondered

> how many of us in social studies actually worked collaboratively with teachers and technologists to not only develop products but thoughtfully and meaningfully research and evaluate the impact of the use of technology and technology enhanced instructional designs within classrooms? (p. 3)

At the very least, the PT3 program helped address Mehlinger's concern about preparing teachers to use technology and pursuing research on the effective use of technology.

By 2003 the field had witnessed elements of all four of Morrissett's futures. Inertia largely had prevailed as the nation's attention turned to standards-based education reform and social studies educators grappled with the consequences of it, such as a diminishing of social studies' curricular status.[6] In one sense the standards based educational reform movement represented the closest the nation ever had come to Morrissett's "agreed upon ideal states," though I doubt that he would agree with the standards movement's conception of an "ideal state." The principles underlying the new social studies, such as inquiry learning, while present, were still "sleeping." Personal computers, coupled with Web 1.0 technology, were now widely available in K-12 classrooms and offered educators the teaching and learning potential recognized by Morrissett, but educators largely had to operate within the existing approach to public education and a standards based curriculum. As a result, in social studies education computers did not yet represent Morrissett's "strong catalyst," a situation not unlike that of the national government and e-government.

CIVIC ENGAGEMENT WITHIN A VIRTUAL WORLD

The American Society for Public Administration (ASPA) and United Nations Division for Public Economics and Public Administration (UND-PEPA) defined e-government as "utilizing the Internet and the World Wide Web for delivering government information and services to citizens" (ASPA & UNDPEPA, 2002, p. 1). E-government during 1990s focused on using the Internet to more efficiently provide services to citizens, rather than as a means for citizens to become politically engaged. This efficiency approach was driven by the 1993 U.S. Government's National Performance Review (Gore, 1993, p. 1), which reflected President Clinton's charge to use technology so as "to make the entire federal government both less expensive and more efficient, and to change the culture of our national bureaucracy away from complacency and entitlement toward initiative and empowerment." The report was based on four principles: "cutting red tape"; "putting customers first"; "empowering employees to get results"; and, "cutting back to basics: producing better government for less" (Gore, 1993, pp. 5-6). Osborne and Gabler (1992) and Milward and Snyder (1996) indicated that information technology would better enable the government to interact with citizens, as well as provide citizens with a means to hold the government accountable for the delivery of services.

During the1990s and into the first part of the twenty-first century, the government largely followed what Coleman and Gøtze (2001) termed a communicative approach to e-government since governmental sites were "an increasingly important vehicle for citizen-initiated contacts with government" (Thomas & Streib, 2003, p. 97). Not surprisingly, research on e-government focused on how well governmental websites provided services to citizens (ASPA & UNDPEPA, 2002; Ho, 2002; West, 2004). Regarding other online technologies, R. Coleman, Lieber, Mendelson, and Kurpius (2008) concluded that the "Internet has properties that make increased participation possible, but currently it is not being used to promote increased deliberation among citizens or between citizens and politicians" (p. 196), which supports Schelin's (2003) contention that "there is marked lag in government adoption of new technologies and methodologies compared to implementation in the private sector" (p. 128). Wiklund (2005), in his study of Swedish municipalities, learned that this phenomenon was not limited to the United States: while "ICT-enabled services have a democratic potential, the services available today only support the realisation of deliberative democratic ideals to a limited extent" (p. 247). Fountain (2001) recognized that the "Internet is often used to reinforce an old institutional structure rather than open the possibility for innovative public service" (p. 250). She also cautioned against resorting to the commercial realm to make better use of online technologies since:

outsourcing information architecture and operations is, effectively, outsourcing of policy making. Public servants and others who hold the public trust bear grave responsibility to forge long-term policy that guards the interest of citizens and that protects the integrity of citizen data and public information. The responsibility may make governments seem slower moving than the private sector, lacking in strategic power, or unsophisticated relative to best practices in the economy. But as we build a virtual state, public servants are needed more than ever to guard the public interest. (p. 250)

For some, online technologies made a more participatory approach to government feasible. The advent of

new, digital technologies of mediation make possible more direct techniques of representation which do not transcend the necessity for representing or being represented in a political democracy, but serve to democratize representation by making it a more direct relationship. (S. Coleman, 2005, p. 178)

S. Coleman suggests conceiving of democracy as lying along a continuum rather than in dichotomous terms, that is, direct and representative democracy. According to Becker and Slaton (2000): "New forms of electronically based democratic political organization will emerge [which] will transform representative government into a system much less responsive to traditionally organized pressure groups and more responsive to a broad base of its citizenry" (p. 81). There is no question that matters of scale, complexity and design impede such a transformation, yet R. Coleman et al. (2008) suggests that "digitally-mediated representation might [enable] a more expansive and interactive kind of accountability ... [accommodate] a pluralistic network of representation ... [and create] new spaces of self-representation" (p. 190). While new technologies offer the potential of a participatory approach to e-government and the injection of more deliberation into U.S. representative democracy, a taste of which the public sampled during Obama's presidential campaign (Rheingold, 1993, p. 1),[7] one needs to consider other parts of the virtual world to gain a sense of how participatory media might help government realize this potential. The emergence of virtual communities offers a starting point since they represent the merger and one of the fuller realizations of participatory media technologies to date.

One of the first virtual communities, WELL—Whole Earth Lectronic Link—was "a computer conferencing system that enables people around the world to carry on public conversations and exchange private electronic mail (e-mail)" (p. 1), which was "established" in 1985. Rheingold's *The Virtual Community* (1993) described both the potential of virtual communities and what people needed to participate in them:

the technology that makes virtual communities possible have the potential to bring enormous leverage, social leverage, commercial leverage, and most importantly, political leverage. But the technology will not in itself fulfill that potential; this latent technical power must be used intelligently and deliberately by an informed population. (pp. 4-5)

Interestingly, replace technology with democracy and communities with society and it reads like a nice justification for citizenship education. As early as 1993, Rheingold expressed caution about the future of virtual communities in light of growing commercial interest in the Internet:

"he odds are always good that big power and big money will find a way to control access to virtual communities; big power and big money always found ways to control new communication media when they emerged in the past. (p. 5)

He believed:

it is still possible for people around the world to make sure this new sphere of vital human discourse remains open to the citizens of the planet before the political and economic big boys seize it, censor it, meter it, and sell it back to us. (p. 5)

Rheingold suggested that computer-mediated communication technology offers "a new capability of 'many-to-many' communication" (p. 12), permitting the creation of a virtual community held together through "three kinds of collective goods ... social network capital, knowledge capital, and communion" (p. 13). He argued that such communication had the potential "to challenge the existing political hierarchy's monopoly on powerful communications media," yet realized that "much of our intimate data and more and more of our private behavior [moves] into cyberspace, the potential for totalitarian abuse of that information is significant" (p. 15). Twenty five years earlier Licklider and Taylor (1968) had predicted what has become another distinguishing feature of virtual communities: "What will on-line interactive communities be like? In most fields they will consist of geographically separated members, sometimes grouped in small clusters and sometimes working individually. They will be communities not of common location, but of *common interest*" (pp. 37-38).

Given people's interest in entertainment and the history of television game shows, it is not surprising that games initially served as the basis for the most widely used type of virtual community. Maze War, possibly the first "online" game, was created in the early 1970s and was a first person shooter game that was played between two connected computers. Over 10 years later John Taylor and Kelton Finn launched *Islands of Kesmai,* an online role-playing game that was based on the popular *Dungeons and Dragons,* on CompuServe. In 1986 Quantum Link, an online service and forerunner of AOL, launched LucasFilm's *Habitat,* an online role-playing game where the user was represented by a game character or avatar. The game's graphics helped make it one of the first commercially successful game oriented virtual communities. Both games were early versions of what came to be known as massively multiplayer online role-playing games (MMORPG). Launched in 1995 Cybertown, which later merged with Colony City, used virtual reality modeling language (VRML) to create a 3D representation of a virtual world. The subscription-based site represented a new direction since users were able to obtain a job, earn money, and make purchases, simulating activities in the face-to-face world. Such games started using chat rooms to enable users to step outside their roles and discuss ways to play the game, allowing users to adopt dual roles within the site's online environment. That same year Worlds Incorporated launched *Alphaworld* where users were able "to build in-world using prefabricated objects" (Damer, 2008, p. 4), eventually leading to the creation of Sherwood Forest Towne, a "purpose-built space" engineered by online users (p. 7). This effort led to "Avatars98," a "full-scale convention within the medium of virtual worlds" where attendees "dialed in over slow modem connections into a single shared 3D space" (p. 5).

The first couple of years of the twenty-first century demonstrated the possible future directions and potential of virtual worlds. According to Bell (2008) a virtual world is a "synchronous, persistent network of people, represented as avatars, facilitated by networked computers" (p. 2), which take several forms. First, there are fantasy game worlds like Runescape, which launched in beta form in 2001 and has become the most popular free MMORPG with over 100 million users worldwide. The game occurs in a fantasy realm and allows players to customize their avatars and to follow a story line largely of their own choosing. A player is able to pursue a "quest" so as to refine certain skills and to receive rewards. An economy, hierarchy and player code of behavior are embedded in the game. The site also contains forums for users to discuss the game or make recommendations on how to improve it. In 2004 Blizzard Enterprises released *Worlds of Warcraft,* a MMORPG set in the Warcraft universe. With over 11 million users *Worlds of Warcraft* is the most popular subscription MMORPG. Second, a year later Electronic Arts released *Sims Online* for Microsoft Windows, which illustrated the shortcomings of situating a virtual world meant to simulate the real world within a game context. While incorporating elements of an online social environment, avatars still were required to follow the offline physical behavior of their offline users, such as their sleep and eating habits, which limited the user's autonomy in the online Sims world. The site was relaunched as EA-Land in 2007, but was shut down in 2008. The fate of *SimsOnline* suggested that users saw a clear distinction between a game and social virtual world and that participants in a social virtual world were more interested in approximating a real life social world than participating in a game-like social world. Damer drew this distinction between the two: "Game-play worlds, while also supporting social interaction and user-created content, have as their primary purpose structured play. For the most part, in a social virtual world users are asked to 'make it all up' for themselves" (p. 2). Third, in 2003 Linden Lab launched a full version of *Second Life*, a virtual world that captured much of what Rheingold described 10 years earlier. As Messinger, Stroulia, and Lyons (2008) note, the "engine behind development of virtual worlds ultimately has been new technologies embodied in successive platforms for participant interaction" (p. 9), moving virtual worlds "beyond the realm of entertainment" so that "much activity in virtual worlds is growing in the realms of business, education, and culture" (p. 6). The elements of virtual worlds identified by Porter (2004), which align well with several characteristics identified earlier, now are possible: purpose, particularly an open one; place or location of interaction, which now can be completely virtual; synchronous and asynchronous interaction; and, a large enough population to sustain a community.

Just as there is an ongoing scholarly debate over whether the more direct democracy features of digital participatory technologies will foster or impair representative democracy, so too there is an ongoing debate over whether shared online activity, such as what occurs in virtual worlds, posting user generated content on sites such as YouTube, and blogging represent forms of civic engagement in an online democratic culture. Barbrook and Cameron (1995) criticized the hacker version of cyberculture characterizing it as "a bizarre mish-mash of hippie anarchism and economic liberalism beefed up with lots of technological determinism." Less critical is Dahlgren (2005), who contended:

> Civic culture is an analytic construct that seeks to identify the possibilities of people acting in the role of citizens. This is a role which can have non- or pre-political aspects, but which may develop toward politics and indeed evolve into formalized politics. (p. 158)

Accordingly, if the

> Internet is at the forefront of the evolving public sphere, and if the dispersion of public spheres generally is contributing to the already destabilized political communication system, specific counter public spheres on the Internet are also allowing engaged citizens to play a role in the development of new democratic politics. (p. 160)

This "new democratic politics" takes the form, in part, of discussion or "talk among citizens" which is "the catalyst for the civic cultures" (p. 160). Blogs, online chat rooms, wikis, and social network sites all represent online forums for deliberation. In that same vein, Gerodimos (2004) cautioned against

> dismissing lay message production on the internet as of limited social importance ... [since to do so] may be missing the point of online communication, which was not to bring about social change through utopian deliberation alone in the first place; rather, to facilitate the cognitive development and political education of citizens. (p. 3)

In turn, specifically referring to MMORPGs, Thomas and Brown (2009) indicated that such games share these characteristics: "a context for experiential learning"; "context for learning that is primarily social in nature"; permit "players who engage in the space to actually *create* and *change* and *evolved* the world they inhabit"; and, "produce a social space around the game that has a profound impact on the game's evolution" (p. 39). Similarly Shaffer, Squire, Halverson, and Gee (2005) argued that MMPORGs enable players: "to *inhabit roles* that are otherwise inaccessible": "to develop *situated understanding*"; "to experiment with new and *powerful identifies*"; and, to develop "a set of *effective social practices*" (pp. 104-105).

At the very least, might such online activity represent informal democratic experiences and precursors for more formal political activity? What might users, youth in particular, gain from such experiences and how might civic educators translate such learning into more formal civic engagement? By about 2004 participatory media technologies such as blogs, wikis, and online games and communities represented an emerging public space characterized by democratic principles with the potential for youth to become civically engaged—but who are these youth that inhabit these online spaces and avidly use communication technologies?

YOUTH'S EMERGING ONLINE LIVES

According to Prescott (2007) four of the top five free virtual worlds sites were youth oriented. The top five sites were: Runescape, which far outpaced the others; Webkinz, designed for 3- to 5-year-olds launched in 2005; Neopets, designed for 5- to 8-year-olds and launched in 1999; Gaiaonline.com, designed for preteens and launched in 2003; and, Club Penguin, designed for 6- to 14-year-olds and released in 2005. These sites illustrate the merging of a commercial culture with a democratic or civic one. The intended audiences of these sites demonstrate the importance of addressing this civic-commercial culture in social studies, as well as heeding Rheingold's premise that citizenship and participatory media education are linked. Consider the relation between an online democratic culture and citizenship education from the vantage point of a 4- to 5-year old whose first experiences with a larger community was becoming a member of the Neopets "community" in 2001. Imagine that several years later the youth joined Gaiaonline, then Club Penguin, and finally, if a 10- or 11-year old girl in 2007, was one of the first 4 million users on Barbie-Girls.com within the first 3 months of the site's launch or, if a boy, had an older brother create an account for him on Runescape. As Subrahman-yam and Greenfield (2008) wrote: "For today's youth, media technologies are an important social variable and ... physical and virtual worlds are psychologically connected; consequently, the virtual world serves as a playing ground for developmental issues from the physical world, such as identity" (p. 124). An unusual child? Hardly!

- According to a study conducted in the United Kingdom, over 60% of 13- to 17-year-olds have profiles on social networking sites (SNS) (Davies & Cranston, 2008, p. 5);
- 97% of teens ages 12-17 play computer, web, portable, or console games (Lenhart et al., 2008, p. i); 48% use a cell phone or hand-held organizer to play games (p. 13); "teens from families earning more than $75,000 annually are more likely to own a cell phone (79% vs. 63%) than teens from families earning less than $50,000 a year" (p. 14); and, teens communicate with each other using a cell phone (67%), e-mail (65%), SNS (61%), IM (60%), and text (58%) (Lehnart, 2009);
- "The majority of youth use new media to 'hang out' and extend existing friendships," while a "smaller number of youth also use the online world to explore interests and find information that goes beyond what they have access to at school or in their local community" (Ito et al., 2008, p. 1), they "create and navigate new forms of expression and rules for social behavior" (p. 1), and "their online "efforts are also largely self-directed, and the outcome emerges through exploration" (p. 2); and,
- Internet (instant message, e-mail, chat) and mobile phone (talk, text) are widely used, mainly to contact friends that live locally, children and young people are making skilful choices regarding the nature of these technologies in relation to the purposes of the communication (Livingstone & Bober, 2006, p. 21).

As these youth mature in "a world in which knowledge production is collective and communication occurs across an array of different media, the capacity to network emerges as a core social skill and cultural competency" (Jenkins, Clinton, Purushotma, Robison, & Weigel 2006, p. 49) the ability to "navigate an already abundant and continually changing world of information" (p. 49) is paramount, as well as the recognition "they will increasingly face risky online situations that require spontaneous decision making to ensure their safety and well being" (Berson, Berson, Desai, Falls, & Fenaughty, 2008, p. 238). Just how different is life for the mobile generation intimately attuned to participatory media that is personal, social and ubiquitous? Consider Solove's (2007) analogy of a person or in our situation, a student, as having both a real world and one or more digital, mobile personas, bearing in mind that a large, growing majority of adolescents routinely enter into commercial, binding agreements which they typically are not capable of doing offline until they turn 18. The Center for Digital Democracy (n.d.) suggests that youth learn to ask questions of their service providers relative to their use of mobile technologies such as those that follow:

1. Do you (or your partners or affiliates) monitor or track my web usage (such as compiling a list of the sites or pages I visit) [or] my cell phone usage and online spending patterns?

2. Do you employ data aggregation and analysis for the purpose of subscriber profiling, and, if so, can I inspect (and, if necessary, correct or suppress) my own profile?

3. Do you permit my user data to be combined with personal information from any other sources—online or off—for marketing or profiling purpose?

4. Do you employ behavioral targeting techniques, including efforts to "personalize" the "user experience" (by selecting or filtering, for example, the mobile content and advertising that I view)?

5. Do you ever use "free offers," discount coupons, online games, and other enticements as a means of securing subscriber permission for data collection and ad-targeting practices?

6. What are my options for protecting myself from these various tracking and targeting practices [and] a short, simple explanation of my privacy rights?

While indicative of how digital participatory media are redefining online space and the lives of youth, the issues raised by the Center pose fascinating questions about youth and citizenship education several of which are addressed in the next section in light of recent developments in digital participatory media and what has come to characterize it.

A CONTEMPORARY LOOK (2004-2009):
CONVERGING FORCES OF YOUTH'S ONLINE LIVES, DIGITAL
PARTICIPATORY MEDIA, AND CITIZENSHIP EDUCATION

While there is no one specific event in social studies that marked the field's shift from a focus primarily on computer literacy to a more holistic approach, which has come to include online participatory media, Bolick's 2004 proclamation that Martorella's "giant may be stirring" has proven accurate. These events included: professional development opportunities for university faculty that addressed the relation between social studies and technology, such as the first couple of College and University Faculty Association's (CUFA) retreats and colloquia conducted by the James F. Ackerman Center for Democratic Citizenship at Purdue University; emerging research on the impact of communications technologies on student learning and civic engagement (boyd, 2008; Heafner & Friedman, 2008; Larson & Keiper, 2002; Raynes-Goldie & Walker, 2008; efforts to situate technology in learning theory (Doolittle & Hicks, 2003); a growing discussion about the relation between technology and citizenship education (Crowe, 2006; Friedman, 2006; VanFossen & Berson, 2008); and, the NCSS 2006 *Technology Position Statement and Guidelines*, NCSS 2007 Bulletin titled *Digital Age*, and 2009 NCSS *Position Statement on Media Literacy*. As Diem (2008) noted, since technology is "ubiquitous within world culture and citizenship" (p. xiii), "how democracy can evolve through technology needs to be part of citizenship education constructs" (p. xx). Since a hallmark of online participatory media's most recent history is the ever increasing convergence of information and communication technologies, the next section addresses this history through the lens of what now characterizes participatory media and online culture and how these characteristics influence the shaping of these "citizenship education constructs" and youth's emerging civic identity, keeping in mind that participatory media still is in a nascent stage.

Online Socialization and the Associative Nature of U.S. Democracy: In 1848 de Tocqueville noted in *Democracy in America* that "Americans make associations ... to found seminaries, to build inns, to construct churches.... Wherever at the head of some new undertaking, you see the government of France, or a man of rank in England, in the United States you will be sure to find an association" (Chapter V, Vol. II, para. 2). What would de Tocqueville think of a MySpace account dedicated to addressing global warming or AIDS in Africa or a section of Second Life for nonprofit organizations? Rainie and Anderson (2008) found that membership in online communities has more than doubled in only 3 years. Some 54% of online community members log on at least once a day, while 71% consider their community as very important or extremely important to them. Since online communities possess many of the characteristics of offline ones, writing within the context of online games, VanFossen, Friedman, and Hartshorne (2008) suggested that a game's "social structure presents an opportunity to examine the importance of citizenship education concepts, such as power of the government, property rights, and consent of the governed" (p. 239).

Participation in an online community affects users' participation in social causes, with 75% indicating they use the Internet to participate in communities related to social causes. More importantly, 87% of those respondents are participating in social causes that are new to them (Rainie & Anderson, 2008, p. 2). Illustrating the blurring of the lines between the offline and online environments, Raynes-Goldie and Walker (2008)

> found that interactive Web sites and online communities aimed at promoting civic engagement, activism, or community involvement among youth are generally facilitators of the civic engagement that occurs in the off-line world, but not necessarily the places where that engagement occurs. (p. 162)

Online sites provide youth with "information, people, and tools to organize" so that "[A]rmed with the support of like-minded individuals, tools to organize, and the right information, youth are empowered by these websites to step into the offline world to volunteer, raise awareness, educate others, and start their own organizations" (p. 162).

Democratization and Generation of Content and Increased Personal Agency: In 2009, London's Royal House announced plans for the creation of the first "online opera story." Using Twitter, individuals could create lines for the opera and thus collaboratively create an opera story, which professionals would then put to music. In 2008, *Encyclopedia Britannica* launched a site that enabled select, expert users to contribute to the encyclopedia. The advent and growth of sites, such as YouTube and Flickr that are devoted to "publishing" user generated content, typify both this phenomenon and time period. New types of sites devoted to the publication of content or creation of intellectual property emerged, such as tagging sites that enabled users to draw upon the online search and review work of other users. While the ability to individually and collaboratively generate content and to create networks of interests serves to empower online users, such activity typically occurs within a commercial as opposed to a public or open-source environment, which has implications for youth. While questions about the posting of copyrighted material largely are resolved, less certain is ownership of user-generated content. The cultural nature of what users produce, for example, recently was recognized in the UNESCO Convention on the Protection and Promotion of the Diversity of Cultural Expressions issued in 2005: "cultural activities, goods and services have both an economic and a cultural nature … and must therefore not be treated as solely having commercial value" (p. 2). While UNESCO seeks to define user generated content in both cultural and economic terms, Google intends to experiment with a subscription based option, which would allow those whose posts routinely have drawn a large number of users to charge such users to view their work, and Google would receive a portion of what such users pay. Personal or user agency now comes in civic, commercial and social flavors!

Increasing Commercialization of the Online Environment: New media or online service provider businesses during the late 1990s and early twenty-first century first sought to build a business model that proved profitable and then began to challenge old media or content providers. Not surprisingly, such models rested on online advertising as represented by Google's 2007 purchase of DoubleCheck and the 2009 announcement that the company had the largest market for pinpoint targeting. While old and new media businesses competed against each other during the late 1990s and first part of the twenty-first century, their interests are now converging, resulting in business partnerships. Google, for example, "entered partnerships with established media interests such as Time Warner AOL, News Corporation, the *New York Times*, and the U.K. *Press Association*" (Gorman & McLean, 2009, p. 253). How well old and new media are able to coexist within the same corporation, particularly since Time Warner and AOL decided to separate, remains an open question. Google's partnership with a company like News Corporation highlights not only the evolution of and relation between old and new media businesses during this time, but the dramatic transition of the Internet from a largely public endeavor to a highly commercial one in less than 15 years. What happened as the online free market system met the hacker culture? One result is "the fusion of consumerism and citizenship," as typified by how the "the discourse of choice has now entered all aspects of human activity and policy-making" (Gerodimos, 2004, p. 4). While making choices is key to personal autonomy and the generation of user content, it is premised upon the user being capable of making well-reasoned decisions. A sound premise for an adult in the online marketplace, but less so for young people, especially when interaction in the environment exposes them to marketing and requires them to enter into agreements.

The above is particularly problematic when youth use commercial participatory platforms for social purposes, the line between online commercial, private/social, and public spaces becomes blurred. As noted by Montgomery (2008): "Market forces are playing a central role in shaping both the online political youth sphere and the new participatory platforms that have come to define Web 2.0" (p. 27). When youth use sites such as Youth Noise and Global Kids (http://www.globalkids.org/), it illustrates the power of digital participatory media to bring youth together to network and act upon social issues since they gravitate to such sites either out of a desire to exercise their public voice due to an interest in a social issue. In such instances youth are shaping this political sphere. "Cause" marketing typifies Montgomery's concern as businesses seek to cultivate brand loyalty by associating either the company or a product with a particular social issue. Within the context of a free market and consumer choice, such behavior is appropriate, particularly in light of youth-directed advertisement on television and radio. Seiter (2005) argues though that the "World Wide Web is a more aggressive and stealthy marketer to children than television ever was, and children need as much information about its business practices as teachers and parents can give them" (p. 100).

Just as direct and representative democracy are best addressed, not as a dichotomous relation, but as the same idea lying along a continuum, the same applies to civic and commercial spheres of the Internet. For example, imagine a group of private individuals create a public MySpace account as a platform to address a social cause and then invites other public MySpace users to become friends. How is their use similar and different from that of an account by a nonprofit organization or a business? What if a nonprofit or business linked their MySpace account to their organization's home page? What if an officer of either organization created a personal account that addressed an issue not on either organization's agenda? For the business what linkage between their advocacy and marketing is appropriate in different online venues? Ultimately, if "the civic identities, political views, and values of young people are rooted in their social relations and the opportunities they have for civic practice" (Flanagan & Faison, 2001, pp. 3-16), what are the implications of the "ubiquitous and integrated nature of marketing in digital political engagement practices" (Montgomery, 2008, p. 33) for the civic education of young people?

Reconciling Youth's Democratic Experiences in a Participatory Online Culture With a Representative Democracy Taking Place Within the Context of Citizenship Education: In "Harnessing Innovation to Support Student Success" (2008), U.S. Secretary of Education Spellings lauded the use of Computer Assisted Instruction (CAI) and Intelligent Tutoring Systems (ITS), which while invaluable tools for differentiating instruction, support a teacher-directed approach to the use of technology. As noted by Bennett (2008a), many youth do not adhere to the traditional model of a dutiful citizen but more to the actualizing citizen model given the breadth and depth of their online experiences (p. 14). Becoming empowered is not something done to a young person but rather something achieved through experiences. Unquestionably, civic educators need to prepare youth to make effective use of digital participatory media for political purposes. More importantly though, we first need to decide how best to do so and then empower youth to become civically engaged in an online environment in preparation for becoming politically engaged. This is not to diminish the importance of the representative democratic process or of youth's involvement in it. Rather, as indicated by Center for Digital Democracy's questions, youth are thoroughly immersed in the civic and commercial spheres of the Internet 24/7. Unless we adopt Parker's suggestion of a participatory approach thoroughly grounded in youth's online lives, we run the risk of preparing them for a life that seems of little relevance to them. The challenge we face is how to promote "participatory democracy ... as an alternative to representative democracy but rather as a complement to it" (Schugurensky, 2004, p. 615).

In addressing this challenge we also need to remember that youth's "democratic" experiences occur primarily within commercial venues. As VanFossen et al. (2008) noted, with commercial virtual worlds there often is a community within a community—a community of users that interact within a critically important, but largely hidden, community of site administrators. VanFossen et al. determined: "by agreeing to the 'End User Licensing Agreement' (EULA) or 'Terms of Service' (which is required in order to register for an account), a user is agreeing to a type of 'social contract' within this virtual government—one that has far-reaching and autocratic powers" (p. 239). Most user agreements authorize the site administrator to terminate an account at any time. There are instances though where users exercised their civic power, such as with FaceBook[8] where users sought to prevent the site administrator from changing the user agreement in a way that was detrimental to them. While on the one hand this situation likely will prove unique since other service providers will adapt their user agreements to avoid the problem, on the other hand an online disagreement between a business and consumers sparks an online response. As noted earlier, the government largely has perceived the Internet as a means to better deliver services, not to civically engage people. One reason for this perception is the government's minimalist online presence. As a result, in the immediate future user-citizens are unlikely to encounter governmental actions that occur only online and that necessitate largely an online response. Such is not the case with users in their relation to online businesses. What might this mean for young people as consumers and citizens as they interact online mostly in commercial places?

At the very least, one option for civic educators to adopt S. Coleman's (2008) "autonomous e-citizenship approach" which while recognizing youth's "limited experience or access to resources" assumes "they possess sufficiently autonomous agency to speak for themselves on agendas of their own making" (p. 191). Supporters of this approach perceive the Internet as a "relatively open public sphere in which the ideas and plans of protest can be exchanged with relative ease, speed and global scope" (p. 192). S. Coleman contends that the "function of e-citizenship is to conceive, create and sustain members of a political community" (p. 201), yet "the terms of citizenship are not static" and citizens need "to contest those terms" (p. 202).

FUTURE DIRECTION AND RECOMMENDATIONS

Establish a Theoretical Foundation and Research Agenda for the Relation Between Citizenship Education and Technology: The field needs to continue to move away from emphasizing a "tools" or computer literacy approach to technology in general and digital participatory media in particular to a more holistic approach as suggested by Berson, Lee, and Stuckart (2001). Otherwise we run the risk of becoming Sisyphus, forever pushing the rock of technology up the school hill, only to have the rock roll back over us as a new technology emerges. Hartley (2002) realized that:

> the research task ... to extend our understanding of access, analysis, critical evaluation, and content creation from familiar to new media ... the latter two ... have proved more contentious; yet these are the most crucial to the democratic agenda. Only if these are firmly fore-grounded in a definition of media literacy will people be positioned not merely as selective, receptive, and accepting but also as participating, critical; in short, not merely as consumers but also as citizens. (p. 11)

Crocco (2001), Doolittle and Hicks (2003), Crowe (2006) and others have recognized the importance of grounding the relation between social studies and technology in theory. What is now needed is to create an interdisciplinary theoretical foundation that integrates learning and teaching, citizenship education with a global perspective, and critical media literacy. Such a foundation, while recognizing the importance of learning how to use information and communications technologies, would place online or digital participatory media into the larger context of schools, society, civic engagement and the lives of youth.

> Rather than dealing with each technology in isolation, we would do better to take an ecological approach, thinking about the interrelationship among all of these different communication technologies, the cultural communities that grow up around them, and the activities they support. (Jenkins et al., 2006, p. 7)

Teasing out and Teaching About Free Market Principles and Democratic Culture in an Online Environment: Features of online participatory media, such as personal autonomy, individual and group interaction and collaboration, undergird both the online free market and democratic culture. Other features though illustrate the divide between the two, such as the generation and democratization of knowledge and intellectual property, and private versus public space. The fluidity of the online environment makes teasing out free market and democratic principles and defining the relation between them highly contentious and contextualized. While the questions posed by Center for Digital Democracy illustrate the need to enable youth, for example, to recognize when they enter into an online commercial agreement to use a SNS or a social contract in a virtual world, and the implications and consequences of both, many instances exist where the line between the two still is evolving. Where is the line, for example, between online cause marketing and cause advocacy? Where is the line between providing commercial virtual world experiences for pre-teens and using such sites to market products to the preteen users? What are the implications of the growth of m-commerce which is "any transaction, involving the transfer of ownership or rights to use goods and services, which is initiated and/or completed by using mobile access to computer-mediated networks with the help of an electronic device" (Tiwari & Buse, 2007, p. 33), given that an ever increasing majority of adolescents use cell phones, the same youth weaned on business sponsored virtual worlds and who routinely release personal information on commercial sites? How do we foster a sense of civic virtue and adherence to democratic values given their experiences within commercially maintained online spaces?

Create Public Spaces for Youth and Opportunities for Purposeful, Relevant Online Civic Engagement: For many early advocates of the Internet, its commercialization represents an unintended consequence of minimizing government's online presence. Ensuring the Internet remained relatively free of government regulation in comparison to the offline environment also meant that fewer public places were created where people might gather for civic and public purposes. According to Bennett (2008b) "We need to develop online environments in which young people can learn civic skills and engage in politics in ways that better reflect their identities and learning preferences" (p. 6).

Ensure Digital Citizenship Education For All: During the 1990s, the national government successfully closed the digital divide between the "have" and the "have not" public school districts. Wartella, O'Keefe, and Scantlin (2000) concluded that "Closing the digital divide will depend less on technology and more on providing the skills and content that is most beneficial" (p. 8). Seemingly a simple matter. Those such as Rock et al.

(2006) and VanFossen (2005) learned though that in the standards-based era elementary social studies risks becoming an oxymoron, a dire situation in high-risk districts where social studies instructional presence is comparable to a shrinking violet. While the description of today's youth demonstrates that digital citizenship education is a K-12 endeavor, young people in high-risk districts who are most in need of citizenship education are least likely to receive it. As Ivey and Tepper (2006) noted:

> those who have the education, skills, financial resources, and time required to navigate the sea of cultural choice will gain access to new cultural opportunities" and "will be the curators of their own expressive lives, while "those citizens who have fewer resources—less time, less money, and less knowledge about how to navigate the cultural system—will increasingly rely on the cultural fare offered to them by consolidated media and entertainment conglomerates. (p. B6)

They question if the United States can "prosper if its citizens experience such different and unequal cultural lives?" Ultimately, "ignoring the literacy demands of new technologies may have especially dire consequences for children in disadvantaged homes and schools" (Tally, 2007, p. 314), potentially providing a new meaning to "no child left behind."

Broadening of Perspectives: SNS

> enable users to articulate and make visible their social networks. While SNS enable interactions and connections between individuals that would not otherwise be made, this is typically not the goal as these meetings are frequently between "latent ties" (Haythornthwaite, 2005) who share some offline connection. On many of the large SNS, participants are not necessarily "networking" or looking to meet new people; instead, they are primarily communicating with people who are already a part of their extended social network. (boyd & Ellison, 2008, p. 211)

This situation raises an interesting challenge for civic educators, particularly since many schools block SNS. If young people's informal, social use of online participatory media is such that they rarely venture outside their personal networks, what is the obligation of educators to use online participatory media to extend youth's experiences with others from a diverse range of life experiences? In turn, what are ways to do so that captures both what makes for good pedagogy and the uniqueness of online spaces and participatory media?

Broaden and Deepen Young People's Democratic Dispositions, Civic Knowledge and Participatory Skills. S. Coleman (2005), Becker and Slaton (2000), and R. Coleman et al. (2008) suggest that the nation is entering an era of a blended form of democracy, one that combines elements of direct and representative democracy. If so, how do we prepare young people for both and to recognize and apply relevant knowledge and skills associated with the relevant type of democracy in appropriate settings? Research, for example, indicates: "efforts in online civic engagement space are often more strongly suited for enabling or more deeply engaging young people who are already civically minded" (Raynes-Goldie & Walker, 2008, p. 161). Does the public nature of such spaces simply make the efforts of such civically minded young people more apparent to a wider population than in the past? If such is the case, how do we broaden the involvement of young people in civic affairs? Reports like the Google Generation illustrate the importance of deepening young people's more academic use of the online environment. Spending a lot of time using certain technological tools, such as text messaging and online social network sites does not mean that they are any better at effectively communicating a reasoned position on gay marriage, undertaking a concerted group effort to address the killing in Darfur, or initiating and guiding a political smart mob to act on a common interest at a given place and point in time. The first two situations require dispositions, knowledge and skills familiar in an offline setting. Initiating a smart mob for civic reasons is a situation relatively unique to digital technology, given the speed with which the smart mob can form and its ultimate size, and raises questions about an adolescent's ability to lead such a group once it materializes. While everyone has sent an e-mail that they instantly regretted, imagine a 15-year old sending a message to a "friends" network of hundreds of people to meet later that night to protest removal of "unhealthy" food from the school's vending machines. While the reason for the protest is somewhat facetious, the point is simple—there is a need to determine how people can use participatory media for civic purposes, particularly in ways unique to an online setting and incorporate such use into citizenship education programs.

Initiate a Public debate: Livingstone and Bober (2006) argue: "a sustained public debate on the nature and provision of the opportunities of internet use for children and young people is lacking" (p. 20). Similar to K-12 education, government has remained caught in a tools approach to digital participatory since most "public policy discussion of new media have centered on technologies—tools and their affordances" (Jenkins et al., 2006, p. 7). As civic educators we need to initiate not only a discussion within a field, but in the larger public, about the issues identified here. As those responsible for preparing our youth for civic engagement, should we not demonstrate how to become civically active about matters related to participatory media, youth and citizenship education and in an online environment? If not us, then who?

CONCLUSION

As noted at the outset, much of what characterizes participatory media aligns with what civic educators hope to cultivate among young people. Online youth face multiple opportunities to choose, which require knowing how and being able to make thoughtful, caring, and well reasoned decisions. Online tools make the generation of content simple, yet young people need to know how to source information, analyze it and then construct it into intelligent, provocative, appropriate, and well researched messages. Collaborating on a common interest to reach an agreed upon goal represents a key aspect of an associative, democratic culture, yet such skills are not innate but are learned—and the list goes on. At the same time an uncertain future lies ahead. A future where the lines between relations such as the public and private and the personal and commercial will continue to blur before a crisper delineation emerges, where the ongoing convergence of information and communications technologies will create a constantly connected, mobile and social generation, and where the giant might fully awake to help develop a citizenship education construct that enables young people, not simply to consume, but to produce democracy in a time and place where the line between an off and online environment no longer exists.

NOTES

1. For the beginning pages of "Man-Computer Symbiosis" by J. C. R. Licklider, refer to http://groups.csail.mit.edu/medg/people/psz/Licklider.html
2. One school of thought is that there always is a certain resistance to any new technological advancement, stretching back to Socrates' critique of the alphabet.
3. As a historical aside, in 1967 Ingraham provided this list of instructional technology: "Film strips, 16 mm. sound films, 8 mm. loop films, transparencies, records, audio tapes, video tapes, film prints, TV programs, flat pictures, slides, cut-outs, games, and realia (artifacts, or models)" (p. 698). According to Ingraham this list represented "software," while textbooks, audiovisual equipment, sound motion pictures, maps and globes" represented the "'hardware'" (p. 699). Compare Ingraham's list with Rheingold's list of participatory media technologies.
4. In 1989 the NCSS board of directors approved the *Teaching about Science, Technology and Society in Social Studies: Education for Citizenship in the 21st Century* where some mention was made of using technology for instructional purposes and the Board endorsed the American Library Association's *Information Literacy: A Position Paper on Information Problem-Solving*.
5. Aside from Diem and Martorella, there were other social studies educators who took an interest in the Internet's potential, such as Braun and Ris-

inger (1999) who authored a NCSS bulletin, Surfing social studies: The Internet book.

6.   The Center on Education Policy (2008), Rock et al. (2006) and VanFossen (2005) concluded that elementary schools had decreased instructional time for social studies so as to provide more time for math and reading.

7.   A Pew Internet Project Data memo dated December 30, 2008 that reported post-election tracking survey results: "Voters expect that the level of public engagement they experienced with Barack Obama during the campaign, much of it occurring online" (p. 1).

8.   In the spring of 2009 while more users were registered with FaceBook than with MySpace, FaceBook generated a third less revenue from ads. MySpace's Terms of Service agreement better enabled the business to post online ads. When FaceBook sought to change portions of the user agreement that would reserve to the company the right to use user content, the membership mounted a campaign against the changes and FaceBook backed away from them.

REFERENCES

Barbrook R., & Cameron, A. (1995). *The Californian ideology*. Retrieved August 6, 2009, from http://www.alamut.com/subj/ideologies/ pessimism/califIdeo_I.html

Becker, T., & Slaton, C. (2000). *The future of teledemocracy*. Westport, CT: Praeger.

Bell, M. (2008). Toward a definition of "virtual worlds." *Journal of Virtual World Research, 1*(1), 1-5.

Bennett, W. L. (2008a). Changing citizenship in the digital age. In W. L. Bennett (Ed.), *Civic life online: Learning how digital media can engage youth* (pp. 1-24). Cambridge, MA: The MIT Press.

Bennett, W. L. (2008b). The generational shift in citizen identity: Implications for civic learning online. *Center for Communication & Civic Engagement*. Retrieved from http://www.engagedcitizen.org

Berson, I. R., Berson, M. J., Desai, S., Falls, D., & Fenaughty, J. (2008). An analysis of electronic media to prepare children for safe and ethical practices in digital environments. *Contemporary Issues in Technology and Teacher Education, 8*(3), 222-243.

Berson, M. J., Lee, J. K., & Stuckart, D. W. (2001). Promise and practice of computer technologies in the social studies: A critical analysis. In W. Stanley (Ed.), *Critical issues in social studies research for the 21t century* (pp. 209-229). Greenwich, CT: Information Age.

Bolick, C. (2004). The giant is waking. *Journal of Computing in Teacher Education, 20*(2), 130, 132.

boyd, d. (2008). Why youth social network sites: The role of networked publics in teenage social life. In D. Buckingham (Ed.), *Youth, identity, and digital Media. The John D. and Catherine T. MacArthur Foundation Series on Digital Media and Learning* (pp. 119-142). Cambridge, MA: The MIT Press.

boyd, d. m., & Ellison, N. B. (2008). Social network sites: Definition, history, and-scholarship. *Journal of Computer-Mediated Communication, 13*(1), 210-230.

Braun, J. A., Jr., & Risinger, F. (Eds.). (1999). *Surfing social studies: The Internet book* (NCSS, Bulletin No. 96, 180.) Washington, DC: National Council for the Social Studies.

Center for Digital Democracy. (n.d.). *Ten questions to ask your cell phone provider—and the online marketers they work with—to protect your mobile privacy.* Retrieved May 27, 2009, from http://www.democraticmedia.org/node/398

Cliff, D., O'Malley, C., & Taylor, J. (2008) *Future issues in socio-technical change for UK education.* Briefing Paper for the Beyond Current Horizons Project. Futurelab.

Clinton, W. J. (1993*). Remarks by President Clinton: Announcing the Initiative to Streamline Government.* Retrieved August 8, 2009, from http://govinfo.library.unt.edu/npr/library/speeches/030393.html

Clinton, W. J. (2000). *State of the Union address.* Retrieved August 8, 2009, from http://usgovinfo.about.com/library/ref/blsoufull.htm

Coleman, R., Lieber, P., Mendelson. A. L., & Kurpius, D. D. (2008) Public life and the Internet: if you build a better website, will citizens become engaged? *New Media Society, 10*(2), 179-201.

Coleman, S. (2005). New mediation and direct representation: Reconceptualizing representation in the digital age. *New Media & Society, 7*(2), 177-198.

Coleman, S. (2008). Doing IT for themselves: Management versus autonomy in youth e-citizenship. In W. Lance Bennett & The John D. and Catherine T. MacArthur Foundation Series on Digital Media and Learning (Ed.), *Civic life online: Learning how digital media can engage youth* (pp. 189-206). Cambridge, MA: The MIT Press.

Coleman, S., & Gøtze, J. (2001). *Bowling together: Online public engagement in policy deliberation.* London: Hansard Society. Retrieved May 11, 2006, from http://bowlingtogether.net

Crocco, M. S. (2001). Leveraging constructivist learning in the social studies classroom: A response to Mason, Berson, Diem, Hicks, Lee, and Dralle. *Contemporary Issues in Technology and Teacher Education* [Online serial], *1*(3). Retrieved from   http://www.citejournal.org/vol1/iss3/currentissues/socialstudies/article2.htm

Crowe, A. R. (2006). Technology, citizenship, and the social studies classroom: Education for democracy in a technological age. *International Journal of Social Education, 21*(1), 111-121.

Cunningham, M. (1995). *WikiWikiWeb.* Retrieved August 4, 2009, from http://c2.com/cgi/wiki?WelcomeVisitors

Dahlgren, P. (2005). Internet, public spheres and political communication: dispersion and deliberation. *Political Communication, 22*(2), 147-162.

Damer, B. (2008). Meeting in the ether: A brief history of virtual worlds as a medium for user-created events. *Journal of Virtual Worlds Research, 1*(1), 1-17.

Davies, T., & Cranston, P. (2008). *How can youth work best support young people to navigate the risks and make the most of opportunities of online social networking.* Leicester, England: The National Youth Agency.

Delli Carpini, M. X. (2000). Gen.com: Youth, civic engagement, and the new information environment. *Political Communication, 17*(4), 341-349.

de Toqueville, A. (1848). *Democracy in America.* Retrieved April 30, 2008, from the American Studies at the University of Virginia website: http://xroads.virginia.edu/~HYPER/DETOC/ch2_05.htm

Diem, R. A. (2000). Can it make a difference: Technology and the social studies. *Theory & Research in Social Education, 28*(4), 493-501.

Diem, R. A. (2008). "Shoulda," "coulda," "woulda": Technology and citizenship education. In P. J. VanFossen & M. J. Berson (Eds.), *The electronic republic? The impact of technology on education for citizenship* (pp. xi-xxii). West Lafayette, IN: Purdue University Press.

Doolittle, P., & Hicks, D. (2003). Constructivism as a theoretical foundation for the use of technology in Social Studies. *Theory and Research in Social Education, 31*(1), 72-104.

Flanagan, C., & Faison, N. (2001). Youth civic development: Implications of research for social policy and programs. *Social Policy Report, 15*(1), 3-16.

Fontana, L. (1988). Television and the social studies. *Social Education, 52*(5), 348-350.

Fountain, J. (2001). The virtual state: Transforming American government? *National Civic Review, 9*(3), 241-252.

Friedman, A. M. (2006). The Internet's potential to affect social studies and democracy. *International Journal of Social Education, 21*(1), 44-58.

Friedman, A. M., & Hicks, D. (2006). The state of the field: Technology, social studies, and teacher education. *Contemporary Issues in Technology and Teacher Education* [Online serial], *6*(2). Retrieved from http://www.citejournal.org/vol6/iss2/socialstudies/article1.cfm

Gerodimos, R. (2004, September). *The interaction of cyberculture and civic culture and its effect on democracy: A research agenda.* Fifth International and Interdisciplinary Conference of the Association of Internet Researchers (AoIR) *Internet Research 5.0: Ubiquity?* University of Sussex, England.

Gore, A. (1993). *Creating a government that works better and costs less: Reengineering through information technology. Report of the National Performance Review.* Washington DC: Government Printing Office.

Gorman, L., & McLean, D. (2009). *Media and society into the 21st century: A historical introduction* (2nd ed.). West Sussex, England: Wiley-Blackwell.

Greenhill, A., & Fletcher, G. (2003). *Social construction of electronic space.* Retrieved May 1, 2008, from http://www.spaceless.com/papers/12.htm

Hartley, J. (2002). *Communication, cultural and media studies: The key concepts.* London: Routledge.

Haythornthwaite, C. (2005). Introduction: Computer-mediated collaborative practices. *Journal of Computer-Mediated Communication, 10*(4), article 11. Retrieved from http://jcmc.indiana.edu/vol10/issue4/haythornthwaite.html

Heafner, T., & Friedman, A. (2008). Wikis and constructivism in secondary social studies: Fostering a deeper understanding. *Computers in the Schools, 25*(3), 288-302.

Ho, A. T. (2002). Reinventing local governments and the e-government initiative. *Public Administration Review, 62*(4), 434-444.

Ingraham, L. W. (1967). The "mixed media" menu. *Social Education, 31*(8), 698-701.

Ingraham, L. W. (1980). Is there a videodisc in your future? *Social Education, 44*(7), 641-643.

Ito, M., Horst, H., Matteo, B., & boyd, d. (2008). *Living and learning with new media: Summary of findings from the Digital Youth Project.* Chicago, IL: The John D. and Catherine T. MacArthur Foundation Reports on Digital Media and Learning.

Ivey, B., & Tepper, S. J. (2006, May 19). Cultural renaissance or cultural divide? *Chronicle of HigherEducation, 52*(37), section B6-B8.

Jenkins, H., Clinton, K., Purushotma, R., Robison, A. J., & Weigel, M. (2006). *Confronting the challenges of participatory culture: Media education for the 21st Century.* Chicago, IL: MacArthur Foundation.

Kendall, D. S., & Budin, H. (1987). Computers in the classroom: Introduction. *Social Education, 51*(1), 32-33.

Kendall, D. S., & Budin, H. (1987). Computers for intellectual regeneration. *Social Education, 55*(1), 34-36.

Larson, B. E., & Keiper, T. A. (2002). Classroom discussion and threaded electronic discussion: Learning in two arenas. *Contemporary Issues in Technology andTeacher Education* [Online serial], *2*(1). Retrieved from http://www.citejournal.org/vol2/iss1/socialstudies/article1.cfm

Leiner, B. M.. Cerf, V. G., Clark, D. D., Kahn, R. E., Kleinrock, D. C., Lynch, J. et al. (2003). *A brief history of the Internet, version 3.32.* Retrieved from http://www.isoc.org/internet/history/brief.shtml

Lenhart, A., Kahne, J., Middaugh, E., Macgill, A. R., Evans, C., & Vitak, J. (2008). *Teens, video games, and civics.* Washington, DC: Pew Internet & American Life Project.

Lenhart, A. (2009). Teens, mobile and games. Washington, DC: Pew Internet & American Life Project. Retrieved on August 9, 2009, from http://www.pewinternet.org/Presentations/2009/28Teens-Mobile-Phones-and-Video-Gaming.aspx

Licklider, J. C. R., & Taylor, R. W. (1968). The computer as a communication device. *Science and Technology, 76,* 21-41.

Livingstone, S. M., & Bober, M. (2006). *Taking up online opportunities? Children's uses of the Internet for education, communication and participation.* Paper presented at the annual meeting of the International Communication Association, New York. Retrieved from the All Academic Research website: http://www.allacademic.com/meta/p11723_index.html

Lunstrum, J. P., & Scheider, D. O. (1969). Commercial television in the teaching of the social studies. *Social Education, 33*(2), 154-160.

Martorella, P. (1997). Technology and social studies-or: Which way to the sleeping giant? *Theory and Research in Social Education, 25*(4), 511-514.

Mason, C., Berson, M., Diem, R., Hicks, D., & Dralle, T. (2000). Guidelines for usingtechnology to prepare social studies teachers. *Contemporary Issues in Technology and Teacher Education, 1*(1). Retrieved from http://www.citejournal.org/vol1/iss1/currentissues/socialstudies/article1.htm

Mehlinger, H. D. (1996). School reform in the information age. *Phi Delta Kappan*, 77(6), 400-407.

Messinger, P. R., Stroulia, E., & Lyons, K. (2008). A typology of virtual worlds: Historical overview and future directions. *Journal of Virtual Worlds Research, 1*(1), 1-18.

Milward, H. B., & Snyder, L. O. (1996). Electronic government: Linking citizens to public organizations through technology. *Journal of Public Administration Research and Theory, 6*(2), 261-276.

Montgomery, K. C. (2008). Youth and digital democracy: Intersections of practice, policy, and the marketplace. In W. L. Bennett (Ed.), *Civic life online: Learning how digital media canengage youth* (pp. 25-50). Cambridge, MA: The MIT Press.

Morrissett, I. (1984). Four futures for social studies. *Social Education, 48*(7), 511-516.

National Center for Educational Statistics. (2003). Internet access in U.S. Public schools and classrooms: 1994- 2002 [Online]. Retrieved from http://nces.ed.gov/pubs2004/2004011.pdf

National Council for the Social Studies. (2006). Technology position statement and guidelines. Retreived from http://www.socialstudies.org/positions/technology

National Council for the Social Studies. (2009). *NCSS position statement on media literacy*. Retrieved from http://www.socialstudies.org/positions/medialiteracy

Open Directory Project. (n.d.). Retrieved from http://www.dmoz.org/about.html

Open Source Initiative. (2007). Retrieved from http://www.opensource.org

Osborne, D., & Gabler, T. (1992). *Reinventing government: How the entrepreneurial spirit is transforming the public sector reading*. Boston, MA: Addison-Wesley.

Parker, W. C. (2001). Educating democratic citizens: A broad view. *Theory into Practice, 40*(1), 6-13.

Pedersen M. (2004, July). *Lessons from cyberspace: The free software movement andconfiguration of ownership*. Second International Conference "Imaging Social Movements," Edge Hill College. Ormskirk, England. Retrieved August 8, 2009, from http://web.archive.org/web/20070224131746/www.edgehill.ac.uk/Research/smg/Conferences2004/info/papers/pedersen.pdf

Pelton, J. N. (1988). Tele-education: The future. *Social Education, 52*(5), 366-369.

Peterson, R. A., Balasubramanian, S., & Bronnenberg, B. (1997). Exploring the implications of the Internet for consumer marketing. *Journal of the Academy of Marketing Science, 25*(4), 329-346.

Porter, C. E. (2004). A typology of virtual communities: A multi-disciplinary foundation for future research. *Journal of Computer-Mediated Communication, 10*(1), article 3.

Prescott, L. (2007). Virtual worlds ranking: Runescape #1. *Hitwise*. Retrieved May 27, 2009, from http://weblogs.hitwise.com/leeann-prescott/2007/04/virtual_worlds_ranking_runesca.html

Rainie, L., & Anderson, J. (2008). *The future of the Internet III*. Washington, DC: Pew Internet & American Life Project.

Raynes-Goldie, K., & Walker, L. (2008). Our space: Online civic engagement tools for youth. In W. L. Bennett (Ed.), *Civic life online: Learning how digital media can engage youth* (pp. 161-188). Cambridge, MA: The MIT Press.

Rheingold, H. (1993) *The virtual community: Homesteading on the virtual frontier.* Reading, MA: Addison-Wesley (Electronic version located at http://www.rheingold.com/vc/book/intro.html).

Rheingold, H. (2008). Using participatory media and public voice to encourage civic engagement. In W. L. Bennett (Ed.), *Civic life online: Learning how digital media can engage youth* (pp. 97-118). Cambridge, MA: The MIT Press.

Rock, T. C., Heafner, T., O'Conner, K., Passe, J., Oldendorf, S., Good, A., et al. (2006). One state closer to a national crisis. A report on elementary social studies education in North Carolina Schools. *Theory and Research in Social Education, 34*(4), 465-483.

Rose, S. A., Brandhurst, A. R., Glenn, A. D., Hodges, J. O., & White, C. S. (1984). Social studies microcomputer courseware evaluation guidelines. *SocialEducation, 48*(7), 573-576.

Search Engine History. (n.d.). *History of search engines: From 1945 to Google 2007.* Retrieved August 3, 2009, from http://www.searchenginehistory.com/

Schelin, S. H. (2003). E-government: An overview. In G. D. Garson (Ed.), *Public information technology: Policy and management issues* (pp. 120-137). Hershey, PA: Idea Group.

Schugurensky, D. (2004). *The tango of citizenship learning and participatory democracy.* Retrieved May 15, 2009, from http://tlc.oise.utoronto.ca/conference2003/Proceedings/s_w.pdf

Seiter, E. (2005). *The Internet playground: Children's access, entertainment, and mis-education.* London: Peter Lang.

Shaffer, D. W., Squire, K. R., Halverson, R., & Gee, J. P. (2005). Video games and the future of learning. *Phi Delta Kappan, 87*(2), 104-111.

Sharples, M., Graber, R., Harrison, C., & Logan, K. (2009). E-safety and Web 2.0 children aged 11-16. *Journal of Computer Assisted Learning, 25*(1), 70–84.

Solove, D. J. (2004). *The digital person: Technology and privacy in the information age.* New York: New York University Press.

Spellings, M. (2008). *Harnessing innovation to support student Success: Using technology to personalize education.* Washington, DC: U.S. Department of Education. Retrieved January 8, 2009, from http://www.ed.gov/about/offices/list/os/technology/reports/roundtable.html

Subrahmanyam, K., & Greenfield, P. (2008). Online communication and adoles-centrelationships. *The Future of Children 18*(1), 119–146.

Tally, B. (2007). Digital technology and the end of social studies education. *Theory andResearch in Social Education, 35*(2), 305-321.

Taney, F. X. (2008). How open source software will affect virtual worlds. *Journal of Virtual Worlds Research, 1*(1), 1-6.

Thomas, D., & Brown, J. (2009). Why virtual worlds can matter. *International Journal ofLearning and Media, 1*(1), 37-49.

Thomas, J. C., & Streib, G. (2003). The new face of government: Citizen-initiated-contacts in the era of e-government. *Journal of Public Administration and Theory, 13*(1), 83-102.

Tiwari, R., & Buse, S. (2007). *The mobile commerce prospects: A strategic analysis of opportunities in the banking sector.* Hamburg, Germany: Hamburg University Press.

United Nations Educational, Scientific and Cultural Organization. (2005). *Convention on the protection and promotion of the diversity of cultural expressions.* Retrieved from http://portal.unesco.org/en/ev
.php-URL_ID=31038&URL_DO=DO_TOPIC&URL_SECTION=201.html

United Nations Division for Public Economics and Public Administration & American Society for Public Administration. (2002). *Benchmarking e-government: A global perspective.*

Valenti, J. (1969). Special statement to readers of social education. *Social Education, 33*(2), 146-151.

VanFossen, P. J., & Berson, M. J. (Eds.). (2008). *The electronic republic? The impact of technology on education for citizenship.* West Lafayette, IN: Purdue University Press.

VanFossen, P. J., Freidman, A., & Hartshorne, R. (2008). The role of MMORPGs insocial studies education. In R. Ferdig (Ed.), *Handbook of research on effective electronic gaming in education* (pp. 235-250). Hershey, PA: Information Science Publishing.

VanFossen, P. J. (2005). "Reading and math take so much of the time…": An overview ofsocial studies instruction in elementary classrooms in Indiana. *Theory and Research in Social Education, 33*(3), 376-403.

VanFossen, P. J., & Shiveley, J. M. (2003). A content analysis of Internet sessions presented at the National Council for the Social Studies annual meeting, 1995? 2002. *Theory and Research in Social Education, 31*(4), 502-522.

West, D. (2004). E-government and transformation of service delivery and citizenattitudes. *Public Administration Review, 64*(1), 15–27.

Whitworth, S. A., & Berson, M. J. (2003). Computer technology in the social studies: Anexamination of the effectiveness literature (1996-2001). *Contemporary Issues inTechnology and Teacher Education* [Online serial], *2*(4). Retrieved from http://www.citejournal.org/vol2/iss4/socialstudies/article1.cfm

Wiklund, H. (2005). A Habermasian analysis of the deliberative democratic potential ofICT-enabled services in Swedish municipalities. *New Media Society, 7*(2), 247-270.

CHAPTER 13

GLOBALLY CONNECTED SOCIAL STUDIES

Making it Real, Making it Relevant

Tim Dove, Jeff Elliott, Merry Merryfield, and Betsy Sidor

There was a time not so long ago when Americans perceived the peoples of Africa, Asia, Latin America, or Europe to be "over there," far away from the United States and unconnected to their daily lives. The issues of those places—dealing with poverty, hunger, old rivalries, ethnic, or religious conflicts—seemed quite apart from the issues faced in their own communities. Up until the late 1980s instructional units and textbook chapters about other world regions often sounded like a fairy tale in a place far, far away as students studied "Nigeria: Tradition and Change," "Japan: Asia's Miracle," or "Israel: A Homeland for the Jews," with little or no connection between what was happening "over there" to the United States or students' own lives.

Then along came major events that demonstrated the increasing interconnectedness of world systems: the seemingly endless flow of manufacturing jobs from the United States to Latin America and Asia, the effects of the global petroleum market on prices in the United States, and the

Technology in Retrospect: Social Studies in the Information Age 1984-2009, pp. 239–260

connections between poverty and violence in other nations and increasing American demographic changes that brought linguistic, ethnic and religious diversity into many American communities. Global warming, the disposal of toxic wastes, overfishing, loss of biodiversity and other environmental issues began to be recognized as unsolvable by one country or even one region. Then we experienced the terror of the 9/11 attacks, wars in Iraq and Afghanistan, and the 2008 world financial crisis. Running parallel to all the political, social, environmental, and economic changes were new information technologies that have literally leapfrogged past old ways of thinking about the cultural, legal or geographic barriers that separate Americans from people and issues "over there." Today American teachers and students know that the world has moved into our towns and neighborhoods, our banks, farms, and factories, into our homes and leisure time. Schools today must educate young people about the world so that they are globally literate and competent to make decisions and solve problems that go beyond their states and nation.

In this chapter we share how we are transforming our teaching and student learning to meet these goals. We reject the "over there" and "over here" dichotomies. We live on planet earth. Our students must be prepared to assess its issues and problems from a global perspective and work collaboratively with diverse people in order to become effective citizens engaged in their community, nation and world. New technologies can make social studies relevant to today's generation and connect them to events and issues across the planet. The chapter is divided into three illustrations of how tech tools can be used to motivate students and help them think critically about their world as they become engaged in mandated social studies content.

- Betsy Sidor shares her experiences using Moodle to develop skills in critical thinking and engagement in global events and issues.
- Tim Dove demonstrates how Skype makes a difference in culture learning and developing skills in cross-cultural interaction.
- Jeff Elliott discusses how his students use several electronic tools to create digital white papers about global issues.

The examples we use come from our courses: middle school world history and global cultures, high school economics, U.S. and world history, and U.S. government. We have organized the chapter around three interrelated goals: making connections with people and primary sources in other world regions, studying global issues and events through multiple perspectives and creating authentic global learning experiences. In each of the sections we begin with a rationale and overview for using a particular technology, followed by a step by step demonstration of how we have implemented it. Each section ends with our reflections and advice.

MOODLE: BETSY'S TOOL FOR
ANALYTIC THINKING AND GLOBAL CONNECTIONS

In the last few decades information technologies have unleashed prodigious economic and cultural energies that have made contemporary society a global one. Brink Lindsey (2008), Vice President for research at the Cato Institute, argues in *The Age of Abundance* that many workers are maladapted to this dynamic, global workplace as few job-seekers have the abilities to think analytically, plan for the long term and work cooperatively to solve local and global problems.

I doubt that most educators are surprised by these abilities, but, as experts on Information Age teenagers, we know that attracting and holding students' attention long enough to develop these traits is difficult. I have noticed that the same learners who passively sit in my classes feverishly engage their digital devices the moment the class change bell sounds. In the 5 minutes that students flow from one room to another, their thumbs tap out text messages, their ear buds flood their brains with exclusive sounds, they pull up their Facebook page, attack an online gaming foe, reset eBay bids, or view a YouTube video. If students gave their schoolwork the same attention that they give their digital devices, educators would be much more successful teaching Lindsey's three skills.

Over the last year I have learned how to use a course homepage in Moodle (see http://moodle.org/), an open-source software package that provides a website for a specific course and allows the teacher and students to post documents, links, RSS feeds, threaded discussions, and use other online communication tools. Moodle centers my classroom in the digital age and connects students to global events and issues every time they go online. Students bookmark my course website and click on Moodle whenever they perform a learning activity. Moodle serves as a course organizer and a digital meeting place where my students and I explore breaking news from around the world and then discuss the "So what does this have to do with me?" questions in Moodle's discussion forums. I have found that by making Moodle a centerpiece for daily research and discussion, my students are enticed to spend more time on academic tasks, think more critically and collaborate on goals that we set together.

Step by Step

Last year my ninth grade students were an academically diverse group who shared a passion for their digital gadgets—cellphones and iPods from home and laptops at school. In order to get world history on their tech radar and scaffold analytical thinking skills, I began using Moodle to organize daily learning activities. As each class started with "Let's Moodle up," the students developed the habit of clicking on "What's in the News" and reading a high interest article that I posted from the *New York Times* or another world newspaper. Together we read the article and studied related maps, photos, links, and statistics that newspapers provided.

After securing the information, students clicked on the Moodle "Forum on the News Article" and responded to an open-ended question, such as one the first week: "To what extent do the Olympic games promote peaceful relations among nations?" Students were asked to develop their ideas with evidence from articles and organize their writing with the Power Paragraph Format, a strategy I use which includes:

Sentence 1: Clearly state your answer to the prompt.

Sentence 2: Qualify and clarify your first sentence.

Sentence 3: Explain why the expert you are citing speaks with authority on this subject.

Sentence 4: Cite evidence from the source that supports your answer.

Sentence 5: Explain how the evidence justifies your answer.

After 7-10 minutes to think, refer to the article and write, students posted paragraphs that others in the class could then read and respond to online. The discussion served to identify interesting ideas and effective use of evidence.

Using Amy Chua's (2008) ideas in *Day of Empire: How Hyperpowers Rise to Global Dominance and Why They Fall* and Howard Spodek's (2008) elements of empire—leadership, legitimacy, administration, economy, and military, we compared the Persian, Roman, Mongol, and American Empires. "Moodle Up" discussions on the Iraq War and past and present qualities of leaders connected the past and present. Political campaigns also offered an opportunity to introduce Jackson and Jamieson's (2007) techniques for "un-spinning" propaganda and recognizing bias. The daily "Moodle-Up" article was selected to reveal multiple perspectives and conflicting sources, some partisan and some nonpartisan. The Forum questions prompted students to write a power paragraph identifying a propaganda technique or the use of political spin. Questions arose comparing the leadership, legitimacy and political behavior of Bush, McCain, Obama to leaders of past empires—Cyrus, Hadrian, or Genghis Khan.

When the world's financial markets crashed, Moodle connected historical events being studied to unfolding news and online resources. Now Spodek's (2008) two elements of empire that had largely been ignored—

administration and economy—were front and center. The media panic over the financial meltdown led to a daily barrage of questions from the students. To help them find objective analysis on the financial crisis, I introduced them to our library's subscription databases, such as *elibray Curriculum Edition* which gives staff and students access to *The Economist* (the analysis is first-rate but the reading level is too advanced for freshman so I paraphrased much of the article.), *Marketplace,* and NPR's *Morning Edition.* The students gravitated to the radio programs and were soon prefacing their comments with "I heard on NPR that …" The bail-outs permeated the students' cyberspace. Now they wanted to know how to determine the credibility of a source, so the Forum prompt demanded not only that the paragraph address the question of the day, but also that it establish the credibility of the source.

How could the skills and knowledge they were learning be assessed? The answer was simple—by asking the class. After a few Forum posts, a student who habitually sneaked to his online gaming site, slapped his head and shouted "now I get it, does Amy Chua thinks the American Empire has lost its glue and is in decline?" With a chorus of affirmations, the students approved the essay question and helped me construct the rubric which required use of three of Spodek's (2008) elements of empire and comparisons to Chua's analysis of the Persian, Roman, or Mongol glue.

Another connection across historical and contemporary events was made when the terrorist attacks in Mumbai, India created teachable moment. When the class met on that Monday morning after Thanksgiving, I never got a chance to say "Moodle Up." One student directed us to the *BBC.co.uk* for a slideshow while another instructed me to load a map of the Mumbai peninsula from *Maps.101.* Yet another was reading from Saturday's *New York Times* and listing the items in the terrorists' backpacks. A consensus suggested that the Forum question ask "Why are the Lashkar-e-Taiba, the Pakistani militant group, so angry with the people of Mumbai?" To help them answer the prompt, I showed them *NewsBank: Access World News,* a subscription database with newspapers from around the world, and randomly assigned students to search newspapers in Mumbai's region—the Middle East, Central Asia, China, South East Asia, India and Pakistan. *NewsBank* has abstracted every article so readers who are not adroit at skimming can sort through the hits more effectively.

Once students found an article, we worked through the bias and credibility issues as a group. Then I gave them time to write their power paragraphs. From the Forum posts and the discussion that followed the students gave me a homework assignment. They wanted to know more about India and Pakistan's relationship with Kashmir. Student interest in the Mumbai terrorist attacks continued, perhaps because they knew about

Hinduism and Islam from world history. The online conversation quickly moved to their interests in jihad and politics.

To work on developing students' global perspectives, I placed on the "Moodle Up" post a list of countries, one for each student, and a Forum prompt, "Why are Muslims so angry?" The assignment was to go to the database *NewsBank: Access World News* and search only newspapers published in their assigned country. It took a good 30 minutes for the students to post their paragraphs as I had to provide the back-story for several issues—such as headscarves in France and cartoons featuring Muhammad in the Netherlands. But the results were impressive. Their answers included "Muslims feel like second class citizens," "they are political minorities and cannot influence their government," and "the Western culture is changing their children." I could not have gotten this result without the use of technology. But, without my direction and background information the students could not have gotten the same results with technology alone.

Moodle continued to provide the content and discussion forums to engage students in world events as they studied world history. The next unit in world history was trade. I set the textbook aside and modeled my activities on William J. Bernstein's (2008) engaging and comprehensive book, *A Splendid Exchange: How Trade Shaped the World*. I assigned a map exercise, called "Pirate Predators, Arrgh! circa 1200 C.E." Working in groups, students competed to get the lucrative job of guarding ships from pirates from the Baltic to the Levant. They researched possible "Choke Points" of the spice trade through historical reference maps from *MAPS 101* (from links on Moodle) and then presented their findings, relevant maps and their security strategy.

As luck would have it, when the students "Moodled Up" they clicked on the front page of the *New York Times* with its coverage of the Somali pirates' hijacking of an oil tanker. Amazed and amused, the students demanded to know how, given modern technology, could pirates still exist? So to answer the Forum question, "Why do pirates operate in Somali waters?" I introduced them to the *CountryWatch* database. Each student was assigned an indicator from the following list: Political Risk Index, Freedom Rankings, Human Rights Index, Government Effectiveness, Economic Performance Index, Control Of Corruption Index, Transparency Index, Rule of Law Index, Human Development Index, Status of Women Index, Energy Consumption Index, and others. The task was to enter the database, search for Somalia, click on the assigned indicator to learn what it measured and Somalia's ranking. Then, in their own words—no cutting and pasting—post to the Forum an explanation of what the indicator revealed about Somalia. We used two projection screens to analyze the results. One screen listed the Forum with the indicators for Somalia and the second the *CountryWatch* page for the United States. As the students shared their indicators, we worked together to analyze the contextual factors of a failed state. For some it was their first experience interpreting data and using it to make comparisons.

Reflections

Teaching thinking and worldmindedness is a long-term process, so set reasonable goals for each day. Start by teaching the power paragraph one or two sentences at a time with one or two resources from other parts of the world. Initially you may ask only for evidence and an answer to the prompt. It may be easier to begin with countries or issues in which students already have a connection. While it is not possible to critique each student each day, work out a rotation so that everyone gets a chance to build a paragraph with class feedback. The learning curve for research and writing may be shorter for some students. Therefore, encourage those who master the objectives to help their classmates. On days when you are pressed for time, ask students to collaboratively construct sentences for the power paragraphs. If you pair up students who disagree they may build proactive answers to prompts. Model an interest in different points of view from other countries so they learn not to assume that all Indians or Russians think exactly the same way.

Once a significant portion of the class has learned to write the power paragraph, focus on developing analytical skills. The Forum now serves as a debating venue and as long as the students are helping you develop the questions the engagement level will remain high. Initially the teacher sets up the debate rules and models questioning techniques that challenge weak evidence, faulty logic, and vague answers. Students quickly learn the analytical process and then the teacher becomes more of an arbitrator during the debate.

Most importantly, do not let the students convince you to let them stop writing the power paragraph. Remember one goal is to develop analytical thinking, and the writing process forces them to justify and clarify every claim that they make. My experience proves that the posted written arguments are more thoughtful and logical than ones that are made orally. The posted arguments also ensure a wider variety of constructive feedback. Even those who do not listen well enough to critique an oral argument can contribute to one that is written.

Experience has taught me that if the world outside the school is engaged in a current issue, then my students will be interested in the topic. So I read world newspapers, pay attention to what the students are discussing outside of class, and work at finding ways to link the topic to the content that I am hired to teach. This approach encourages the students to question, research, think deeply and teach each other. Providing I select the right topic, the engagement level will be high and students will spend the time on the learning activities to master an aspect of the problem. Collaborative activities such as debates and discussion forums put students in the role of a teacher, and when students reconcile facts that contradict their thinking they learn to analyze issues.

SKYPE: TIM'S WORK ON CULTURAL UNDERSTANDING AND REAL TIME CONNECTIONS

How can we teach students to gain an understanding of diverse world cultures? I remember my students' frustrations years ago as they struggled to overcome stereotypes and misinformation as we studied Africa. They could identify how cartoons, Hollywood films, missionary tales or the "exotic" nature of some *National Geographics* had shaped their mental images. But what was frustrating to my students was that they didn't know where to turn to redefine their understandings of diverse cultures and geographic regions across the continent. I found that inviting people from other countries to come in and interact with my students was one of the most powerful strategies I had. Eventually my students would come to the point when inquiring about a new place or people that they would say, "Let's talk to someone from there and find out!"

Today people can "visit" our classroom from Germany or Japan as there are many different ways to communicate electronically with people across the planet. From teleconferencing to asynchronous discussions, new technologies are connecting students with people across town and across oceans. We have found Skype, a free software package, to work well as it gives users free voice and visual communications as it links computers of registered users (see www.skype.com). Skype has the potential for overcoming some of the resource dilemmas of the past as it requires only a computer (although Skype can be used on a PDA or cell phone), an online connection, a webcam, and a microphone. I have had students pull together the needed hardware from garage sales.

The opportunities to use Skype as a productive educational tool are limited only by the imagination. I first used Skype with my students while attending a Civic Education Conference in Morocco in 2008. My colleagues and I (we are an interdisciplinary seventh grade team at Phoenix Middle School[1]) saw this trip as an opportunity to share primary source information with our students at home in Ohio and test the viability of Skype for cross-national learning. After downloading Skype onto my own laptop and my classroom computer (which connects to a 6 x 9 ft screen), my colleagues and I practiced talking to each other at home and at work. Then with some coordination of time (a great way to teach about time zones), I was able to talk face to face with my classes in real time from Marrakech, and my students were able to have conversations face to face with teachers from Sudan, Ukraine, Morocco, and England whom I had met at the conference. Morocco was no longer just a page in the textbook. As I moved the webcam on my balcony, my students could look around the neighborhood where I was staying and view the everyday activities (students walking home from school, shoppers choosing fruit, business-men with their briefcases) that were both alike and somewhat different from ones in Worthington, Ohio.

What makes such experiences more than just an interesting activity? My colleagues and I see such connections as an authentic way to begin to facilitate their understanding of what we like to call "Internal Culture" (Hanley, 1999). Unlike the surface culture of clothes, food, architecture, holidays, and music that often passes for culture study, internal culture is made up of the beliefs, values and norms (how people act related to time, space, age, gender, authority, self vs. the group, etc.) that they would need in order to work collaboratively over time with people from that culture. My colleague, Beth Cullinan, uses a version of Merryfield and Wilson (2005) iceberg image to help students analyze differences between surface and internal culture. As students discuss what they can see when visiting another culture (or people from other countries can see when they visit us), they organize items for the cultural iceberg (see Figure 13.1).

Internal culture is not an easy concept, so we have them apply the idea to a topic under study. For example, our students were completing a unit of study about contemporary China, and a student chose the "Three Gorges Dam" to work on for her comparison of surface and internal culture. As an explanation of surface culture, she listed the plans for construction and images of landforms. Within the internal culture explanation, she discussed the tension between values of flood control and power needs with traditional Chinese beliefs in home and community, ties to the land and the treasuring of archeological sites.

Students quickly learn that it is very difficult to write a long list of internal culture components of another culture if they do not have access to primary sources. As one student said, "This is hard. You can't assume from the surface that you know a culture." Other assignments that followed helped students move from identifying their own lack of understanding to devising the kinds of questions necessary to engage a person in a conversation about cultural norms, values and beliefs. These experiences led students to recognize the implicit value of talking online to people in another country and created excitement about the opportunities afforded by Skype.

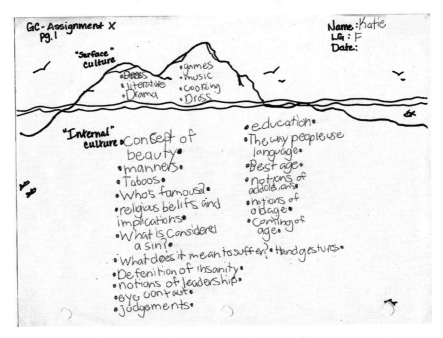

Figure 13.1.   Example of student work on culture.

My colleague, Robert Estice, and I wanted students to check out the intricacies of working with Skype. We started a "Skype Club" to try out different uses with small groups. We contacted a friend in Atlanta who owns an art gallery. Students easily recognized that seeing an art gallery online is fine, but having an interactive conversation with the owner about the art while "walking" through the gallery is a much better learning experience.

We also had a series of conversations with an elementary school principal (a friend of an American friend) and his 14-year old son in Taiwan. It was fascinating to watch the nonverbal reactions of the son. The conversation began between the adults—teachers at my school and the principal in Taiwan. We then moved the conversation to the students (see Figure 13.2).

The young Chinese boy's hair was unkempt, he had glasses on and his non-verbal actions gave the impression he was not all that interested in talking to Dad's friends. However, after some of our Chinese American students began to talk with him in Mandarin Chinese and this young man saw an articulate pretty young lady speaking back to him, the boy disappeared for a moment from the camera. When he returned, the glasses

Figure 13.2.   Photos of Taiwan and Columbus interaction.

were gone, the hair was combed, and a very animated young man contin-ued the conversation. The visual transformation was interesting, but the depth of the conversation changed as well. All of these experiences were prepped and debriefed with students under the guise of understanding surface and internal culture. We also discussed what questions are needed to help move the conversation into a deeper understanding and how to read nonverbal language.

Students then helped each other set up accounts and practice on dif-ferent machines throughout our school building and then with individu-als at home. They discussed how to present oneself online and what information should or should not be shared given issues of privacy and security. We also addressed questions such as: What do parents need to know so they will be supportive? What is appropriate behavior on the web and why?

Next we built on what we had learned to use Skype to have students identify and act on universal concerns. Students wanted to connect to stu-dents from other regions of the United States and other countries. The idea was to make introductions, move through surface culture informa-tion, discuss topics related to internal culture and then begin to identify local issues or concerns students could work on together to help their local communities. Further student conversation generated the idea that if a more diverse group of people looked at universal concerns from dif-ferent experiences, maybe we could learn from one another ways to attack problems in our own community. To this end, a letter of introduction was created by the team inviting other schools to consider talking with us online.

The letters went out to 28 schools that families and friends had contacts with as well as ones identified during Internet searches. It became clear that a personal connection to the school created easier initial contact.

Students and teachers then designed the "Hello" conversations. We found that it is best if students design the questions through a Socratic method as they need to wrestle with how people should introduce themselves to a stranger and in what ways they could be themselves while also being sensitive to other culture's norms. Conversations have developed in Atlanta, Taiwan, and Syria over Skype. We are in year 2 of using Skype and are excited about the early outcomes.

Reflections

There are three aspects of this work that need assessment: (1) student skills in communicating with Skype, (2) how use of Skype affects cultural learning and thinking skills, and (3) what other understandings and actions result from conversations through Skype. Figure 13.3 displays an overview of the implementation and assessment process.

Each section needs to have its own assessment through conversation, minute papers, demonstrations and/or reflective assignments. Our action plans will not go into effect until next school year. We see three critical issues to keep in mind as teachers begin working with Skype. First students must understand the implications of information on the web usually not being private. Second, students need a specific context and learning experiences to ground their understanding of how Skype can create important understandings that would be difficult without direct contact. And once contact has been made with other groups, teachers need to plan scaffolding activities to move communication beyond "What's your favorite music and food?" Classrooms of the twenty-first century need real-world connections as they prepare students to be adults who can work effectively in cross-cultural situations in their communities and around the world.

ONLINE DATABASES, GOOGLE DOCS, I-MOVIE AND MORE: JEFF'S DIGITAL WHITE PAPERS

As teachers we want our students to understand the joys and sorrows of the human condition and be cognizant of how societies and the physical planet are changing. We want them to use this knowledge as they work with others in making their world a better place. Sometimes such broad goals seem hard to reach when we find ourselves competing for students' attention with texting, online videos, web-surfing or social networking websites. Let's face it, textbooks, overheads, worksheets, teacher talk or even educational videos appear to our students as relics of a pre-elec-

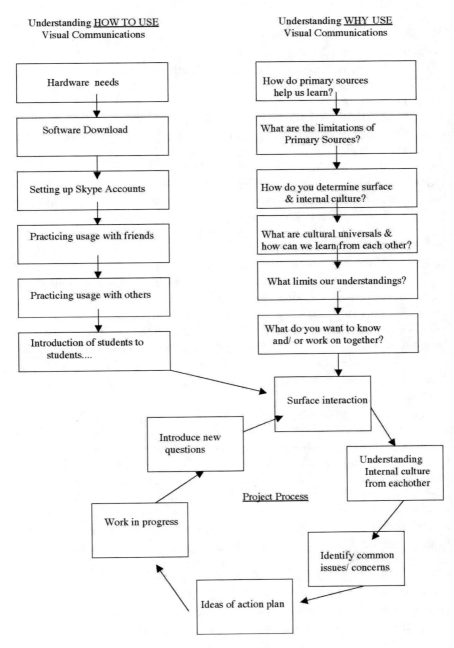

Figure 13.3.   Implementation and assessment process.

tronic age. In order to motivate students to master curriculum mandates and become engaged as citizens of a global age, we need to develop learning experiences that allow students to apply the best of the digital world with its collaborative and knowledge-sifting facets to the essential questions of the social studies. Technology can connect their personal worlds to critical issues in our content so that students learn how to find and evaluate information and collaborate with others to address real-life problems. Through several tech tools, students can create digital white papers that address these goals.

At Metro High School[2] our students take a 2 hour block of social studies everyday in their sophomore year. During Fall and Winter quarters we focus on integrated American and World History and then government/civics in the Spring. In the last unit of World History students study globalization and create a culminating project that targets an enduring global human problem. Then during the last unit of the government/civics course, they develop a "digital white paper project" that advocates a specific solution to a global problem through public policy. We call these "white papers" as this is the name traditionally given to persuasive research documents that seek to affect public policy. They are usually created by government or corporate entities that seek to change legislation and political realities. In their white papers students take a position based on evidence and attempt to convince their audience of the benefits of adopting a proposed course of action. These are *digital* white papers as they are developed through use of electronic databases and online discussions using Google docs and presented by digital tools from podcasts to iMovie.

Our digital white paper project was based on the World Millennium Development Goals (MDGs) which 192 member states of the United Nations and 23 international organizations have agreed to achieve to improve life on the planet by 2015.[3] There are seven goals which include eradication of extreme poverty and hunger, providing universal education, improving gender equality, improving child and maternal health, combating HIV/AIDS, working towards environmental sustainability and developing global partnerships. Students research an MDG of their choice, analyze possible courses of action, develop an argument for a specific legislative solution and present it to an authentic audience—using digital tools at each step. Finally they submit their digital white paper to the local, state, or federal legislative committees most appropriate for passing that legislation. As an assessment piece, it is an authentic use of technology much like adults might adapt in a local or global political process.

Step by Step

The skills and knowledge applied in the digital white paper are developed incrementally over a school year from unit to unit as students are taught increasingly complex skills in identifying and searching electronic databases and analyzing and synthesizing conflicting data and then organizing it through Google docs to make cogent arguments using Smart-Boards. They develop a basic understanding of globalization and some global issues through U.S. and world history. Because they already have foundational skills (in thinking, analyzing, and using digital tools) and knowledge, the digital white paper itself takes about 8 days of double-blocked periods.

The first day we discuss the project overall, including the assessment rubric. The requirements of the white paper include an abstract at the beginning of the paper, an explanation of the global issues surrounding the MDG that the student has chosen, data supporting a specific legislative solution, and an analysis of the national and global benefits gained from adopting that solution. All data must be supported with footnoted references and analysis, plus an annotated bibliography.

ELECTRONIC DATABASES, ONLINE JOURNALS, SMARTBOARDS

Once they understood the scope of the digital white paper, I taught a lesson using a SmartBoard on the relational and interactive nature of global dynamics and resources for researching contexts of global problems. I took an enduring human problem and had the class examine how it has been shaped by historical contexts, cultural diffusion and assimilation, politics and economics, human rights, and security issues. This process refreshes and extends everyone's skills in thinking globally, accessing interactive web resources and databases, scanning academic journals and analyzing flash-animated maps and graphics. As a class we built a resource base of appropriate journals and international databases for particular millennium goals and tried different approaches for finding useable data. For example, we began by thinking through what descriptors would be most productive in searching electronic databases such as JSTOR (http://www.jstor.org/), or what online journals would be productive of all those listed in the Ohio State University libraries homepage. They learned that Freedom House and the Social Science Research Council might be very useful for the study of human rights and conflict, whereas the World Bank, UNESCO, and UNDP databases were more relevant for global poverty.

With practiced access to online resources at Ohio State University, students were responsible for using a variety of data sources. Scientific journals and studies as well as public policy journals and government publications were to be used in order for the paper to be considered credible. Students were expected to demonstrate that no public policy happens in a vacuum so they needed to assess political institutions and actors (public and private) who could be relied on to support or oppose the legislation.

We spent some time examining how mass media outlets heavily influence knowledge frameworks. We discussed "the political animals"—groups, institutions and realities which have created or shaped public policy. The challenge for the students was that as they were learning these concepts they were required to incorporate an understanding of these groups and realities into their white paper and analyze which public interest groups would be supportive of their legislation. At the conclusion of these interactive lessons, students chose the enduring global problem they wanted to pursue and we discussed the three core questions that would guide their inquiry:

1. Identify *why* the issue of their MGD is such an enduring human problem. How does this issue impact my community and me?
2. Which public and private individuals and institutions are taking steps and making investments to meet the goal by 2015—and how can they be influenced? Also, identify current legislation that is being introduced in regards to my issue and evaluate its efficacy to meeting the MDG.
3. What still needs to be done? Find quantitative and qualitative data that illustrates the gap between what is being done and what more needs to happen for the MDG to be met by 2015.

Then we turned the students loose to research, chat with experts, download the latest journals, and create their papers. One day before the "first final draft" was due, students used Google docs as wikis to upload and edit each other's papers. We learned that this collaborative process continued well after students went home for the night.

It took my students about 7 days (of double-blocked periods) to complete the research and answer those questions. The final step was for them to consider alternatives and push for a specific legislative in a persuasive paper designed to influence public policy in the United States. Their three options were to (1) directly support an existing piece of legislation currently being considered by either a local, state, or federal legislative body, (2) identify and seek to repeal (remove) a law currently in effect that is detrimental to the success of their MDG or (3) create a piece of legislation and formally present it to a local, state, or federal legislative representative. The research at this stage included interviews (face to face or online) with at least two experts in the field in order to give weight to their arguments. These experts had to be from appropriate government, scientific or academic fields.

Digital Graphic Organizers

At the beginning students created a project plan based on a template developed by Battelle Research Institute in which they broke down their tasks and set benchmarks. I find some students always need structure in organizational skills. We developed a simple graphic organizer that helped students to deposit links, cite them properly, keep track of sources, organize data by questions and then analyze the evidence for each alternative. We e-mailed it to students so they could cut and paste, expand the borders of the text boxes and so on. The versatility of the organizer was a big success. Students who were fairly new to advanced research could gather data without the fear of forgetting what it was about or how it was connected to the questions they were to address. Most of my students had no prior experience with annotating a bibliography. I set a requirement for annotating at least three resources in MLA style. We followed the online writing guide "OWL", a great web resource at Purdue.[4]

Google Docs

After the lengthy process of gathering data, analyzing their findings and building an annotated bibliography, students compiled their work into a 4-minute informational lecture organized around the three central research questions. Then they uploaded all their work into Google documents (Google docs for short) for feedback and discussion with me and others in the class who were also researching their MDG. Google docs are secure webpages where students can store their research as digital notecards and then "invite" group members to look at their work and post comments.[5] When students were able to view and instantly comment on each other's work, I found that they often inserted helpful links and information, added details to each other's bibliographies or offered creative suggestions. Instant collaboration! Then when students were satisfied with their work, they submitted it to me via e-mail.

iMovies

At Metro students meet the requirement of digitally communicating information through a variety of tools: creating websites with Google Pages and Google Maps, iMovie documentaries and podcasts with still images and slideshows using Google Picasa (a digital photo organizer with slideshow ability). In the digital white paper, students used a variety of tools to communicate their ideas with decision makers in the larger world. Some chose to post their iMovie videos on YouTube while others e-mailed them to appropriate researchers at Battelle or elected official with jurisdiction to pass the legislation.

In the planning phase, students defined and wrote up their goals and objectives. As in all projects, students needed to think about their goals and plan what they were going to do before they began. These plans included content standards, student-generated deadlines or benchmarks and overall goals.

In order to prevent students from ad-libbing their lines and ignoring the rubric, I required that they write out the scripts for their videos word for word before they began to film. Scripts were used to check to what degree the work addressed the rubric. Students included props, music, or sound effects on their script and storyboard as these details need to be included in the planning stage.

In the filming/editing phase students found an appropriate place to record, filmed their movie and then edited it by cropping and moving clips, adding music and voice-overs and creating title scrolls, credits, and transitions. When students were ready to publish their work, iMovie saved it as a .mov file, which was burned onto a DVD (using the simple program iDVD). Some students chose to publish their new movie to YouTube. Instant fame and glory in the digital age!

For their final presentation I invited appropriate people from Cardinal Health, Ohio State University, Battelle, Columbus City Council, and the Ohio Department of Education as well as teachers, community professionals, city government officials to observe the students' presentations as an authentic audience. Since our task was authenticity in advocacy, our students became aware that if their work was going to mean something to real people, then our representatives in government who are working on these issues and fighting for or against this legislation had to hear their findings.

Reflections

My students appreciated the relevancy and deeply authentic nature of the project. Global issues were at the forefront of their minds. Said one young man, "Writing the White Paper taught me that ordinary people like me can fairly easily do research on world issues and present an idea to congressmen that could potentially change policies in my life." Students voiced new insights, such as: "[The white paper project was] an eye-opening experience because I never really thought about gender equality around the world—or here in Ohio." For many the exposure to humanity's core struggles—and realizing they could do something about these struggles—brought about epiphanies in their education. One student in the class was so moved by what she had learned that her career path goals were altered. "The White Paper project helped me realize that I want to be an advocate, maybe a professional lobbyist, for global health and global development once I am older."

Authenticity was a primary concern. Technology made a huge contribution to making it real for our students. The pressing immediacy of the issues created a reality that students crave as they love being in the *now*. Global education brings engagement in critical real-world issues into students' lives.

When students shared correspondence from their elected representatives, strong roots of civic engagement were valued. For example one e-mail shared by a student read:

> Hey, I just got a letter from Sherrod Brown in the mail responding to the white paper I sent him. VERY COOL =] He reassured me that he was doing everything he could to help what I was in support of, and why wouldn't he? I'll be voting soon =] haha.

Students made gains in efficacy: "I realized that I can accomplish things that are challenging and come up with a good product in a short amount of time." "It expanded my comfort zone. I didn't feel capable at the beginning of the project but I learned that I could do serious research and writing if I wanted to." These students would not have had anything close to an experience in global interconnectedness without being able to explore the World Health Organization's publications, Jeffrey Sach's speeches, the World Bank's databases, the French newspaper *Le Monde*, and the latest research from the Ohio State University's political science department.

There are some issues that I continue to wrestle with as students will always want more time, and marshalling all necessary skills is truly difficult for many. More troubling was the problem of reverting back to Google—away from the journals and online databases—as a default when things got tough. Predictably those students that relied on Google had a very difficult time getting the information they needed. The online journals and databases had much more to offer students, but they are new to students, and reading is at a higher level. Conceptually some students needed assistance trying to wrap their brains around such an enormous task. They had difficulty understanding the ultimate goals, even after much scaffolding and support in the early stages. As teachers, we felt we never took our eyes off the proverbial ball—that is, the advocacy angle—but a few students were lost at times.

Despite these limitations, we enjoyed the outcomes immensely as students were "going deep" and becoming thrilled with making true-to-life advocacy projects, improving their writing researching and presenting skills, and immersing themselves in global issues and the actions of becoming better global citizens. The digital white paper project became a capstone for the year's content, research, writing and thinking skills.

The reward for this culminating project is seeing the joy on students' faces as they received feedback from their audiences and realized the value of their own perseverance in creating something difficult yet significant. They knew they were stronger as they gained the courage to move beyond their comfort zones to learn from people and organizations across town and across the planet. In speaking of the Millennium Goals, they echo the sentiments of citizens of the world who are using their minds to create positive change. As an authentic experience, the digital white paper project can give your students the relevance they want in the social studies by using today's electronic tools to help people in a very real way.

CONCLUSION

Across these three illustrations are many common threads. Tech tools make learning more relevant and motivating to today's digital natives. Whether Moodle, Skype, Google docs, iMovies or online databases, these new technologies bring the world and its people into the classroom and infuse global perspectives into the social studies. Today events in Beijing or Cairo can be followed almost as well as events in a neighboring city or state. And students have access to how people in Brazil or Japan are working with Europeans to preserve fisheries or control global warming. The potential for students making real-life connections with people in different world regions or working with organizations that share their political goals is here, now.

Jeff tells the story of two young professionals who had been sent from Cardinal Health to observe the school. The women came into his classroom as the lights went down for a student to show his exquisite iMovie documentary. As the eloquent 15-year old (who looked like the fourth Jonas Brother) began discussing his research on global poverty and public policy in the Obama administration, the women's mouths actually fell open. My colleague walked over and whispered, "I know what you're thinking, and the answer is yes. He made that himself." In a conversation afterwards it became clear that these health professionals had no idea tenth graders could do such research, develop such policy choices or produce such media. Yet their lesson is one for all of us. With the right tools and instruction, over time our students will produce high quality work that has profound meaning in the real world.

NOTES

1. Phoenix is a new middle school that draws students from across Worthington School District. See http://phoenixms.org/
2. Located in Columbus, Ohio, Metro Early College High School was initiated by the Educational Council of Franklin County as a STEM (science, technology, engineering, mathematics) high school. From its first ninth grade class of 100 students in 2006, Metro has grown to 400 students in Grades 9-12 in the fall of 2009. Metro is a public school option open to any student attending one of 16 participating school districts within Franklin County, Ohio. Metro is partnered with many institutions, including the Battelle Institute, The Ohio State University, and the Bill and Melinda Gates Foundation. See also http://www.themetroschool.org/
3. See http://www.un.org/millenniumgoals/ for details.
4. http://owl.english.purdue.edu/owl/resource/614/01/
5. A link to Google documents and a tutorial video can be found here: https://www.google.com/accounts/
   ServiceLogin?service=writely&passive=true&nui=1&continue=http%3A%2F%2Fdocs.google.com%2F&followup=http%3A%2F%2Fdocs.google.com%2F&ltmpl=homepage&rm=false

REFERENCES

Bernstein, W. J. (2008). *A splendid exchange: How trade shaped the world*. New York: Atlantic Monthly Press.

Chua, A. (2007). *Day of empire: How hyper powers rise to global dominance and why they fall*. New York: Doubleday.

Hanley, J. (1999). Beyond the tip of the iceberg: Five stages toward cultural competence. *Reaching Today's Youth, 3*(2), 9-12.

Jackson, B., & Jamieson, K. H. (2007). *Un-Spun: Finding facts in a world of [Disinformation]*. New York: Random House.

Lindsey, B. (2008). *The age of abundance*. New York: Harper Collins.

Merryfield, M. M., & Wilson, A. (2005). *Social studies and the world: Teaching global perspectives*. Silver Spring, MD: The National Council for the Social Studies.

Spodek, H. (2008). *The world's history*. New York: Pearson Prentice Hall.

RESOURCES

Congressional Digest: Pro-Con Online (http://pro-and-con.org)
CountryWatch (http://countrywatch.com)

Dismal Scientist. Moodys. (http://www.economy.com)
Elibrary Curriculum Edition (http://www.proquestk12.com)
Gale Group Virtual Reference Library (http://infotrac.galegroup.com)
MAPS 101 (http://www.maps101.com)
NewsBank: Access World News (http://infoweb.newsbank.com)

CHAPTER 14

MEDIA CONVERGENCE
AND THE SOCIAL STUDIES

Jeremy Stoddard

As a young middle school social studies teacher in the 1990s, I was the first in my department to use the LCD projector in my classes to display student projects, show video clips, and yes, to project the occasional PowerPoint presentation. At the time these uses of media delivery technologies were still relatively rare and were viewed as being "cutting edge." I quickly realized, however, that often times the use of technology and various forms of media took away from more challenging and intellectually rigorous activities. Asking students to add images to a PowerPoint presentation did not require the same types of intellectual work as a critical inquiry lesson did; however, there was a motivational aspect of these lessons for students that was hard to ignore, and they were gaining authentic skills in media production, knowledge construction, and distribution through, at that time, very rudimentary web pages.

As an educational technology professional development specialist years later, projectors were less rare and PowerPoint presentations almost ubiquitous. I also noticed that most teachers had adopted the technologies to deliver media in essentially the same way that they used the overhead projector that had preceded it. Teacher practice still largely consisted of

Technology in Retrospect: Social Studies in the Information Age 1984-2009, pp. 261–284

lecture and recitation. The increased availability of technology and access to media did not seem to be transforming their practice as was promised by technophile policymakers. In fact, the technology was rarely in student hands, and students were not being taught the critical analysis skills or production skills necessary to become information and media literate (Buckingham, 2000, 2003). At the same time, societal interactions with media and technologies outside of the school changed rapidly. The expansion of the Internet, cellular technology, and wi-fi networks has transformed how Americans interact with information on the World Wide Web and with each other (Jenkins, 2006).

In his book *Convergence Culture: Where Old and New Media Collide*, media scholar Henry Jenkins (2006) explores how this rapid evolution and convergence of media, technology, and society has impacted American culture. For Jenkins, media convergence is the "flow of content across multiple media platforms, the cooperation between multiple media industries, and the migratory behavior of media audiences who will go almost anywhere in search of the kinds of ... experiences they want" (p. 2). This chapter explores Jenkins conceptualizations of media convergence and convergence culture and examines the current and potential impacts of this culture on democratic citizenship, one of the main goals of social studies education, and the practice of social studies teachers and students. The concept of convergence is useful in examining the evolution of media and teacher, and student interactions with media, in the social studies classroom over the years and provides a different perspective from previous studies in the literature that focus more specifically on technology use. It also provides a framework for thinking about how to develop and utilize media effectively in the social studies classroom in the years to come.

MEDIA CONVERGENCE AND CONVERGENCE CULTURE

The convergence of media and the technology that provides the opportunities to interact with media have evolved greatly over the past 25 years inside and outside of the classroom. No longer do social studies teachers need to have separate overhead projectors, filmstrip projectors, audiocassette players, videodisc players, television and VCR players, 8 mm film projectors, or polycom teleconferencing units. All of the functions of these various pieces of equipment can now be easily conducted using a laptop computer and projector in the classroom—and will likely eventually be done through smaller handheld computers or smart devices. Although there has been a rapid evolution of technology in and out of schools, the media that are delivered through these technologies has remained virtually the same—albeit in an evolved form. As Jenkins (2006) notes, history teaches us that old media never die—and they don't even necessarily fade away. What dies are simply the tools we use to access media content— the 8-track, the Beta tape. These are what media scholars call delivery technologies…. Delivery technologies become obsolete and get replaced; media, on the other hand, evolve. Recorded sound is the medium. CDs, MP3 files, and 8-track cassettes are delivery technologies. (p. 13)

For example, the classic educational film or film strip, once delivered via an 8 mm projector, film strip projector, and then VHS or DVD can now be accessed and streamed over the web through sources such as the *Public Broadcasting System* (PBS) website or through subscription services such as Discovery Education's *Streaming* (formerly *United Streaming*), a site that is replacing the old video library services commonly used for decades.

The evolution of delivery technologies and modes of delivery has changed rapidly, as has the access to larger and larger amounts of media, but the form of media has evolved more slowly. The nature of the educational filmstrip, with its progression of still images and anonymous voice-over narration is still present in many of the videos available via *Streaming*, which houses short video clips of content largely created for the *Discovery Channel* family of cable networks. These clips are catalogued using searchable tags for content and even for alignment with various state academic standards so that teachers can efficiently find and select relevant clips for their classes. Therefore, this converged media source still promotes the use of video clips as part of a lecture on "what happened" in the past that is aligned to state standards and that does not necessarily engage students in viewing the media critically or even in constructing their own knowledge of an event. Media convergence on its own does not provide for a shift in pedagogy that represents the other two tenets of the convergence culture, participation and collective intelligence (see Figure 14.1).

Other documentary or news style video that are not packaged for traditional classroom use but have educational aspirations have gone through a more thorough stylistic change. They have adopted the production, narrative, and editing styles more attune to the "MTV" generation and then to the more current "YouTube" generation. This evolution of media form has been driven in part by the nature of what is viewed as motivational or entertaining. No longer would sitting quietly in front of a dry "talking head" documentary be viewed as motivational by today's youth. In the United States many students want to be actively engaged or at least view media with a faster pace and shorter segments, a more dramatic narrative structure, and characters that they can better relate to (Selwyn, 2005; Smith, 1995). In a study I conducted, I found that students gained little knowledge from viewing traditionally styled documentary films, in large part because the teacher did not have students engage intellectually with the material. A number of students in the class I observed did not even remember watching the dry documentary on the Great Depression two weeks after it was viewed (Stoddard, 2010).

The change in student demand for a different style of media, in particular video, has apparently taken effect as newer films produced for classroom use move at a faster pace and often include dramatic reenactments of events, a hip soundtrack, or digital recreations to show what something may have looked like in the past (Stoddard, 2009a). This convergence of media forms can be problematic when examining the veracity of media as a source of history. In one case, that of the documentary *The Children's March* (2004), which won the Academy Award for best short subjects documentary in 2005, the film uses recreated scenes interspersed into the real footage of the events in Alabama in 1963. The film does not acknowledge to the audience what is actual footage of the protests against segregation that occurred and what was recreated with period cameras specifically for the film. Therefore, with this evolution of media, as digital forms similar to video games converge with video of events and special effects, the distinction between "reality" and construction is becoming less clear—posing a challenge for social studies teachers and media educators.

The convergence of media reflects the overall changes in the role of media in culture, especially our interactions with media and with each other through new media. The convergence culture that Jenkins (2006) describes goes far beyond the evolution of hardware and software that allows us to listen to music, watch a video, and chat (in writing or verbally) from the same handheld device. This convergence occurs "through social interactions with others" as part of a "participatory culture" that Jenkins describes as the convergence culture (p. 3). As an example of this, I am currently writing this chapter on my laptop in England, keeping up with news from the states via my *New York Times* Reader (powered by Adobe) while talking with my wife on her mobile phone in Virginia via *Skype*. At the same time I am also tracking stage 14 of the Tour de France via a feed from *ITV* (a British sports station) online and chatting about the race with friends all over the United States—as well as updating my wife on how far ahead a break away group of riders is from the peleton (the main pack of riders in a bike race). This kind of simultaneous interaction between multiple people all over the world, multiple types of media, and multiple forms of information all channeled through one delivery technology (i.e., the laptop) would have been unheard of 20 years ago and likely even unimaginable.

In addition to using media in intended ways as part of a participatory culture as described above, Jenkins (2006) uses the example of how new media are used in unintended ways, especially in the production and dissemination of new media forms. He presents the example of the now infamous series of images of *Sesame Street* (1970) character Bert pictured alongside Osama bin Laden and titled "Bert is Evil" as an example of the convergence culture in action. The high school student who produced the images had also used Photoshop to create collages of bin Laden that later ended up on t-shirts and posters during anti-American demonstrations in several Islamic countries alongside the "Bert is Evil" image, much to the disgust of the producers of *Sesame Street* when the images were displayed on CNN. This example illustrates how media convergence, in this case media used in unconventional or unintended ways, can lead to an international controversy when part of a participatory culture. Another familiar example of convergence culture is the use of film clips that are manipulated and then distributed via YouTube to express frustration with everything from the nature of American politics to frustrations with working in academics. For example, one clip from the end of the film *Downfall* (2004) that depicts the final days of Hitler in his Berlin bunker has been dubbed with subtitles and used to depict events ranging from Sarah Palin being the downfall of the Republican party to a scenario critiquing the process of scientific peer review with Hitler as the lead professor on an article that received a bad review from the notorious reviewer number three (http://www.youtube.com/watch?v=-VRBWLpYCPY). These media are shaped and distributed among niche groups using new media forms and delivery technologies as well as culturally specific symbols and meanings.

The conceptualization of media not as a strict form (e.g., television, radio, film) but instead as a cultural system that evolves from the original technology is helpful in understanding how media shapes and is shaped by society over time. Jenkins (2006) defines a medium as

> a technology that enables communication; … a medium is a set of associated "protocols" or social and cultural practices that have grown up around that technology…. Delivery technologies come and go all the time, but media persist as layers within an even more complicated information and entertainment stratum. (pp. 13-14)

For example, the advent of television did not kill radio or the theatre, but it did propel the shift of the content and role of those media in culture. Theatre shifted from being an entertainment form for the masses to a source of entertainment for a smaller niche of theater-goers, and the content of radio shifted from radio plays and variety shows to more talk, news, and music. This trend is also evident in schools. For example, the introduction of educational television did not drastically impact the way classes were taught despite the hopes of many for a rapid transformation of pedagogy (Cuban, 1986). Instead, participants in the culture of education appropriated educational television as part of their existing pedagogy that then slowly evolved as the medium was incorporated for various purposes.

CONVERGENCE CULTURE AND DEMOCRATIC CITIZENSHIP

The convergence culture, introduced above, is a result of the intersection of media convergence, participatory culture, and collective intelligence (Jenkins, 2006 p. 2) (see Figure 14.1), and the impact of this culture on democratic citizenship and democratic participation has been startling. Even while we see democratic participation in traditional means (e.g., participation in local organizations, voting) in decline, participation through new media has emerged quickly and with great effect in recent years. This emergence erupted as media designed for particular purposes have been appropriated toward democratic goals. As Jenkins argues, the convergence culture has emerged "where grassroots and corporate media intersect, where the power of the media producer and the power of the media consumer interact in unpredictable ways" (p. 2).

The evolution of the convergence culture in how media is used for democratic purposes may be most apparent in a comparison of the Tiananmen Square Massacre of 1989 and the repression of demonstrators in Iran after the disputed presidential election 20 years later in 2009. The violent events of June 4th, 1989 ended a month and a half long period of pro-democracy demonstrations in Tiananmen Square, located in the heart of Communist China's capital city of Beijing. Once the repression of Chinese protestors, made up primarily of students, began there was little

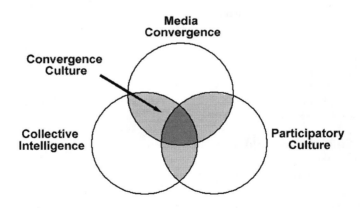

The Emergence of the Convergence Culture (Jenkins, 2006)

Figure 14.1.   Diagram of convergence culture.

news of what occurred. Even today, the estimates of those killed during the government crackdown vary (Hua, 2009). The primary source for video footage and information outside of China was the Western media. One of the most powerful scenes of the events, now iconic in its own right, was a videotaped encounter between a protester and a line of tanks moving into the square. However, the authoritarian Chinese regime was adept at maintaining a firewall that kept most information from leaving the country, and those in the West could only speculate as to the fate of many of the protestors for years after the event.

By comparison, the events following Iran's 2009 presidential election demonstrate just how powerful media convergence and the convergence culture have become in terms of shaping politics, democracy, and world history. Despite Iran's record of being a regime as equally adept at controlling the flow of information as China, the organized protests and massive retaliation of Iranian militias against the protestors were broadcast around the world via nonofficial media outlets. After the disputed election, protesters and media reporters covering the protests filled the streets in Tehran as well as the pages of the social sharing site *Twitter* via cellular phones and other handheld smart devices with updates about when and where rallies would be held. As days passed and the protests continued, Twitter was used to document the violent retaliation by various Iranian police and militia members against the protesters. Because the government could not block the Twitter messages, this medium was used to organize and report what was happening. Even as official Western media sources were being cut off from broadcasting the events, the world followed what was unfolding through nonofficial participatory media sources. This method of communication was deemed so important that the U.S. government even asked Twitter to hold off on a scheduled software update that would have shut down the site for a number of hours in the middle of the protests (Grossman, 2009). Here the convergence culture, which had formed already in certain sectors of the Iranian population, appropriated the medium of Twitter for their pro-democracy pursuits. This use of Twitter went far beyond what its designers could have imagined, and it illustrates Jenkins' assertion that in a convergence culture participants use media designed for more corporate or commercial pursuits for their own reappropriated purposes. This is not to say that Twitter is a democratizing force, especially as its role was likely exaggerated by the Western media who were the ones most taking advantage of the media, but it does reflect the potential for how media and democratic citizenship may converge in the future.

Previous to this grassroots illustration of how convergence culture aligns with democratic citizenship, the 2008 presidential campaign of

Barack Obama revealed a knowledge of and much more purposeful use of the convergence culture in the United States. In part powered by young staffers and volunteers, the Obama campaigned utilized every technological resource at its disposal (e.g., *Facebook*, *Twitter*, *MySpace*) to recruit, communicate with, and connect supporters. These efforts were rewarded with record turnouts of young people who felt like they were part of a movement because of the participatory nature of the campaign. Obama's campaign staff fully exploited its understanding of the convergence culture as it was both highly organized but also vastly participatory at all levels. The Obama website allowed volunteers to share information and communicate with each other, to arrange and advertise gatherings, and even to track where campaign signs were being taken from supporters' yards. This use of media to connect with participants and to allow participants increased interactions with the campaign beyond going to a rally, donating money, or knocking on doors (although these were done as well) paid off, especially with younger potential voters who felt that they were actually part of a movement. Because of their knowledge of the convergence culture, Obama's campaign changed the way politicians must interact with their supporters in future campaigns.

In addition to these specific examples, the low cost of media production coupled with ease of distribution makes media convergence a democratizing movement. Groups who have been traditionally marginalized by mainstream media and Hollywood have opportunities to produce and distribute their own media. Further, as the Iranian example shows, media convergence has made the world smaller in terms of the ability to communicate across vast spaces and connect with people who share different views. Rather than being limited to the three or four newspapers in stock at the local gas station, the World Wide Web allows access to news and opinions from around the globe from different perspectives. This explosion of media also provides sources for social studies teachers to include perspectives in their classes from otherwise marginalized groups or voices (e.g., Hicks & Ewing, 2003).

In addition to the impact that media convergence may have on what media are available in and out of the social studies classroom, Jenkins' conceptualization of the convergence culture is a potentially useful framework for democratic education and social studies education—especially in how teachers use media and technology as part of their pedagogy. The three tenets of the convergence culture (media convergence, participatory culture, collective intelligence) are also the hallmarks of authentic quality social studies education. Media convergence allows for a multitude of perspectives and the ability to communicate easily between and among groups across the country or planet. Being part of a participatory culture where ideas are discussed, action is taken, and consensus and community is developed is key to good democratic education. Collective intelligence is at the heart of quality constructivist teaching that emphasizes student intellectual work and a classroom that fosters student learning from and with each other, or with others from outside of the school (e.g., experts, students from other countries). Therefore this notion of a convergence culture is helpful in terms of what social studies teachers may want to foster as part of their pedagogy. Unfortunately, many social studies classrooms do not currently include these three aspects of convergence culture.

CONVERGENCE CULTURE AND THE SOCIAL STUDIES CLASSROOM

Unlike the dynamic examples of how the convergence culture and media convergence have impacted democratic participation outside of school, there has been far less of an impact documented in most social studies classrooms (Swan & Hofer, 2008). In their review of research on technology use in the social studies, Swan and Hofer found that technology has not been the catalyst for transforming teacher pedagogy or engaging students in democratic participation in the outside world that it was promised to be. Similar to the findings of Cuban (1986, 2001) and others, this lack of impact may be in part because the focus is on technology (e.g., hardware and software) and not on the use of media in the classroom as part of pedagogy. However, the impact of media convergence and the rapid changes in delivery technologies are very apparent in today's social studies classrooms. The media that is consumed in social studies classrooms using these devices has also converged—with many affordances for social studies teaching and learning—but also with some constraints. The evolution of a convergence culture involving a participatory culture, media convergence, and collective intelligence in these classrooms is harder to find. In fact, some of the impacts of new technologies and media convergence outside of the classroom may be having negative implications for how media is used as part of teacher pedagogy inside of classrooms in today's educational context of standardized curriculum, network filters, and high stakes testing.

As noted above, the technology employed in social studies classrooms and the information that this technology makes accessible has changed rapidly over the past 25 years. In the early days, Apple and MS-DOS microcomputers were used primarily in schools to type papers, play games such as *Oregon Trail*, or maybe analyze small data sets in a spreadsheet. Since the days of these first Apple II computers, teachers' and students' capacity to access, produce, and distribute information via media has grown exponentially. Over the decades, more complex uses of media and technology in the classroom have emerged, although in many schools the basic function of the computer lab as a place to have students type essays still exists. Many teachers have created more dynamic uses for the computers in their classrooms and for their visits to a school's computer labs. For example, Webquests and Web Inquiry Projects (Molebash, 2004; Molebash & Dodge, 2003), multimedia supported historical inquiry (Doolittle & Hicks, 2003; Saye & Brush, 2005, 2006, 2007), the use of GIS (geographic information system) data and distance learning technologies to make geography instruction more authentic (Doering, 2007; Heafner, 2009), and student produced documentaries (Hofer & Swan, 2008-2009) have all been integrated into social studies classrooms using constructivist models of teaching and new media available via the World Wide Web or student and teacher produced media.

Educational media producers who have traditionally provided educational video and audio resources in the form of older delivery technologies are now making media more accessible and more expansive through media convergence. In addition to subscription streaming video sources such as Discovery's Streaming, PBS provides much of its media online for use in classroom settings, including documentaries, resource lists and bibliographies, images, and more interactive games. These sites provide more media and resources for teachers to be able to create dynamic and rich lessons for their classes. The sites often create spaces for teachers to share lesson plans or implementation ideas or for students to share their ideas related to the project or any final media products that they may have created. In addition, several sites provide podcasts and other forms of media, created by experts, teachers, or students, that enable the sharing of historical research or inquiry on a social or political issue (Swan & Hofer, 2009). Individual schools have also created their own media sites highlighting powerful social studies media projects. For example, the Urban School in San Francisco has an ongoing video/oral history project called *Telling Their Stories* (http://www.tellingstories.org) that engages classes of social studies students in researching and conducting interviews with various groups from the past ranging from survivors of the Holocaust to former residents of Fillmore, a traditional African American neighborhood in San Francisco, who were moved out of their homes in the name of urban development. This project utilizes the power of media convergence and all of its affordances.

Traditional educational media producers are also attempting to keep themselves relevant as the convergence culture emerges. For example, the Corporation for Public Broadcasting (CPB) created an initiative in 2007 focused on history and citizenship education. The goal of this initiative is the development of new media for teaching American history and civics— both in schools and out. They have invested millions of dollars in a number of research and media development projects. One of the requirements for the grant project is that funded projects must find ways to integrate media from the various Corporation for Public Broadcasting outlets (e.g., PBS, National Public Radio). The hope for CPB is that these projects, which include various forms of video games, simulations, and even massively multiplayer online games, will incorporate video from programs such as *Newshour* or *Frontline* to engage students in important historic or present day issues. In order to maintain its own relevance in and out of the classroom, CPB is encouraging the blending of old media with new, or in new forms and through new delivery technologies.

Whereas some media producers have taken conscious steps to converge and redesign media, other producers continue to simply add on new media to existing projects as they are developed. Colonial Williamsburg's Electronic Field Trip program is a good example of how media producers are attempting to take advantage of new media, and see the value of new media in education, but have not gone so far as to adopt principles of the convergence culture to try to transform social studies teaching and learning. Colonial Williamsburg is a living history museum that focuses on interpreting life in Virginia's colonial capital during the period immediately preceding the American Revolution. Started in the early 1990s, the Electronic Field Trips were designed to allow students from across the United States to experience what Colonial Williamsburg has to offer without leaving the classroom. The original version of the field trips, which were broadcast only via participating PBS stations and satellite, were done live in the streets of Colonial Williamsburg and included call in segments during which students from classes around the country could "call in" to ask questions of the historical interpreters and Colonial Williamsburg historians. Since that initial season, the Electronic Field Trips have evolved to include multiple pre-produced dramatic segments that are interspersed with the live call in segments—although in addition to calling in, students can also e-mail questions for the panel of "experts" and vote online on questions that appear intermittently during the broadcast. Much of the video, other than the live segments, can be streamed on demand from the project website. Resources, teacher lesson plans, and supplementary games and web activities can also be found on this site. In addition to the call-in segment, there are also opportunities for students to communicate with experts and other students via e-mail and a discussion board.

Despite all of these additions to the Electronic Field Trip program, the new forms of media are rarely used by the teachers with their classes, other than some of the video games (Stoddard, 2009b). The Electronic Field Trip program is just one example where media convergence has impacted the nature of the project, but the aspects of collective intelligence and participatory culture have not emerged as strongly and therefore limit the impact of media convergence. The process of continually adding on new media to existing curriculum or educational media without also restructuring the curriculum to become more centered on student participation and construction of knowledge, and without conducting professional development to support teacher use of the media, does not have the transformative pedagogical effect that is intended. Here we see how new media, when not utilized with the convergence culture in mind, fails to be effective as a site of teaching and learning.

As these examples illustrate, social studies classrooms have changed immensely in many ways over the past 25 years, in make up of students, in curriculum, in pedagogy, and in the use and availability of a range of technologies and media. However, pedagogy and use of technology in the classroom still varies greatly and in many ways has been slow to change. Technologies are not necessarily viewed or utilized as part of a student-centered curriculum. In fact, in many schools there has been little change in how technology has functioned as a part of pedagogy, in part because students are rarely allowed to use it. This has not changed much over the past 25 years (Cuban, 1986, 2001; Hobbs, 2006). Too often media such as film, video, or various interactive video games and simulations are used as a "baby-sitter" or reward instead of as part of authentic activities (Hobbs, 1999, 2006). Also, students in different schools or even classes within a school (e.g., remedial, honors) may receive different experiences with media than others (Dewitt, 2007).

The presence of technologies in the classroom, and overall access to technologies and the internet has grown exponentially in the past 2 decades (Cuban, 2001; Margolis, Estrella, Goode, Holme, & Nao, 2008), but unfortunately the digital divide has now shifted to a pedagogical divide in how students are engaged with media and technology in the classroom (Dewitt, 2007; Margolis et al., 2008). Dewitt notes that access to technology and media is not as big of an issue now in schools as it once was, but the larger issue remains teacher pedagogy and teacher expectations for students with media and technologies. In his study of technology use in high school social studies classes, he found notable differences in how technology was used as part of teacher pedagogy in schools and classes that served students from different socioeconomic classes. Similarly, Margolis et al. (2008) argues that the digital divide, which traditionally denotes the lack of access to technology and information media access through the Internet, notes that being wired is not as big of an issue as what types of skills are being developed by students in urban areas with technology. Overall, urban and low socioeconomic status students, and students of color in particular, are not getting the same experiences with media or developing the same skills in critical analysis or production as students who attend schools in the neighboring suburbs.

These findings also resonate with emerging findings from a study I am currently conducting. As part of this study, I have surveyed secondary social studies teachers from several school districts regarding their use of media. One of these districts is exploding with technology. Each middle and high school social studies teacher surveyed ($n = 27$) teaches in a classroom with a projector mounted in the ceiling, a laptop loaded with software including access to two video libraries, Discovery's Streaming and *Safari Montage*, a document camera, and four student computer work stations. Early results show that the primary use of all of this technology and media access is teacher lecture. These lectures are media rich and often include presentations loaded with images and streaming video or other media. Students are generally asked to simply listen and take notes. The vast quantity of available technology in these schools has not shifted or transformed teacher pedagogy, and in fact may be reinforcing existing pedagogy behavior similar to what Dewitt (2007) refers to as "technology enhanced traditionalism." So why has technology not been the transformational tool it was promised to be?

In the case of the teachers in this particular school district several influences appear to be impacting student lack of engagement with media. In addition to the resilience of teachers to change their own pedagogy that Cuban (2001), Dewitt (2007), and others describe, these teachers are also influenced by a high stakes testing environment and a lack of professional development that focuses on pedagogy with technology and media. The emphasis on testing, and in this case a low level multiple choice Virginia state standardized exam, is often used as justification for a teacher-centered classroom style where knowledge is focused on in a rote fashion and presented by the teacher for student consumption. Use of media as a one-way delivery tool via the mounted projector is the result. In addition, the professional development offered to these teachers has focused largely on using the hardware and software and not on ways to successfully integrate the technology. This was the most often stated reason for why few of the teachers have actually had students use the four work stations in the room, with the exception of allowing students to do independent research. Despite a convergence culture that has emerged outside of the schoolhouse doors, the presence of media convergence in the classroom has not led to the participatory culture and collective intelligence that are its two other tenets.

In addition to a lack of teacher professional development and pressures to "teach to the test," there are also other institutional factors limiting the emergence of a convergence culture inside social studies classrooms. The teachers in the above study also reported not being able to access certain media sources because of network filters. Certain social sharing sites such as YouTube are often blocked and the teachers reported that technology staff members were often reluctant to allow even teachers to access them in the school. Although there may be some justification in limiting access to sites that may have inappropriate material, there is no reason that teachers should not be able to access these sites so that they can show appropriate material in class—especially material that may be teacher or student created.

The impact of official or unofficial barriers to media use is a continued trend in schools. Although the delivery technologies may be new, there have always been barriers placed on media and technology use because of fears of expensive equipment being damaged or by beliefs about what types of media should be allowed into the classroom. Twenty years ago, staff may have been reluctant for students to use a VHS camcorder for fear that it might get broken, even though the camera was purchased with the intent of student use. In other cases, administrators or school boards have banned films and other media because what they contained was viewed as controversial. In many cases, decisions are being made by people who have a particular, and generally outdated, vision of what social studies classrooms are supposed to look like and a limited understanding of how learning best occurs.

In addition to the pedagogical and learning limitations, the use of filters and approved or subscribed services such as Discovery's Streaming also creates ideological issues. Although media convergence can prove to have a democratizing effect, in some cases the lack of contact with multiple viewpoints and ability to chose and limit your sources of information can lead to someone's engagement consisting of a more narrow viewpoint than before. In *Republic.com 2.0*, Sunstein (2007) argues that the explosion of media has also led to our need to filter out information for fear of overload and to instead frequent specialized or niche media producers which tend to only present narrow points of views in order to attract their niche audience. As someone is now able to select out particular cable, satellite radio, and news feed sources via the Web for viewing, the convergence of media may be having an antidemocratic effect on some sectors of society. Even when a participatory culture and collective intelligence exist, it may exist only within smaller select communities who believe roughly the same things and who can now connect via numerous media channels. Sunstein provides the example of members of a conservative political group who tend to limit their news consumption to a few like-minded sources. Someone in this group could feasibly exist in the world while rarely being exposed to alternative viewpoints if they chose—and when alternative views are linked from their sites of choice, it is "often to show how dangerous, or how contemptible, competing views really are" (Sunstein, 2007 p. 51).

Similarly, if teachers only utilize Discovery Streaming as their source of video, and use only videos aligned with their state standards, the ideological viewpoints introduced in their classroom and construction of the past or present may be limited as well. In order to combat this impact, Hess (2007) suggests that media such as film need to be viewed as value laden and that teachers should explicitly select media that represent legitimate but varying perspectives. This is not a new problem in education. For decades, private corporations or interest groups have been producing curriculum or media as a way to gain entrance into the nation's classrooms. A prime example is *Channel One*, a news program offered to schools for free along with televisions and other equipment since the 1980s. In order to take advantage of the free technology, schools had to agree to show a short news program every morning that also included several minutes of advertising targeted toward student audiences (Blokhuis, 2008). This arrangement targets poor schools overwhelmingly as they lack the funds for new technology. The use of Channel One limits not only the information about current events students in these schools are getting to one limited perspective, but also exposes students to commercial advertisements.

Today, many websites and other outlets include advertising and value-laden perspectives in media intended for educational use. *The History Channel* website has webisodes titled "This Day in History" that provide a one minute overview of what historic events have occurred on the date, some significant and some inconsequential. Surrounding the video are advertisements for *History Channel* programs and merchandise and advertisements for other companies such as Hyundai and Lowe's. Sources such as these that appear to be documentary or news style sources in general present a major challenge for teachers. As in the example of *The Children's March* above, these media range in quality of production and in the blurring of fact and representation of events for entertainment purposes. They are viewed as being objective sources of information, however, as they come from what is seen as a legitimate source in the *History Channel* (Mangram, 2008; Stoddard, 2009-2010), and because people in general trust documentary style media to be accurate and objective (Rosenstone, 1995).

Even if teachers select media with varying perspectives and from various sources, issues may still remain. The expanded use of media in the classroom has highlighted the ever important need for students to develop skills in critical literacy. Teachers often assume that because students are media savvy that they are also able to differentiate between sources accessed through the web or that they understand the different ways in which history is constructed in a feature versus documentary film. Although the analysis of primary sources has been a major initiative in history education over the past two decades, and research has examined how media can be used to engage students in this kind of historical thinking (Doolittle & Hicks, 2003; Saye & Brush, 2006, 2007), this type of analysis has not naturally led to media literate or critically literate students (Stoddard, 2010).

In a study I conducted of two teachers and how they used various types of historical "media" in their classrooms as part of their pedagogy, I found that the teachers' believed that some sources represented the past more objectively (e.g., textbook, documentary film), while other sources need interpretation as primary sources (e.g., speeches, images, documents), and others served as a more conceptual representation of the past (e.g., feature film) (Stoddard, 2010). The beliefs about these various media led to pedagogy that emphasized the objectivity of textbooks and documentary films and thus reinforced their students' beliefs about how these media represent the past. This pedagogy can become problematic when students believe that only particular types of sources should be analyzed critically while others are viewed as "truth." As Barton (2005) suggests, all sources should be examined with a critical eye and be looked at as evidence, taking into account the nature of the evidence and authorial perspectives that the source may reflect. In this same way, it may be helpful to look at all sources of historical information as media, as they all represent or communicate about the past in some way but are also all impacted by the nature of the particular medium through which the representation is encapsulated (McLuhan, 1964).

So what can be done to help students develop better critical literacy skills in a media rich world? Some new research in the literature provides frames for utilizing the convergence culture and popular culture to develop democratic citizens. In order to counter the impact of media on students' beliefs about the world and lack of critical literacy, S. Matthews (2009) advocates for the use of popular media, such as reality programs, to interrupt students' beliefs about the world around them. In particular, she proposes using *The Amazing Race*, a television series that tracks contestants as they engage in a world-wide treasure hunt of sorts, to help interrupt students ethnocentric "culture-gazing" through popular culture. In addition to critiquing media representations, other researchers advocate for student production of media outside of the traditional disciplinary lenses of history and geography. Budin (2005) and Cramer (2005) offer models for engaging students in journalistic pursuits through both developing critical perspectives about the role of media in a democracy and using new media to publish via the web on student constructed pages or blogs. Both argue that using these new media channels to reach authentic audiences outside of brick and mortar schools will go a long way to developing active and media literate citizens for the twenty-first century.

Similarly, Yow and Swan (2009) provide a case study of one teacher's attempt to engage students in the role of photojournalists and documentary film makers to learn geographic skills and content related to their local surroundings. These epistemic frames for viewing the world begin to take advantage of the convergence culture and use media to engage students in authentic problems that go beyond textbooks and classrooms.

SOCIAL STUDIES AND
MEDIA CONVERGENCE OUTSIDE OF THE PHYSICAL CLASSROOM

Outside of the traditional classroom setting, media has been utilized more recently to transform ways of interacting and learning about past and present societies and engaging in the practices of citizenship. When outside of the confines of the classroom and limits of the school day schedule, numerous projects involving student production of media or use of media to connect with others have been more effective in utilizing media convergence as part of more authentic pedagogy. J. Matthews' (2009) study of using handheld computers for Augmented Reality gaming is an example of how media convergence, in this case handheld GPS enabled devices, enabled students to interact with their environment and each other around a place-based historical inquiry. As part of his study, Mathews had small groups of students interact with various sites on the University of Wisconsin-Madison campus related to the anti-Vietnam War era protests that had occurred there. Students were able to access primary documents and other media in order to answer inquiry questions while they also analyzed the physical environment around them. For example, they were asked to read the account of the 1970 Sterling Hall bombing in newspaper articles while standing outside of the actual building. Although done with classes of students, this project had to first break free from the confines of the classroom to be successful. Field trips and place based education have long been part of the social studies curriculum (Bellan & Scheuerman, 1998; Noel & Colopy, 2006), and Matthews study shows how much more powerful and authentic these activities can be when students can interact with multiple sources of information and authentic inquiry while surrounded by history.

In addition to place based augmented learning, simulations have also long been a social studies staple. New models of simulating expertise and the thinking of professionals have also emerged along with the convergence of media. Bagley and Shaffer (2009), in their study of how activities modeled after the practices of urban planners, found that civic knowledge and civic skills can be learned through simulating professional practice.

This game, *Urban Science*, asked students to take on the role of an urban planner while wrestling with all of the data, decisions, and partnerships necessary for this kind of work—developing civic knowledge and skills along the way. As part of the simulation, students worked in teams modeled after the profession and used multiple complementary media ranging from handheld GPS units to *iPlan*, a software program that allowed students to redesign "State Street," a pedestrian thoroughfare in Madison, WI, in order to make it more attractive, safe, and sustainable. Included in this civic related work was the utilization of surveys to help inform decisions regarding the preferences of local constituents and stakeholders for the State Street corridor and also to provide a sense of what they would likely be able to build consensus around in order to be approved by the city and Urban League. Because of the nontraditional curricular nature of this project and the need for long chunks of time for student participation, this study was done on the weekend with a small group of students ($n = 12$).

These out of school examples of how media convergence has been applied toward social studies goals share several similarities. Both utilize media heavily but do not focus on the delivery technologies. Both have students actively constructing knowledge, or at least provide the potential for students to construct knowledge. And both include opportunities to interact with others, and especially people from outside of the school, on real or simulated—but real world—problems. Unlike most of the in class examples of student engagement with media, these two projects are illustrative of what social studies education could look like when incorporating all aspects of convergence culture, not just in response to media convergence.

THE FUTURE OF MEDIA AND CONVERGENCE IN THE SOCIAL STUDIES

So what is the future of social studies and democratic education in a convergence culture? There is great potential for innovation in pedagogy with media toward goals of social studies and citizenship education. The concept of convergence may help teachers and teacher educators better integrate the use of media in the context of pedagogy that also encourages and actively requires participation and is centered around collective intelligence. The participation and collective intelligence may take place either with students in the class or, when appropriate, with others from outside of the class (e.g., other students, experts). This pedagogy could include engaging students in using media for purposes of developing grassroots support for local and national social and political issues; communicating and networking with others who are interested in particular historical periods, places, people, or events; building social media sites with shared expertise, data, and knowledge in a fast moving global society; and utilizing media to model professional practice using various forms of simulations or experiential media. As convergence is an organic process that relies on intersecting corporate media and grassroots interests, it will continue to evolve more quickly than classroom practice. However, that does not mean that aspects of convergence cannot be used in educational media or pedagogical designs.

One example of a program modeled on convergence tenets that may show us a glimpse of this future is *Oceana: A Virtual Democracy*. This project, currently being developed by the Center on Congress at Indiana University, is a massively multiplayer online role-playing game (MMORPG) that places students in a virtual island democracy with a government modeled after the United States. In different levels of the game students may be engaged as citizens, legislators, lobbyists, or journalists as they learn social studies content and skills in inquiry, deliberation, and consensus building. As students are engaged in researching and then advocating for or against various relevant real world issues (e.g., immigration policy), they are also utilizing media from a variety of ideological diverse sources such as news magazine programs like *Frontline* to more specialized news sources from special interest groups in order to collect background information on their issue. They may also create their own in-world media in support of their position for viewing by other inhabitants of *Oceana*. Students are engaged in actively participating through their role—campaigning for their issues and eventually taking the role of a member of the legislature who needs to deliberate and work toward consensus with other lawmakers. In the initial version, the world will be set up for internal classroom use where students from the same class can participate in their own world. However, later versions of the game will allow students from classes all over the country or even the globe to discuss, deliberate, and build consensus for important issues of the day. Students will have to write speeches, hold news conferences and rallies, and write stories for partisan or non-partisan outlets in the Oceana game-world. As Oceana's system of government is modeled after the U.S. government, students will learn about important issues, structures of government, and democratic citizenship skills. Other games built with similar attributes, and especially interactions between students from around the world and centered on building collective intelligence, have been extremely successful in areas such as science and engineering education (e.g., Quest Atlantis). *Oceana* has the potential to fully implement the tenets of the convergence culture in a way that also works toward the knowledge, skills, and dispositions goals of democratic citizenship and social studies education.

The advocacy of using MMORPGs or other multiplayer online games in the social studies is not unique. However, most of the literature explores and advocates the use of commercial games (e.g., Squire, 2004; VanFossen, Friedman, & Hartshorne, 2008). Commercial games can be problematic for some of the same reasons identified above with other media—especially in issues of representations and the blurring of reality. Many video games, especially those that feature history related themes, incorporate cinematic elements along with the more interactive digital simulations to create their game worlds. In addition, the rules designed for a game are created with the goal of motivating a player's interest and desire to keep playing—and do not necessarily simulate the world accurately. Sid Meier's *Civilizaiton III*, for example, does not necessarily represent a realistic model of how societies develop, even though it may include a lot of factually accurate material. This is not to say these games are worthless as pedagogical mediums, but they are likely going to be more problematic than a game such as *Oceana* that is designed from the ground up for social studies and democratic education goals.

My purpose in writing this chapter is not to argue that the concept of convergence culture is going to transform education forever, nor is it to claim that there are not limitations to a convergence culture framework. Examples identified in this chapter focus more on production and consumption of knowledge through media than the critical analysis of the media itself and what (and who) the media represent. The lack of critical media literacy skills in our society represents real challenges for the future of our democracy. There are also issues of power and access when it comes to media, critical literacy, and media production skills. As Margolis et al. (2008) point out, too often lower income youth and youth of color will not have the same access or experience to develop media related skills that will help them later in life as their wealthier and often white, suburban counterparts. Jenkins (2006) also identifies the issue of access as a downside of the convergence culture writ large.

> Not all participants are created equal. Corporations—and even individuals within corporate media—still exert greater power than any individual consumer or even the aggregate of consumers. And some consumers have greater abilities to participate in this emerging culture than others. (p. 3)

Therefore, any model of pedagogy that utilizes a framework of convergence also needs to include the development of critical literacy skills in order to avoid the issues both Margolis et al. (2008) and Sunstein (2007) identify.

If Jenkins' (2006) observations about an emergence of a convergence culture hold true, it will not be a question as to whether or not some of these elements will eventually filter into education, as many already are. The larger point I have attempted to make here is that by using a framework of convergence when designing educational media or making pedagogical decisions, teachers, policymakers, and educational media producers may be able to better focus on what is really important in social studies and teaching with and about media. Specifically, the focus on the intersection of media convergence, participatory culture, and collective intelligence may provide a better framework than the largely technocentric models of technology integration that are currently being used in education. This framework also provides a foundation for developing or even adapting media that exist to work towards social studies goals, and it promotes the active role of teachers in the community of learners instead of placing technology at the center of the pedagogy. The focus is on students, their interactions, and how they can collectively develop skills and a knowledge base for being democratic citizens. These knowledge and skills will maintain their relevance in society long past any piece of technology that currently exists or is even currently being imagined.

REFERENCES

Bagley, E., & Shaffer, D. W. (2009). When people get in the way: Promoting civic thinking through epistemic gameplay. *International Journal of Gaming and Computer-Mediated Simulations, 1*(1), 36-52.

Barton, K. (2005). Primary sources in history: Breaking through the myths. *Phi Delta Kappan, 86*(10), 745-753.

Bellan, J., & Scheuerman, G. (1998). Actual and virtual reality: Making the most of field trips. *Social Education, 62*(1),35–40.

Blokhuis, J. (2008). Channel one: When private interests and the public interest collide. *American Educational Research Journal 45*(2), 343-363.

Buckingham, D. (2000). *The making of citizens*. London: Routledge.

Buckingham, D. (2003). *Media education: Literacy, learning, and contemporary culture*. Cambridge, England: Polity Press.

Budin, H. (2005). Democratic education and self-publishing on the web. In M. S. Crocco, (Ed.), *Social studies and press: Keeping the beast at bay* (pp. 189-198). Charlotte, NC: Information Age.

Cramer, J. (2005). Blogs in the machine. In M. S. Crocco (Ed.), *Social studies and press: Keeping the beast at bay* (pp. 199-214). Charlotte, NC: Information Age.

Cuban, L. (1986). *Teachers and machines: The classroom use of technology since 1920*. New York: Teachers College Press.

Cuban, L. (2001). *Oversold and underused: Computers in the classroom*. Cambridge, MA: Harvard University Press.

DeWitt, S. (2007). Dividing the digital divide: Instructional use of computers in social studies. *Theory and Research in Social Education, 35*(2), 277-304.

Doering, A. (2007). Adventure learning: Situating learning in an authentic context. *Innovate-Journal of Online Education, 3*(6). Retrieved from http://innovateonline.info/index.php?view=article&id=342&action=synopsis

Doolittle, P., & Hicks, D. (2003). Constructivism as a theoretical foundation for the use of technology in Social Studies. *Theory and Research in Social Education, 31*(1), 72-104.

Grossman, L. (June 17 2009). Iran protests: Twitter, the medium of the movement. *Time Magazine*. Retrieved from http://www.time.com/time/world/article/0,8599,1905125,00.html

Heafner, T. (2009). Utilizing the power of technology for teaching with geography. In J. Lee & A. Friedman (Eds.), *Research on technology in social studies education* (pp. 207-230). Charlotte, NC: Information Age.

Hess, D. (2007, May/June). From "*Banished*" to "*Brother Outsider*," "*Miss Navajo*" to "*An Inconvenient Truth*": Documentary films as perspective-laden narratives. *Social Education, 71*(4), 194-199.

Hicks, D., & Ewing, E. T. (2003). Bringing the word and the world into the classroom: Using global newspapers for teaching social studies. *Social Education, 67*(3), 134-140.

Hirschbiegel, O. (Director). (2004). *Downfall* (Der Untergang). (Distributed in the United States by Sony Pictures Home Entertainment, http://www.sonypictures.com)

Hobbs, R. (1999). *The uses (and misuses) of mass media resources in secondary schools.* Washington, DC. (Eric Document No. ED439452).

Hobbs, R. (2006). Non-optimal uses of video in the classroom. *Learning, Media and Technology 31*(1), 35–50.

Hofer, M., & Swan, K.O. (2008-2009). Technological pedagogical content knowledge in action: A case study of a middle school digital documentary project. *Journal of Research on Technology in Education, 41*(2), 179-200.

Houston, R. (Director). (2004). *Mighty times: The children's march* [Film]. (Available from Teaching Tolerance: A Project of the Southern Poverty Law Center, http://www.tolerance.org)

Hua, Yu (2009, May 30). China's forgotten revolution. *New York Times*. Retrieved from http://www.nytimes.com/2009/05/31/opinion/31yuhua.html?_r=1

Jenkins, (2006). *Convergence culture: Where old and new media collide.* New York: New York University Press.

Mangram, J. (2008). Either/or rules: Social studies teachers' talk about media and popular culture. *Theory and Research in Social Education, 36*(2), 32-60.

Margolis, j., Estrella, R., Goode, J., Holme, J. J., & Nao, K. (2008). *Stuck in the shallow end: Education, race, and computing.* Cambridge, MA: MIT Press.

Matthews, J. (2009, April). *A window to the past: Using augmented reality games to support historical inquiry.* Paper presented at the annual meeting of the American Educational Research Association, San Diego, CA.

Matthews, S. (2009). Disrupting *The Amazing Race*: Education, exploration and exploitation in reality television. *Theory and Research in Social Education, 37*(2), 247-272.

McLuhan, M. (1964). *Understanding media: The extensions of man.* New Yoek: McGraw-Hill.

Molebash, P. E. (2004). Web historical inquiry projects. *Social Education, 68*(3), 226-229.

Molebash, P. E., & Dodge, B. (2003). Kickstarting inquiry with webquests and web inquiry projects. *Social Education, 67*(3), 158-162.

Noel, M., & Colopy, M. (2006). Making history field trips meaningful: Teachers' and site educators' perspectives on teaching materials. *Theory and Research in Social Education, 34*(3), 553-568.

Rosenstone, R. A. (1995). *Visions of the past: The challenge of film to our idea of history.* Cambridge, MA: Harvard University Press.

Saye, J. W., & Brush, T. A. (2005). The persistent issues in history network: Developing civic competence through technology-supported historical inquiry. *Social Education. 69*(4), 168-171.

Saye, J. W., & Brush, T. A. (2006). Comparing teachers' strategies for supporting student inquiry in a problem-based multimedia-enhanced history unit. *Theory and Research in Social Education. 34*(2), 183-212.

Saye, J. W., & Brush, T. A. (2007). Using technology-enhanced learning environments to support inquiry in social studies classrooms. *Theory and Research in Social Education. 35*(2), 196-230.

Selwyn, D. (2005). Give us 8 seconds and we'll give ... the business. In M. S. Crocco (Ed.), *Social studies and press: Keeping the beast at bay* (pp. 141-158). Charlotte, NC: Information Age.

Smith, M. (1995). *Engaging characters: Fiction, emotion, and the cinema.* New York: Oxford University Press, Inc.

Squire, K. D. (2004). Sid Meier's Civilization III. *Simulations and Gaming, 35*(1), 135-140.

Stoddard, J. (2009a, April). *The "History Channel effect" and the challenge of the documentary for social studies teaching and learning.* Paper presented at the annual meeting of the American Educational Research Association, San Diego, CA.

Stoddard, J. (2009b). Toward a virtual field trip model for the social studies. *Contemporary Issues in Technology and Teacher Education, 9*(4). Retrieved from http://www.citejournal.org/vol9/iss4/socialstudies/article2.cfm

Stoddard, J. (2009-2010). The history channel effect. *Phi Delta Kappan, 91*(4), 80.

Stoddard, J. (2010). The competing roles of epistemology and ideology in teachers' pedagogy with historical media. *Teachers and Teaching: Theory into Practice, 16*(1), 133-151.

Sunstein, C. (2007). *Republic.com 2.0.* Princeton, NJ: Princeton University Press.

Swan, K., & Hofer, M. (2008). Technology and social studies. In L. Levstik & C. Tyson (Eds.), *Handbook of research in social studies education* (pp. 307-328). New York: Routledge.

Swan, K., & Hofer, M. (2009). Trend alert: A history teacher's guide to using podcasts in the classroom. The entity from which ERIC acquires the content, including journal, organization, and conference names, or by means of online submission from the author. *Social Education, 73*(2), 95-102.

VanFossen, P. J., Friedman, A. M., & Hartshorne, R. (2008). The emerging role of synthetic worlds and massively-multiplayer online role-playing games (MMORPGs) in social studies and citizenship education. In R. Ferdig (Ed.),

Handbook of research on effective electronic gaming in education (pp. 235-250). Hershey, PA: IGI.

Yow, S. H., & Swan, K. O., (2009). If you build it, should I run? A teacherís perspctive on implementing a student-centered, digital technology project in his ninth-grade geography classroom. In J. Lee & A Friedman (Eds.), *Research on technology in social studies education* (pp. 155-172). Charlotte, NC: Information Age.

CHAPTER 15

SOCIAL AND CULTURAL IMPLICATIONS OF TECHNOLOGY INTEGRATION IN SOCIAL STUDIES EDUCATION

Cheryl Mason Bolick

The past several years have exhibited vertiginous change, surprising novelties, and upheaval in an era marked by technological revolution and the global restructuring of capitalism. This "great transformation" comparable in scope to the shifts produced by the Industrial Revolution, is moving the world into a postindustrial, infotainment, and biotech mode of global capitalism organized around new information, communications and genetic technologies. (Best & Kellner, 2001, p. 1)

The chapters in this book highlight many of the exemplary uses of technology integration in the social studies. Yet, the reality of integration of technology in the classroom lags behind many of these exemplars (Dede, 2008). To examine technology integration, we must consider what technology schools have access to and how technology is used to promote student learning in the twenty-first century (Cusi, 2007; Margolis, 2008). This chapter will explore technology integration, technology literacy, and

Technology in Retrospect: Social Studies in the Information Age 1984-2009, pp. 285–294

the social context of technology integration through the lens of social studies education.

Learning in the twenty-first century involves a new series of skills that are integral to successful technology integration. Our schools have fallen short of integrating these skills into the curriculum. As the National Research Council states (NRC),

> while we attempt to ensure that every American child has a quality educa-
> tion in the traditional basic subjects, other countries have recalibrated their
> educational institutions to respond differently to the challenge of learning
> for the 21st century ... our students may lack the skills that are critical to
> succeeding in the new global marketplace that places technology and com-
> munications at the center of work and learning. (NRC, 2006, p. 3)

According to the National Council for the Social Studies (NCSS, 2009), "social studies educators teach students the content knowledge, intellectual skills, and civic values necessary for fulfilling the duties of citizenship in a participatory democracy" (para. 1). Given the unique relationship between technology and citizenship education, it is essential for social studies educators to examine the social and cultural implications of technology integration in our schools.

Only 45% of children in low-income housing have access to computers at home. Yet, 100% of these students have access to technology in their classrooms (Pew Research Center, 2008). This would seem to be a statistic that schools could be proud of. Schools are providing technology access to children who otherwise would be left behind in today's technology driven economy. However, an examination into how technology is integrated into instruction reveals a stark disparity between how upper-income students use technology versus lower-income students (Becker, 2000; Margolis, 2008). Students in upper-income classrooms use technology for higher-order thinking activities, whereas students in lower-income schools use technology for basic skills. Given the purpose of social studies education and the phenomenon of twenty-first century tools redefining what it means to be a citizen in our society, we must examine the realities of technology integration in all schools.

> People in the 21st century live in a technology and media-suffused environ-
> ment, marked by various characteristics, including: 1) access to an abun-
> dance of information, 2) rapid changes in technology tools, and 3) the
> ability to collaborate and make individual contributions on an unprece-
> dented scale. To be effective in the 21st century, citizens and workers must
> be able to exhibit a range of functional and critical thinking skills related to
> information, media, and technology. (Partnership for 21st Century Skills,
> 2009, p. 5)

TECHNOLOGY INTEGRATION

Even with the technology infrastructure building that occurred in the 1990s, most schools "could not yet be described as well equipped because they did not permit routine integration of computer technology into the learning activities of most classes" (Becker, 2000, p. 46). This is due, in part, to the difficulty schools have in keeping technologically current as technology is constantly changing. Many teachers feel pressured for content coverage. There is a gap in the research literature as to how current high stakes testing and accountability have affected technology integration in schools. The "great" barriers to technology integration reported by teachers were not enough computers or outdated computers, lack of release time for teachers to learn how to use computers or the Internet, and lack of time in schedule for students to use computers in class (Becker, 2000; National Center for Education Statistics [NCES], 2000). Increasingly, teachers cite high-stakes testing demands as barriers as well (Friedman, 2004; Maddux, 1998).

Given that the classroom is often the pivotal space in which children develop technology skills, we must carefully examine how technology is being used with *all* children (Gorski, 2009). Many educators believe that social progress naturally comes with technological progress (Gorski, 2009). Simply adding access to technology does not level the playing field for all children to use technology. Contextual factors (economic, political, historical, and social) provide an explanation for the lack of widespread transformative use of technology and curriculum integration. Cuban (2001) wrote that "the striking emergence of a large, diverse ad hoc coalition seeking to replicate in public schools the technological transformation that had occurred in the corporate workplace" (p. 156) was responsible, in part, for the emphasis of educational technology in the past two decades. It was believed that higher productivity could be achieved by introducing new technologies into schools and therefore America wanted high tech schools. For many, a "good" school has become synonymous with a technologically equipped one.

Cuban (2001) has argued that computers are generally incompatible with the demands of teaching, and that, for the most part, teachers will shun their use by students during class. A critic of educational technology zealots who encourage school decision makers to wire classrooms, purchase hardware and software, Cuban has been skeptical of these reform efforts because the nature of traditional school and classroom organizations do not easily allow for computers to be used for knowledge construction. The integration of technology into the curriculum is a complex process. Given the rapid speed of evolutionary technologies, the technology tools are perpetually changing. As the tools change, the skills that are needed to use technology are changing. This new set of technology-based skills has been defined as technology literacy. The following section will examine this concept.

Technology Literacy

To integrate technology into the curriculum, teachers must possess a certain amount of technology literacy. Similarly, in order to learn with technology, students must possess an amount of technology literacy. The question of how technology should be integrated into the curriculum depends on how one defines literacy. The increasing emphasis on technology in education has prompted a new definition of what it means to be literate.

As technology becomes more and more ubiquitous in classrooms and in our society, the term *literacy* continues to evolve and change. We are in the midst of a historic transformation in which technology is redefining literacy. Literacy was once limited to text-based or oral instruction. As means of communication have evolved with technology, literacy has evolved to include hypertext documents, multimedia projects, and online communication. Coiro (2005) explains that the changes may be categorized into four challenges for students: to search for, navigate, critically evaluate, and synthesize information. This redefinition holds the potential of making drastic changes in education and society.

Educators can no longer assume students will master information literacy skills in the context of learning traditional school subjects. Rather, information literacy skills must become a deliberate component of the school curriculum. Too often, teachers assume that because students are able to navigate web pages or play and develop multimedia games, they have technology literacy skills. More often than not, however, students do not possess sufficient technology literacy skills to facilitate learning. The nature of information literacy skills calls for educators to rethink literacy in our schools. The new literacy skills in the twenty-first century include the ability to solve problems quickly by accessing information and communicating solutions. Leu (2000) states, "it may become unimportant to demonstrate the advantages of new technologies for educational contexts if its already clear those technologies will define literacies of our students' futures" (p. 762).

Leu (2000) presents a framework to help make sense of the interrelationship between technology and literacy. His framework consists of the transformative, transactional, and deictic method of thinking about these relationships. The transformative perspective is based upon the notion that technology helps reshape literacy. According to the transactional view, technology and literacy shape one another. The deictic perspective incorporates both and emphasizes the constantly evolving forms and functions of literacy. Students must be able not only to locate appropriate information but also to critically read, analyze, evaluate, and make inference within the different curricular fields. This reconceptualization of literacy calls for a redefinition what it means to develop social studies skills for citizenship.

SOCIAL CONTEXT OF TECHNOLOGY AND SCHOOLING

Paradigm shifts such as the one discussed above must be examined through the lens of social context. Bruce (1997) suggests that the cultural contexts of literacy and technology hold potential to transform our society. The impact of technology on our society is not unlike the impact the printing press had on fifteenth century society. The discovery of the printing press brought about a paradigm shift in the way information was organized and disseminated. As we investigate the links to the curriculum and the new paradigm shift, social and cultural impacts of technology emerge. To understand the impact of technology on schools, we next examine social and cultural impacts of technology in schools.

The impact of technology on schools is much more broad than educational policy and curriculum integration. The literature reflects that the impact of technology encompasses societal and cultural aspects. Our society is in the midst of transitions that will be as far-reaching as the Renaissance. The transitions propelled by technology are intertwined with education, politics, economics, and culture. The all-encompassing nature of technology diffusion is referred to as technoculture. The proliferation of technology within society has far-reaching effects on social and cultural aspects of society. Despite these effects, the diffusion of technology has not occurred for all students in schools. There is a well-documented divide of technology access and usage within schools.

Digital Divide

The digital divide is a term often referred to as the "the gap between the technology *haves* and *have nots*. The digital divide first became an educational issue in the 1980s when Apple computers entered the classroom. Within 3 years of having computers in the classroom, 67% of high income schools had computers while only 40% of lower income schools had computers, making the gap between the technology *haves* and *have nots* obvious. The digital divide can be used to discuss inequalities between

individuals within a society or between developing or developed countries. For the purpose of exploring technology in U.S. schools, however,
this discussion will be limited to the digital divide within the U.S. and the
implications for education.

The National Telecommunications and Information Administration
(NTIA) first reported on the digital divide in 1995, with their report, *Falling Through the Net: A Survey of the "Have Nots" in Rural and Urban America*.
The term digital divide attracted mass media attention in 1998 when the
NTIA used "digital divide" in the title of its second national survey. The
NTIA has continued to publish reports in 1998, 1999, and 2000. Taken
together, the four reports implicitly tell a story of technological determinism: that technology is not so much revolutionary as it is evolutionary, and
that evolution is inevitable, inevitably progressive, and progressively
desirable.

Digital divide is typically based on ethnicity and socioeconomic status.
Therefore access to computers and connectivity is often seen as a remedy
to the digital divide. There are numerous reports that illustrate the obvious gaps in access and connectivity between the *haves* and *have nots* (Compaine, 2001; Judge, Puckett, & Cabuk, 2004; Norris, 2001).

NCES (2005) reports that K-12 students whose families were in poverty
were less likely to use the Internet at their homes than K-12 students
whose families were not in poverty (47% compared with 82%). Minority
children and children of low socioeconomic status are less likely to have a
computer in their home. Thereby, children and adolescents whose parents have at least some graduate education and whose families have
incomes of $75,000 or more per year are more prone to use computers at
home (NCES, 2005).

Despite the many reports that illustrate the blatant gaps between the
haves and *have nots*, there are other reports that demonstrate that the gap
is narrowing. The U.S. Department of Commerce study *A Nation Online:
How Americans Are Expanding Their Use Of The Internet* (2000), reported
that Internet use by the lowest income households (those earning less
than $15,000 per year) increased by more than twice the rate of the high-
est income households (those earning more than $75,000 per year) from
1998 to 2001 The study also found that Internet use among African
Americans and Hispanics increased 30 to 33%, a rate higher than the
annual rate for Caucasians.

Using reports such as these, the U.S. Department of Commerce and
others purport that the digital divide no longer exists and is not a societal
issue. The gap between access and connectivity may indeed be shrinking,
resulting in a narrowing of the digital divide when it comes to access and
connectivity. However, access and connectivity alone will not resolve the
underlying issues surrounding the digital divide. Despite the progress we

have made in closing gaps of access and connectivity, approximately fifty percent of adults are still "disconnected" at home (Jackson et al., 2003). Access is dependent on socioeconomic status, gender, race, age, and place of residence, and how an individual uses the computer. For example, better educated individuals are more prone to use the computer for tasks related to work, education as well as political and social engagement.

Jackson et al. (2003) found that historically, race and age were the only predictors of Internet use. Their study found that African Americans and older participants used the Internet less than Caucasian participants and younger participants. Jackson et al. offers three explanations for why African Americans use the computers less than Caucasian Americans, when access is not an issue: cultural differences in preferred communication modalities and partners, lack of individuals to engage in online communication, aesthetic preferences and web design, high need for technical support. The results of the study emphasize the need to further study cultural factors as they related to use of technology,

> a reconceptualization of the digital divide that focuses on race rather than access may be helpful in distributing the benefits of technology to all. Such a reconceptualization directs research attention to cultural factors that influence the extent and nature of technology use. (p. 157)

Today, many educational leaders frame the discussion around how underrepresented groups are using technology in schools, rather than just about access to technology (McLeod & Vasinda, 2008). A snapshot of this is seen when we look at wireless technology in schools. Wireless connections are in found in schools serving more affluent students two-thirds more often than in schools serving less affluent students (Parsad & Jones, 2005).

Recognizing that the digital divide is about more than access we are prompted to consider digital equity. Digital equity refers to equitable access to computers and connectivity and to culturally relevant technology. Digital equity embraces the principles of social justice to see that not only does everyone have access to technology, but that they have skills to use the technology, and that the means and materials are culturally relevant. Digital equity recognizes the notion that when underrepresented groups use technology, technology is often used to reinforce low-level thinking skills and stereotypical patterns of representation (McLeod & Vasinda, 2008).

McLeod and Vasinda's (2008) work suggests that technology in schools is actually contributing to inequity, rather than disrupting the inequality. The phenomenon of Web 2.0 tools is one case in which technology is further contributing to digital equity. One of the objectives of Web 2.0 is to democratize information exchange on the Internet. Web 2.0 provides users the opportunity to participate in diverse online interchanges in which users have equal voices. Yet, we know that 90% of users of Web 2.0 are and can still be labeled as consumers while only 2% could be defined as producers (Bull, Hammond, & Ferster, 2008).

The National Institute for Community Innovations identified five dimensions of digital equity: content creation, effective use, quality content, cultural relevance, and technology resources. It is imperative that educators go beyond the issue of access and consider the dimensions of digital equity. Schools should be using technology to help students become editors and creators of information, rather than just consumers of information (Bull et al., 2008). Otherwise, access to technology could intentionally or unintentionally continue to further promote social inequity.

CONCLUSION

Schools have long been guilty of perpetuating social inequality in our society (Anyon, 1980). Unequal access and unequal use of technology in our schools is reproducing the status quo in our society. Reform has concentrated on economic aspects of schooling rather than on the purpose of schooling in a democratic society perpetuates (Tyack & Cuban, 2004). Coming back to the purpose of social studies education as preparation of citizens, we must consider technology integration in context of our society. The field of social studies education is uniquely positioned to assist in this regard. When considering integration of technology into the field, we must consider not only the curricular points of integration. Many of these curricular points of integration have been highlighted in this book. They are dynamic and transforming for the field. However, the field must go one step further to successfully integrate technology into the social studies content.

As the field of social studies education reflects on where we have been and where we will go in the future, social studies educators must consider the social and cultural aspects of reform. Our teacher educators, teachers, and students should develop an awareness of the social and cultural aspects of technology integration. We must work to insure equitable access to networks, equipment, and content for the development of effective citizens in the twenty-first century.

REFERENCES

Anyon, J. (1980). Social class and the hidden curriculum of work. *Journal of Education*, *162*(1). Retrieved October 14, 2008, from http://www-scf.usc.edu/~clarkjen/Jean%20Anyon.htm

Becker, H. (2000). Who's wired and who's not: Children's access to and use of computer technology. *The Future of Children, 10*(2), 44-75.

Best, S., & Kellner, D. (2001). *The postmodern adventure.* New York: Guilford Press.

Bruce, B. C. (1997). Literacy technologies: What stance should we take? *Journal of Literacy Research, 29,* 289-309.

Bull, G., Hammond, T., & Ferster, B. (2008). Developing Web 2.0 tools for support of historical inquiry in social studies. *Computers in the Schools, New York, 25*(3/4), 275-287.

Coiro, J. (2005). Every teacher a Miss Rumphius: Empowering teachers with effective professional development. In R. A. Karchmer, M. Mallette, J. Kara-Soteriou, & D. J. Leu, Jr. (Eds.). *New literacies for new times: Innovative models of literacy education using the Internet* (pp. 199-221). Newark, DE: International Reading Association.

Compaine, B. (2001). *The digital divide: Facing a crisis or creating a myth?* Retrieved (April 29, 2005, from http://ebusiness.mit.edu/research/papers/130%20Compaine,%20Digital%20Divide.pdf

Cuban, L. (2001). *Oversold and underused: Computers in the classroom.* Cambridge, MA: Harvard University Press.

Cusi, R. C. (2007). *Technology and equity: Explaining differences between elementary teachers' use of computers in low-income Latino and middle class schools.* Unpublished doctoral dissertation, University of California, Irvine.

Dede, C. (2008). Reinventing the role of information and communication. In G. Fenstermacher (Ed.), *Yearbook of the national society for the study of education* (pp. 11-38).Hoboken NJ: Wiley-Blackwell.

Friedman, A. M. (2004). *Digital primary source use in world history and world geography.* Unpublished doctoral dissertation, University of Virginia, Charlottesville.

Gorski, P. (2009). Insisting on digital equity. *Urban Education, 44*(3), 348-364.

Jackson, L. A., B. Gretchen, B. Frank, Z. Yong, von Eye, A., & Fitzgerald, H. E. (2003). Home internet use in low-income families: Implications for the digital divide. *IT & Society, 1*(5), 141-165.

Judge, S., Puckett, K., & Cabuk, B. (2004). Digital equity: New findings from the early childhood longitudinal study. *Journal of Research on Technology in Education, 36*(4), 383-396.

Leu, D. (2000). Literacy and technology: Deictic consequences for literacy education in an information age. In M. L. Kamil, P. D. Pearson, & R. Barr (Eds.), (Ed.), *Handbook of Reading Research* (Vol. III, pp. 743-770). Mahwah, NJ: Erlbaum.

Maddux, C. (1998). Barriers to the successful use of information technology in education. *Computers in the Schools, 14*(3/4), 5-11.

Margolis, J. (2008). *Stuck in the shallow end: education race and computing.* Cambridge, MA: MIT Press.

McLeod, J., & Vasinda, S. (2008). Critical literacy and Web 2.0: Exercising and negotiating power. *Computers in the Schools, 25*(3-4), 259-274.

National Center for Education Statistics. (2000). *Teachers' tools for the 21st century* (No. NCES 2000-102). Washington DC: U.S. Department of Education.

National Center for Education Statistics. (2005). *Internet access in U.S. public schools and classrooms: 1994-2003* (No. NCES 20005-15). Washington DC: U.S. Department of Education.

National Council for the Social Studies. (2009). *About the National Council for the Social Studies.* Retrieved August 31, 2009, from http://www.socialstudies.org/about.

National Research Council. (2006). *ICT Fluency and High Schools: A Workshops Summary.* Washinton, DC: National Academies Press. Retrieved October 10, 2008, from www.nap.edu/catalog/11709.htm

National Telecommunications and Information. (1995). *Falling through the Net: A survey of the "have nots" in the rural and urban America.* Washington, DC: U.S Department of Commerce.

Norris, P. (2001). *Digital divide: Civic engagement, information poverty, and the internet worldwide.* New York: Cambridge University Press.

Parsad, B., & Jones, J. (2005). Internet Access in U.S. Public Schools and Classrooms: 1994-2003 (NCES 2005-015). U.S. Department of Education. Washington, DC: National Center for Education Statistics.

Partnership for 21st Century Skills. (2009). *Skills framework.* Retrieved June, 5, 2009, from http://www.21stcenturyskills.org/

Pew Research Center. (2008). *Teens and social media.* Retrieved September 1, 2008, from http://www.pewinternet.org/reports/index.asp

Reinking, D. (Ed.). (1998). *Synthesizing technological transformations of literacy in a post-typographic world.* Mahwah, NJ: Erlbaum.

Tyack, D., & Cuban, L (2004) Tinkering toward utopia: A century of public school reform. Excerpts from a conversation at the Askwith Education Forum. *Harvard School of Education, HGSE News.* Retrieved October, 1, 2008, from http://www.gse.harvard.edu/news/features/utopia03012004.html

U.S. Department of Commerce. (2000). *A nation online: How Americans are expanding their use of the internet.* Retrieved April 28, 2005, from http://www.ntia.doc.gov/ntiahome/dn/nationonline_020502.htm

Warschauer, M. (1999). *Electronic literacies: Language, culture, and power in online education.* Mahwah, NJ: Erlbaum.

CHAPTER 16

SOCIAL STUDIES AND TECHNOLOGY 2009-2034

David Valdez, B. Justin Reich, and Michael J. Berson

The preceding chapters have traced the contours of the use of technology in the social studies over the past 25 years, a period marked by unprecedented technological change. Together, our collaborators have shown us compelling exemplars and illustrative failures; they have provided detailed maps of well-studied terrain and sketches of frontiers yet to be explored; and they have provided a clear portrait of the present and the cutting edge. Our task now, is to project further into the future. What will learning and teaching with digital technologies in the social studies look like in the next 25 years?

We approach this chapter with the belief that we must not let the future simply evolve. To reach a point where technology cannot be described as "oversold and underused" (Cuban, 2001), we must learn from our past to enhance the learning and educational experiences of future generations of social studies students. In this final chapter, we provide a hopeful vision of how, over the next 25 years, social studies educators might integrate emerging technologies into their learning environments. We offer this vision as a starting point for a larger conversation among social studies educators about what the future of learning in the social studies ought to

Technology in Retrospect: Social Studies in the Information Age 1984-2009, pp. 295–309
Copyright © 2010 by Information Age Publishing
All rights of reproduction in any form reserved.

look like, what role technology will play, and what we need to do in classrooms, teacher education programs, publishing houses, and public policy to bring about the best possible environments for nurturing young citizens.

Envisioning the classroom of tomorrow poses fundamental questions about how technology will shape future society. For decades artists have been imaging how networked computer systems will change our lives. At one extreme is a *Jetsons*-like world with brightly colored flying cars and mechanical assistants that help us to dress and do household chores. The *Jetsons'* technology is benevolent and allows for greater luxuries and human freedoms. The other extreme is the dark apocalyptic vision of *Blade Runner* where machines are necessary for survival, and the mystique of a Big Brother presence pervades technological innovations. We admit that our presentation here is more like the *Jetsons*: where technology makes certain facets of life easier and richer, but does not replace the fundamental tensions, drama, and comedy of the human experience. The *Jetsons* was funny, after all, because we still recognized ourselves in their transformed world. In this short chapter, we present a similarly aspirational vision, although certainly one role of social studies instruction in the decades ahead will be to prevent the scenarios of *Blade Runner, 1984*, and other technological dystopias from being realized.

The typical school morning in the year 2034 is not without similarities to today's classroom. The final bell rings, and a handful of flushed students are tardy to class. In some classes, students immediately pull out their networked devices, and log in to the online learning environment prepared for class by their teachers. In other classes, the period begins with the human connection that has been the hallmark of education for millennia, and screens and projectors remain dark as teachers and students connect and prepare for the day's tasks. Some things may never change, but by 2034, technology has enabled a more efficient classroom and pedagogical approaches that are personalized to student needs.

SOCIAL STUDIES IN CLASS

Let us imagine a class period in the day of the life of one student, George, and his teacher, Jane. As George is sitting down to class, Jane asks her students to log into the landing page for her class in the school's learning management system, and students pull out their web-enabled devices. In George's school, every student has been issued a hand-held mobile device. This device, about the size of today's iPhone, has nearly all the functionality of a phone and laptop computer.

The cell phones of today have two major limitations: awkward data entry and limited screen size. The small keyboard size even on devices with QWERTY-style keyboards is cumbersome for anything more than limited text messages or keyword searches. In addition, the size of the visible screen limits how much data is displayed and how quickly a user can scan for relevant information. In 2034, these obstacles will be overcome with several different new technologies.

George can use his mobile device as a handheld and interact with a touch screen in his hand. The device even has "gestural interface," which was pioneered at MIT beginning in 2009. George's handheld recognizes his natural hand gestures in order to take and edit photographs, navigate the internet, and access databases, using the mobile phone as the processing unit (Mistry, 2009).

George can also project a real-scale virtual keyboard onto any flat surface, like his desk or a wall, and type naturally. His handheld can also project an image as small as a piece of paper or as large as a wall. George's desk has a white panel built into the surface that he can flip up to use as a screen. With this handheld device, George has the option of remaining constantly connected with his learning environment. The types of handheld devices vary depending on student needs and customization features. There are some high-end products like tablets and cell phone interface tools as well as traditional mini-netbooks. In much the same way students have various calculators with multiple features and accessories, so too do students of the future have handheld devices with multiple price points and accessibility features.

At other schools, George's friends use touchscreen tablets rather than the handhelds. Some schools maintain rigid regimes for ensuring that all students use the same platform, and at other schools, students and classes use differing devices but are united by the same platform. Some schools conduct all technological support and device repair on site, while others require students to be individually responsible for their own machines. Issues of equity remain, but the dramatic drop in the costs of these devices means that every student in the country is accessible to a machine for online communication, writing, and research.

As students log in, Jane asks her students to spend the first few minutes of class working on a "Do Now," a brief activity to reorient the student towards the class period. For the previous evening's homework, Jane asked her students to view a short web video about a new law that Congress passed and then to read a related *Wall Street Journal* article. Their assignment was to then find a related news video, online article, or paper clipping about the same story from another country and to compare/contrast the two pieces. Today's Do Now is to review their previous night's assignment, and to write a metacognitive reflection about how they completed the assignment, focusing on the skill of "transmedia navigation," the ability to follow a story line across multiple media (Jenkins, 2006).

Completing the Do Now is a seamless process, and individualized for each student. George's class interface automatically retrieves his completed homework assignment, and opens up a new entry in his online notebooks. A few of George's classmates have not finished the assignment and, with the touch of a button from her administrative controls, Jane temporarily grants students web access to catch up on the homework rather than complete the Do Now. As in the past, illness, family challenges, motivation problems and other issues mean that students do not always complete their homework, but technology enables Jane to more efficiently use their time together to be sure that each student has meaningful learning opportunities throughout their class time together.

Before class even begins, Jane knows quite a bit about what her students did for homework and where they are in their learning process. The teacher spends no time collecting homework. She has already worked with her learning management system (LMS) to evaluate the class's homework, and she has a great deal of data at her fingertips in terms of who completed the assignment and what the students learned in the process. When she awoke this morning, her learning management system gave her a homework report, providing details about which students had completed the homework the evening before. The report notes what time the assignment was submitted, and utilizing a word count rubric and content evaluation application, the report indicates which students only partially finished the assignment. Each assignment is evaluated by a plagiarism detection tool that prevents multiple students from submitting the same assignment or copying material from the web. Since the teacher has given a similar assignment several times in years past, the LMS's natural language processing software can use the teacher's previous grades to identify which assignments are likely to be of high and low quality. Software tools also compare this assignment to each student's previous assignments to evaluate spelling, grammar, length, usage, and so forth. Automated writing evaluation remains primitive, but teachers can still use this basic data to help chart each student's progress and provide strategies for differentiated instruction. Later this evening, Jane will post brief feedback on each student's assignment. Using natural handwriting on her touchscreen tablet, Jane's feedback will be included in each student's online portfolio for students and parents to review.

Since the teacher does not need to spend any time collecting homework, she can use her report to instantly connect with the few students who did not turn anything in or turned in substandard work. She spends the period of the Do Now connecting with students who are falling behind, rather than figuring out who is. After resolving their individual issues, she returns to her desk station and announces to students that they have one minute to finish their journaling.

After a minute, she tells students to save their work, and then she sets up the students' interface for class. When students are in her class, Jane can control each student's mobile device. When the Do Now period ends, Jane calls up an interface for George and his peers which includes the class outline and objectives on the left margins of the screen, and the essential question for the day across the top. Access to e-mail, texting, the Web, and other programs is locked and unlocked by the teacher as necessary during class.

In order to facilitate discussion about transmedia navigation, the teacher asks one student to take notes. George volunteers, and Jane sets her classroom projector to project directly from George's mobile device. The teacher then darkens all other students' computers, so the pupils focus on the discussion in that room among their peers. Sometimes the most important skill in teaching with technology is knowing when to turn it off.

During the discussion, several students describe the challenges that they faced in finding media from other countries. Some simply found media that was published in English, but others wanted to get perspectives from different cultures. Some of these students used online translation tools to read print reports or listen to news videos; others asked friends in other countries to give a brief synopsis. Many of George's classmates have participated in virtual exchanges with students in other countries since their earliest years in elementary school, and virtually every student keeps up with friends around the world. Jane facilitated a conversation about the strengths and weakness of these approaches to translation and more broadly of the different media that students discovered, from the traditional media conglomerates to local citizen journalists reporting collaboratively around the world.

After reviewing specific dimensions of transmedia navigation, the teacher shifts the discussion to another skill: comparing and contrasting. In reviewing the assignments over her morning coffee, Jane noted that many students described both articles or videos rather than actually comparing or contrasting them, so she chose three exemplary assignments which she projects on the whiteboard and on her students' screens. The class discusses the assignment for a few minutes, and collectively they clarify how to compare and contrast effectively. The teacher then assigns different students to different tasks. Those who did an exemplary job on their assignment are asked to make an update to the "Compare/Contrast" article on the class' "Social Studies Skills and Habits of Mind" wiki. Most of the other students are tasked to revise their assignment, and the few who didn't turn their work in have a few additional minutes to catch up.

A small flashing light appears on Jane's handheld computer indicating that class is halfway over. Even in 2034 with nearly all of the logistical work taken care of automatically, teachers are still pressed for time, so she gives students a few more minutes to work on their revision before changing the activity. For the second half of class, students are put in groups and asked to create a graphical organizer to compare the various international responses to the new American law. Students use a digital collaborative mind-mapping tool to organize their various articles and videos, categorizing the responses as supporting versus opposing and further delineating the opposing responses as procedural versus ideological. Each topic on the mind map is linked back to the original article or video, as students will be required over the next few nights to write a paper synthesizing the international responses to the new law. The essential question of the class period, "How is American domestic legislation shaped by foreign policy?", remains at the top of students screen during the entire exercise. As the teacher wanders the room offering guidance and feedback, she continues to point students towards the essential question to keep their discussions focused. She also regularly glances at her own mobile device, which she has set to scroll through the screens of each of her students. When students appear to be off topic or off task, she wanders towards their desks to help them regain focus. Technology has not replaced classroom management strategies in 2034, but it has enhanced teachers' awareness and ability to handle off-task behaviors.

Three beeps from Jane's handheld indicate that only five minutes are left in the period, and she reviews the assignment for the next day. The notes that George has been recording are archived to the class wiki site and made available for students from other periods. George's handheld interface now includes an exit card which has a brief poll about the day's lesson and a space for an open response. Before leaving, he completes the poll and writes a few sentences about what he is eager to learn more about. All of the feedback is uploaded to the teacher's desktop and stored for her review. George and his friends move on to their next class. Some students move to the school's computer lab/media center where they are enrolled in online advanced placement (AP) courses that are not offered at their brick-and-mortar school.

In another social studies classroom exploring the same compare/contrast assignment, similar technology is in use. The teacher moves to the front of the room where a web-enabled wipeboard is positioned. The teacher projects some students' homework onto the board. One student provides a link to an online German news article about the new U.S. law. The article was originally posted in German, but using translation software, the student was able to successfully understand the story. The teacher navigates to another student's submission. This time, it is a Japanese television news clip that has been posted online. The teacher shows the clip with English subtitles and asks students whether they felt the clip was balanced. Using a web-based polling system, the teacher asks students to use their cell phones to text their vote. Real-time data is projected onto the wipeboard. The class discussion is productive. A few students use their mobile phones and tablets to find additional materials and begin to e-mail their findings to the shared bulletin board on the class management site. Toward the end of class, the teacher reminds the class about the new homework assignment that has already been posted to the class site. The websites, news programs, and polling results were captured and stored on the class website. One student who was absent from class today will be able to go online and access the content, including the wipeboard comments from the day's lesson, and review the material at a later date. Another student who was present is convinced that one of the sites the class visited today was also discussed a few weeks earlier. He is able to go online and review the class archives of previous discussions and captured slides to check out his hunch.

ON AUTHENTIC WORK

In the social studies classroom of 2035, a considerable amount of time is spent doing real and authentic work. Jane and her teacher colleagues have recognized that the classroom walls which sequestered students from meaningful community involvement could be breached with online technologies. Increasingly, businesses, governments, nonprofit groups, and other communities recognize the hunger that young people feel to solve pressing problems and engage with the world, and Internet connections allow school-community partnerships to flourish.

Through partnerships with local historical associations, history students comb online archives of audio, visual, and document materials, interview community elders, and piece together the stories and life histories of their communities. Through online forums, they share these stories back with the broader community who can provide meaningful feedback and critiques that let even young students feel a genuine sense of audience and purpose as they write. In the social studies class of 2034, students are dramatically involved in the fabric of their community, both physical and digital, and the effective use of technology allows students to meaningfully contribute, document, participate, and analyze the dimensions of their identities.

Civics students poll community members about local concerns, contribute to government forums about youth issues, and analyze publicly available data about government and business to better understand their towns, counties, and country. Geography students using geographic information systems (GIS) help local governments better understand traffic patterns, help scientists produce detailed maps of reserve sanctuaries, or track recycling trends in a given neighborhood.

Students studying global issues routinely interact with students across the world, and it's as common for students to work in groups with students on multiple continents as it is for them to work in their own classrooms. One of the highlights of George's year is when the school holds a lock-in where students sleep in the gymnasium and arise in the early morning to talk and work synchronously with their colleagues in Shanghai, Abu Dhabi, or Jaipur. Overseas teachers align curriculum goals with George's teachers each year to plan for topics of discussion and transcontinental live-video presentations. Later in the second-half of the academic year, the process is reversed.

Nearly all of this intellectual endeavor happens in the public sphere. The notion of handing a final performance of understanding to a single teacher is reserved only for very personal kinds of assignments in health or English/language arts classes. For the most part, everything students produce has an audience, and students are used to having their work evaluated by school peers, students in other schools, experts and professionals who give their time to review student work, and parents who have a window into school life.

All of these projects and performances do not entirely replace time devoted to the study of core, foundational knowledge. Economics students still study supply and demand, and U.S. history students still study the Civil War. But whenever possible throughout the year, social studies teachers motivate the study of these subjects with an authentic project-based approach in which students apply disciplinary knowledge to tackle real world challenges.

SOCIAL STUDIES BEYOND THE CLASSROOM WALLS

Later that evening, George will be able to check his mobile device for his homework and additional communications from his teachers. Each student will consider his or her phone an essential classroom tool. With parent permission, teachers will regularly send text messages to students about homework, project deadlines, and even pop quizzes. When Jane finishes grading the day's homework, she can upload scores and comments to the school's server. This sends a message to a student's mobile device and to the parents as well, so George and his parents have real-time access to information about his class performance.

Since schools keep central databases for each student, Jane can use her mobile device to check educational applications that contain information about the learning style, personal strengths, and academic challenges of each of her students. As students enter each class for the first time, she downloads each student's profile. Instantly, she is made aware of how best to differentiate instruction for students while maintaining each student's privacy. Jane can continue to update the student profile so that other teachers can monitor the student's performance in all of his/her classes and provide necessary support. Teachers can send personalized messages to students about their performance, praising them for their participation or encouraging them to keep trying. Parents can be kept abreast of their student's performance and follow the profile of their child. Each of these tasks is no different from what motivated teachers do today. They check in with students about how well the material is being received and how to improve delivery of content. They consult with other teachers about students of interest. They contact parents and students to give feedback and address concerns. Utilizing technology like mobile phones will allow teachers to carry out many of the tasks they already do, but do so with greater ease and faster results.

The technology will also allow teachers to better communicate with families for whom English is not their native language. Improved translation applications will allow teachers to send basic communications to students and parents. As teachers post private feedback to each student about assignments or send comments about academic achievement, students and parents will be able to access the teacher comments in a variety of languages. For some families, this will become a valuable means by which to stay connected and informed about teacher expectations and student performance. Reciprocally, parents will be able to send communications to teachers in their native language, and the teacher will be able to use basic digital translation tools to comprehend the e-mail. There will continue to be a need for translation aides to assist during parent-teacher conferences or phone calls to home, but by 2034, there will be improved efforts in basic tools of communication for common school-related expressions and scenarios. In this way, Jane is able to assist her students in the mainstream classroom and can continue to provide differentiated instruction for all learners.

In the evening, as George is completing the night's homework, he logs onto the class website and reads the assignment. He has a question about the task. He is not quite sure if he can work with a partner to complete the assignment. The student checks his instant messenger service but sees that Jane has not logged on. The student then accesses the virtual teacher assistant from the class website. This avatar has been preprogrammed with responses to commonly asked questions from students and is accessible during after-school hours. Avatars are used as digital representations of a person and may be accurate or fictitious projections of the person in a digital environment. Avatars have moved from gaming features to business applications, and Yahoo Inc., which has approximately 7 million users each month on its avatar-creation site, has licensed with private corporations for commercial marketing programs that guide online users through products (Noguchi, 2005). George uses natural speech or writing and asks his question to the avatar. This digital virtual teacher assistant clarifies the assignment parameters, and a log of the communication is captured and delivered to the teacher's digital dropbox.

Currently, avatars are used as facades for some instant messenger features or as an application in games and social networking sites, but it is likely that the future classroom will also have a supplemental cyberclass. Some classrooms, especially at the university level, are a hybrid of brick-and-mortar classrooms as well as some online class feature. This model will continue to expand to the secondary level. Not only may teachers post assignments, study guides, syllabi, and FAQs as they might today to their class website, they will also interact after school with students by use of an avatar. Although it may seem that the teacher is working extra hours from home, it will be possible for the teacher-avatar to operate independently from the teacher actually being online. The teacher-avatar will already be preprogrammed with a host of question-response scenarios, capable of transcribing student questions so the actual teacher may later read the dialogue and follow up with students in class or online. While the avatar may not be able to explain as clearly or completely some aspects of the curriculum, it will allow for some degree of nonschool hour instruction to continue, which may benefit some students who need to be reminded of assignment details or for students who may have missed class. The avatar will also be able to make some natural language translations for English Language Learners who may want to review the assignment at their own pace or practice their English. The teacher can assume control of the avatar at anytime and may arrange reviews or special discussions with virtual visitors.

These various features will break down the classroom constraints of time and space and allow students to engage in the social studies anytime, anywhere.

ON PRESERVICE INDUCTION, IN-SERVICE TRAINING, AND EDUCATION RESEARCH

Jane did not develop her technology integration skills on her own. Throughout her preservice and in-service training, our teacher had both powerful role-models and effective instruction in theoretical frameworks and pragmatic concerns with implementing technology in the classroom.

Up until 2009, teachers' abilities to effectively integrate technology in social studies classroom were severely curtailed by the almost total absence of effective technology integration in preservice and in-service training. The teacher educators of 2009 were nearly all products of an educational system without technology, and as a result they had little personal experience with using computers or mobile devices within their teaching. Indeed, many teachers associated fear, anxiety, and worry with introducing new technologies in class, which required new preparation, new pedagogies, new conceptions of knowledge, and new ideas about student authorship and audience.

In those early years of the new millennia, however, teacher educators recognized a troubling disconnect between the media saturation in the lives of a new generation of "digital natives" and the technological isolation of the classroom. Some teacher educators held out hope that this divide would organically wane over time as younger, more tech-savvy teachers entered the profession, but the early results were not promising. Even as the oldest "digital natives" began entering the profession, their classroom experience and preservice training did not include examples of how to effectively integrate technology into teaching and learning. As a result, young teachers with great technological fluency and media saturation in their personal lives implemented methods that were well established during the nineteenth century. They continued to utilize the same format and tradition of classroom instruction they had personally experienced.

So what inspired teacher educators to commit to the hard work of transforming their curricula to include more technology integration, thereby providing models of excellence for preservice teachers? It was not the surfeit of new information available, or the radical shift of commerce into an online environment, or the convergence of print and online journalism, or the transformation of social lives and identity through social networks. The critical shift was in American politics, as politicians united their supporters through social networks, communicated directly to constituencies through *YouTube* and *Facebook*, and pushed forward a good governance initiative closely tied to generating transparency by publishing information online. Moreover, interest groups and civic leaders used the same tools to organize their supporters, volunteers, and advocates. Once Web 2.0 tools became firmly ensconced in the civic sphere, social studies teachers felt a compelling responsibility to immerse students in online communities and help prepare them for their roles and responsibilities as citizens in the twenty-first century.

Making this transformation required teacher educators to return to their syllabi and lesson plans, and begin modeling lessons that thoughtfully and effectively incorporated various technologies- computers, projectors, interactive whiteboards, mobile devices, and so forth. Since many teaching colleges and preservice teachers have better access to technology than many schools and K-12 students, teacher educators designed lessons that could be accomplished not just by students with 24 hour access to networked computers, but by students who might need to go to a library or stay after school to get access to computers. By being immersed in these classroom experiences as students, preservice teachers had the chance to experience and then design technology rich lessons that allowed students to access diverse sources, collaborate, and co-construct knowledge and understanding. These experiences in methods classes at the university level were supported by induction into teaching frameworks and pedagogical ideas that many preservice teachers learned in special courses focused on methods with technology.

Education researchers played a critical role in helping to advance pedagogy as this transformation was taking place. Many researchers continued in the rich tradition of design research (Dede, 2005) that had been developed over the previous decade, where researchers experimented with new methods and pedagogy and reported on their efficacy. Nearly all social studies methods teachers were involved in these efforts on one scale or another. In addition to these design methods, researchers recognized that extraordinary innovations were happening across the country in technology integration, and qualitative researchers developed a rich repertoire of case studies describing these efforts. At the same time, researchers also recognized that the continuous, real-time data produced by online learning environment would enable entirely new approaches to education research, where longitudinal analyses of usage statistics or semantic analysis of content could allow quantitative research to provide some context about the entire universe of wikis that offered some perspective of qualitative case studies. Innovations in technology-rich pedagogies sometimes emerged from concentrated research along any one of these methodological lines, but more often came about as a result of drawing insights across these differing kinds of studies.

By 2034, through a difficult period of growth, social studies educators have closed the media chasm between classrooms and the rest of the world, and technology and social media is an essential part of school life. To be sure, much about classrooms remain unchanged—the virtues of face to face exchange, debate and discussion, close relationships between students and teachers, the need to make content themes relevant, and the close reading of print text remain essential parts of school life. But these time-honored methods are complimented and accentuated by the new methods and pedagogies enabled by emerging technologies.

All of these important developments in teachers colleges and research universities are supported by professional development efforts within schools. Jane takes considerable personal responsibility for her own professional development. She has carefully designed her personal learning network to sensibly absorb information from several sources helpful for social studies teachers: some professional historian newsletters, blogs from other educators, and the National Council for the Social Studies Ning social network (ncssnetwork.ning.com). Her colleagues are members of similar networks, and so they regularly have shared texts to shape their discussions in department meetings. These teachers continue to share resources with one another and adapt ideas to their own needs—much as teachers of today foster a collegial respect for one another.

In addition to her personal learning network, Jane also has regular in-service trainings provided by her school district. Recognizing that hardware and software investments are worth little without developing the humanware of learning, federal, state, and municipal technology grants have been radically refigured over the last decades to require that technology purposes are paired with professional development training, to avoid the "oversold and underused" phenomena that dominated the end of the twentieth century and the beginning of the twenty-first century (Cuban, 2001). Some of Jane's professional development is presented through face to face sessions on her campus, but she also regularly participates in webinars and online minicourses that she can complete, at least partially, on her own schedule. Professional development opportunities encourage effective infusion of technological resources and create productive systems of digital resources.

Every year, Jane's school or department picks a theme to organize professional development so that the school is collectively making progress towards "the next level of work" (City, Elmore, Fiarman, & Teitel, 2009). Some years the focus is exclusively on an issue entwined with technology, some years the focus touches upon technology, and some years the focus is elsewhere. These regular professional development opportunities allow our teacher to continue to develop her skills with new media and new technology even as the digital landscape changes around her.

CONCLUDING THOUGHTS

This chapter offers a glimpse into the future, yet this collective vision is a conjecture of just one of many possible scenarios that optimize the diffusion of technological innovation in our society and its translation into educational applications. No one knows for certain what the future will bring, and emerging technologies and revised pedagogic approaches to teaching could make the best-laid plans obsolete. What is inevitable is that change will occur. The question is how proactive a role educators will take in ushering in a new age or whether they will hold tight to traditional practices and ways of thinking.

Although new media are not a panacea for education, technology innovation may offer rich and constructive experiences that extend beyond the potential of traditional media that has been a mainstay of teaching for centuries. Schools need to embrace the important shift toward digitally connected and mobile technologies that are pervasive in the lives of children. These tools provide an opportunity to not just support learning, but also they may guide and enrich students' experiences with access to ideas on a global scale, active engagement through critical analysis of information, and participation in inquiry and discovery that leads to the creation and dissemination of new ideas. Let us learn from our past, and embrace the future so that we can reap the benefits of the unprecedented technological change. Our students are counting on us to guide them into the future, their future. They rely on the skills that teachers foster, the examples that are modeled, and the ideas that are nurtured. The future offers a tremendous opportunity to be responsive to a world that has been transformed by technology. It is time to embrace this change and create learning experiences that are more extraordinary than anything we have yet imagined.

REFERENCES

City, E. A., Elmore, R. F., Fiarman, S., & Teitel, L. (2009). *Instructional rounds in education: A network approach to improving teaching and learning.* Cambridge, MA: Harvard Education Press.

Cuban, L. (2001). *Oversold and underused: Computers in the classroom.* Cambridge, MA: Harvard University Press.

Dede, C. (2005). Why design-based research is both important and difficult. *Educational Technology, 45*(1), 5-9.

Hanna, W., & Barbera. J. (Executive Producers). (1962). *The Jetsons* [Television series]. Los Angeles: Taft Broadcasting.

Jenkins, H., Clinton, K., Purushotma, R., Robison, A., & Weigel, M. (2006). *Confronting the challenges of participatory culture: Media education for the 21st century.* Chicago, IL: The MacArthur Foundation. Retrieved November 4, 2009 from http://www.digitallearning.macfound.org

Mistry, P. (2009). *Sixthsense: A wearable gestural interface.* Retrieved from www.pranavmistry.com/projects/sixthsense

Noguchi, Y. (2005, November 22). Self 2.0: Internet Users Put a Best Face Forward Web Chatters Upgrade Their Identities for Virtual Life. *Washington Post,* p. A01. Retrieved on December 1, 2007, from http://www.washingtonpost.com/wp-dyn/content/article/2005/11/21/AR2005112101787.html

Orwell, G. (1949). *1984.* United Kingdom: Secker and Warburg.

Scott, R. (Director). (1982). *Blade Runner* [Motion picture]. United States: The Ladd Company.

ABOUT THE AUTHORS

Marsha Alibrandi is associate professor of secondary education at Fairfield University in Connecticut, and author of *GIS in the Classroom* (2003) and coeditor of *Digital Geography* (2008). She taught 9-12 grade geography and social studies at Cape Cod Tech, and has taught undergraduate and graduate courses in geography and social studies education since 1990. While associate professor at North Carolina State University, she offered a GIS in education course between 2000 and 2005. She continues to seek, support, research and report on classroom applications of geospatial technologies (GSTs) nationally and internationally, and is interested in comparing spatial and linguistic cognition, and the critical, ethical and equity issues inherent in GSTs. Her publications have been targeted on integrating GSTs in social studies education and she can be contacted at marsh@cape.com

Linda Bennett is the associate dean, director of the Teacher Development Program, and an associate professor of social studies education at the University of Missouri. Through her efforts, the university offers an online master's degree in social studies education and her innovations in technology are integral to preparation of elementary social studies teachers. She is editor of *Social Studies and the Young Learner* and publications range from integration of technology in elementary social studies to teacher preparation. She has made numerous international and national technology related presentations. She can be contacted at lb@missouri.edu

Ilene R. Berson is an associate professor of early childhood education in the Department of Childhood Education and Literacy Studies at the University of South Florida. She has extensive experience working with children ages birth to eight, and she is a nationally certified and state licensed school psychologist. Her research focuses on prevention and intervention services for young children at imminent risk for socioemotional challenges associated with child maltreatment and other traumatic events. She leads collaborative reform initiatives, forging linkages between early childhood, child welfare, and health care systems, as well as international studies on the engagement of young children with digital technologies. Dr. Berson has extensively published books, chapters, and journal articles and has presented her research worldwide. Dr. Berson embodies the characteristics of an engaged scholar who works closely in reciprocal relationships with practitioners and policymakers to develop innovative solutions for emerging and long term issues to promote young children's well being. She can be contacted at iberson@usf.edu

Michael J. Berson is a professor in the Secondary Education Department at the University of South Florida and a senior fellow in The Florida Joint Center for Citizenship. He instructs courses in social science methodology and is the coordinator of the doctoral program in social science education. His award-winning courses have been acknowledged for integrating emerging technologies into instruction and modeling dynamic and fluid pedagogy. Dr. Berson has extensively published books, chapters, and journal articles and presented worldwide. His research on child advocacy and technology in social studies education has achieved global recognition. He can be contacted at berson@usf.edu

Cheryl Mason Bolick is an associate professor in the school of education at the University of North Carolina at Chapel Hill. Her areas of scholarship include the social studies, teacher education, teaching and learning with technology, and integrating technology into the social studies. She can be contacted at cbolick@unc.edu

June Byng is a doctoral candidate at the University of Texas at San Antonio in the Department of Educational Leadership and Policy Studies. She holds principal, classroom teacher, and special education certifications from the Texas State Board of Educator Certification. Her most recent publication includes coauthorship of a book chapter in Marshall and Oliva's (2010) *Leadership for Social Justice: Making Revolutions in Education*. She has also collaborated with her professors, Dr. Elizabeth Murakami-Ramalho, Dr. Encarnacion Garza, and Dr. David Thompson, on a study of principal preparation programs in Texas: *Effective Leaders Impacting*

Schools: An Overview of Principal Preparation Programs in Texas. She presented findings from this study during a poster session at the annual UCEA conference in November, 2008 and facilitated a roundtable discussion of the same study at the annual conference of the NCPEA in August, 2009. A recipient of the UCEA Barbara L. Jackson Scholar Award for 2009 to 2011, she is also the founder and director of a local 501(c)(3) nonprofit organization, Light the Borders, which supports impoverished communities along the Texas-Mexico border by providing distributions of food and other items, special camps for children and families, and free Spanish/English translation services. She can be contacted at jbyng@juno.com

Richard Diem is currently dean of the Honors College and professor of education at The University of Texas at San Antonio. In addition to his work at UTSA, he has also taught at in the public schools in suburban Chicago, Northern Illinois University, Texas Women's University, and the Escola de Superior in Viseu, Portugal. He is a graduate of Bradley University where he earned his undergraduate degree in history. He completed a master's degree in education from Southern Illinois University, Carbondale, a master's in history from Colorado State University and a PhD from Northwestern University in education and anthropology. His professional work includes 4 books, 95 articles, 100 papers, and 5 million dollars in grant and funded awards. In addition he has received two Fulbright-Hays professorships as well as numerous other honors. He has also served as president of the National Council for the Social Studies. Diem's major research interests have been the application of technology to educational environments and the cultural implications of information and technological dependence in school settings. He can be contacted at: Richard.Diem@utsa.edu

Timothy M. Dove is a social studies and technology teacher at Phoenix Middle School in Worthington, Ohio. He is working on educational reforms for secondary education, including but not limited to mastery assessments, appropriate use of different technologies, advisory groupings and curricular integration. He can be contacted at DovePHX@gmail.com

Jeffrey Elliott is a social studies educator at the Metro Early College High School in Columbus, Ohio. He is involved in school reform, integration across content areas, using technology to reach students and moving to online platforms for teaching and learning. He can be contacted at elliott@themetroschool.org

Adam M. Friedman is an assistant professor, director of social studies education, and director of secondary education at Wake Forest University. He instructs undergraduate and graduate secondary social studies methodology courses, an undergraduate elementary social studies methodology course, as well as a course in descriptive research in social studies. Dr. Friedman's research interests include studying the impact of technology use on the teaching and learning of social studies, particularly Web 2.0 applications. He has published a wide variety of book chapters and journal articles, and delivered numerous professional presentations. He can be contacted at amfriedman@wfu.edu.

Thomas C. Hammond is an assistant professor in the Teaching, Learning & Technology Program at Lehigh University. He recieved his doctorate in instructional technology in 2007 from the University of Virginia. Prior to entering academia, he taught social studies, language arts, and computer science for 10 years in the United States, Haiti, and Saudi Arabia. He currently teaches social studies methods, instructional technology classes, and classroom research methods. While at the University of Virginia, he was a member of the PrimaryAccess design team. His current research focuses on technology-mediated social studies instruction and teacher education. He can be contacted at tch207@lehigh.edu

Vanessa Hammler Kenon has served in the areas of higher education academics and research, student services, career services, industry and community relations, and education leadership for over 19 years. In her current position she serves at the University of Texas at San Antonio as the project director for Upward Bound Math and Science. Kenon is a graduate of Trinity University where she earned degrees in communications and English. She served on the Trinity University San Antonio Chapter Board of Directors for 2 years and the university's National Alumni Board for 6 years. Kenon earned a master of arts degree in education with a concentration in adult and higher education and recently completed her doctorate in educational leadership, both at the University of Texas at San Antonio. Access to global education and social justice issues in education serve as Kenon's area of interest and research. Her paper on global access utilizing networked global learning communities was accepted and presented at the 5th International Workshop on Higher Education Reform at East China Normal University in Shanghai, China and was also accepted and presented at the Network Ethics: The New Challenge in Business, ICT and Education Workshop at Catholic University in Lisbon Portugal. Recently, Kenon was named by the University Council of Education Administrators as a 2008 UCEA Barbara Jackson Scholar and also selected as a 2009 David Clark Scholar by the American Education Research Association. She can be contacted at vanessa.kenon@utsa.edu

John Lee is an associate professor of social studies and middle grades education. He conducts research on digital history, and is specifically interested in the development of innovative ways for supporting teachers and students as they make use of online historical resources. He is also involved in efforts to theorize and develop tools and materials related to new literacies. Dr. Lee is the codirector of the New Literacies Collaborative online at www.newlit.org. He also directs the DigitalHistory and Pedagogy Project at www.dhpp.org. For more see www4.ncsu.edu/~jklee/. He can be contacted at john_lee@ncsu.edu

Meghan McGlinn Manfra is an assistant professor of secondary social studies education at North Carolina State University. She received her doctorate in 2006 from the University of North Carolina at Chapel Hill. Before becoming a professor, she taught high school American History and World History (advanced placement) for 5 years. She currently teaches secondary social studies methods, curriculum foundations, and social studies education theory and research. Her primary research interest is the integration of digital history to make social studies instruction more authentic and meaningful for students. A second line of inquiry focuses on teacher research for professional development. Using critical theory as the guiding framework, she is researching the manner in which teacher-directed inquiry can create more democratic classrooms. She can be contacted at meghan_manfra@ncsu.edu

Merry M. Merryfield is a professor of social studies and global education at The Ohio State University. Her research examines teacher decision-making in global education, cross-cultural experiential learning, and online pedagogies. She can be contacted at merryfield.1@osu.edu

Andrew J. Milson is an associate professor in the Department of Teacher Education and Administration at the University of North Texas. He teaches undergraduate courses in secondary education and graduate courses in curriculum studies. His research interests include the implementation of inquiry learning methodologies in secondary schools and the integration of the Internet and geospatial technologies into social studies education. He served as coeditor of the volumes *Readings in American Educational Thought* (Information Age, 2004) and *Digital Geography* (2008) and has published articles in journals such as *Theory and Research in Social Education*, *Journal of Educational Research*, *Educational Policy*, *Social Education*, and *The Social Studies*. He can be contacted at amilson@unt.edu

Joe O'Brien is an associate professor in the Department of Curriculum & Teaching at the University of Kansas. He instructs courses in instructional practices, research and theory in middle and secondary social studies and has received numerous teaching awards. His research interests include the relation between digital participatory media and civic engagement and the use of historical thinking to learn about presidential actions related to different phrases of the Preamble to the U.S. Constitution. He can be contacted at jeobrien@ku.edu

Patrice Preston-Grimes is an assistant professor in social studies education at the University of Virginia's Curry School of Education, where she teaches undergraduate and graduate courses in social studies methods and research, cultural geography, and the history of American education. Her research interests include civic education, African American educational history, the sociocultural contexts of teaching and learning, and more recently, the uses of technology in social studies instruction. A former middle grades language arts and social studies teacher, she is the recipient of the 2007 Exemplary Research in Social Studies Award by the National Council for the Social Studies (NCSS) and has published articles, commentary and presented her work at numerous national and state conferences. She can be contacted at pgrimes@virginia.edu

Justin Reich is a doctoral candidate at the Harvard Graduate School of Education, the project manager for the Digital Collaborative Learning Communities Project funded by the Hewlett Foundation, and the codirector of EdTechTeacher.org, a technology integration consulting firm. Along with his colleague Tom Daccord, he is the webmaster of *The Best of History Web Sites* (besthistorysites.net) and *Teaching History with Technology* (thwt.org) and coauthor of *Best Ideas for Teaching History with Technology; A Practical Guide for Teachers, by Teachers.* His scholarly writings have appeared in *Environmental History, Social Education,* and *World History Connected,* and his opinion writings have appeared in the *Washington Post,* the *Christian Science Monitor,* the *Providence Journal,* and the *Worcester Telegram and Gazette.* He can be contacted at bjr795@mail.harvard.edu

Eui-kyung Shin is an associate professor of social studies education in the Department of Teaching and Learning at the Northern Illinois University. She teaches undergraduate courses in elementary education and graduate courses in global education. Her research interests include the integration of Geographic Information System (GIS) into elementary classrooms and the infusion of global perspectives into the elementary curriculum. She has published articles in journals such as *Journal of Geography, Theory and Research in Social Education, Action in Teacher Education,*

The Social Studies, and *Social Studies and the Young Learner.* She can be contacted at ekshin@niu.edu

Betsy Sidor teaches economics and American studies at Upper Arlington High School in Columbus, Ohio. Her research interests include using inquiry based instruction to integrate the social studies and language arts curricula and employing twenty-first century technologies to develop authentic audiences for assessment. She can be contacted at bsidor@uaschools.org

Jeremy Stoddard is an assistant professor in the School of Education and an associated faculty in the Literary and Cultural Studies/Film Studies Program at the College of William & Mary, where he also directs the secondary history and social studies education program. He is a graduate of the University of Wisconsin-Madison, and is a former middle school history and social studies teacher and curriculum and technology specialist. His research uses critical and sociocultural frameworks to analyze the role of media in teaching and learning in history and democratic education. He is coauthor, along with Alan Marcus, Scott Metzger, and Richard Paxton, of the book *Teaching History with Film: Strategies for Secondary Social Studies,* published by Routledge (2010). He can be contacted at jdstod@wm.edu

Cheryl A. Franklin Torrez is an assistant professor in the Teacher Education Department at the University of New Mexico. She instructs courses in curriculum and instruction and social studies education. Her research interests focus on technology integration in elementary classrooms and in teacher education. She can be contacted at catorrez@unm.edu

David Valdez is currently teaching AP and IB psychology at a magnet school in Pinellas County. He is currently pursuing a PhD in curriculum and instruction at the University of South Florida. His interest include practical applications and the effective infusion of technology into social studies classrooms. Mr. Valdez is currently researching the ways in which social networking sites are utilized as tools to aid in the developmental process of adolescent identity. He can be contacted at dvaldez2@mail.usf.edu

Phillip J. VanFossen is the James F. Ackerman professor of social studies education, director of the Ackerman Center for Democratic Citizenship, and associate director of the Purdue University Center for Economic Education at Purdue University. VanFossen is also serving as the interim department head for the Department of Curriculum and Instruction. He is the program author for a recently released high school economics textbook. His research interests include how social studies teachers use the Internet, digital media, and virtual worlds (e.g., MMORPGs such as *World of Warcraft*) in their teaching. He has authored 3 books, numerous chapters, and more than 25 refereed articles on these topics. He can be contacted at vanfoss@purdue.edu